HISTORY'S FOOLS

DAVID MARTIN JONES

History's Fools

The Pursuit of Idealism and the
Revenge of Politics

OXFORD
UNIVERSITY PRESS

OXFORD

UNIVERSITY PRESS

Oxford University Press is a department of the
University of Oxford. It furthers the University's objective
of excellence in research, scholarship, and education
by publishing worldwide.

Oxford New York

Auckland   Cape Town   Dar es Salaam   Hong Kong   Karachi
Kuala Lumpur   Madrid   Melbourne   Mexico City   Nairobi
New Delhi   Shanghai   Taipei   Toronto

With offices in

Argentina   Austria   Brazil   Chile   Czech Republic   France   Greece
Guatemala   Hungary   Italy   Japan   Poland   Portugal   Singapore
South Korea   Switzerland   Thailand   Turkey   Ukraine   Vietnam

Oxford is a registered trade mark of Oxford University Press
in the UK and certain other countries.

Published in the United States of America by
Oxford University Press
198 Madison Avenue, New York, NY 10016

Library of Congress Cataloging-in-Publication Data is available

ISBN: 9780197510612

Printed in India

For J, B, L.

CONTENTS

There is some grandiose ludicrousness in the spectacle of these men...
submitting often from one day to the other, humbly and without so much
as a cry of outrage, to the call of historical necessity...they were fooled by
history, and they have become the fools of history.

(Hannah Arendt, *On Revolution*, 1963)

ACKNOWLEDGMENTS

This book arose from a conversation with Michael Dwyer of Hurst in Riyadh in 2017. A visiting Professorship in the War Studies Department, King's College, London proved a congenial home for writing it and the head of department, Professor Michael Rainsborough, an exceptional host. At Hurst, Lara Weisweiller-Wu, Miah Bains and Daisy Leitch oversaw the book's editing and production with efficiency and panache. The project draws upon a number of articles written in *International Affairs*, *Studies in Conflict and Terrorism*, *International Security*, *Quadrant*, *The National Interest* and *The American Interest* over the last two decades. Some of these articles were co-authored, several with M.L.R. Smith and one with John Bew. They bear no responsibility for the argument, structure or limitations of the current work. Former students, Lana Starkey in Brisbane and Rhiannon Emm in London, helped with research and the bibliography. My wife, Jo, endured my craft and sullen art and supported the endeavour throughout.

INTRODUCTION
PROGRESSIVE HUBRIS AND THE POST-HISTORICAL MOMENT

'History is being driven in a coherent direction by rational desire and rational recognition', Francis Fukuyama wrote in 1992. He added, 'liberal democracy in reality constitutes the best possible solution to the human problem'.[1] Reflecting on the spirit of the times in 2010, Tony Blair, wrote that 'for almost twenty years, after 1989, the West set the agenda, to which others reacted. Some supported us, and some opposed us, but the direction of the globe, the destination to which history appeared to march, seemed chosen by us'.[2]

The end of the Cold War announced a New World Order. For a brief, unipolar moment, liberal democracy flourished and ideological conflict abated. World politics, channelling Francis Fukuyama, embarked on a path leading to the promised land of a secular, cosmopolitan, market-friendly, end of history. Even though civilizations might still clash, political scientists were convinced that the 'snowballing effect' of democracy's third wave would prove irresistible.[3] Or so it seemed.

A quarter of a century later, a liberal worldview premised on shared norms, open markets, open borders and an abstract commitment to social justice lay in tatters. The progressive world order that lay before us like a land of dreams, various, beautiful and new, mutated, after 2001, into a darkling plain, where an exhausted West struggled to contend with ignorant armies clashing by night. In 2018, Freedom House and the Economist's Intelligence Unit vied with each other to demonstrate the extent of democracy's global 'crisis', whilst Harvard and Oxbridge political scientists speculated about how democracies suffer trauma and die.[4]

How, we might wonder, did an abstract commitment to universal values – multiculturalism at home and military intervention abroad, founding a liberal order – come, paradoxically, to undermine the progressive faith in an international community? Why did an apparently shared, universal, cosmopolitan ideal inexorably advancing regionalism, international law and human rights come to grief? In the illiberal new world shaped by social media, renewed ideological rivalry and the revenge of revisionist powers that emerged from the liberal end of history cocoon, what, if anything, of its moral legacy, and its political legitimacy survives the wreckage?

In order to explore this Panglossian adventure in political thought and conduct, this book examines how a progressive understanding of 'a post historical world'[5] sought 'to construct' – to use one of its favourite infinitives – a shared public morality fit for a secular, multicultural, socially just and borderless world. In order to unpick its ruling assumptions, we shall trace the manner in which, after 1989, a powerful consensus in the mainstream media, in business, finance, and government promoted a new liberal economic and political ideology. In this enterprise, Western academia, functioning as a state-funded cheerleader for 'democracy and the global order',[6] witnessed liberal scholars of various hues, as well as various congeries of cultural Marxists and post-structuralists, busily constructing and deconstructing the lineaments of the cosmopolitan, post historical, *Weltanschauung* necessary for the borderless, twenty-first century world that the end of history made possible.

Ultimately, as we shall see, the new, progressive liberalism of the 1990s suffered from a relic of magical thinking concerning conduct. As a post-modern ideology it viewed, in its various manifestations, order, both local and global, as the product of a 'determinate, independent instrument' and contended that 'the rational way of going about things is to go about them under the sole guidance' of this rational progressive instrument.[7] Taking an excessively long view of the future and a short view of the past, the new liberal end of history mentality had the debilitating habit of restricting, and misrepresenting, the West's actual predicament in a contingent world after the dissolution of the Soviet Union in 1991.

Somewhat problematically, 'the rest' of the world, or the non-Western 'other', to use the liberal relativist's participle of choice, failed to embrace the secular progressive understanding of the historical process. As one of the more sceptical connoisseurs of this style of instrumentalist thought observed, 'a single homogeneous line of development is to be found in history only if history is made a dummy upon which to practice the skill of a ventriloquist'.[8] As in a tragedy of Aeschylus, incoherence and political confusion were the inevitable consequence of such Olympian hubris.[9]

Yet the West has been here before. The triumph of the West is invariably accompanied by the fear of impending crisis and doom. Triumph and Decline are enduring themes in the history of western thought. It may be traced to St Augustine's commentary on the contrasting fates of *The City of God* and the city of man.[10] In its more recent, secular, version, Oswald Spengler's *Decline of the West* (1918) anticipated the West's 'megapolitan' decay, whilst Arnold Toynbee's multivolume *A Study of History* (1934–61) identified a 'cyclical pattern to the rise and fall' of all 'civilizations'.[11] In this vein, James Burnham contemplated *The Suicide of the West: An Essay on the Meaning and Destiny of Liberalism* (1964), whilst Samuel Huntington's *The Clash of Civilizations and the Remaking of World Order* (1996) detected a shifting balance of power among civilizations, with the West inexorably 'declining in relative influence'.[12] As the tide of history turned once more, after 2016, Jonah Goldberg (2018) also anticipated *The Suicide of the West* coinciding with 'the rebirth of tribalism, populism, nationalism, and identity politics'.[13]

The problem, as Leo Strauss saw it, at the height of the Cold War, was that the West had once seemed 'certain of its purpose', 'a purpose in which all men could be united'. The undoing of the assumption of its universal purpose, to bring 'progress toward a society embracing equally all human beings', then as now, engendered a sense of crisis.[14] How, we shall also consider, might what Strauss identified as a 'practical particularism' that accepts that a political society, remains what it always has been, 'a particular society'…'whose most urgent and primary task is its self-preservation and whose highest task is its self-improvement',[15] abate the 'mid-life crisis', to use David Runciman's phrase, that now faces a distracted and confused, democratic West?[16] To embark on this inquiry into how an all-pervasive, liberal, progressive and ultimately Olympian ideology assumed a seemingly impermeable form, out of various currents of liberal and radical thought flowing through Western universities, we shall first examine its structural preconditions in the apparent triumph of the open market and a borderless world that terminated the Cold War.

2

THE END OF HISTORY AND THE KANTIAN MOMENT

At the end of the short twentieth century (1914–1990), liberal democracies emerged as the richest and most powerful states the world has ever seen. But success came at a cost. It encouraged the belief that there existed no problem that the liberal mind could not overcome. The liberal *persona*, its ruling assumptions and the global landscape it believed it inhabited, form the *mise-en-scène* of the first act of this melodramatic exercise in omniscience. Dusting down copies of some of the definitive works of the 1990s affords a revealing insight into the character of the Western progressive illusion that marked the end of history.

Fukuyama's *The End of History and the Last Man* (1992), based on an earlier, more querulous essay, 'The End of History?' (1989), forms the starting point for this journey through the intellectual labyrinth of the time. Fukuyama asks at the outset: 'By way of an introduction'… 'whether at the end of the twentieth century, it makes sense for us to speak once again of a coherent and directional History of mankind that will eventually lead the greater part of humanity to liberal democracy'. The answer came in the affirmative and for two reasons. 'One has to do with economics and the other' with what Fukuyama termed 'the struggle for recognition'.[1]

More precisely, economic, scientific and technological presuppositions underpinned a universal yearning for recognition, *thymosis*, which only a liberal democratic regime could fulfill. By 1989, 'capitalism', or, more accurately, free trade and open markets, had proved 'more efficient than centrally planned economic systems in developing and utilizing technology, and in adapting to the rapidly changing conditions of a global division of labour, *under the conditions of a mature industrial economy*'.[2]

Looking around the world, Fukuyama also found a correlation between 'advancing socio-economic modernization and the emergence of new democracies'.[3] He was not the first to identify this trend. US political scientists, such as Samuel Huntington and Michael Doyle, had already identified a Cold War 'wave' of democratization that showed liberal democracies growing from thirty-six states in 1960 to either fifty-nine or sixty-one by 1990.[4]

Fukuyama's interest in this correlation reflected a wider Cold War, American intellectual infatuation with democratization and political change that had informed the study of comparative political science as a discipline since the early years of the Cold War. From the 1960s, the US government-sponsored comparative Social Science Research Council (SSRC) generously funded the study of the relationship between modernity and the advancement of democracy. In particular, modernization theory, which came to dominate the understanding of area studies and comparative politics, as those fields of social scientific endeavour flourished on American campuses in the course of the 1950s and 1960s, informed a post-war liberal understanding of political development and democratic change.[5]

Comparative political theory situated the non-Western or developing world within an evolutionary paradigm. This approach, which owed much to Talcott Parsons and Edward Shils' synthesis of the foundational sociologies of Max Weber and Emil Durkheim, initially tried to identify the structures and functions that framed pluralist, modern, social action. As the programme unfolded and 'the change to change' appeared more challenging than initially assumed, a later generation of political scientists tried to establish the preconditions, processes, sequences, and crises that promoted or inhibited the always anxious transition from tradition to modernity.[6]

This Cold War methodological edifice affected and informed a Western liberal understanding of the world's evolving politico-economic character. As such it was preoccupied both with the pattern of the past and evaluating the relative impact of internal and external tensions affecting revolutionary transformation in the developing world.

The answers given to three methodological questions came to dominate the comparative politics research programme. Firstly, what policies and processes affected what Walt Rostow identified as industrial 'take off' in late developing economies;[7] secondly, what was the relationship between economic and political development; and thirdly, to what extent did culture and/or contingent historical experience impede or promote development? This approach fashioned alternative answers to the crucial fourth question: did modernization necessitate democratization?

Events in Eastern Europe and East Asia in the late 1980s provided fertile, empirical grounds for potentially confirming a liberal democratic response to the fourth question. The surprising, and unanticipated, collapse of the Soviet Union and its ramifications inspired academic entrepreneurs and their institutions to found journals devoted to exploring the phenomenon. In 1990, Johns Hopkins University founded *The Journal of Democracy* as an offshoot of the National Endowment for Democracy. It rapidly established itself, its promotional literature claimed, as both 'the world's leading publication on the theory and practice of democracy' and 'amongst the most influential of social science journals'. The journal engaged with 'both activists and intellectuals in critical discussions of the problems and prospects for democracy around the world'. It explored 'the establishment, consolidation, and maintenance of democracy, including political institutions, parties and elections, civil society, ethnic conflict, economic reform, public opinion, the role of the media, and constitutionalism'. It also covered 'questions of democratic theory and culture'.[8] A few years later the University of Warwick launched *Democratization* (1994), studying the 'processes' diffusing 'democratic norms, institutions and practices both within and across national boundaries',[9] particularly in the developing world. Both journals assumed pre-eminence in this new field of endeavour and in turn influenced the media and liberal governmental response to the importance, not only of understanding the democratization process, but also of promoting democratic programmes and democratic activism.

This academic enterprise that Fukuyama packaged for public consumption found an equally salient correlation between globalization and a decline in authoritarian regimes. Indeed, by the end of the 1980s, notwithstanding the brutal suppression of the 1989 Tiananmen Square 'incident' in China, the People's Republic of China (PRC), the Soviet Union, and the Warsaw Pact countries of Eastern Europe were, it seemed, succumbing 'to the economic logic of advanced industrialization'. Rapidly unfolding, 'technologically driven economic modernization' created strong incentives for developed and developing countries 'to accept the basic terms of the universal capitalist economic culture by permitting a substantial degree of economic competition and letting prices be determined by market mechanisms'. There was no alternative path toward 'full economic modernity'.[10]

The World Bank agreed. Its report on *The East Asia Miracle* (1993) found the High Performing Asian Economies (HPAEs) of the Pacific littoral, a curious bestiary of emerging 'dragon' and 'tiger' states, already making considerable strides along this increasingly well-trodden path. By the mid 1990s, it had become received academic and liberal media wisdom that the embedded liberalism of the post-1944 Bretton Woods multilateral trade regime had enabled East and South East Asian states, first Japan and subsequently South Korea, Taiwan, Singapore, Hong Kong, Thailand, Malaysia and even Indonesia to develop export-oriented growth models.

Like a flock of flying geese,[11] as one Japanese economist observed, these developing economies first exported labour-intensive and subsequently high value-added electronic and manufactured goods throughout the developed world in general and to the open US market in particular by targeting specific industries or 'picking winners' and restricting imports.

Over time, these stable, developing states created a virtuous circle of an educated and cheap labour force and high domestic savings rates enabling manufacturing industries to establish a comparative advantage in overseas markets and attract foreign direct investment from both investment funds and transnational corporations (TNCs) looking for offshore bases. This success demonstrated the triumph of capitalism, deregulation and the market over planned or import-substituting alternatives to economic development.

The flexibility of 'competition states' and city regions in the emerging interconnected, global financial order further undermined the economic sustainability of rigid, bureaucratically overloaded systems. The rise of the Asian dragons and the opening of five mainland Chinese economic zones to investment after 1978 also falsified the claims made by Marxist world systems theorists that globalizing capital merely enabled a core of Western states to exploit a neo-colonial, non-Western 'periphery'.[12]

In other words, the development of the market state or 'Anglo-Saxon' economic model, and the deregulation of transportation, telecommunications and finance in the 1980s, in the aftermath of the Plaza Hotel Agreement (1985) and the Louvre Accord (1987), created conditions for the globalization of financial markets and the rapid appreciation of the Japanese yen. This big bang financial and technological revolution, coupled with the collapse of the Soviet Union and the fall of the Berlin wall in 1989, constituted the economic and political preconditions for a tsunami of deregulation, foreign direct investment (FDI) and democratization globally.

By 1991, the former nuclear engineer and managing director of McKinsey, Japan, Kenichi Ohmae, could identify a 'triad' of advanced, interlinked economies comprised of Japan (and the newly industrialised economies (NIEs) of East Asia), the United States and Europe forging a globalization process that would render closed authoritarian governments and planned economies unsustainable. The future was borderless. In this brave new world, governments played an important but 'diminished role': educating the workforce; providing a stable and supportive infrastructure; and protecting the environment.

In a letter co-authored with fellow McKinsey directors for Europe and the globe, as an addendum to the 1991 edition of *The Borderless World,* Ohmae promulgated a 'Declaration of Interdependence' toward 'the world' that he foresaw emerging by 2005. The declaration predicted that 'the weave of economic and intellectual interdependence', rather than superpower rivalry, would 'enhance' global security as well as individual and institutional well-being. Global financial interdependence would create 'no absolute losers nor winners, as market mechanisms (would) adjust participating nations' competitiveness fairly through currency exchange rates and employment.

9

In this global financial order, the 'efficient nation state' would play a 'diminished' role. The state's role in the borderless world was to allow access 'to the best and cheapest goods and coordinate activities with other governments to minimize conflict arising from narrow interests'. The 'leading nations', promoting the process, would enhance networking and develop a new global framework 'to deal collectively with traditionally parochial affairs, such as tax…and laws governing mobility of tradable goods, services and assets'.

Emerging multilateral regimes and their institutions, like the World Bank, the International Monetary Fund (IMF), Asia Pacific Economic Cooperation (APEC) and the World Trade Organization (WTO), together with the development of economic and, over time, politically integrated regions like the European Union (EU), North American Free Trade Association (NAFTA), and the Association of South East Asian Nations (ASEAN) mutating into an East Asian Economic Community (EAC) would not only create wealth, but also, Ohmae and McKinsey contended, address the earth's environment, help underdeveloped nations and 'advance human rights and dignity' everywhere.[13]

McKinsey's Declaration became the default position of the Davos World Economic Forum which, in the course of the 1990s, assumed a prominent role in promoting both the economic and political virtues of globalization, and the role of transnational institutions many of which, like the WTO (1994), APEC (1989), EU (1993),[14] and NAFTA (1994) appeared on the global scene for the first time.

Modernization, Globalization and Political Legitimacy

Following Max Weber and Barrington Moore, it had become social science orthodoxy that the emergence of an urban middle class in the west created 'the material conditions for democracy'.[15] Yet although globalizing trade and investment certainly created wealth, and its distribution enabled the growth of an educated urban, Asian middle class, it didn't necessarily guarantee democratization. 'An economic account of history gets us to the gates of democracy, but it does not quite deliver us to the other side', Fukuyama observed. 'The process of economic modernization', he continued, briefly restating Talcott Parsons' 'normative' modernization theory of the 1950s, transforms traditional 'tribal and agricultural societies into urban, educated, middle-class ones'.

But democracy also requires democrats, or, more precisely, citizens demanding 'recognition' as individual stakeholders in society bearing equal constitutional rights. Despite the obstinate attachment to cultural difference and the continuing appeal of religion and ethnicity, Fukuyama nevertheless detected a liberal *Geist* at work in the dialectical process governing world history. He argued that the Enlightenment understanding of liberal democracy and its commitment to equality, liberty and the rule of law reflected a universal 'human desire for recognition'.[16] 'The desire for recognition then', Fukuyama claimed, channelling Alexander Kojève's post-war adaptation of Hegel's *Philosophy of Right*, represented 'the missing link between liberal economics and liberal politics'.[17]

'Mankind', Fukuyama prognosticated:

> will come to seem like a long wagon train strung out along a road. Some wagons will be pulling into town sharply...while others will be bivouacked back in the desert, or stuck in ruts in the final pass over the mountains. Several wagons, attacked by Indians, will be set aflame and abandoned along the way. There will be a few wagoneers who, stunned by the battle, will have lost their sense of direction and are temporarily heading in the wrong direction while one or two wagons will get tired of the journey and decide to set up permanent camps at particular points back along the road.[18]

Nevertheless, 'the great majority of wagons will be making the slow journey into town and most will eventually arrive there'. The town, of course, was the promised land of liberal democracy or what Robert Dahl identified as 'polyarchy'.[19] While the wagons might be painted different colours and constructed of 'varied materials', they are all similar.

History ends, then, with a somewhat parochial US Western frontier analogy. Its provisional character, the fact that some states or 'wagons' were stuck in ruts or bivouacked in the outback, reflected the fact that, although the Asian economic miracle had industrialised, modernized, and opened that region to FDI, they had still not arrived in the happy town of polyarchy.

Moreover, and somewhat problematically, although former Warsaw Pact states, from Poland to Hungary, had staged velvet revolutions after 1989 that led to liberal democratic constitutions, their economic development remained somewhat etiolated. By contrast, East Asian states, with varying degrees of success, had assembled illiberal, politically unaccountable developmental coalitions of bureaucratically guided conglomerates and labour unions in collectively mobilized enterprise associations based on the model of Japan Incorporated. In Japan, Singapore, Taiwan, and Malaysia, it was single party dominant regimes that oversaw the modernization process. Meanwhile, in South Korea, Thailand and Indonesia, the military enforced variations on authoritarian rule by market friendly, and US approved, monarchs and presidents.

In fact, as Fukuyama, *The Journal of Democracy*, and democracy theorists reluctantly acknowledged, there existed 'considerable empirical evidence to indicate that market oriented authoritarian modernizers do better economically than their economic counterparts'.[20] Paradoxically, as the cases of Singapore, Taiwan, South Korea and Thailand testified, 'authoritarian regimes' were in principle 'better able to follow truly liberal economic policies undistorted by redistributive goals that constrain growth'.[21] Authoritarian capitalists from Singapore to Seoul, Taipei and Beijing enjoyed 'the best of both worlds', capable of enforcing a high degree of discipline upon their labour force, whilst permitting sufficient freedom to encourage technological innovation.[22] As *The Economist* observed in 1986, 'happy is the country that the rest of the world finds boring. It quietly gets on with its business in life, which mostly is business. Every so often a dazzled economist, or a stranded journalist, marvels at its growth rates and per capita everythings'.[23] The HPAEs emerged, as the same journal remarked a decade later, under the cloak of a 'boringness factor' made possible by a felicific calculus of United States aid, protection and market access.[24]

In 1992, Fukuyama, following the prevailing liberal perplexity, observed that although there was an unquestionable relationship between economic development and liberal democracy, 'the Mechanism underlying our directional history leads equally well to a bureaucratic-authoritarian future as to a liberal one'.[25] Moreover, whilst

Fukuyama, the *Journal of Democracy*, the *Economist* and the *Far Eastern Economic Review* assumed the interdependence of liberal democracy and globalization, a countervailing Asian school of shared, but distinctive, Asian values asserted that 'paternalistic authoritarianism', rather than individualism, better suited modernizing Asia's Confucian, Muslim and Buddhist traditions of harmony and consensus.

The first premonitory snuffling of a moral and political rejection of the universal claims of liberal democracy in the post-Cold War era may be found in the writings of Singaporean scholar bureaucrats like Kishore Mahbubani, Chan Heng Chee and Bilhari Kausikan, Harvard neo-Confucians like Tu Wei Ming, as well as philosophically inclined authoritarian leaders like Lee Kuan Yew and Mahathir Mohamad.[26]

In the immediate aftermath of the collapse of the Soviet Union, the Pacific Rim's ruling elites rejected both the political practices and constitutional legacy bequeathed to them by their former colonial masters. Pan-Asianists like Malaysia's Mahathir Mohamad, Japan's Shintaro Ishihara, and Singapore's Goh Chok Tong and Kishore Mahbubani considered that, without elite guidance, democracy, equal rights and civil liberties caused economic stagnation, inner city chaos and monstrous regiments of single parent families.[27]

The translation of these Western values to Pacific Asia, moreover, constituted an insidious ploy to undermine, or, worse, recolonize, the recently developed states of the Pacific littoral. Instead, the Pacific Asian region placed its faith in what might be termed post-Confucian characteristics, adumbrated in South East Asia by a syncretic overlay of moderate Islamic and Buddhist values such as 'social cohesion, subordination of the individual, bureaucratic tradition and moralising certitude', which as the Sinologist Roderick Macfarquhar observed, offered a 'potent combination for development purposes'.[28]

Moreover, the successful translation of traditional high cultural values of Islamic, Buddhist and Confucian provenance into programmes of mass education and bureaucratic practice offered the intriguing illiberal prospect of a potentially enduring, but distinctively Asian modernity that effectively synergized the extended order of the market with the bounded governance structures of traditional culture.[29]

Ironically, this modern Asian illiberalism had risen and evolved into successful administrative states under the benign aegis of

American containment, a policy premised upon entirely different, liberal ideological assumptions. Could the Asian values that American hegemony and the openness of western markets had inadvertently facilitated sustain a new, soft authoritarian, Pacific Asian order in the post Cold War era?

The Rise and Fall of Shared Asian Values

Prior to 1997, Asian, and a small coterie of Western, scholars infatuated by Pacific Asia's rapid economic development, maintained that this was indeed the case. They emphasised the functional utility of a uniquely Asian approach to regional economic growth and problem solving. Thus, Noordin Sopiee, Director of the Malaysian Institute of Strategic and International Studies (ISIS), observed that the 'Cartesian' Western approach to international relations and political economy depended upon 'legalistic forms, agreements, contracts, institutions, and structures'; by contrast, the Asian approach 'relies more on the meeting of minds and hearts, on consensus building, peer pressure and on unilateral good and proper behaviour'.[30] While Pacific Asia had no supranational institutions comparable to NATO or the European Union, it had evolved instead informal 'networks that are inclusive rather than exclusive'.[31] These distinctive and shared values informed, it was maintained, evolving regional, economic and security structures like the ASEAN Regional Forum (ARF), and APEC's Bogor Declaration of 1994. Indeed, they constituted what Singapore's Minister for the Arts at the time, B.G. Yeo, considered to be a common cultural area that presaged the emergence of a new Pacific community, a 'return to the time when Asia was the cradle of civilization'.[32] In the view of the then Deputy Prime Minister of Malaysia, Anwar Ibrahim, these non-liberal values formed the basis of an Asian Renaissance.[33]

In 1992, even Fukuyama reluctantly admitted that Asia faced a 'critical turning point in respect of world history' where the pull of hierarchy, family and group identity might negate the appeal of individual rights and the need for recognition.[34] Globalization had, in fact, incubated a 'curious double phenomenon'. On the one hand, economics, technology and the spread of the idea of 'rational recognition as the only legitimate basis of government' engendered the growing homogenization of mankind; but on the other, there appeared 'resistance to that homogenization and a reassertion, largely on a sub-political level, of cultural identities that ultimately reinforce existing barriers between peoples and nations'.[35]

In a similar vein, Benjamin Barber reflecting, in *Jihad versus McWorld* (1995), upon the wars of ethnic and religious dissolution that balkanized the former secular, Communist state of Yugoslavia, wrote that the New World Order appeared 'Janus faced'. It offered the integrationist blandishments of McWorld – fast food, mobile phones, MTV and Nike trainers – 'pressing nations into one homogenous theme park'.[36] At the same time, globalization created the conditions for groups to separate themselves from the larger communities to which they had previously been connected, retribalizing society and fragmenting nation states. The anxious recourse to the primordialist certainties of 'Jihad', Barber's somewhat clumsy term for identity politics, occurred alongside the appeal of McWorld and often, as Barber observed in Sarajevo in 1994, at the same time.[37] Somewhat differently, Samuel Huntington, disillusioned with the way third wave democracy had ebbed, foresaw, instead, a growing clash of civilizations.[38]

This evident dissonance at the end of history notwithstanding, a liberal orthodoxy, enhanced by the CNN effect, one that transnationally promoted liberal, secular democratic values via the reach of global satellite TV, remained committed to the 'trickle down' effect of global growth. In stable and open economies, development, the liberalizing mantra held, presaged the emergence of an urbanized and educated middle class, creating inexorable pressure to democratize into a homogeneous and increasingly borderless world.

As Philip Cerny observed in 1997, 'globalization as a political phenomenon' basically meant that 'insulated units', that is states, could no longer determine the shape of the political playing field. Globalization was itself a 'process of political structuration'.[39] In the course of the 1990s, the most successful states, Cerny observed, enforced decisions which arose from world markets. In the West this meant the globalization process favoured the flexible adaptability and transparency of 'competition states', like the US and UK, that rendered post-war welfare mechanisms increasingly superfluous.[40]

However, it was the Asian Financial Crisis (AFC), which began with a run on the Thai baht in July 1997, that gave empirical substance to this globalizing process, exposing both the economic limitations and the weak political legitimacy of the illiberal, Asian model.

The first financial crisis of the globalization era, in other words, reinforced the end of history thesis and the inexorable link between globalization and democratic political development. The AFC enhanced the cachet of competitive openness, transparency and accountability at the expense of Asian style authoritarianism and its face-saving predilection for the corrosive vices of what the Malaysian opposition to Mahathir's enlightened Asian despotism termed in 1997 'KKN' (*Korrupsi, Kronyism dan Nepotism*). [41]

In August 1997, a month after the outbreak of bahtulism in Bangkok, the casual reader could walk into the *Kinokuniya* bookshop in the Shaw Centre on the corner of Singapore's Orchard Road to witness 'the great Singapore sale'. In the current affairs section of the shop, despite a radical markdown, piles of John Naisbitt's *Megatrends Asia: The Eight Asian Megatrends that are Changing the World* (1996), and Jim Rohwer's analogously euphoric *Asia Rising: How History's Biggest Middle Class will Transform the World* (1996) could not be sold. Alongside the pile of remaindered Naisbitts, but not on offer, the economic bestsellers of 1997 mirrored the region's financial angst. Leo Gough contemplated *Asian Meltdown: The End of the Miracle* (1997), Callum Henderson asked rhetorically *Asia Falling? Making Sense of the Asian Currency Crisis and its Aftermath,* and R. Gill pondered *Asia Under Siege: How the Asia Miracle Went Wrong*. East Asia, it seemed had for three decades boomed the boom only to 'bust the bust'.

The prevailing academic wisdom on the character and sustainability of illiberal East Asian economic and political development underwent an analogous change. Uncritical acceptance of the virtues of the close relationship between state linked banks and conglomerates had facilitated the accumulation of debt to equity in what was always misleadingly referred to, in East and South East Asia, as the 'private sector'. [42] Public sector technocrats and politicians entangled with private sector business established the distinctively 'crony' character of the Asian developmental model. As a result, the easily available credit of the *endaka*-led financial wave decade, 1985–95, left littoral

Pacific Asia sitting on a property bubble that extended from Tokyo to Jakarta.

The moral hazard of easy credit meant that the miracle states of the Pacific Rim failed to develop either a corporate or a government bond market, leaving capital little option but flight at the first indication of financial difficulty.[43] In other words, outside of still British administered Hong Kong, one of the devices long established in the West to hedge states and corporations against the consequences of an economic downturn exercised little appeal to the Confucian technocrats who determined the long term growth strategies of the Asian miracle economies. Moreover, the close relationship between bureaucrats and business that characterized East Asian development rendered conglomerates from Fuyo and Mitsubishi in Japan to Kia in South Korea, Charoen Phopkand in Thailand, Renong in Malaysia or the family cartels of the Suhartos in Indonesia, unaccountable both to shareholders and normal practices of accounting and, in the absence of any effective hedging instruments, vulnerable to capital flight. When global markets questioned the premise of growth based on the mobilization of inputs and the risk attached to investing in such opaque and over-exposed arrangements, financial crisis ensued.[44]

Significantly, the political arrangements that most successfully weathered the meltdown were ones where democratization had most advanced. Thus, the growing elite tolerance of multi-partism and electoral contestation in some Asian countries enabled non-violent transition from economically discredited ruling parties or presidents to market friendly reformers like Kim Dae Jung in South Korea or the liberal coalition led by Chuan Leekpai's Democrats in Thailand.

By contrast, democratically deficient and Sultanist Indonesia, which looked to the *dwifuncsi* of the *Angatan Bersatu Republic Indonesia* (ABRI – the armed forces) to guarantee order by military force when the economy stalled, witnessed the fall of New Order President, Suharto, a sustained period of economic and political chaos, followed by an uncertain but ultimately sustained lurch towards democratic, constitutional reform. In other words, as global financial markets became increasingly integrated and hedge funds explored the possibilities of derivative and option trades, the AFC and its political fallout allayed Fukuyama's residual hesitancy regarding the Asian

17

model. The most successful states to weather the crisis were those with flexible capital and labour markets that had most effectively marketized their bureaucracies.[45] In Pacific Asia, the meltdown least affected small, pragmatic technocracies like Taiwan, Hong Kong and Singapore which demonstrated the necessary flexibility to adapt to the requirements of the volatile mood swings of international finance.

Even though Taiwan and South Korea had undergone only very recent democratic transitions in 1997, the AFC nevertheless seemed to vindicate, or at least offer some evidence of a link between globalization and democratization. By the end of the decade, Thomas Friedman's *The Lexus and the Olive Tree* (1999) could update and reinforce Fukuyama's 'definition of the real character of the new world order'.[46] Friedman identified an economic 'golden straitjacket' that all states now had to wear in order to achieve continuous growth and investment and avoid the kind of financial crisis that briefly paralyzed Asian development in 1997. The emergence of global finance and stock markets 'that never slept' resolved, as if by an invisible hand, globalization's 'double phenomenon' that prior to 1995 left some developing states 'stuck in ruts' (Fukuyama), locked in 'jihad' (Benjamin Barber) or obsessing over olive trees (Thomas Friedman).

As US Treasury Secretary Larry Summers observed, 'it was surely no accident that communism, planning ministries and corporate conglomerates all ran into great difficulties in the same era'.[47] The former South Korean Prime Minister, Lee Hong Koo, agreed: 'We didn't realize that the victory of the Cold War was a victory for market forces above politics. The big decisions today are whether you have a democracy or not and whether you have an open economy or not'.[48]

The Myth of the Golden Straitjacket

Friedman's revision of the liberal democratization thesis sought to demonstrate how 'large historical forces produced'...'today's global market system', and their most notable features the Fast World, the Golden Straitjacket and the Electronic Herd.[49] In the increasingly Manichean division between those countries pursuing the McWorld and Lexus and those who opted for jihad and olive trees, a globalization friendly state had to adopt, or be moving toward, a radical financial and economic reform agenda that made:

> the private sector the primary engine of its economic growth, maintaining a low rate of inflation and price stability, shrinking the size of its state bureaucracy, maintaining as close to a balanced budget as possible, if not a surplus, eliminating and lowering tariffs on imported goods, removing restrictions on foreign investment, getting rid of quotas and domestic monopolies, increasing exports, privatizing state-owned industries and utilities, deregulating capital markets and making its currency convertible, opening its industries, stock and bond markets to direct foreign ownership and investment, deregulating its economy...opening its banking and telecommunications systems to private ownership and competition and allowing its citizens to choose from an array of competing pension options.

If a state stitched 'these pieces together', it wore the 'Golden Straitjacket'.[50] Shifting and mixing metaphors from clothing to ice cream and transport, Friedman contended that there were no strawberry, raspberry whirl or mint choc chip alternatives to free market vanilla. 'You can adjust your society to it by going faster or slower'. However, if 'you want a higher standard of living, in a world without walls, the free market' remained the only economic alternative left. 'One Road. Different speeds. But one road'.[51]

Three global forces drove this homogenizing, 'one size fits all', model: the democratization of technology, finance and information. They also gave birth to 'a new power source in the world', the 'Electronic Herd'. This little understood financial phenomenon, outside direct political control, assessed state progress in adhering to, or trying on, the straitjacket. The herd comprised 'the faceless stock, bond and currency traders sitting behind computer screens all over the globe' moving money electronically from mutual to pension to emerging market funds and pioneering exciting new financial products like derivatives and collateralized debt obligations. Meanwhile, multinational corporations spread production around the world, shifting factories to the 'most efficient low-cost producers'. The faceless herd rewarded with investment capital countries that put on the Golden Straitjacket and 'kept it on'. Those who did not, as happened in South East Asia in 1997, got whacked.

The straitjacket also applied, and democratization theory more generally, Friedman maintained, to the rapidly growing Chinese economy.[52] Although largely unaffected by the AFC, and, as the Electronic Herd took flight from the former 'miracle' Asian economies, a large-scale beneficiary of global FDI after 1997, the PRC would inexorably face 'a difficult adjustment'. It would be a mistake to assume, contended political scientists and economists at the time and for two decades after, that China would become 'a richer and richer authoritarian system with the Chinese Communist Party' maintaining authoritarian political controls. 'Either China won't get richer, or it won't be as authoritarian as it is now...because what the Chinese government can get away with now is very different from what it will be able to get away with once it is fully integrated into the herd'.[53]

From the perspective of the omniscient liberal redoubts of Davos, *The Economist* and *The Financial Times*, China, like the Asian miracle economies, would eventually come into the purview of the Electronic Herd and their independent credit rating enforcement agencies: Moody's, Fitch, and Standard & Poor's. These prowled the globe assessing competitiveness and productivity, doling out performance grades ranging from triple A to junk bond status.

At the millennium, it seemed, the global system reflected the complex interaction between the Electronic Herd, nation states and the Golden Straitjacket. Moreover, by 1999, as the internet achieved 'critical mass', it increasingly defined commerce and transaction, exercising a vice-like grip, tightening the system, shrinking the globe, making it 'smaller and smaller and faster and faster with each passing day'.[54] As Klaus Schwab, founder and chairman of the Davos World Economic Forum observed, we have moved into a new world, 'in which it is not the big fish that eat the small fish, it's the fast fish that eat the slow fish'.[55]

Plugging into the system, as it increased its interconnected velocity, however, merely intensified the pressure to democratize. Responding to the Electronic Herd required the flexibility, legitimacy and sustainability that only liberal democracy could deliver. Thus Larry Diamond, founding editor of *The Journal of Democracy*, asserted that 'nations that plug into the herd with good software, rule of law and accountability – but with no regular free elections' could not keep up in the long run. Whilst the fast world of the internet, and the technological, political and economic revolution it entailed could not be halted or even stalled, Friedman, like Barber, nonetheless recognized that this came at a cost to traditional communities who valued their 'olive trees' as much as their free market 'Lexus'.

Technological innovation, as a wealth-creating and democracy-enhancing project, necessarily disrupted traditional hierarchies and values. It also created economic losers as well as winners, and not only in the developing world. Economists Robert H. Frank and Philip J. Cook portrayed its emerging character in The Winner Takes All Society.[56] Globalization, they found, played 'an important role in the expansion of inequality' by creating a winner takes all market for the globe.[57] Between 1971 and 1995 the income of the poorest fifth of the US population dropped by twenty-one per cent, while the income of the richest fifth jumped by thirty per cent over the same period.

The first signs of a backlash against the process of globalization, moreover, was itself felt both locally and globally. It affected redundant steelworkers in the US and Europe, crony capitalists in Malaysia, Indonesia and Thailand and 'angry young men' across the developing world. The potentially violent character of the backlash appeared most acutely in corrupt, authoritarian, but developing, states like Egypt, where although its 'small, cell phone armed, globalizing elites were definitely pushing to get online and onto the global economic train… others feared they would be left behind or lose their identity trying to catch it'.[58]

The globalization process that brought about an interconnected, but by no means integrated, global society, induced countervailing political resistance to this all-consuming process of creative destruction. At its most violent, it took the form of what Friedman termed, with his penchant for capitalization, 'Super-Empowered Angry Men' who viewed the 'United States, IBM, The New York Times, Wall Street and the global economy…[as] all part of one power edifice' that needed taking down. This polymorphous, fragmented, but angry, resistance ranged from Aum Shinrikyo, the Japanese cult, the environmentalist Unabomber in California, Osama bin Laden's 'gang in Afghanistan', and 'the Ramzi Yousef Group' that first bombed New York's World Trade Center in 1993.[59]

Interestingly, Friedman not only failed to observe that the fast world had facilitated links between Yousef, his mentor Khalid Sheikh Mohammed in the Philippines, and bin Laden's 'gang' in Afghanistan; he also considered Yousef, a graduate of Swansea University in Wales, rather than bin Laden, the scion of a rich Saudi business family, as the 'quintessential Super Empowered Angry Young Man'. Unlike Cold War era terrorists, from the PLO to Brigate Rosse and the Provisional IRA, 'who wanted many people watching' and 'not many dead', Yousef's group had opted for a new, hypermegalomanic terror. Yet, in 1999, it seemed the new terrorism, unlike the Cold War variety, was merely nihilistic. It was 'not trying to change the world'. 'They know they can't so they just want to destroy as much as they can'.[60]

This protean, apocalyptic response, however, had one obvious target – the West or, more precisely, the United States. The Cold War Middle Eastern rebels with a religious cause, who assassinated Egyptian President Anwar Sadat in 1981, initially believed they had to overthrow Arab nationalist rulers and impose a purified Islamic order across the Middle East. Similarly, the Taliban, who overthrew the Soviet backed regime in Kabul in 1992, sought to impose on Afghanistan the Salafi ideals they had imbibed in Arab sponsored madrassas across the border, in Pakistan.

Globalization, however, had also transformed the Cold War project of Islamism in one country. Paradoxically, the fast world that had undermined the Soviet Union now made it possible for transnational Islamism, of the Salafist variety, to attack the western Great Satan itself and in its own backyard. As Stephen P. Cohen observed: 'Globalization not only makes it possible for them to attack the United States', it was also logical. The logic assumed that nation states no longer represented the real power structure. 'The relevant power structure is global'. But if one country enforced it, it was 'the American superpower'.[61]

Yet despite the backlash from disparate groups, left behind, offended or marginalized by globalization, there existed, the prevailing liberal consensus contended, neither a shared interest, nor the collective resources, for a 'new coherent, universal ideological reaction to globalization'. Redundant steelworkers had little in common with environmental activists or Middle Eastern jihadis. Whilst the first era of global capitalism had witnessed universalist Marxist, socialist and fascist ideological alternatives to market capitalism, Friedman concluded, like Fukuyama, that no ideology, other than a liberal democratic one, could 'remove all the brutality and destructiveness of capitalism and still produce steadily rising standards of living'.[62]

In order to mitigate the disruptive and creatively destructive impact of globalization, the process needed, therefore, to become more inclusive, both at the level of the state and transnationally. A progressive commentariat maintained that avoiding a global, Manichean division between winners and losers required a new international social contract between 'workers, financiers and governments' to ensure 'sustainable globalization'. The liberal pursuit of a wealthier, socially just and sustainable new world order required, paradoxically, the abridgment of the free market policies that had made globalization possible and successful.

Market or competition states, promoting private sector reform and 'neo-liberal' attitudes to investment, welfare and finance had created the preconditions for globalization in the 1980s. However, as the 1990s unfolded, the political, fiscal and economic thinking of those who advised the Conservative and Republican administrations of Margaret Thatcher in the UK and Ronald Reagan in the US traded at a political discount. The 'pure market vision', its critics alleged, had socially divisive and politically unsustainable consequences both globally and locally. At the same time, the return to a paternalistic, or socialist, cradle to grave welfare state was no longer politically or economically feasible in the era of the Electronic Herd.

To give it moral as well as political legitimacy, liberal democracy therefore required a new 'social compact that both embraces free markets, but also ensures that they benefit and are tolerable for as many people as possible'. Globalization had to be democratized to make 'it work for more and more people'. Commentators like Friedman, Joseph Stiglitz and George Soros wrote that the only way to balance the forces of globalization was the centre left or social democratic project in Clinton's America, Tony Blair's UK and Gerhard Schröder's Germany that attempted to harmonize and democratize globalization. This new 'third way' sought an equilibrium between open markets, the fast world, and those marginalized by the process. The conundrum of how to humanize the consequences of globalization meant both centre left and, in time, centre right, Western democratic governments pursued a magic formula that, whilst embracing globalization, provided a social safety net for those marginalized by the process, 'because without integration with the world you will never generate the incomes you need to keep standards of living rising and to take care of the left behinds'.[63] Evidently, the developed economies required a redistributive, socially just way to achieve equitable, as well as progressive, economic development and promote what Soros envisaged as a global open society that transcended the evidently anachronistic sovereign nation state system.[64]

Beyond the West, somewhat differently, sustainable globalization required a total democratic transition to universal norms. Soft and not so soft authoritarian regimes in East Asia, South America and Eastern Europe discovered that the impact of globalization was challenging, destabilizing and ultimately delegitimizing. In a borderless world, without an external, authoritarian hegemon, the floating masses could no longer be coerced into passive acquiescence. The pursuit of legitimacy and growth within the golden straitjacket inevitably accelerated the replacement of illiberal governments in developing states that embarked on the globalization path by others that sought to adjust its burdens. Regime transition, once achieved, gave the people ownership of the political process. As Larry Diamond explained, 'as a result of the opportunity to participate in the process and throw out people who they felt had moved too harshly... or corruptly', the globalization process achieved 'greater political legitimacy and thus more sustainability'.[65] This, the emerging liberal consensus maintained, was what happened in Eastern Europe after 1989 and would happen in East and South East Asia after 1997.

Nevertheless, as sustainable globalization established the economic preconditions that demanded greater democracy, it also required a benign hegemon and a stable power structure to sustain it. As Robert Kagan observed, 'good ideas and good technologies also need a strong power that promotes those ideas by example and protects those ideas by winning on the battlefield'.[66]

The United States, as the sole hyperpower, thus assumed a disproportionate burden for sustaining globalization and the open, borderless economic order it announced. The US, therefore, sought to fashion the process in its liberal, democratic self-image. This required US commitment to, and investment in, a rule-based order and multilateral institutions like the United Nations, the IMF, NATO, WTO and the World Bank. These institutions, the liberal US foreign policy establishment believed, gave those nations 'adapting to American geopolitical leadership some sense that they have a voice in the decision making'.[67] John Ikenberry discovered an 'institutional logic' in this postwar 'liberal institutional order' which was 'reinforced but not caused by the Cold War'. 'Power disparities', Ikenberry thought, were 'rendered less consequential, reducing the incentives for states to move toward...hegemonic and balance of power orders'.[68]

In what history subsequently revealed to be a largely mistaken scenario for the evolution of world politics in the twenty-first century, Friedman claimed, with typical bravado, that:

> In the globalization era, counterinsurgency is out; baby-sitting is in. House to house fighting is out; cruise missiles are in. Green Berets are out; UN blue helmets are in. In today's world there is no war that America can lose for long abroad and no war it can sustain for long at home. So when the American President is faced with a military threat his first question is not 'what strategy will work to put an end to this threat?' Rather his first question is, 'How much do I have to pay to get this show off CNN so I can forget about it?'[69]

Clinton's ill-fated 1993 adventure in Somalia seemingly confirmed a pre-millennial reluctance for US foreign adventure, no matter how ethically justified. Subsequently, convincing the US public of the need for an active foreign policy of 'humanitarian intervention' to maintain 'the minimal necessary rules and norms' of the international order seemed to liberal internationalists a difficult, but not necessarily insurmountable task.

After all, American hegemony, or what its critics termed 'Empire', benefited most from the fact that, as the world fell forward towards liberal democracy, integrated markets and the international rule of law, it relegated violence to the periphery.[70] Progressive thought, idealistically assumed this rendered inter-state war redundant as an instrument of policy. Immanuel Kant's neglected *Perpetual Peace: a*

Philosophical Sketch (1795) appeared increasingly prescient. Revised for contemporary consumption, constitutional republics, accountable to their citizens in accordance with a constitution 'based on *cosmopolitan right*', would see individuals and states co-exist in 'an external relationship of mutual influence' conducive to a perpetual peace.[71] Friedman's 'golden arches theory' translated Kantian peace into a popular idiom. Friedman's version held 'that no two countries that both have McDonalds have ever fought a war against each other since they each got their McDonalds'.[72]

The Third Way Moment

A post-Cold War, progressive, transnational consensus emerged in the course of the 1990s. It dominated government thinking in both Europe and the United States for a quarter of a century. At the millennium, it was both academically and politically fashionable to assert, as Anthony Giddens did, that the developed states of the fast world were now 'without enemies'. Globalization and the interconnected market rendered large-scale, inter-state war, if not impossible, then increasingly 'unlikely'.[73] Paul Hirst and Grahame Thompson considered 'armed forces'…'an irrelevance for the major advanced states in dealing with one another'. Although advanced states might still face threats, nevertheless in golden arched McWorld governments were unlikely to have 'to call on the lives and properties of their citizens for war'.

Moreover, 'without war', the nation state 'becomes less significant to the citizen'.[74] Summarizing this perspective at the end of the twentieth century, John Baylis and Steve Smith contended that accelerated globalization 'reduced the chances of major…war' and 'incentives for states to embark on territorial conquest'. Ultimately, 'interstate warfare generally advances little purpose for – and sooner positively harms – global capitalism, global environmental management, global tourism and so on'.[75]

As planning for inter-state war ceased to be a critical factor in government calculation, it also seemed 'no longer utopian to connect issues of national and global governance'.[76] In an interconnected world, the relationship between the global and the local became an all-consuming progressive political, financial and academic shibboleth.

The key progressive political question was how, as Giddens' *Polity Press* co-founder, David Held contended, to 'embed utopia' in order to create sustainable 'economic improvement in global markets while not sacrificing the basic cohesion of developed and developing societies'.

Although at the time these writers seemed to occupy a small intellectual theoretical enclave, detached from the political mainstream, this utopian project came to influence a post-millennial generation educated in its preoccupations with global justice, cosmopolitan democracy and emancipation from the thrall of the otiose nation state. How, we might wonder, did this evolution in thinking come about?

3

THE PROGRESSIVE MIND AND THE
ISLAMIST CHALLENGE

At the dawn of the new millennium, a progressive intellectual consensus assumed an increasingly ideological form that affected and sometimes constrained Western democratic behaviour domestically and transnationally. It came to influence government policy in both Europe and the United States for over two decades. It assumed that history had ended and the world moved according to a teleological timetable towards an inclusive, secular, socially just, human rights based, borderless world where globalized economic dynamism unleashed 'creativity and innovation'. The latter phrase appeared in the European manifesto *Europe: The Third Way-Die Neute Mitte* that British Prime Minister Tony Blair and German Chancellor Gerhard Schröder issued in 1999. This global, progressive movement went 'beyond left and right'. It also went beyond the nation state.[1]

'Hubristic' is the epithet that springs to mind to describe the imposition of a norm-based, transnational rule that transcended conventional Western party political lines and the state-based international order. US Democrats like Bill Clinton; Tony Blair's New Labour; Schröder's SPD (*Sozialdemocratische Partei Deutschlands*); and, in Australia, John Howard's Liberal coalition government, all promoted, by various means, global democratic integration, as did their twenty-first century Republican, Democrat, Conservative, Labor, Liberal, and Christian Democrat successors: George W. Bush and Barack Obama in America, David Cameron in the United Kingdom, Angela Merkel in Germany, and Kevin Rudd and Malcolm Turnbull in Australia. The third way accepted market economics, but rejected 'market society', preferring instead a 'new politics',[2] which, Tony Blair maintained, transcended conventional party politics and partisanship.[3]

An emerging international elite in the mainstream media, business, finance and government, as well as academia, thus promoted a model of 'cosmopolitan governance' for a borderless twenty-first century world.[4] As 'chief architect' of the third way, Anthony Giddens,[5] observed in 1998, developed states were 'without enemies'. Consequently, the key political issue was how, as David Held contended, to sustain 'economic improvement in global markets while not sacrificing the basic cohesion of developed and developing societies'.

Although the Anglo-Saxon, libertarian market state had unleashed globalization's economic potential, from the mid-1990s progressive, cosmopolitan, communitarian, deliberative and radical democratic thought held that the free market required tempering by 'solidarity in social relations'.[6] Unlike old style socialism, the new perspective accepted the market, but insisted that it required regulation to guarantee a set of desired outcomes. Its amalgam of market economics and progressive policy viewed these outcomes in terms of enhancing social justice; recognizing difference; regionalism and transnational governance; and transforming the outmoded sovereign state. Progressive states and international legal regimes implemented these desiderata, and with every implementation the individual became both a citizen of the world and a pensioner ever more dependent upon an administrative bureaucracy.

As Ralf Dahrendorf observed, there was already something 'slightly contrived, almost elitist' about a concept which attracted attention through 'evangelistic methods of communication'. Third way thought deflected criticism by 'an amalgam of spin, diffidence and dogmatism'.[7] Its emancipatory, or, to use Tony Blair's term, 'modernization' agenda[8] viewed 'cosmopolitan pluralism' and 'democratizing democracy' as a progressive way of 'responding structurally to globalization'.[9] To modernize the UK, for example, required 'upward' and 'downward' reform. It required devolution of authority to the subnational level in Scotland and Wales, whilst alienating sovereignty from Westminster 'upward', to regional, supranational European governance structures in Brussels, the Hague and Strasbourg. It offered the prospect of 'the movement of governance to a world level and diffusion downward to the local level'.[10]

Cosmopolitan democracy, unlike the traditional political variety, welcomed the dilution and fragmentation of state sovereignty, replacing it with an oxymoronic 'cosmopolitan nation in a cosmopolitan democracy operating on a global scale'.[11] As Held conceived it, global democracy could only be 'sustained by ensuring the accountability of all interrelated and connected power systems'. The 'people would enjoy multiple citizenships... They would be citizens of their immediate political communities and of the wider regional and global networks which impacted upon their lives'. The cosmopolitan polity would reflect and embrace the 'diverse forms of power and authority that operate within and across borders'.[12]

Against this 'background...the nation state would in due course wither away' or be 'relocated within an overarching democratic law'.[13] Former Australian Foreign Minister and director of Human Rights Watch Gareth Evans considered that membership of the emerging transnational order required a new category of 'good international citizens' dedicated to human rights promotion and global norms. Critical theorists like Andrew Linklater explained what such 'cosmopolitan citizenship' entailed, namely 'dispositions and practices that can be harnessed to transform political communities and the global order so that they conform with universalistic moral commitments'.[14]

International or regional organizations like the United Nations or the European Court of Human Rights, abetted by congeries of international lawyers rather than elected parliaments, enforced these overarching transnational commitments. The NGOs and INGOs, the UN, IMF, WTO, and the EU Council of Ministers, which were either established or acquired increasing regional or international authority in the 1990s to advance this 'ethical ambition' and 'emancipatory intent', were also liberated from irksome popular democratic control.[15]

International decision-making, on this level, inevitably entailed a loss of democratic accountability at the state level. State decentralization, subsidiarity, and modernization rarely meant a gain for liberty, transparency or political accountability. Among the problems it created, law and order, homegrown terrorism and uncontrolled migration flows stood out, while the solutions proffered were bureaucratically guided, ethically ambitious programmes beyond civil control.

Across Europe, the operation of this ethically activist, political and bureaucratic elite increasingly resembled a less efficient version of Singapore's illiberal administrative state model. As Ralf Dahrendorf, a keen observer of the European Union's authoritarian tendencies, noted in 1999, 'the temptations of leadership and the comforts of public apathy' combined to form a 'perilous attack upon liberty'.[16] The new liberalism, as it evolved from a series of progressive intimations into an ideological form, sat uncomfortably with the sovereign, democratic nation state and its conventions of individual liberty, equal citizenship, and exclusive political allegiance.

The modern, Cold War era, liberal democratic state was an association of individuals in which each person was both a subject and a citizen, on the one hand, and a member of civil society on the other. The new activist regionalism, by contrast, moved away from the rule of law, administered through sovereign assemblies, towards a practice of bureaucratic management in order to achieve equality of outcome and social harmony. The European managerial class in politics, public administration, the media, and academia increasingly resembled an enlightened despotism. Its rule possessed 'two general characteristics': pursuing the 'politics of perfection' and 'the politics of uniformity'. The essence of this rationalist managerial style was the combination of the two.[17]

The third way approach to democracy and global order was replete with rationalist temptation masquerading as multicultural sensitivity and uncoerced deliberative and communicative reason. It solved all conflict through an amalgamation of state and civil society. It organized society according to a single rational progressive principle, converting the state and ultimately the globe into a managerial enterprise. In the process, it dissolved the political distinction between public and private life. Its rule was of course benevolent, but despotisms seldom claim to be malevolent.

The third way understanding, through its abstract ethical claim to advance global democracy and international good citizenship, assumed forms that undermined traditional understandings of the democratic state and the citizenship or equal membership of the constitutional order that accompanied it. Liberated from the Cold War restraints that the Western democratic state had placed upon it, the progressive mind explored these abstract global and ethical possibilities.

The Construction of the New Liberal Persona at the End of History

Despite the practical success of the Cold War market state order, the new liberal progressive soteriology, with its penchant for rational harmony and openness to the notion of equal dignity and the need 'for secure and separate cultural identities',[18] invited the questioning of its ruling assumptions.[19] Founded on an intellectual compromise so extensive that it tries to include all the guiding beliefs of Western opinion, the new liberalism came, as we have seen, to accommodate a relativist and critical response to liberal certainty and establish it as the premise for its latest ethical and emancipatory programmes.[20]

The modern liberal identity grew out of an Enlightenment, secular and improving sensibility that found the present condition distasteful, not because it is dull, comfortable, or transient, but because it contains suffering. In its nineteenth and twentieth century rationalist pursuit of both truth and improvement, it evinced a growing distaste for what Kenneth Minogue termed 'suffering situations'.[21] The enhanced liberal progressive character, reformulated after 1990 as the international or cosmopolitan 'good citizen', was, like its radical democratic counterpart, ill at ease in the nation state. It found victims everywhere and sought universal norms to alleviate their pain and voice their voicelessness, both locally and globally.[22]

In 'a post-historical world', the new liberalism, therefore, tried to establish the rational secular basis for a shared public morality calibrated to the needs of a cosmopolitan, multicultural, borderless, fast, transnational order. It promoted an abstract global ethics emanating from a single rational viewpoint that sought to harmonize all human relations. As it turned into government policy in the last decade of the twentieth century, its meliorist conception of improvement required

33

managerial systems to measure performance and impose morally improving behaviour upon the general population.

It was not the principle of liberty, therefore, that, after 1990, absorbed the official mind. Instead the emancipation of minorities, their recognition and compensation for past suffering preoccupied third way governance. The identity/oppression syndrome captured the dilemma that cosmopolitan ethics encountered in its attempt to achieve an inclusive, egalitarian and harmonious global order, freely obeyed by 'diverse' but nevertheless 'cherished' communities of difference.

The liberal always searches for and eventually finds solutions, particularly in open societies, which permit, acknowledge and respond to its criticism. The rational solution inevitably requires measurement, an index of suffering and an appropriately calibrated response. A brief excursion through recent developments in progressive thought since the end of the Cold War explains how oppression and victimhood replaced a shared understanding of national belonging and citizenship.

In the aftermath of 1945, Western liberal elites initially identified equality of opportunity as the challenge to future progress and sought to assess and promote ability, regardless of race, creed or gender. However, in the post-1968 world of emancipation, and rainbow coalitions of feminist, civil, gay and minority rights advocates, the liberal *persona* progressively lost its enthusiasm for equality of opportunity and focused instead on the problem of diversity and equality of outcome. John Rawls' *A Theory of Justice*, as we have seen, first captured the new taste for social justice, and bureaucracies busied themselves with finding criteria for measuring need based on exclusion and discrimination.

This ethical pursuit, one that came to dominate academic political theory and, in time, government practice, found the legal proceduralism that sought to establish the abstractly just procedures to govern conduct nationally and internationally too rigid. Consequently, a more culturally empathetic liberalism emerged in the 1990s, one that attended to the specific grievances of excluded minorities. Pursuing this progressive line, public sector jobs increasingly required applicants not only to state their gender, but also their ethnicity, rather than their citizenship. Adverts for tertiary education posts announced that due to gender imbalances, appointment committees would look to appoint female candidates. The criteria soon expanded to include ethnicity, disability and sexual orientation.

At the same time, radical London boroughs, North American Ivy League universities, and the Canadian and Australian governments began experimenting with projects that cherished diversity rather than ability, correcting institutional racism and sexism and quantifying the change in terms of equality of outcome, rather than opportunity. Branded, in the 1980s, a utopian fantasy of 'the loony left', this approach to measuring oppression, representing it by recognizing its difference, eventually achieved the status of academic and political orthodoxy.[23] The ethical truth embraced was not empirical, but criteriological. Once established as a policy conviction, 'the revelation floats free of any evidence'; more precisely, 'it *determines* the evidence'.[24]

As it dawned on the improving post-colonial progressives that addressing oppression both globally and locally was not only virtuous and just, but also lucrative in terms of public sector and academic preferment, a bureaucracy devoted to diversity and difference emerged. The brave new world of recognition management and policy bureaucracies devoted to measuring and improving the oxymoronic inclusionary diversity state thus turned the suffering, the migrant and the victim into an assessable and evolving moral system devoted to their emancipation. At the same time, it diluted, or in its preferred argot, 'transformed' the classical notion of equal citizenship of a constitutionally limited state into something global, amorphous and borderless.

In the perfected community of the socially just, all the abstract classes which sought public visibility and voices, whether as oppressed women, minorities, or the disabled, would be respected. Consequently, they would deserve, as a group entitlement, all the kinds of success admired in a nation that the arts, government and science conferred, thereby generating a full range of successful people prospering in the admired professions. The progressive society moves away from individual ability towards collective self-worth. The more collectively people thought, the more one of the new liberalism's basic ambitions would be achieved, namely the abolition of failure.

The allocatory bureaucracy of the evolving cosmopolitan order reduced formerly equal and free individual citizens to subjects, requiring management, education and guidance. Classical liberalism, which pioneered the idea of individual liberty, by a process of rational critique, metamorphosed into an ethical activism that inhibited both individual liberty and freedom of expression. Born with an Enlightenment contempt for tradition and a critical attitude to present imperfections, the liberal mind always sought and fought for causes. Indifferent to the open society that made it possible, the new normativism of the post-Cold War era restlessly pursued the emancipation of the oppressed; the more alienated from the prevailing secular order, the better. To question the progressive critic merely demonstrated the ignorant response of the unenlightened to suffering victims.[25]

Whilst the suffering might be real, the policies to address it demanded the management of the population in depth and detail. Seduced by the empty kisses of abstraction and assuming all problems available to rational solution, the progressive liberal mind dismissed objections to multiculturalism, group rights, social justice, and an evolving international community of shared norms as at best irrational, at worst racist.

The Islamist Challenge

The case of Islam, in its evolving encounter with the borderless, secular West, crystallized the illusions that beset the liberal mind in its attempt to establish an inclusive order, freely obeyed. At the end of history, the old media, government, and academia dismissed, or discounted the fact that progressive multiculturalism had incubated a distinctive style of thought and practice that radically questioned its basic teleological assumptions. Political Islam, in a soteriological mood, found the West's commitment to secularism, normativism and internationalism not progress but, to quote its most influential thinker, Sayyid Qutb, 'hideous schizophrenia'.[26] From this politically religious perspective, only 'terror in the mind of God',[27] or violent *jihad*, could rectify this condition of hubristic ignorance. Ironically, while Western theorists contemplated the end of history in Enlightenment, thymotic, and secular terms, the Islamist mind considered itself locked in a Manichean struggle to establish a *Dar al-Islam*, confronting Western secularism and offering an eschatologically validated alternative to it.

Islamism, as an evolving understanding, responded to the West's global ethics by selectively manipulating elements of Sunni and Shia teaching, amalgamating them with nihilist and illiberal thought of a Western critical and postmodern provenance to craft a very different ideology or, to use Eric Voegelin's term, a new 'political religion'.[28] Like the Western ideological formations that it selectively drew upon, Islamism also possessed a triadic structure, couched in a religious rhetoric, one that disclosed past oppression, requiring violent struggle (*jihad*) in the present, to achieve a final, apocalyptic emancipation. This millenarian vision proved in time both adaptable and appealing to the new global audiences that the borderless world and a protean, virtual, social media environment ironically brought into being after the Cold War ended.

The new, catastrophic terror that threatened the post-Cold War democratic state order was, to some extent, the price paid for the way the Cold War ended. The limited strategy of Cold War terrorism, which sought media attention but limited casualties, rapidly assumed a transnational form facilitated by the end of the Cold War balance of superpowers and the spread of low intensity ethno-religious conflicts in failing states and states of concern. The new interconnectedness, brought about by the revolution in communications, facilitated trade, population flows, economic growth, and anxiety. It also enabled transnational criminal activity, notably people, drug, and weapons smuggling, and the transnationalization of what Raymond Aron termed 'polymorphous' violence organized via diaspora communities, greater interconnectivity, and the emerging borderless world that progressive commentators and business elites in the 1990s had enthusiastically welcomed.[29]

Prior to 2001, despite evidence to the contrary provided by failing states like Somalia, Rwanda, and the former Yugoslavia, and the fallout from the Asian financial crisis (1997), this period of *Zeit* without *Geist* in hindsight represented the highpoint of the argument for global, liberal, democratic convergence and the end of history, where all *isms* became *wasms*. Europe *sans frontières*, along with the development of regional groupings like ASEAN's (the Association of Southeast Asian Nations) expanded Pacific community offered the premonitory intimation of a post-nation state constellation. Yet whilst an ASEAN or EU-style post-national, managerialist bureaucracy sought to erase the potential for conflict via empathy, ethical aid, and emancipatory discourse, the new terror without a signature or acknowledged source sought catastrophic impact to convey its non-negotiable, apocalyptic message.

Initially, the new warfare scenario confined itself to states or regions 'of concern' – Afghanistan, the Balkans, the Middle East – but circumstances and technology afforded the opportunity for the failed state world, fuelled by myths of ethno-religious purity, to hit back at the borderless world of the progressive visionary.

As the strategy became more unpredictable and asymmetric over the first decade of the twenty-first century, it also became more protean. Al-Qaeda, and subsequently Islamic State in Iraq and the Levant (ISIL), represented the most significantly evolved proponents of this polymorphous, increasingly social media-dependent strategy. It operated increasingly as a franchised and de-territorialized arrangement found in states of concern, but with elements of its command and control situated in multicultural, cosmopolitan cities like London, Kuala Lumpur, Jakarta, New York, Paris or Sydney.

In fact, in its most interesting post-9/11 and post-Iraq war form, the congeniality of multicultural global cities for the support networks of transnational ethno-religious struggle over time promoted a *sui generis* militancy in the diaspora, characterized by groups like *al-Muhajiroun* (the Migrants), based in London from the mid-1990s until the UK government curtailed their activities in the wake of the 7 July 2005 attack on the London underground.

Islamism and Modernity

> Colonialism and its followers, the apostate rulers, then started to openly erect crusader centres, societies, and organizations like Masonic Lodges, Lions and Rotary clubs, and foreign schools. They aimed at producing a wasted generation that pursued everything that is Western... Allah's enemies plotted and planned, and Allah too planned, and the best of planners is Allah.[30]

As this quotation from a 1998 al-Qaeda training manual indicates, post-Cold War Islamist ideology categorically rejected Enlightenment faith in secular reason and progress. Instead, new technology, particularly social media and the internet, fuelled a retreat into a primal narcissism that responded directly to the growing anxiety globalization created. The recourse to such violent Islamic identity politics evolved from the failure of a variety of illiberal nationalist and pan-nationalist projects in the Muslim world after 1945, further exacerbated, in the Middle East, by the goad of Israel and the enduring sore of Palestine.

To address this failure within the post-colonial Muslim world, various reformist groups began to view *jihad* or violent struggle as a necessary precursor to a purified new order. The Afghan war against the Soviet Union (1979–89), culminating in the defeat of the Soviet Satan, vindicated this interpretation. The Afghan war, and the globalizing opportunities made possible by the end of the Cold War, enabled a network of disparate revolutionary groups to evolve into an Islamist *Internationale*. It formed al-Qaeda (the base) as a new force outside the international order. Europe, the United States, South East Asia and even Australia became important and evolving nodes of autonomous organization and recruitment. While Western analysts considered the Soviet reversal a result of imperial overstretch, intimating the imminent demise of liberal democracy's main ideological competitor, from the Islamist perspective, the successful *jihad* against the Soviet Union left only the western 'spider house' standing. The 'collapse' of the twin towers on the morning of September 11, 2001, exposed its ultimate fragility.[31]

After 1990, the non-Arab Muslim world, particularly its European extension, evolved an especially intractable version of an Islamist ideological style that legitimated catastrophic violence, one which, as Olivier Roy observed, 'has nothing to do with importing Islamic radicalization to Europe'. On the contrary, it evinced a *sui generis* process of ideological radicalization with the potential for projecting catastrophic violence globally.[32]

An ascetic, militant brand of Islam successfully promoted its appeal first across the Muslim world and, via the processes of globalization post-1990, established itself amongst diasporic communities in Europe, the United States, and Australia. This evolution was both ironic and troubling. It was ironic because many scholars and media commentators on Islamic development assumed that the dominant Sunni model of Islam would prove responsive to development and be modernity-friendly. The case of Southeast Asian Islam, for example, was widely promoted in the 1990s as amenable to capitalism, benignly syncretic, and immune to Middle Eastern-style religious fundamentalism.[33]

Yet what happened in Southeast Asia in the wake of the Asian financial crisis cast doubt on these assumptions. The discovery of the al-Qaeda franchise *Jemaah Islamiyah* (Islamic Group) in December 2001, and the bombing in Bali in October 2002 revealed that, even here, Islam harboured a significant minority committed to an exacting, puritanical version of the faith that required *jihad* to bring about a *Darul Islamiya* (an Islamic realm) stretching from Cambodia to Kalimantan.[34] That the greatest catastrophe in this area of the global campaign occurred in Bali, the most tolerant and least Islamized province of Indonesia, reinforced the point.

It was troubling because both the 9/11 attacks and those in Southeast Asia together with the European experiences of Madrid 2004 and London 2005, among others, cast doubt on the mainstream analysis of Western modernization, democratization and liberal development theory. The Southeast Asian case shook the heretofore unshakeable shibboleth of modernization theory and liberal orthodoxy: that democratization in the non-Western world would engender social and intellectual pluralism (even with its corresponding discontents), not a socially centrifugal identity politics.

Analogously, the European case undermined faith in the idea that rich, developed polities could unproblematically integrate different ethnic and religious minorities through instituting equal opportunity policies and diversity awareness training, cherishing minorities that would progressively engender commitment to a communitarian and cosmopolitan democratic ethic.[35]

Yet, rather than give up these articles of progressive faith, Western commentators turned to a narrowly socio-economic explanation to account for the special circumstances that facilitated the call of militant Islam in the developed and developing world. In the UK, the Home Office and other ministries maintained that it was amongst the alienated and ghettoized communities of Brick Lane or Bradford, or among the ranks of petty criminals in H.M. Prisons with little hope of anything beyond the dole or casual employment, that radical Islam recruited its foot soldiers, like the shoe bomber Richard Reid.[36]

In Southeast Asia, meanwhile, there existed a correlation between the proliferation and popularity of radical Islamic groups and the simultaneous faltering of the economy during the Asian Financial Crisis of 1997. We could be witnessing, then, an example of James C. Davies' 'J-curve', where popular disillusion and a propensity for rebellion correlate not with absolute standards of living, but with the incendiary gap between rising expectations and a sudden decline of performance.[37]

But correlation is not cause, and a predominantly economic explanation for millennial woes and the global appeal of radical Islam appeared worryingly incomplete. It could account for riot and discontent, but not for New York, Bali, Jakarta, Madrid, London, Paris or Brussels' distinctly Islamist idiom of expression and social profile. Government reports underlined the disturbing deficiency in official understanding before and after 9/11 in New York, London and Paris. The UK government's Home Office considered the problem of Muslim alienation nothing that a few action-plans, 'outreach' programmes, and 'one-stop shop' resource interactive CD-ROMs could not remedy, even if this eventually evolved into a strategy to *contest* radicalism or violent extremism.[38] Governments in the US, and across Western Europe and Australia, devised similar programmes.

However, the deracinating, globalizing experience of recent years in the developed and developing world seemed the fuse rather than the ammonium nitrate itself. The turn toward an ideological Islam amongst the global Muslim community has, in fact, more to do with the consequences of the slow motion collision between modernity in its globalized form and an Islamic social character. The fact that standard-issue Western modernization theory has been wrong about other Islamic societies in the Middle East and South Asia as well suggests that this is a line of analysis worth exploring.

Students of Islamic societies stress their many cultural differences.[39] Yet too great an insistence upon distinctions risks missing commonalities of equal importance. It is mostly among middle-class males under forty that previously proscribed Islamist groups in the Middle East, South and Southeast Asia, and their confrères in North America, London, Paris, Hamburg, and Madrid found recruits to an uncompromising ideology of *sharia* discipline.

In mid-2002, the Surabaya and Jogjakarta regional heads of *Laskar Jihad* (Holy War Troopers), an Indonesian Islamist group dedicated to advancing the Quran by the Kalashnikov if necessary, were a Western-trained engineer and a medical doctor, respectively. Analogously, in the UK, suicide bombers like Omar Sharif or al-Qaeda operatives like Omar Sheikh came from wealthy middle-class backgrounds. In Sheikh's case, he attended the fee-paying Forest School in north-east London, and had completed the first year of a BA in statistics at the London School of Economics.[40]

Other London universities played host to recruiters on behalf of the nominally non-violent *Hizb ut-Tahrir* and *al-Muhajiroun* (the Migrants), an al-Qaeda front organization.[41] Membership of *Hizb ut-Tahrir* was notably middle-class. It included business economics graduates, IT specialists and financial advisers.[42] A similar kind of campus extremism in the 1960s found solace in revolutionary left organizations like the International Socialists, the International Marxist Group, and even Irish Republican groups.[43] In other words, although radical Islam remains a minority avocation, globally its appeal to an educated, but deracinated, middle class shared an affinity with the composition of al-Qaeda and later mutations like al-Nusra and the Islamic State networks – whether in their Saudi, Egyptian, German, Pakistani, Algerian, Syrian, Iraqi, French, British, US or Southeast Asian franchises.

At the same time, the popular recourse to religious purificationism in Southeast Asia also repeats a pattern found elsewhere in Asia and the Middle East. Whenever centralizing secular authoritarian regimes in the Muslim world have experienced rapid growth and attendant social change, they are invariably confronted by a fundamentalist challenge. That challenge is everywhere accompanied by a significant middle class retreat into a closed world of sectarian identity. Progressive secularism has everywhere failed to thrive in the modernization processes of late-developing Muslim-majority states. In some cases, as in Iran, fundamentalism achieves power. In others, it achieves a capacity to blunt the power and programmes of the secular state, and to retard the liberalization of civil society. Even apparent long-term successes are not immune from such challenges, as the recent political history of Turkey shows.

A different process, however, occurred in Europe and to a lesser extent in North America. Here, second and third generation migrants found solace not in the bland joys of secularism, or in nostalgia for the struggle in the homeland, but in a re-Islamization that favours 'supranational [Islamist] organizations instead of 'national' Islamic movements'.[44] *Hizb ut-Tahrir* (Party of Liberation) exemplified this transition from a diasporic to a universalist mode of Islamic identity politics. As Olivier Roy explains:

> [this] fundamentalist party based in London...was originally set up as a Palestinian Islamic movement in 1953. Officially non-violent, its ideas are nevertheless very radical. It advocates the immediate re-establishment of the caliphate...and the ultimate conversion of the entire world to Islam. *Hizb ut-Tahrir* is now a genuinely international movement.[45]

And it was increasingly from London, with its global links, that it promoted its agenda internationally, without fear of surveillance or prosecution, establishing branches in Sweden and the Netherlands as well as throughout the UK. Indeed, as Ed Hussein, a former member, observed, *Hizb ut-Tahrir* 'borrowed' its organizational structure and confrontational tactics from radical socialists.[46] As an elite vanguard party, it recruited on university campuses, whose diversity and tolerance it found particularly congenial. As Hussein again observed, 'at many universities the tactics of confrontation and consolidation of Muslim feeling under the leadership of *Hizb* activists were being adopted... What dumbfounded us was the fact that the authorities on campuses never stopped us'.[47] Between 1997 and 2012 the party also opened branches in Sudan, Uzbekistan, Pakistan, Malaysia, Indonesia (until 2017), and Australia. In fact, the Pakistani branch seemed 'to have been set up at the instigation of the London leadership. During a trial for sedition in Lahore in 2002, the defendants were British born Muslims who only spoke English with an East London accent'.[48]

Civilization and its Discontents

If standard Western theories of modernization are powerless to explain such broad phenomena, where else might we look for help? It is tempting to join the queue of those who would cast Francis Fukuyama's End of History thesis against Samuel Huntington's theory of the Clash of Civilizations,[49] but it is a temptation worth resisting.[50] Fukuyama pointedly identified the Muslim world as the likeliest source of long-term resistance to his vision. As for Huntington's clash, it focuses on Islam's relations with the non-Islamic world, not on the sociology of Islam itself. It is a little hard to see why so many turn for guidance to these two approaches, neither of which centres on the puzzle at hand. Besides, grand theorizing is vulnerable, almost inevitably, to a specious form of reductionism. As Pieter Geyl observed of the early twentieth century proponents of civilizational history, Oswald Spengler and Arnold Toynbee,[51] their civilizational sweep suffered from 'fallacious arguments and spurious demonstrations'.[52] It is therefore somewhat misleading to ask if the supranational Islamist case merely indicates a temporary subsidence on the path to polyarchy at the End of History, or rather foreshadows an inexorable clash of civilizations in a dichotomized global order on the model of Benjamin Barber's *Jihad versus McWorld* or Thomas Friedman's *The Lexus and the Olive Tree*.[53]

If one nevertheless conducts a thought experiment where the sociology of Islam in its supranational, ultra orthodox, and perennially jihadist mode is framed as a test between Whiggish optimism versus Spenglerian pessimism, one does not need Fukuyama or Huntington to proceed. Such thinking has an old (and oddly neglected) pedigree. Take Fukuyama's essential case for liberal optimism, for example. Analysing the decline and fall of the Roman Empire from the security of a politically liberal, rapidly developing, but undemocratic, London in 1776, Edward Gibbon concluded that modern Europe possessed a prophylactic against external and internal threat that Rome had lacked. Rome, of course, fell to a combination of barbarians without and a loss of belief within. Thus, the glory that was Rome 'insensibly declined with their laws and manners'. By contrast, Gibbon considered that the threat posed by barbarism to modernizing eighteenth century Europe had 'contracted to a narrow span'. This was for two reasons.[54]

First, in the spirit of liberal twentieth century modernizing secular ethical theory *avant la lettre*, Gibbon contended that Europe was 'secure from any future irruption of barbarians; since before they can conquer, they must cease to be barbarous'. Modernization, in other words, required civilization; gaining power meant undergoing a process that would eviscerate the motive to use that power in ways inimical to mainstream civilizational institutions and values. Gibbon, and the British Enlightenment generally, believed that they had identified a serendipitous developmental paradox: civilization's schooling of the passions generated a scientific and technological advantage that could only be learned by adopting the soft civilized ways of the modern city. The Highland clan, the migrant minority, and the Bedouin tribe alike had to abandon simple traditional values, brush their hair, trim their beards and go to school, lest they be permanently entrapped in a cake of backward custom. It is essentially the same notion of process that stands at the centre of Fukuyama's contentions, as well as Tony Blair's third way, in politics after 1997, that did much to fashion the once chic Cool Britannia's multiculturally conscious diversity.[55]

Somewhat differently, Gibbon also argued that both Europe and the New World of America – what we now term 'the West' – enjoyed an unassailable technological edge unknown to Rome: 'mathematics, chemistry, mechanics, architecture have been applied to the service of war'. This meant that those disposed to the joys of civilization could not be 'displeased that the subversion of a city should be a work of cost and difficulty; or that an industrious people should be protected by those arts which survive and supply the decay of military virtue. Cannon and fortification', Gibbon pontificated, 'now form an impregnable barrier against the Tartar horse'.[56]

Here, perhaps, is where Gibbon's analysis breaks down, but, in so doing, it illuminates what is unique about our own globally interconnected, but by no means politically or ideologically integrated condition. Unlike Gibbon's eighteenth century faith in the ultimate protection afforded by the civilizing social, educational, and technological setting of the advanced modern city, we have no impermeable barrier against the contemporary equivalent of the Trojan horse – the suicide bomber. By a little understood process, the jihadi warriors of our day have managed to circumvent the 'civilizing' process to which Gibbon alluded. Instead, they employ the West's technology, most notably the internet and social media, but they violently reject the values of the society that produced them.

45

How could such a thing happen? Ernest Gellner, the pioneer of what might be called a clash theory of Western versus Muslim society, proposed an answer many years before Huntington, Fukuyama, or Friedman began asking such questions. As an anthropologist and sociologist, Gellner was acutely aware of the main economistic tenets and epistemological tendencies of Western thinking about development. But he was also sensitive to the fact that these tenets could not explain the modernizing Muslim, or East Asian, world.

From his sociological perspective, Western civil society differed fundamentally from traditional societies in that it required 'modularity', a distinctive capacity to combine in effective associations with others, but without any one of these associations subsuming or defining the rest. Traditional society was stable, but also immobile, because external structures fixed people's definitions of their own identity, and then, for lack of any alternative point of reference, those definitions were internalized. Western individualism, by contrast, enabled a variety of roles in society (religious, ethnic, political, social, occupational), and these increasingly defined identity rather than ascriptive characteristics assigned at birth. This for Gellner was the 'miracle' of modernity that broke the Malthusian trap and the closed circle of traditional society. It happened only once, in England, under the exceptional political conditions that prevailed there in the eighteenth century.[57]

While observing that a vast chasm separated modern flexibility from traditional immobility, rather along the lines of Karl Popper's 'open' and 'closed' societies,[58] Gellner recognized, *contra* Gibbon, and contemporary comparative political scientists and normative international relations theorists, that modernization – what he called 'the deadly angel who spells death to economic inefficiency' – was 'not always at the service of liberty' or secularity.[59] Gellner observed that Islam's encounter with modernity had led it to grow both stronger and purer in the nineteenth and twentieth centuries.[60] Islamic societies seemed to be secularization-resistant; they sidestepped the development of modularity even as they assimilated many modern modes of conduct, including scientific methods.

Islamism and Modernity: From Afghani to jihad.com

This evolving dialectic between a felt need to purify Islamic thought and practice and the experience of modernity in its Western guise is, moreover, by no means a recent phenomenon. In fact, from the middle of the nineteenth century, if not before, Muslim intellectuals grappled with the social facts of modernity and colonization and the weakness of the Muslim response to the Western challenge. Some, like Kemal Atatürk, who dissolved traditional arrangements like the caliphate in 1924, maintained the necessity of adopting Western forms of bureaucracy, secularism and the nation state in order to create the conditions for mobilizing Muslims towards developmental goals.[61] Those who followed the Atatürk route replaced traditionalism with Western educational, administrative and corporatist developmental programmes to modernize post-colonial societies, as the *Front de Liberation Nationale* (FLM) did in Algeria, Gamal Abdel Nasser did in Egypt, and Saddam Hussein in Iraq.

Others, however, considered this route one of pagan ignorance. Following the example of Muhammad ibn Abd al-Wahhab (1702–91)[62] in Arabia, they either maintained the need to purify and codify an Islamic response stripped of traditional accretions, or like Jamal al-Din al-Afghani (1838–97),[63] sought to 're-open the gates of *ijtihad*', enabling independent reasoning regarding the Muslim response to modernity.[64] They prescribed an Islamic formalism to address the challenge posed by a progressive and increasingly secularized modernity, held responsible for the decline of Muslim civilization, remedying the failed Muslim response to the Judaeo-Christian, Western civilizational challenge through a return to a stricter piety and the original Islamic teachings, stripped of later accretions.[65]

Subsequently, those influenced by Afghani and his Egyptian disciple, Mohammed Abduh, also assumed this reinterpretation to require a return to the purity of the early teachings, initially intimated by the strict, Hanbali school jurist, Ibn Taimiya (1263–1328), during the decaying Abbasid dynasty.[66] This style of thought led Middle Eastern scholars in the 1920s and 1930s, like Mohammed Rashid Rida (1865–1935) in Syria and Egypt, to promote the revival of a reformed caliphate implementing the pure teaching of the first rightly guided or pious ancestors (*al-salaf al-salih*, whence 'Salafist') and the stricter jurists who interpreted their *ahadith* (sayings of the Prophet, sing. *hadith*). This intellectual effort to combine modernity with Islamic authenticity found its initial political form in the shape of Hasan al-Banna's (1906–49) Muslim Brothers (*al-Ikhwan al-Muslimun*), whose programme insisted upon the complete and holistic nature of revealed Islam, encompassing *din* (religion), *dunya* (life), and *dawla* (state).[67]

Elsewhere in the Muslim world Abu al-a'la Mawdudi (1903–79), founder of the *Jaamat-i-Islami* (Islamic Party), maintained, in the context of the partition of India, that the new Muslim state of Pakistan should, after 1947, adopt an Islamic constitution. This required, Mawdudi contended, the creation of a total ideological state that vested absolute sovereignty (*hakimiyya*) in God, mortals merely being delegated to implement the holy law. Only thus could the Muslim world escape the current condition of *jahiliyya* (ignorance).[68]

Mawdudi's views profoundly influenced the most important theorist of a politically religious Islam, Sayyid Qutb (1903–66). Qutb's later work, notably *Milestones* (*Ma'alim fi al-Tariq*, 1964) brought out the Manichean distinction between the properly constituted *dar al-Islam* and the condition of almost universal ignorance in which the world, both Muslim and *dhimmi* (non-Muslims living in Muslim states), resided. 'Everything around us', Qutb maintained, 'is a *jahiliyya*...even much of what we think of as being Islamic culture, Islamic sources, or Islamic philosophy and thought is the making of this *jahiliyya*.'[69] The way out of this condition of ignorance required total submission to the sovereignty and rulership of God; or more precisely, as Qutb explains, 'the wresting of power from the hands of its human usurpers to return it to God alone.'[70] For Qutb and his successors, the 'correct order for the steps of the Islamic method' was first to remove the non-Islamic regime and establish Islamic society. Only later would the revolutionaries consider the mundane details of social organization.[71]

Via Qutb and Mawdudi, Islamic reform assumed the character of a political religion. Yet, paradoxically, its desire to build an Islamic state along Islamically planned, rational lines indicated the impact not only of the West but of ideological thinking of a totalitarian character upon a generation of Western-trained Muslim scholars. It is after Qutb that we can refer to Islamism not as a traditional religious form but as an ideology, or more precisely, to use the terminology of Eric Voegelin, a political religion.[72] Like the totalitarian movements of the twentieth century that influenced this style of thought, it assumes an activist mysticism and a specialized knowledge or Gnosis 'of the method of altering being.' As Voegelin explains, in 'the Gnostic attitude' we recognize the 'construction of a formula for self and world salvation, as well as the Gnostic's readiness to come forward as a prophet who will proclaim his knowledge about the salvation of mankind'.[73] Under the influence of Qutb and subsequently Taquiuddin al-Nabhani, the founder of *Hizb ut-Tahrir* in 1953, Islamism became both a system (*nizam*) that immanently critiqued the contradictions in modernity, Islam's relationship with modernity, and the means of radically transforming it via struggle. As Nabhani explained, in *The Way of Revival,* 'The Islamist does not flatter the people, is not courteous to the authorities, or care for the people's customs and traditions... Rather he must adhere to the ideology alone'.[74] Consequently, Nabhani argued for a complete destruction of the existing political order, particularly in Muslim countries, and its replacement by the caliphate or '*khilafah* system'.[75]

The evolving militancy associated with this programme of Muslim authenticity in its confrontation with secularizing modernity reflected the political oppression that groups like the Muslim Brothers encountered in Egypt and Syria from the 1960s onward. In this context, Qutb's successors, like Muhammad Abd al-Salam Faraj and the *al-Jihad* (Holy War) organization, rendered explicit Islam's neglected duty of *jihad* or violent confrontation with the infidel for the imminent establishment of the purified Islamic state by direct action.[76] The failure of the corporatist, nationalist, state model in the Middle East; these states' growing corruption; defeat by Israel in 1967; and failure to address the problem of Palestine, only amplified the divisions within the Muslim world. It was in the aftermath of the assassination of Anwar Sadat in Egypt in 1981, and the suppression of the Muslim Brothers in Syria, that Islamists like Ayman al-Zawahiri and the Palestinian Abdullah Azzam sought to internationalize the struggle and establish, as Zawahiri explained in his *Knights Under the Banner of the Prophet*, a new force 'outside the new international order' designed to release the world from 'domineering Western enslavement'.[77] In order to achieve this transformation to a religiously immanent world order, Zawahiri's group broke with the more pragmatic Muslim Brotherhood and joined with the Arab *mujahideen* in Afghanistan and Pakistan, sponsored by Osama bin Laden after 1988, in order to establish the lineaments of al-Qaeda.[78] The promotion of this ideology and the struggle to realize it was facilitated by the New Islamic Order of Hassan al-Turabi in Sudan, after 1990, the Taliban in Afghanistan after 1996, and, after 2014, by the caliphate of Islamic State in Iraq and the Levant (ISIL). Significantly, and in keeping with its evolving ideological character, the increasingly protean organization and universalization of the Islamist message now occurred outside the Middle East – in South Asia, Southeast Asia, North Africa and, of course, Europe.

This Islamist style global project openly opposed the West's inclusive, cosmopolitan, secular alternative. Prior to his death in 1996, Gellner's attempt to understand why this evolution had occurred led him to develop a sociology of Islamic neo-orthodoxy that describes what developed in South and Southeast Asia, North America, Paris, Brussels, and London at the end of history. Gellner surveyed the macro-social realities of the twentieth century Muslim world and identified a mass movement from the illiterate folk Islam of the countryside to the high, literate, Islam of the city. Urbanization and increased literacy encouraged a shift from a mimetic form of learning to an analogic process defined by abstractions available only to those who could reason through symbols – that is, those who could read and follow the precepts of the Book.[79]

Gellner saw that in the course of the twentieth century neo-orthodox Muslims came to associate greater piety with upward mobility. This involved a process in which the authority defining Islamic piety passed from the clan elder to the literate cleric or imam at the school or the urban mosque, and in which standards of conduct were learned from the printed page rather than through oral tradition. In their own cultural framework, this was advancement – indeed, it was modernization – and it applied with special power to the role and status of women.[80]

If, in the postmodern, post-colonial world, identification with scripturalist high culture becomes the hallmark of Islamic urban sophistication, then it follows that the bourgeois, Muslim woman in London, Karachi, Jakarta or Sydney wears the veil or the headscarf, not because her mother did so, but precisely because she did not. The way 'up' for women is within a newly mobile traditionalism, not outside it. There was nothing explicitly political about the processes of neo-orthodoxy, but Gellner anticipated a number of its political implications. As long as clan groups and tribal affinities remained more or less stable, the processes of neo-orthodoxy would be buffered by local or indigenous tradition and the constraints on behaviour that it imposed. But if the literal community was disrupted sufficiently, or if the migrant energies of modernization ejected individuals and families from it, new possibilities emerged – and here we come to the sociological underpinning of Islamic fundamentalism, or reformed Islam in a globally de-territorialized form that is more accurately termed 'Islamism'.

Islamism is identified most closely with the strain of Islamic thinking called 'Salafism'.[81] While neo-orthodoxy evinced a tendency toward scripturalism and puritanical theology, fundamentalist formalism represented a modern political impulse that re-constructed Islam not in a traditional, but in a *faux* traditionalist way, turning it into a *nizam*, a total ideological system of ultra orthodoxy.[82] This became first evident in the thinking of the Egyptian Islamic Brotherhood, the Pakistani *Jaamat-i-Islami*, and Nabhani's *Hizb ut-Tahrir* in Jordan in the 1950s. It suggests that this Islamist social vision, while founded on a pre-industrial scripturalism, thrives best under social conditions formed by modernization: the specialization and compartmentalization of work associated with industrialization and the transformation of communications. By the late 1990s, each *jihadi* group from Southeast Asia to Western Europe had its own website and was comfortable with mobile phones and soon adept with social media. What these groups envisaged, then, was not the establishment of just any global caliphate, but a cyber-caliphate, networked and organized through websites like umma.net or Azzam.com run, until 2004, by Babar Ahmed through Imperial College, London's computer system.[83] After 2014, Islamic State dramatically developed this strategy. By 2015, its official media organization produced 'slick content' from thirty-eight different media offices from West Africa to East Afghanistan, deploying communication not just as a recruiting tool, but as a mode of governance.[84] At its peak Islamic State promulgated an estimated

90,000 posts a day, in the process creating a 'generation jihad' that complemented its management of savagery within the Islamic State between 2014–19.

Welcome to the Cyber-caliphate

Purificatory Islamism, from Europe to South Asia, seeks to cleanse the message from the accretions of backward tradition and turn it into a rule-based social order that stands beyond temporal power and existing political authority. It seeks to globalize Islam's pre-modern scriptural injunctions transcending the bureaucratically centralizing post-colonial arrangements in the developing world, or the multicultural injunctions of postmodern Western democracies, establishing, via modern communication systems, a transnational network – the cyber-caliphate. Again, this is hard to achieve in a coherent community where tradition and family associations mingle with the transformational impulse. It is much easier when that coherence breaks down, when individuals live outside such real communities, and where an abstract or virtual *asabiyya* (clan or community) takes their place. One would therefore expect more extreme examples of neo-orthodoxy among those uprooted from community and tradition, and more plentiful recruits to its neo-orthodoxy among those living, literally, outside of community and tradition. And this is exactly what we, in fact, find.

Thus, across the interconnected Muslim world, at the millennium, it was typically urban, male university graduates who discovered in the strict formalism of neo-orthodox teaching the simplicity and certitude to cushion their education in science and technology, which was also an education in falsifiability and doubt. Outlining the belief that science can only be civilized through faith, Qutb maintained that only the genuine practice of a pure Islam could heal the unnatural breach between religion and scientific materialism. The 'ideological ideal' of Islam alone could 'rescue humanity from…the barbarism of technocratic culture', from the vice of an authoritarian nationalism imposed by a Nasser, a Suharto or an Atatürk, 'and from the stifling trap of communism'.[85]

Such a system, thought Qutb, required a unified *ummah* in the novel sense of a trans-territorial ideocracy. Politically, this means that the boundaries of the *ummah* reflect the extent of the doctrine's acceptance. Where it is a majority, it rules; where it is not, it struggles. As Gellner pointed out, this Islamist self-reformation addresses directly the predicament of Muslim backwardness and inner city deprivation. It offers scripturalism, asceticism, rule orientation and aversion to regressive local particularisms, all of which, he wrote, 'may have elective affinities with the virtues required to surmount the arduousness and strains of the long march to disciplined, modern industrial society'.[86] Islamism promotes a rule-governed, illiberal arrangement in which society is organized 'by networks, quasi tribes, alliances forged on the basis of kin, services exchanged…common institutional experience, but still, in general, based on trust, well founded or not, rather than on formal relations in a defined bureaucratic manner'.[87] In its most extreme form, as in al-Qaeda and subsequent mutations that have the propensity to engage in catastrophic violence, the new 'community' is forged on mafia activities and terror franchises rather than on traditional pastoral-based clan affinity. This is how al-Qaeda and subsequently Islamic State came to operate whether in Raqqa, Paris, Madrid, Hamburg or London.[88]

Islamism thus bulges with paradox. It exemplifies a network-based social order without a real society. It is atomized without individualism. It can operate effectively in a bewildering diversity of settings. Against the civilizational prophylactics identified by Gibbon, and liberal progressive secularists, Islamism has no need of the doubtful joys of modularity, and has developed, via jihad.com, an asymmetric capacity to turn the West's technological and cybernetic edge against it. It devastated a large part of the downtown area of a modern cosmopolitan city like New York, a backpacker's holiday playground like Kuta Beach in Bali, and London's creaking transport infrastructure with conspicuous ease. If this sociology of political Islam is correct, then traditional, even very pious, Middle Eastern Islam as such is not the problem. Terror-prone Islamism does, of course, arise in a remote sense from the least traditional, most fundamentalist Muslim state, Saudi Arabia, but Islamism's active nodes and cells are not located in Arab countries. As we have seen, many are evolving in Southeast Asia, but the most dangerous networks are located in the West, or more precisely in Western Europe. As we have suggested, *dar al-Islam* is no longer a simple geographic concept; the virtual world of the cyber-caliphate knows no conventional boundaries. Therefore, to understand what is happening in North Africa, the Middle East, and South and Southeast Asia, we also have to look at what goes on, for example, in London, New York or Paris.

Hamburg Technological University served as a perfect location for Mohamed Atta to plan his towering day in history. Islamist cells remain active in Germany, Spain, Italy and France. But it is in Britain that perhaps the most acute cognitive dissonance may be observed. While former Prime Minister Tony Blair remained steadfast in his commitment to the war on terror abroad, until 2004 the Home Office permitted self-styled sheikhs Abu Hamza al-Masri and Omar Bakri Mohammed to recruit for al-Qaeda from their state-subsidized mosque in Finsbury Park, North London, and Abu Qatada to operate as al-Qaeda's *emir* in Europe.[89] These leading figures in the protoplasmic al-Qaeda network promulgated the achievement – by *jihad*, if necessary – of a unified Islamic world that would include among its future member states the Islamic Republic of the United Kingdom. Groups like Omar Bakri Mohammed's *al-Muhajiroun*, its breakaway factions and front organizations like the *Saviour Sect, the Shariah Project, Islam4UK* and *Need for Khilaffah* dismissed more moderate voices in British Islam who rejected their promotion of a de-territorialized Salafist utopia as 'chocolate Muslims'.[90]

This dismissal of Muslims who practiced a traditional understanding of the faith revealed and reinforced the Gnostic character of 'Euro-Islam'.[91] The Islamist, unlike the conventional believer, drew a distinction between the experience of mundane reality and the second or transformed reality that the imaginative projection of the political religion promises. This second reality, as Voegelin explains, 'screens the First Reality of common experience' from view. Violence, from this perspective, is both necessary and justifiable to immanentize, that is, realize in this world, the Gnostic dreamer's truth.[92] As Voegelin explained in *The New Science of Politics*, 'Gnosticism as a counter-existential dream world can perhaps be made intelligible as the extreme expression of an experience which is universally human, that is of horror of existence and a desire to escape from it'.[93] Translated into a political religion or total ideology in the context of modernity, the

Gnostic impulse is inherently Manichean, and violent. Immanentizing the transformational end justifies the violent means. Moreover, the end community to which the ideologist aspires has natural enemies, notably those who accept the world as it is with all its messy secularism and pluralism. From the Islamist's apocalyptic perspective, the violence or other 'types of actions which in the real world would be considered as morally insane because of the real effects which they have will be considered moral in the dream world because they intended an entirely different effect'.[94] Combining Gellner's sociology of Muslim reformation with Voegelin's understanding of Gnosticism reveals Islamism as a distinctive but comprehensible, universal, but secularism-resistant, ideological formation.

Yet prior to the London bombings of July 2005, the Metropolitan Police, the Mayor of London, and the UK government more generally, did little to discourage Islamist activism or attempt to sanction its more questionable premises.[95] In this the UK experience only represented a more acute form of a wider Western practice of tolerant indifference. Such a complacent reaction to the Islamist call enabled groups like *al-Muhajiroun* and *Hizb ut-Tahrir* to get a head start in the battle for hearts and minds amongst second and third generation Britons and Europeans of Muslim heritage. Illustrative of what, at the time, would have been seen as progressive sensitivity to and tolerance of diversity and difference, a Metropolitan Police-approved rally held in Trafalgar Square on August 25 2002 captured the evolving character of generation jihad at the millennium. Clad in a variety of colourful *thowbs*, the crowd resembled something from a hippie counterculture revival festival. Instead of love and peace, however, they chanted 'Osama, Osama, Osama'. Religious enthusiasm accompanied the flowing robes and beards.[96] In four green tents marked 'Islam', 'Capitalism', 'Democracy', and 'Globalization' – located just behind the backs of the statues of two heroes of empire, Sir Henry Havelock and Sir Charles Napier, whilst Admiral Nelson turned a blind eye from atop his pedestal – the radically chic disciples of the Islamic *internationale*, stylishly accoutred in black headscarves and matching Ray-Bans, promulgated their ideological vision. Handouts like 'A Call to Boycott America and Israel' excoriated the 'hyenas and vultures which operate under the guise of the coalition against terrorism'.[97] This heady mixture of transformational utopianism, over time, appealed to a younger generation of Muslim-European youth, recruited to the apocalyptic messaging in growing numbers. Why? And, one might ask, why London?

First, as Gellner suggested, the attractions and opportunities of Western life lure young diasporic Muslims away from traditional ways of life and communal attachments. Those championing the transnational *ummah* consequently addressed the universal and spiritual yearning of young, European Muslims 'who cannot identify with any specific place or nation'.[98] For the postmodern Islamic masses, 'the high spiritual clarity (of the message) is made bearable through a connection with the neither high nor especially spiritual extension of God's realm by force of arms over the ecumene'.[99] Secondly, and more prosaically, because states from Algeria, Egypt and Jordan to Singapore, Malaysia, Indonesia, China or Russia exercise a far greater degree of control over radical Islamist activity than occurred in Western Europe generally, and London in particular. Illiberal states control their press, limit internet access, and are not overly concerned about violating civil liberties, as the experiences of Chechens in the Russian Federation or the Uighur population of Xinjiang in China all too vividly demonstrate.

Not so in the United Kingdom, where liberal guilt about Britain's colonial sins increasingly trumped common sense both prior to and after the bombings of July 7 2005.[100] Indeed, after al-Qaeda moved its centre of operations from Sudan to Afghanistan in 1998, a number of disgruntled operatives, alarmed by the primitive conditions in Kabul, proposed re-locating to London. This led Ayman al-Zawahiri to rule that 'a brother may travel to London to collect funds, but may not stay there or seek asylum'.[101]

Al-Qaeda's leading strategist assumed that the Home Office would unhesitatingly grant asylum if requested, and he was undoubtedly correct. As Mohamed Sifaoui, an Algerian journalist who penetrated a Parisian al-Qaeda cell in 2002, revealed, Euro-Islamists consistently looked to London for guidance after the French began deporting radical clerics following the Parisian Metro bombings of 1995. Sifaoui, working undercover, encountered 'Islamists from all over the world' at the supposedly moderate Central Mosque in London's Regent's Park. These included the Algerian *Groupement Islamic Armée* (GIA) leader, Abdellah Anès, former *mujahideen* and co-founder (with Abdullah

Azam, Ayman al-Zawahiri and Osama bin Laden) of the strategy for internationalizing jihad.[102] Anès reminded Sifaoui, 'Don't forget that all the brains are here in London'.[103] It was Sifaoui who coined the term 'Londonistan' to capture the capital's congeniality to the promulgation of the new political religion.

The End of History, Identity Politics, and the Management of Savagery

The 'brains' included a new generation of jihadi thinkers attuned to Western norms, the progressive ideological commitment to inclusivity and diversity, and the opportunities a borderless world offered for their totalitarian alternative. A new generation of Western educated proponents of jihadism, like Abu Musab al-Suri and Anwar al-Awlaki, found London's multiculturalist, migrant-friendly, global interconnectedness peculiarly favourable to promulgating the revolutionary call in an English online medium that combined Salafist concepts with street argot to enhance jihad's global appeal amongst an anxious and anomic diaspora. The Yemeni-born, US-educated Anwar al Awlaki, who moved to London in 2002 to avoid 'persecution' by the FBI, before relocating to the Yemen to co-ordinate al-Qaeda in the Arabian Peninsula, particularly facilitated an English online media strategy transmitting the purificatory and apocalyptic message to a global market.

Awlaki quickly identified the marketing opportunity that the social media revolution begun by Facebook andYouTube in 2004 afforded for intensifying, simplifying and disseminating the jihadist call. After 9/11 Salafist jihadism turned to social media. The new medium carried the message to a global audience. There were no gatekeepers to inhibit its promulgation. Messages posted from one remote or hidden location reached an audience counted in millions.

In innovative publications like *Constants* and the Islamist online journal *Inspire*,[104] Awlaki's online journalism promulgated, in an amended and accessible form, the latest advances in Islamist thought, notably Abu Musab al-Suri's *Call to Global Islamic Resistance* (2005) and Abu Bakr Naji's *The Management of Savagery: The Most Critical Stage Through Which the Ummah Will Pass* (2004), a virtual blueprint for building a caliphate and a guiding text for Islamic State's leadership after 2014.[105]

Al-Suri possessed impeccable Islamist internationalist credentials. Syrian in origin, he acquired Spanish citizenship through marriage in 1984. Subsequently he spent time in Peshawar, Pakistan, as al-Qaeda began to take shape under the guiding hand of Osama bin Laden's spiritual mentor, the Palestinian Abdullah Azzam. Moving to London in the early 1990s, al-Suri joined the al-Qaeda linked group *al-Muhajiroun*.[106]

After 2003, al-Suri recognized that the global Islamist resistance movement required a more sophisticated strategy than the one al-Zawahiri and Osama bin Laden pursued before and after 9/11.[107] The new third generation jihadism turned instead to social media in English to promote a strategy of lone actor attacks and 'leaderless' resistance via an online *Global Call*. It asked for spontaneous, self-radicalized actions 'which will wear down the enemy and prepare the ground for waging war on open fronts…[W]ithout confrontation in the field and seizing control of the land, we cannot establish an [Islamic] state, the strategic goal of the resistance'.[108] The leaderless resistance that al-Awlaki and al-Suri envisaged across the west, and which Islamic State (IS) promoted through its media arm after 2014, complemented the management of savagery within its newly acquired territorial realm.

In June 2014, at Mosul in northern Iraq, Islamic State in Iraq and the Levant (ISIL) announced both the rebirth of the caliphate and the end of the Sykes-Picot era that had seen the partition of the Ottoman Empire and the dissolution of the caliphate. From the perspective of twentieth century Islamic thinkers like Rashid Rida, Sayyid Qutb, and al-Mawdudi, the Treaty of Lausanne (1923) had inaugurated the decadence that led to the proliferation of pharaonic and idolatrous (*taghut*) regimes. The Afghan war and 9/11 had begun the reversal of the process of decay. The inauguration of the Caliph Ibrahim in 2014 symbolised not so much the end of history, but the beginning of the end of the West's colonial dominance. In this teleological context, managing violence, whether in the West or in Syria, would secure the borders of Islam. The chaos of savagery represented the intermediate stage of state breakdown, which the revolutionary cadre must manage *en route* to the purified final historical stage that would immanentize, in Voegelin's terms, the eschaton of the Islamic realm. As Naji explained, 'if we succeed in the management of savagery, that stage will be a bridge to the Islamic state which has been awaited since the fall of the caliphate'.[109]

Significantly, this revolutionary and eschatological approach to the conduct of jihad applied Mao Zedong's thinking on protracted warfare to the condition of Islam globally.[110] Applying the revolutionary dialectic with Islamist characteristics, Naji distinguished between the stage of state breakdown, characterised as one of 'vexation and exhaustion' where the failing state's power, as in Afghanistan, remains contested, and the subsequent stage of 'savage chaos', where the people 'yearn for someone to manage the savagery', before the transition to the final historical stage of the reborn caliphate.[111] As with earlier theorists of revolutionary, ideological war, IS considered the control and support of the masses, through armed struggle, necessary to achieve unity and power.

Violence, as with earlier, twentieth-century totalitarian styles, therefore, was a crucial feature of Islamism's pure theory. Any backsliding or 'softness' would 'be a major factor in the loss of the element of strength'. Moreover, it did not matter if the caliphate was not achieved immediately. Indeed, 'the more abominable the level of savagery is', it was still less abominable than enduring stability under 'the order of unbelief, the *nizam al-kufr*, by several degrees'.[112]

Significantly, in developing Islamist political thought on confronting and combating the Western secular oppressor, the new, activist, global jihadist movement (GJM) also played the West's 'political game'. It was vital, as the cosmopolitan third generation jihadists recognized, to exploit the Western democratic political process and its progressive secular understanding of justice for purposes of infiltrating and manipulating the population. The jihadist online strategy stressed the importance of infiltrating the military, police, civil institutions and, of course, secondary and higher education, where Western communitarianism proved particularly amenable to the 'trojan horses' of the purified politically religious programme.[113]

In its ideological reading of Islam, the global jihad movement further maintained that, as Mohammed used small bands against his enemies during the *hijra*, small bands of committed jihadists groomed online became the approved military model for conducting jihad in the West. As Naji observes, 'the rate of operations escalates in order to send a practical message to the people that the power of the *mujaheds* is on the rise'.[114]

In the evolution of the jihadist ideological alternative to new liberal progressivism, those like Awlaki increasingly came to discriminate between the military strategy, the media strategy, and the planning for the effects of these strategies in the aftermath, for example, of a successful attack, such as those undertaken in Paris in 2015, Brussels 2016 or successive London attacks also in 2016.

Here once more the revolution in social media played a crucial role not only for promoting the transformational values of the political religion, but also for recruitment to the cause and the justification and intensification of purificatory violence. After June 2014, the IS online journal *Dabiq* presented jihad as liberating and the actions of foreign fighters recruited from Europe and North America a source of inspiration that gave apocalyptic meaning to otherwise meaningless lives – a simple, but evidently persuasive appeal to young Muslims unconvinced by the multiculturalism and tolerance of Western modernity.[115]

At the same time, Awlaki and his online successors, like the former West Sydney male stripper and boxer, Feiz Mohammad, or Melbourne rapper Neil Prakash aka Abu Khalid al Cambodi, used social media to brand their product. IS considered this aspect of their movement important enough to establish, in August 2014, the Anwar al-Awlaki brigade, to promulgate the message and its online recruitment strategy.

The global jihad movement developed this strategy not only to project its ideology, but also to package it for Western consumption. Segueing off a *L'Oreal* advert, for instance, a 2015 recruitment message, targeting young, western educated Muslim women, ran 'Cover Girl, No, Covered Girl Yes. Because you're worth it'. The flow of young second generation Muslim men and women brought up in secular Western multicultural societies to Islamic State attested to the success of the appeal. Whether it was the transgressive violence of a Westminster University graduate like 'Jihadi John' (Mohammed Emwazi) or a fourteen-year-old schoolboy from Blackburn, England, grooming an attack on Melbourne on ANZAC day 2016, myth and symbolism were vital to the action and the message it conveyed.

Western governments seemed as shocked by the cultic appeal of IS as they were surprised by the rapidity and lethality with which it achieved *de facto* authority over territory in Syria and Iraq.

60

Significantly, in rejecting the decadent, progressive values of the third way, the ultraviolent messaging of IS directly contrasted the emancipatory, liberal, secular belief in life, human rights and the pursuit of happiness, with a cult of death. As early as 2004, after the Madrid bombings, apologists for the atrocity clarified the divide between a pluralist secular international order and their brand of apocalyptic millenarianism in the formula: 'you love life, we love death'. This slogan went through several variations over time, including versions like 'The Americans love Pepsi, we love death'. In essence, however, this thanatic aesthetic deliberately defined itself against a secular Western Enlightenment belief in how we might live the good, or ethical, life.[116]

Fascism, the Italian philosopher Umberto Eco observed in a different ideological context, engaged in political necrophilia.[117] A taste for killing and martyrs represented its purest form. Islamism as it evolved from Qutb to Naji became similarly obsessed. It means, as the slickly produced IS YouTube videos demonstrated, adoring and serving death. Beatifying violence reinforced the non-negotiable, politically religious commitment. Indeed, to love death, as jihadism does, is to say that it is beautiful to receive it and to risk it and that, somewhat perversely, the most beautiful love is to distribute it. This death wish is evident today across the Middle East and amongst those seduced by its online appeal in the West. It is a form of political nihilism made possible by both the deconstruction of traditional order and the sanctification of violence.

This aspect of jihadism and the capacity of its version of Islam to endorse the cult of death does not desensitize youth (as mainstream newspaper opinion pages allege), but rather renders violence purificatory and sacred. Sadistic cruelty and the addictive death-craving it elicits, moreover, serve the broader ideological struggle to achieve apocalypse now. In this, the Islamist alternative to the end of history again dramatically contrasted itself with the core Western liberal value, one that Richard Rorty, following Judith Shklar, identified as cruelty being 'the worst thing we can do'.[118]

Third Generation Jihadism and Global Ethics

There is a continuous and often little remarked self-critique focusing on violent conduct that occurs in exchanges between jihad's true believers. An example of this was a 2005 letter sent by Ayman al-Zawahiri to Abu Musab al-Zarqawi, the leader of al-Qaeda in Iraq, and an early pioneer of ultraviolence. Zawahiri questioned the harshness of Zarqawi's methods in leading Iraq down the path of sectarian war. The criticism was not about ends, but means. The killing of unbelievers and apostates is a process that needs appropriate management to achieve ideological goals.[119]

Western media commentary often dismissed attacks such as those that took place in cities such as Boston, London, Ottawa, Sydney or Paris after 2014 as the product of 'lone wolves' or 'stray dogs'. In fact, these actions served a wider strategic purpose that reflected the evolving illiberal thinking about the utility of extreme violence to bring about the final apocalyptic confrontation between Islam and ignorance.

The *jahiliyya* Western world is fragile, lacking cohesion, and easily divided. Islamists, according to Naji, therefore pursue a doctrine of 'paying the price, that is: you bomb us and we'll bomb you, especially in your heartlands where we know you are weak'. In this understanding, the Global Jihadist Movement (GJM) is acutely aware that it is engaged in a 'political game' where 'rough violence in times of need' is part of the policy of 'paying the price'. Moreover, whilst the rightly guided are driven by political religion, the West is vitiated by self-interest. Naji, in this respect, even quoted Palmerston's dictum that there are no permanent enemies or permanent friends, only permanent interests, which the politically aware, Western trained, jihadist must exploit.[120]

Extending from its politico-religious base, Islamist ultra-orthodoxy derived its ideological formula from both Western and non-Western sources that it amended to its distinctively utopian project of social perfection. Its Manichean, rather than inclusive, worldview invites an activist style that legitimates violence to embed its version of the desired this-worldly utopia. The critical political difference between Islamist and fascist totalizing visions is that Islamism currently lacks the resources afforded by a modern state to prosecute its total solution,[121] thereby compelling a recourse to asymmetric means.

In this evolution of jihadist practice, al-Qaeda, Islamic State (IS) and the GJM are not only influenced by a modern business theory of franchising, but also by the tactics formulated by groups equally opposed to pluralist, secular, progressive, liberal, borderless modernity.

These groups range from cults like *Aum Shinriyko* and white supremacist movements like Aryan Nation and their European neo-Nazi affiliates, to the practice of alienated, lone wolves like the radical environmentalist Unabomber. In fact, it was American Aryan Nation strategist Louis Beam who first identified the potential of a leaderless resistance where 'individuals and groups' commit random acts of violence, but 'operate independently of each other' to serve the ideological purpose.[122] Random actors responding violently in the name of the organization multiplies the effect of the ideology with which they identify. It is how the clean skins and lone wolf phenomena evolved across Western Europe and the United States after 2003.[123] Beam's strategy particularly informed post-Abbottabad al-Qaeda as well as IS tactics, as attacks between 2013-16 in Boston, Ottawa, Paris, Central and South East London, Brussels, and Nairobi demonstrated.[124] Dramatically enhanced by social media, leaderless resistance made previous modes of revolutionary organization to bring about utopia increasingly redundant.[125]

The first post-Cold War manifestation of leaderless resistance occurred, however, in the US Mid-West. It took the form of Timothy McVeigh's 1995 Aryan Nation-influenced attack on the Alfred P. Murah Building in Oklahoma City. Interestingly, the media, security agencies and academia did not consider McVeigh insane. Instead they took both the bomber and the ideology motivating his right-wing extremism seriously.

By contrast, faced with a far more determined and ubiquitous jihadist threat, a liberal commentariat presented the wave of homegrown attacks in Western Europe and the United States between 2005-15 as isolated events, ignoring Islamism's broader strategic thinking and disregarding the politically destabilizing consequences of asymmetric violence. As a consequence, there arose a disjuncture between what Islamists openly said, had said for a while, and actually have carried out, and what the government, media, academia and security community say they really mean.

International Relations theory and progressive liberal commentary post-9/11 assumed that the homegrown, but global, jihadist tendency would wither on the vine or, at some point, adopt a more moderate and negotiable position. To end ideologically motivated armed conflict, Tony Blair's long serving political adviser Jonathan Powell maintained, you had to talk to terrorists.[126] From this progressive, communicative perspective, Islamic State's self-styled Caliph Ibrahim would eventually morph into a version of Gerry Adams, but with a better beard. Why did the elected representatives of secular, progressive western democracies do so little to defend a secular, progressive and nominally inclusive way of life against the promulgation and growing appeal of this non-negotiable alternative to its global ethics and progressive secular vision of a borderless world? It is to this curious response that we shall next attend.

4

THE INCOHERENCE OF THE PHILOSOPHERS[1]
OR, THE WEST AND THE REST

After the millennium, confusion over the theory and practice of war abroad and countering terrorism at home haunted the official mind and the progressive conscience: who or what was the enemy? How should war be prosecuted and justly conducted after 9/11? Did home-grown attacks represent an existential threat to the West or a mere blip on the teleological expressway to the end of history? And what might the answers to these questions portend for future international, political and social organization?

These questions arose as the 'War on Terror', declared in September 2001, degenerated into a series of long and inconclusive engagements. The answers they received, however, slowly unravelled the illusions about identity, social justice and multicultural harmony that held the new liberal, progressive vision together. In particular, the refusal of the progressive mind to accept, let alone refute, illiberal belief systems that proposed a very different and apocalyptic end to history appeared both intransigent and misconceived. The incoherence of the response dates from the weeks after the 9/11 attacks on the World Trade Centre and the Pentagon. As we observed in the previous chapter, a *sui generis* species of politically religious fanaticism had, by the 1990s, identified the United States in particular and the West generally as its far enemy, even as it domiciled itself within its capital cities. Prior to 9/11 the prevailing progressive worldview dismissed the threat or, if it did recognise it, considered it both peripheral, external, and a response to Western colonialism.[2] This perspective continued to shape the official mind after 2001, despite the regular discovery of Islamist inspired plots to commit catastrophic attacks on North American, Australian and European secular and civilian targets.

In other words, the Western response, in either its more aggressive neo-conservative, or in its non-confrontational, radical pacifist modes, demonstrated a curious insouciance that, despite evidence to the contrary, refused to entertain the possibility that a premodern or, to use Fukuyama's term, 'nonviable' belief system could represent an enduring threat to domestic order, or upset the secular and normative processes determining a global end of history.[3]

Le Monde editorialised on 12 September that 'We are all Americans now', but the Western strategic response and its justification quickly demonstrated a singular lack of unity.[4] On 14 September 2001 President George Bush declared at the National Cathedral in New York that 'the conflict was begun on the timing and terms of others [but] it will end in a way, and at an hour of our choosing'. The chosen hour never arrived. Instead, the US prosecuted an ill-defined war against 'terrorist organizations with global reach' that led it into long and inconclusive wars in Afghanistan, Iraq and Syria.

US determination to put boots on the ground and keep them there, despite mounting casualties, did at least falsify Friedman's pre-millennial assumption that the US hyperpower had little appetite for overseas military engagements. To forestall future domestic terror attacks, successive administrations also revised, centralised and expanded the homeland national security apparatus. Nonetheless, almost two decades later, despite the killing of Osama bin Laden in Abbottabad in 2011, and the degradation of the Al-Qaeda network, 'terrorist organizations with global reach' had only mutated and grown.[5]

In the course of the long war, a number of strategic enthusiasms came and went. The neo-conservative doctrine of pre-empting external threats, designed for a new and different kind of war 'to be prosecuted with determination and patience' enjoyed a brief, but costly, ascendancy.[6] So, too, did the once fashionable doctrine of counter-insurgency or COIN that succeeded it. COIN endeavoured to capture the hearts and minds of the population, to whom the US and its coalition partners brought forcible regime change, through the provision of security, accountable institutions and welfare. David Petraeus' enthusiastic promotion of his version of armed social work in Iraq after 2007 collapsed with the rise of IS and the continuing and intractable presence of the Taliban in Afghanistan.

The US and its allies ostensibly conducted these wars of choice to achieve modernization, pluralism and democratic transition, but the Arab Spring nevertheless came and went. The outcome of coalitions of the willing and UN-approved 'Responsibility to Protect' campaigns altered into unstable, costly and ultimately unsustainable interventions. The prosecution of long wars of choice also revealed the infirmity of institutional arrangements designed for the different circumstances of the Cold War. The US determination to prosecute external war against an apparent 'axis of evil' fractured the relative harmony sustaining Western diplomacy and the conduct of international affairs during and immediately after the Cold War.

Disagreement over the legitimate use of force exacerbated this emerging dissonance. Irrespective of the merits of unilateral action versus a UN Security Council-approved consensus for legal intervention and the conduct of just war abroad, Cold War international institutions increasingly functioned in a bewildering geopolitical landscape. The burgeoning divide in strategic thinking and practice between a growing US predilection for unilateralism to maintain the international *status quo* and what Donald Rumsfeld dismissed as an Old European propensity of France and Germany for diplomatic negotiation and UN-sanctioned police missions came, over time, to jeopardise the ideals and institutions of a progressively evolving, liberal multilateral order.[7] To understand how this liberal world order began to unravel, we shall first examine the different traditions informing the US and Western European approach to foreign affairs after 1945 and their effect upon the conduct of the war on terror both at home and abroad.

US Exceptionalism and the Roots of Western Disharmony

The European official mind, committed, post-1951, to a project of European integration, drew, from the experiences of the nineteenth and twentieth centuries, the lesson that interstate war was futile. The losses France and Germany sustained in terms of men, matériel, empire, and *gloire*, in the first half of the twentieth century, prompted a postwar generation of western European politicians and administrators like Robert Schuman, Jean Monnet and the original progenitor of the end of history thesis, Alexander Kojève, to conclude that rational planning, enlightened bureaucracy, regional institutions, technology, and diplomacy could manage most problems, whilst violence, especially the inter-state kind, solved nothing. This approach to European and, by extension, global problems through multilateral institution building, compromise, negotiation and a fashionable soupçon of uncoerced communication increasingly informed the thinking of a post-1990, third way, progressive, consensus.

Yet, paradoxically, bureaucratically planned supranational arrangements like the European Union only emerged from the chaos of inter-state war because a US protectorate, expressed through NATO, facilitated it. The US security umbrella afforded the stability and investment for post-war Western European reconstruction. Consequently, Franco-German misgivings concerning Bush and later Trump era unilateralism looked through some American eyes, in the wake of 9/11, like ingratitude. The fraying of US-European ties began in 2003, and by 2016 had led to Donald Trump questioning the continuing US commitment to NATO, which underpins the sense of collective Western security as well as the foundation of a progressive international order.

This unintended consequence of the war on terror also exposed the great divide between modern American and European thinking about the experience of war and the use of force in conducting foreign relations and securing the national interest. From its inception, the United States considered itself exceptional. It was either a promised land or a crusader state and sometimes it was both.[8] After 1776, the US expelled the British imperial presence, and explored the implications of the Monroe doctrine for the American continent.

In the twentieth century, war in Europe and Asia, as well as more recent foreign policy adventures, firmly established an often overlooked but distinctive Jacksonian tradition in US foreign policy.[9] This accepted the necessity of force to pursue the United States' manifest destiny. It required security at home and, from time to time, promoting freedom and democracy abroad, whilst avoiding 'entangling alliances' particularly with potentially duplicitous Europeans.[10]

During the Cold War, the possibility of Mutually Assured Destruction put this distinctively American foreign policy tradition on hold. The neo-realist strategy of deterrence and containment required a global architecture and a global commitment. Even here, however, the eventual collapse of the Soviet Union vindicated the superiority of the American way. After September 11, and the dramatic emergence of an asymmetric international terrorist threat, rendered more potent by the dark side of global interconnectivity, Bush and, after 2016, Trump era strategists, revived this unilateral tradition. It particularly informed post-9/11 Republican thinking about the appropriate use of US military force. In Paul Wolfowitz's neo-conservative view, it was always better for the US to fight small wars now than big ones later.

The renaissance of US unilateralism in foreign policy sat uneasily with a growing European and progressive commitment to regional and international regimes. It also contrasted with the prevailing liberal institutionalist worldview that the State Department and the US foreign policy establishment espoused during the Cold War. This Wilsonian liberal tradition assumed that the US, as the essential power, advanced its interests by enhancing multilateral regimes governing everything from trade to the environment. The way that the Cold War ended gave liberal internationalism additional impetus prior to 9/11 and its aftermath. After 2008, the Obama administration tried to revive and reinvigorate this commitment to the international community and the edifice of multilateral institutions that the US had constructed during the Cold War.

This liberal institutional perspective, premised on the need for negotiated consensus before resolutions could be passed or action taken, morphed, in the last decade of the twentieth century, into an idealist, progressive, and constructivist practice advancing universal norms and international law. After a brief neoconservative and unilateralist interlude, the Obama presidency reinvigorated the progressive commitment to inclusivity, human rights and social justice, along with the US' continuing attachment to multilateral regimes and international institutions. To the European Union, and progressive new liberals everywhere, the Obama doctrine came as a welcome relief. Despite the continuing war on terror, Obama represented, for a progressive transnational elite in business, academia, and the media, an enlightened return to global norms, social justice and an inclusive end of history.

However, Obama's rhetoric notwithstanding, the incoherent approach to intervention in the rest of the world after 9/11 generated political and economic tensions in the West that the progressive teleology informing the end of history underestimated to its eventual cost. Islamism in particular exposed internal and external contradictions in the new liberal normativist vision, which required hard choices rather than the preferred third way amalgam of spin, diffidence and dogmatism.

Global Ethics Fights the War on Terror

Despite evidence to the contrary, the global ethical perspective maintained that it was not terrorism, post-9/11, that threatened an emerging normative order, but 'power pragmatic' nation states, particularly the US and its coalition partners. These global tensions could only be assuaged, the liberal progressive view maintained, when 'large, continent wide, actors like the EU and ASEAN' evolved into 'empowered regional actors' affording the UN 'a base for the implementation of high minded programs and policies'.[11]

This task became even more urgent after 9/11. Unprepared for the new transnational Islamist challenge to world society, progressive opinion adapted to the latest manifestation of globalization with a mixture of insouciance, moral relativism and political equivocation. On the one hand, progressive ideologists acknowledged the profound impact of 9/11, but, at the same time, sought both to minimize it, whilst empathizing with the suffering situation that provoked such otherwise irrational acts of violence.

An edited volume published in 2002[12] established the lineaments of what would become progressive orthodoxy concerning asymmetric attacks upon Western civilian targets. Summating the progressive mood post-9/11, Ken Booth and Tim Dunne contended the attacks on New York and Washington represented not a clash of civilizations, but an unfortunate 'collision' that exposed the West's difficulty in 'understanding colliding thought-worlds'. It also graphically illustrated how 'the rest' of the non-Western world hated the US. Steve Smith argued that the prevailing Western understanding of the other provoked these 'collisions' and urged a renewed engagement with cultural difference and 'alternative rationalities'.[13] Terrorism 'must be countered', but the progressive mind considered social injustice and environmental harm far graver threats. 'Poverty' was, after all, 'the biggest killer'.[14]

The evolving progressive response to Islamically-sanctioned, catastrophic violence of the al-Qaeda and IS variety thus entailed a far from compelling mix of queasy agnosticism, euphemism, moral equivalence and logical *non sequiturs*. Attempting to contextualize the threat, progressive opinion also adopted a neutral, non-judgmental stance in assessing the recourse to violence by non-state actors. This gave its pronouncements a rhetorical aura of objectivity and professional expertise. Whilst not condoning 9/11, or subsequent attacks in Madrid, London and Paris, the progressive perspective acknowledged that Western democracies also engaged in acts of state terror. Moreover, given the evident power imbalance between the West and the rest who, Noam Chomsky, asked rhetorically, was the real global terrorist?[15]

Moral equivalence, premised on a radically sceptical relativism, achieved growing progressive academic and media acceptance in the wake of the invasion of Iraq and the subsequent insurgency that culminated in the rise of IS and its short lived caliphate (2014–18). 'Fundamentalism', Jürgen Habermas opined in 2003, appeared 'on the world historical stage' only as a dialectical response to oppression, fear and, of course, miscommunication. Meanwhile, it was the US and its allies that responded with 'the civilized barbarism of coolly planned death'.[16]

Addressing the latest global crisis, therefore, required progressive philosophers, Europeans and cosmopolites to promote, not Western secular values, but an enhanced commitment to the transformative politics of global emancipation. Habermas prognosticated in 2003 that although US hegemonism had attempted to divide and weaken the West by invading Iraq, it would only make more enlightened Europeans conscious of their common political fate. Consequently, Europe, with its continuing commitment to human rights, social justice and open borders, had 'to throw its weight on the scale to counterbalance the hegemonic unilateralism of the United States'.

To facilitate this, the founding fathers of critical global discourse ethics and radical deconstructive scepticism, Habermas and Jacques Derrida, promulgated a manifesto for integrating Europe and embedding a utopian politics founded on communicative reason. This would occur if 'core Europe', namely France and Germany, promoted the deepening of European institutions and adopted a common foreign and security policy through an inclusive European constitution that expressed a common European progressive will. From this cosmopolitan perspective, the European Union, its commissions and regulatory bureaucracy, constituted the basis of an enlightened European identity that transcended its dark twentieth-century past and fulfilled its Kantian promise as the progressive harbinger of a global federation. The Europe-wide protests against the Iraq war on 15 February 2003 announced, Habermas and Derrida averred, the birth of a new European public sphere. Ever closer European Union, from the progressive new liberal perspective, offered a form of 'governance beyond the nation state' which set a precedent for a 'post-national constellation'. Distinguishing itself from the US 'behemoth', integrated Europe could eventually 'defend and promote a cosmopolitan order on the basis of international law against competing visions'.[17]

Significantly, this cosmopolitan worldview considered rule by bureaucratic committee or 'comitology' a practical basis for a more deliberative, communicatory, post-national order than the backward nation state.[18] A core Europe that was inclusive and 'acknowledges the other in his otherness' as the basis of a common identity, naturally appealed, and offered ideological legitimation, to the European administrative class's project of an integrated Europe *sans frontières*. After 9/11, this deliberative cosmopolitan approach to international relations also appealed to the UN in its attempts to implement international and human rights law. After 2008, its transformative assumptions also influenced the Obama administration. Thus, despite its ostensibly critical stance, the progressive worldview assumed an increasingly elitist, idealist and managerial form of rule in both the style of thought it encouraged as well as the cosmopolitan order it promoted after the events of 9/11 and 2003.

The global ethical perspective post-9/11 thus found Europe, its supranational institutions and courts of international justice rather more congenial than the United States and its regime of homeland security, at least before the emergence of Obama. Despite mounting global disorder after 2008, the new liberal progressivism assumed that all international issues could be solved through open communications and inclusive dialogue that would lead to a set of universally agreed norms, rationally applied by a global elite and their enlightened ethical counsellors. From this perspective nation states, particularly powerful Western ones, suffered from the morally defective pursuit of national interests. Self-interest inhibited the free communication that would enhance the pursuit of an enlightened, just, cosmopolitan and normative order. The post-Westphalian state system had been judged by those who observed 'the tide of history' and found wanting.[19] Therefore, it must inevitably be replaced by something more inclusively supranational. From this teleological perspective, US hegemony represented a graver threat to world peace than either al-Qaeda, Islamic State, or the rising power of China or a revisionist Russia.

The evolving cosmopolitan transnationalism ultimately offered a mixture of therapy and a marriage guidance council approach to international relations. All the world's problems might be solved through uncoerced communication, arriving at mutually acceptable norms. Violence, itself a construct of the otiose nation state, would disappear from the world stage. This understanding reflected the tendency in the Western third way of governance that decided 'the calculation of pure power politics simply does not compute'.[20] The emerging, socially just global order would instead require only 'therapeutic' intervention or the odd, UN approved, police action to enforce, reluctantly, its shared norms. University presses and academic journals like *Millennium* and *Critical Security* devoted themselves to works advocating liberal or 'positive' peace studies and *Justice, Dialogue and the Cosmopolitan Project*.[21]

9/11 and the End of History

September 11 and its aftermath transformed the institutions, conventions and assumptions that underpinned international relations and the conduct of democratic politics. However, this only appeared clearly after 2016, as the owl of Minerva spreads its wings with the falling progressive dusk. In the wake of the first Gulf War (1991), the Clinton administration in the US and the Blair government in the United Kingdom shared a pursuit of ethics and human rights in foreign policy that promoted ethical intervention abroad allied to a multicultural, diversity-conscious sensitivity at home.

After 9/11, the evolution of this policy of military intervention and regime change abroad coupled with state neutrality and liberal tolerance at home strained, but by no means broke, faith in the progressive pursuit of global ethics and the project of embedding utopia. Although the official European faith in international law and peace through conversation clashed with a more assertive neo-conservative view of how to promote global norms, the arrival of Barack Obama in the White House after 2008 revived a shared Western progressive pursuit of global ethics, minority rights and social justice. International law and multilateral regimes reasserted themselves, not only in the US foreign policy establishment, but as a progressive, imperialist, global project.

The ambiguous and increasingly incoherent Western response to domestic terror attacks reflected this progressive worldview. Western governments assumed, for a long time, that the asymmetric attack was alien in provenance and externally manageable. Consequently, the regular identification of 'cleanskin', home-grown, and lone actor terrorists from diasporic communities who engaged in random, but cumulative, acts of violence against iconic secular targets in cosmopolitan capital cities posed a dilemma for the progressive mind and its longstanding commitment to 'cherishing' and enhancing the self-worth of culturally distinct minorities.[22] Ironically, the political and ethical dilemma this posed and the ambivalent response it elicited was exposed most cruelly not in the United States, with its more robust policing of homeland security after 9/11, but in old Europe, most notably in the UK. The successive UK administrations of Tony Blair, Gordon Brown, David Cameron, and Theresa May from 2001–

18 pursued what Sayyid Qutb might have diagnosed as a hideously schizophrenic approach to the war on terror.

The British case was all the more poignant as it gave credence, if credence were needed, to Dean Ascheson's observation, in 1962, that 'Great Britain has lost an empire and has yet to find a role'.[23] UK foreign policy after Suez (1956) prioritised its 'special relationship' with the US. Blair and Cameron, like Harold Macmillan before them, formed close, but not particularly special, relationships with successive Republican and Democratic presidents. Unlike core Europe, Britain actively participated in US-led coalitions to 'drain the swamp' of terrorism in weak states where it proliferated, whilst offering core elements of Islamism's ideological infrastructure empathy, safe havens and welfare at home.

Blair and, later, Cameron's attempts to straddle a US propensity to unilateralism whilst maintaining a European commitment to internationalism rendered their progressive pursuit of social justice at home and an ethical foreign policy abroad disjointed and ultimately incoherent. American neo-conservatives and French Gaullists, who agreed on little else, all considered Britain a soft touch for international terrorists. In a *Weekly Standard* 'Letter from Londonistan', Irwin Steltzer observed in 2005 that '[w]hen it comes to issues such as immigration, extradition and the application of power of the state at home, he [Blair] is torn between humanitarianism and civil rights principles, and the need to wage war against Britain's domestic enemies'.[24]

While the Bush presidency adopted a war mentality at home and abroad, the UK's official position and that of the progressive, liberal commentariat post-9/11 was far more circumspect. Successive UK governments after 2001 accepted the moral and strategic necessity of the war on terror, the deposition of Saddam in Iraq and Gaddafi in Libya, and the overthrow of IS, in order to promote a universal, liberal order. However, the official UK mind sedulously distinguished between war's external and internal prosecution.[25] More precisely, the European Courts, the progressive media and the new profession of terror expert eschewed the US 'war on terror model' with its propensity to 'internment and torture'.[26] Somewhat perversely, the UK government considered the adversary within its territory a lesser threat and treated this aspect of the 'war' as a criminal act best left to the police and judiciary.

In conditions of deep pluralism, the progressive, new liberal theories that envisaged an impartial, socially just state giving legal force to policies of reverse or positive discrimination and group or minority rights, John Gray predicted, 'is likely to further fragment us' and 'evoke more intolerance among us'.[27] The modernization programme of multiculturalism, open borders, free movement of labour and devolution of sovereignty that Tony Blair embarked upon and David Cameron and Theresa May continued between 1997–2018 offers a particularly interesting test for whether the new liberal policy experiment of multicultural diversity recognition, as opposed to a more traditional *modus vivendi* that sought to assimilate minorities by recognizing and balancing moral and cultural incommensurabilities, fragmented communities along cultural lines, rather than integrating them.[28] The case of Islamism and the conduct of the war on terror raised the issue of social and political fragmentation in a particularly acute form. Did the progressive policies adopted by successive UK governments after 2003 enhance or undermine political and democratic solidarity? We would assume from what we have argued thus far that the answer might be in the negative. And, in fact, this is what we find.

The Unbearable Lightness of Being European

The UK's conduct of the war on terror according to normative and progressive criteria led to a series of moral and political contortions that left an enduring and turbulent political legacy. Empathizing with cultural difference required, from the outset, a political language that distorted the reality of the modern Western cosmopolitan cityscape in order to maintain the fiction of inclusionary, multicultural development in what Tony Blair declared was his 'progressive' vision animated by a 'boundless' and 'manic lust for modernization'.[29] It led, over time, to official practices that reflected core assumptions informing the new liberal progressive ideology of the post-Cold War era and the rhetorical and practical equivocation they necessitated.

In its manifestation as a security doctrine, Blair's third way post-1997, and Cameron's way after 2010, required Britain to prosecute forcefully the war against those who resort to jihad abroad, actively participating in coalitions of the willing whether in Afghanistan or Iraq, whilst affording some of Islamism's key ideologists and strategists a high degree of latitude and permissive tolerance in the United Kingdom itself.

Rather than acknowledge this strategic incoherence, the UK government, media and security agencies resorted to a practice of dissimulation, dismissing militant revolutionaries based in London like Omar Bakri Mohammed, Abu Hamza al Masri (aka Mohammed Kemel) and Anjem Choudary as fantasists and losers rather than, ideologists with a coherent but apocalyptic worldview and a strategy designed to achieve it. Between 2001–5, the media routinely dismissed Salafist jihadi preachers like Abu Qatada and Omar Bakri Mohammed, both afforded asylum in Britain, as 'loud-mouths',[30] describing Abu Hamza's inflammatory oratory at Finsbury Park mosque before 2005 as that of a harmless 'clown'.[31]

The Western intelligence community maintained the fiction that Muslim terrorists would 'attack us from abroad', as happened in America on 9/11, or as the 'gang of Moroccans' who perpetrated the Madrid train attacks did in 2004.[32] *Hizb ut-Tahrir* and *al-Muhajiroun*, until the latter was banned in 2005, operated openly across the UK and, by extension, in the more tolerant states of Europe under what Omar Bakri assumed was a 'covenant of security'.[33] The covenant assumed that in return for the tolerance and subsidies the diversity-sensitive government afforded, *al-Muhajiroun* and its affiliates would refrain from attacking the United Kingdom.[34]

The assumption was by no means misplaced. In 1998, Home Secretary Jack Straw appointed Bakri's aide, Makbool Javid, to the UK Race Relations Commission.[35] Indeed, in the course of the 1990s, the Home Office, Department of Education, Department for International Development, and Labour-led local authorities in London, Luton, Birmingham, and Manchester, under the auspices of cherishing diversity, had directly and indirectly subsidized the activities of Islamists, like the alleged spiritual head of al-Qaeda in Europe, Abu Qatada.[36] Granted political asylum, and in some cases, British citizenship, these activists not only used the UK as a base from which to rally support for the jihad abroad,[37] but also, in the course of their proselytizing mission, to take control of mosques across Britain and

Europe. From these bases in North London, Birmingham, Leeds and Manchester, they preached their distinctive brand of de-territorialized, purificatory Islamism to a generation of alienated, diasporic Muslim youth, some of whom proved willing recruits to the cause.[38]

The imputed covenant between Islamism and Blairite multiculturalism only came under threat when the government attempted, half-heartedly, to restrict Salafi jihadist preaching after 2001, and then only at the behest of more moderate members of the Muslim community, who expressed concern at the impact of its proselytizing upon British Muslim youth. In April 2004, Omar Bakri Mohammed declared that the covenant of security had lapsed. Asked whether an attack on London was likely, Bakri responded that it was, in fact, 'inevitable'.[39]

Euro-Islam, in other words, played 'the political game'. It exploited the fact that whilst third way governance acknowledged that 'today, conflicts rarely stay within national boundaries' and 'interdependence defines the new world we live in', it also wished to 'celebrate the diversity in our country' and draw strength 'from the cultures and races' in its midst.[40] Islamism exploited the practical limitations of this abstract, theoretical commitment to a multicultural complex of communitarian, cosmopolitan, inclusive, but diverse, attachments. New liberalism presumed that 'communities with separate identities can live together peacefully, united only by the weakest of national identities'.[41] The presumption informed the programme to modernize British institutions after 1997. Officially, it took the form of policies promoting cultural diversity, rather than a shared understanding of nationality that had traditionally sought to assimilate minorities within a condominium British identity. Incorporating the European Convention on Human Rights and the rulings of the European Court of Justice into British common law, third way modernization also eroded the sovereignty of parliament and the authority of the UK government. The overall effect dissolved a British identity into a much vaguer, protean, European one.[42]

The accommodative character of multiculturalism resulted in official vacillation between, on the one hand, prosecuting those within Muslim communities prepared to wage external and internal jihad as a reflection of their cultural identity, to, on the other, celebrating their diversity as refreshingly postmodern.[43] This constitutive ambivalence remained central to the progressive political agenda, despite the fact that some cultures drew upon their politically incommensurable understanding of religion, and the interdependent and transnational character of conflict, to render Europe's infrastructure and civilian population a soft but morally defensible target.

Rather than address this incoherence, the British government consistently opted to ignore it. It discounted the rise of Euro-Islam during the 1990s, when it first emerged, then after 9/11 and the London bombings of 2005, and even after the rise of Islamic State in 2014. As early as December 1998, members of Abu Hamza's *Supporters of the Sharia* were arrested in connection with kidnapping and terrorist attacks in Yemen, which Hamza had already identified as a potential location from which to launch global jihad.[44] The same month that Hamza developed the Yemen front also found him organizing a boot camp for potential jihadists at the North London Mosque in Finsbury Park, since 1996 controlled by those committed, like him, to a non-negotiable understanding of an Islamist political religion.[45]

British authorities calculated that perhaps as many as 600 British Muslims, influenced by radical imams exiled from the Middle East and granted some form of asylum in the UK, had undertaken training in al-Qaeda training camps in South and Southeast Asia between 1996 and 2004.[46] Even by the flexible standards the European Union applies to the significant minority of alienated Muslims practicing a distinctive version of Euro-Islam in its midst, cosmopolitan London stood out for its indifference to diaspora communities committed to violent struggle at home and abroad.[47] The UK, of course, has a long history of granting asylum to political dissidents, from Marx and Lenin to those who resisted Communism in the Cold War.

However, unlike an earlier generation of political revolutionaries, the modern Islamist revolutionary character was committed to acting both globally and locally in support of a supranational, ideological Islamic brand.[48] Thus, when on 7 July 2005 a series of coordinated bombings disrupted the London transport system, killing fifty-six commuters, two facts quickly emerged. Firstly, the previously unheard-of 'Secret Organization Group of al-Qaeda in Europe', which claimed responsibility for the bombing, had planned the operation to cause maximum panic and loss of life.[49] The success of what Oxford University's Professor of Contemporary Islamic Studies, Tariq Ramadan, euphemistically termed 'interventions'[50] dramatically illustrated the vulnerability of soft targets like mass transit systems to those prepared to countenance mass casualty terror.[51] They also achieved the saturation media coverage that organizations that have recourse to extremist violence crave.[52] Secondly, and more alarmingly, the United Kingdom's security forces were well aware of the possibility of an attack. Then Director General of MI5 Eliza Manningham-Buller had announced in 2004 that an al-Qaeda franchised attack on London was 'only a matter of time',[53] whilst the former Commissioner of the London Metropolitan Police, John Stevens, considered it 'inevitable'.[54] Why were the agencies charged with national security resigned to a mass casualty attack on London's transport system and to subsequent attacks and foiled plots on UK infrastructure thereafter?

Third way commitment to diversity meant, in effect, that to be forewarned was not to be forearmed. Although after 2011 David Cameron sought to distance his coalition government from the state-led multiculturalism that, he argued, facilitated 'radicalization', official policy remained, at best, ambivalent.[55] Cameron's government failed to curtail the spread of violent extremism, of both the Islamist and, after 2016, the white supremacist variety, which, both he and German Chancellor Angela Merkel agreed, multicultural policies had failed to curb.[56]

Meanwhile, the European Research Council (ERC) continued to reward with large grants teams of sociologists demonstrating that, despite some 'concern' over events post 9/11, Britain was, still, in 2012, a model of successful multiculturalism.[57] The shibboleth of the impartial state cherishing minority rights and cultural diversity meant that, after 2005, it became official and academic orthodoxy to deny any direct connection between Islam and acts of home-grown terror. Immediately after the London attacks, Assistant Deputy Commissioner of the Metropolitan Police, Brian (subsequently Lord) Paddick, asserted that 'Islam and terrorism don't go together',[58] later adding: 'We've got Londoners, faith groups, everybody being united in adversity as a result of the attacks rather than fragmenting'.[59]

Ultimately, the official mind was more concerned with preserving harmony than identifying the source and motivation for the attack. Progressive governance demanded the following formula: ensure good community relations; London and the country were robust and resolved;[60] and the attack had nothing to do with religion.[61] The formula required citizens to be resilient, rather than protected. Over the next decade, police spokespersons, the media and government officials wheeled out this tried, and increasingly failed, recipe whenever a new 'intervention' occurred.

The progressive orthodoxy that good community relations prevailed throughout multicultural Cool Britannia contributed greatly to the initial disbelief that the London attack could be home-grown. After the discovery that the London bombers hailed from Leeds, in Yorkshire, BBC's *Newsnight* interviewed a variety of prominent local figures. They all applauded the harmonious state of community relations.[62]

However, investigative journalists revealed a rather different picture. Inter-communal relations in the former mill towns of Yorkshire and Lancashire were often tense, and reflected the social fact that 'white and ethnic communities lead largely separate lives'.[63] Revelations of the real state of community relations, as opposed to the official myth, led some commentators to question the progressive enthusiasm for multiculturalism. Mick Hume wrote that 'the celebration of diversity increasingly served as a substitute for any more coherent worldview within the British elite'. Consequently politicians, the media and academia invariably emphasized the importance of tolerance, implying that the core, perhaps sole, British value was that 'we tolerate the values of others'.[64]

The official commitment to tolerance and community resilience sought to pre-empt those who might exploit any terrorist incident to foment xenophobia, suspend civil liberties and seek revenge.[65] The fact that groups like the British National Party and, in the course of the decade, the English Defence League and National Action made political capital out of domestic attacks and linked them to large scale immigration reinforced this apprehension.[66]

To assuage apprehension, police and government spokespersons and experts asserted the peaceful character of Islam[67] and the plight of ordinary Muslims.[68] Senior community leaders reinforced the view that the British Muslim population lived in a state of siege. In July 2005, at a press conference chaired jointly by Birmingham city council and West Midlands police to demonstrate harmonious community relations, Mohammad Naseem, the senior Islamic cleric in Birmingham and chairman of the city's central mosque, claimed: 'There seems to be a directive to target Muslims... Muslim bashing seems to be more earnest than the need for national unity and harmony'.[69]

However, this discourse had countervailing and ultimately divisive consequences. As David Goodhart noted at the time, 'If you are constantly being told by even moderate Muslim leaders [along with most of the media, legal and academic commentariat] that Britain is a cesspit of Islamophobia and is running a colonial anti-Muslim foreign policy, you might as well conclude "...I would like to give blood"'.[70] Interviews with Muslim youth from the Leeds suburbs where the 7/7 bombers planned their attack revealed both alienation and a burgeoning sense of shared Muslim oppression. One youth told the *Independent* journalist Shiv Malik, 'Look how many Muslims are dying and no one cares. One gora [white] person dies and it's on the TV all day'.[71]

The focus on the question of Muslims' treatment in Britain in culturally sensitive government, academic and media commentary impeded society from confronting the evident ideological problems posed by the dissemination of a Salafist political religion for a secular liberal democracy. Progressive commentators increasingly emphasised a hitherto neglected Islamophobia that vitiated the institutions and practices of Western and, more particularly, given its history, European society. Repeated in schools, universities and the media, this perspective inculcated a growing contempt for a neo-colonial and decadent host society. At the extremes, among the more volatile and impressionable proponents of Euro-Islam, it gave politically religious justification for those disposed to murderous rage to settle their grievances.

Events in Afghanistan, Libya, North Africa and Syria between 2007 and 2014 exacerbated this sense of resentment, whilst the rise and fall of Islamic State merely compounded it. In May 2013, British Islamists Michael Adebolajo and Michael Adebowale justified their murder of Lee Rigby as 'simply retaliation for your oppression' and the 'invasion of our lands'.[72] By 2014, British, French and Australian intelligence services expressed growing concern at the more than 300 British, 200

French, and 200 Australian citizens, some as young as sixteen, fighting with jihadist groups in Syria who would eventually return home, 'trained in the latest terrorist techniques'.[73]

Root Causes, Progressive Guilt and Muslim Grievance

The new liberal, post-Rawlsian assumption of the progressive compatibility of all values at the end of history increasingly confronted an uncomfortable political fact. As Ernest Gellner observed, 'the tolerant endorsement of human diversity becomes very tangled if one realizes that very many past and alien visions have been internally inclusive, intolerant and ethnocentric; so that if we, in our tolerant way, endorse them, we thereby also endorse or encourage intolerance at second hand. This might be called the dilemma of the liberal intellectual'.[74] The dilemma was further compounded by the multicultural paradox of the post-1989 period. This held that whilst Western cosmopolitanism must tolerate non-Western minorities in the name of diversity, it was not incumbent upon the minority to adapt to the practices and values of their country of adoption.

To address this evolving predicament, the governmental response to the London bombings, and subsequent attacks, oscillated between a curious mixture of coercion and tolerance. The oscillation arose from the conflict between a need to deter what most Western governments, after 2005, termed 'radicalization' or 'violent extremism' in its midst and the continuing progressive belief in a politics of diversity and inclusivity that the European political class, the wider media and academic commentariat assumed would eventually engender the harmonic convergence of communities in multicultural moderation at the end of history.[75]

Rather than identify Islamism as an ideological threat to secular pluralism, Western governments instead proscribed a generic political crime of terrorism that functioned as an expanding and all-purpose category that avoided connecting a violent anti-Western ideology to groups organized within the indigenous Muslim community. Consequently, when scholars in the rapidly evolving field of terror studies revealed motives other than religion to account for Euro-Islam's propensity to political violence, they found a ready welcome among progressive opinion-makers in academia, branches of government, and the mainstream media seeking to discount any universal religious motivation for the recourse to asymmetric, but purificatory, violence. Academic experts like Louise Richardson, Robert Pape and David Kilcullen first disclosed a variety of alternative explanations accounting for the actions of jihadists, attributing them to contingent factors like nationalism, alienation and minority oppression.[76] In this way, the abstract noun, 'terror', that merely denotes fear, could be connotatively adjusted to disclose its true, but concealed roots. This identification required an interpretive expertise that disclosed an otherwise overlooked causal motivation.[77]

At the same time, a discrete new field of critical terror and security studies evolved additional techniques of 'self-reflexive' inquiry and methodological pluralism 'to establish the requisite impartial understanding of the suffering situations that inspired the recourse to otherwise irrational violent acts'.[78] In this hermeneutic endeavour, new academic journals, devoted to critical and emancipatory international relations, like *Critical Studies on Terrorism*, and *Critical Studies on Security*, proposed a radical transvaluation of the new terror's true roots.[79]

Prominent public intellectuals, usually of a Middle Eastern, Asian, or moderate or non-practicing Muslim provenance, provided the authority for this idealist interpretation of post-9/11 terrorism. The Palestinian Christian Edward Said,[80] who had first deconstructed the 'Orientalism' that distorted Western scholarship of 'the Arab mind'; Ziauddin Sardar, who asked, rhetorically, 'Why Do People Hate America?' (2003);[81] Tariq Ramadan, Oxford professor and adviser to the UK government;[82] Tariq Ali;[83] and Tarak Barkawi revealed that the real terror emanated from the West with its long-established history of orientalizing the other in order to subjugate and colonize it.[84] From this relativist and deconstructive perspective, 'the inability of Western elites to see themselves as others see them [stood] directly in the path of a clear-sighted appreciation of the nature of the current conflict'.[85] In fact, 'the root causes', Barkawi wrote, 'of the current situation lie in the working of long-term histories of Western expansionism and their dynamic interaction with the Islamic world'.[86] Al-Qaeda and its mutations, in other words, represented only a distinctively postmodern and hybrid form of colonial resistance.[87] Consequently, the progressive mind needed to 'find the requisite empathy to understand why men dedicated to the betterment of their peoples and willing to sacrifice their lives…found it necessary to fly jet aircraft into buildings or to blow themselves up in the compounds of humanitarian organizations'.[88]

The necessity for empathy soon became an essential prerequisite for the critical appreciation of this new form of hybrid resistance. Critical theorists like Richard Jackson and Ken Booth contended that 'responsible research' now required an empathetic 'ethics of responsibility to the terrorist other'.[89] In a similar vein, Anthony Burke argued that a properly self-reflective normativism required the engaged analyst not only to critique the 'strategic languages of the West' but also to 'take in' the 'side of the Other' and 'engage' with the 'highly developed form of thinking' that provided movements like al-Qaeda with 'legitimizing foundations and a world view of some profundity'.[90]

Critical and emancipatory theory thus cast the threat and its resolution in terms of Muslim victimhood. It discovered the roots of contemporary 'resistance' in a genealogy of trauma that dated from the earliest Christian encounters with Islam and particularly from the eighteenth-century European colonial exploitation of the declining Ottoman Empire, as well as its more recent and indirect manifestation in the form of a borderless world of global capitalism.[91] Professor Booth adjudicated that *'terror has multiple forms and the real terror is economic'*.[92] Stretching the concept of an abstract terror and then reducing it to a mixture of inequitable globalization, non-Western othering and geographic ethnocentrism served the progressive purpose of both minimizing and dissipating the identification of an escalating threat.[93]

Prior to 9/11, international relations theory and global ethics had evinced a predisposition to read events through an impartial but critical 'lens' that deconstructed the false consciousness of liberal democracy to expose the instrumental rationalism that informed it. It had already deconstructed western, particularly US, foreign policy to reveal the discourses that created threats through 'practices of differentiation and modes of exclusion'.[94] The dissolution of Cold War verities had provoked an insecure West to search for a new discourse of danger. After 1990, this search elevated the importance of new non-traditional threats to the international system. In this context, an amorphous 'terrorism' linked to a shadowy global Islamist *Internationale* neatly filled the vacancy left by the former Soviet Union.

Turning the legitimate security concerns of Western democracies upside down, IR theory revealed the West's terror discourse to be 'Islamophobic'. It cast Muslims as 'incomprehensible, irrational, extremist' and 'threatening'.[95] The intimidation that individual British and European Muslims may have encountered does not mean that there existed an institutional Islamophobia driving counter-terrorism policy. Yet Islamophobia, a term first coined in the context of the Iranian revolution to discredit critics, was deployed by critical theorists and the UK Commission of Race Relations after 1996 to account for the new politics of fear that had come to distort the priorities and practices of western governments after 9/11.

Paranoid Politics and the Logic of Appeasement

Rather than accept the existence of a politically religious threat, the progressive and critical mind instead shifted the focus from the violent action to the democratic reaction. Public intellectuals, progressive politicians and media commentators, including the liberally disposed British and Australian national broadcasters, argued that Western governments exaggerated an amorphous terror in order to curtail legitimate dissent and the civil liberties of oppressed minorities.[96] In his bestseller *Dude, Where's My Country?*, Michael Moore popularized this view, maintaining: 'There is no terrorist threat. Why has our government gone to such absurd lengths to convince us our lives are in danger? The answer is nothing short of their feverish desire to rule the world, first by controlling us, and then, in turn, getting us to support their efforts to dominate the rest of the planet'.[97]

Progressive commentary after 9/11 labelled the liberal democratic state's legitimate and, in Europe, half-hearted, and incoherent, efforts to curb the spread of Islamism, the 'politics of fear'. Western governments had conjured the spectre of Islamically-inspired violence for the purpose of advancing an omniscient surveillance state. After 2005, Western governments had persuaded their gullible publics to accept an illiberal extension of state power on the grounds of pre-empting potential terrorists. UK government proposals to introduce identity cards, extend detention of terrorist suspects without trial, and curtail the expression of views calculated to inflame hatred, reflected the new authoritarian disposition. Ironically, the thesis required fear, in this case that of an Orwellian dystopia, to sustain it.

In this increasingly paranoid critical style, Anthony Burke detected an omnipresent Western war against the other. Revealing the conspiratorial relationship between 'freedom's freedom: American Enlightenment and permanent war',[98] Professor Burke maintained that an 'onto-technology of freedom through US history, the Cold War and the War on Terror' demonstrated 'the multiple dangers posed by the aggressive assertion of a simultaneously instrumental and universalizing image of historical action and inevitability that rejects any restriction of its powers and any responsibility for their effect'. This and equally adventurous exercises in critical security analysis revealed that the modern liberal democratic state and its 'violent and exclusivist' understanding of sovereignty, 'linger[s] like a latent illness in the very depths of modern cosmopolitanism'.[99]

Consequently when US National Security Agency (NSA) contractor Edward Snowden leaked classified intelligence files to *The Guardian* and *The Washington Post* in May and June 2013, revealing the extensive covert surveillance of internet communications by the NSA and the UK's GCHQ,[100] it seemingly confirmed this critical reading of Western government policy. Western democracies had abandoned constitutional safeguards on privacy in order to become surveillance states in an era of 'turnkey tyranny'.[101] Although the UK Director General of Intelligence, Andrew Parker, dismissed the view that 'we monitor everyone...browsing at will through people's private lives' as 'utter nonsense',[102] the United Nations' senior counter-terrorism official, Ben Emmerson, QC, contended that Snowden had disclosed issues at the 'very apex of public interest concern', rather than, as MI5 claimed, providing 'a gift to terrorists'.[103]

Between 2003 and 2016, critics in academia and the mainstream media consistently promulgated the view that a nebulous Islamic terror functioned as an omnipresent fear licensing both internal surveillance and external war. The BBC series 'The Power of Nightmares' broadcast in early 2005 revealed 'how the idea that we are threatened by a hidden and organized network is an illusion. It is a myth that has spread unquestioned through politics, the security services and the international media'. Pre-publicity presented the threat as a 'fantasy' which 'politicians then found restored their power and authority in a disillusioned age'.[104] The politics of fear influenced mainstream media commentary, and boosted the critical deconstruction of the alleged Western roots of terror on UK, European, Australian and US campuses.[105] Nor was the evolving consensus confined to academic and media commentary. This interpretation found growing support amongst European administrators, European courts, members of parliament and at the highest level of the UK judiciary.

Both the British High Court and European Courts of Justice and Human Rights detected the politics of fear at work in the proclivity of European governments to hand out deportation or extradition orders to suspects wanted in third countries for terror related offences.[106] In 2004, the UK Law Lords questioned the state's right to detain without trial terror suspects like Abu Qatada under the provisions of the Terrorism Act (2000). Lord Hoffman found that: 'The real threat to the life of the nation, in the sense of a people living in accordance with its traditional laws and political values, comes not from terrorism, but from laws such as these'.[107] In his judgement, Hoffman pronounced that 'fanatical groups...do not threaten the life of the nation... Terrorist crime, serious as it is, does not threaten our institutions of government or our existence as a civil community'.[108]

Hoffman asserted as a constitutional fact what could only be an expression of political faith. In a similar vein, security experts like Bill Durodié 'lismissed the pretensions of Islamism's putative UK franchise as a 'conspiracy of dunces'. Assessing the 'sheer naivety and incompetence of all these so-called al-Qaeda operatives', like Richard Reid, the 'dim-witted shoe bomber who had trouble with matches', Kamel Bourgass and Sajid Badat, Durodié concluded that, 'if that is the best of what the supposed massed ranks of al-Qaeda have to offer after [9/11]...we should have little to fear. But the media, politicians and the policy have sought to portray the situation differently'.[109]

The London bombings of 2005 and subsequent attacks on soft targets in the UK, Europe, Australia and North America between 2005 and 2016 should have discredited the politics of fear and falsified the evaluations of both the BBC, law lords like Hoffman, and security analysts like Durodié. They did not.[110] The politics of fear proved extraordinarily resilient. Thus terror analyst Sarah Oates, in a Chatham House briefing paper issued after 7/7, avowed that 'the politics of fear can often overshadow a more informed discussion'. 'It is easy', she wrote, 'to slip into prejudices and assumptions about the "enemy" rather than focusing on any erosion of citizen's rights resulting from the war on terror'.[111]

Here, the terror expert once again offers a different and purportedly deeper insight into the root causes of terror and the rational or correct way to respond. Bill Durodié maintained, in the same briefing paper, that the best way to reassure the public and build community resilience against the threat was to assume that there wasn't one. 'We should remind ourselves that there have been few significant terrorist attacks in the developed world. To suggest otherwise', he asserted, is both 'alarmist and disingenuous'.[112]

Rather than assess the character and extent of the threat to public order, terror expertise displaced responsibility for the attack from the actual intervention and its aftermath to Britain's involvement in the Iraq war. Serving as the US's main coalition partner and participating in the occupation of Iraq after 2003 constituted, in this view, the external cause of domestic terror.

Jihadist groups had, as we saw in chapter 3, looked to exploit the coalition's occupation of Iraq to legitimate attacks on soft Western civilian targets on the grounds of moral equivalence. In July 2004, the Abu Hafs al-Masri Brigade warned: 'Withdraw your troops from Iraq and walk in the path of those who preceded you, lest you taste the bitter fruits of blood'.[113] Similarly, in September 2004, Omar Bakri Mohammed justified attacks upon UK targets because 'Britain has carried out attacks in Iraq'.[114] In July 2005, George Galloway, the Respect Party MP, along with radically pacifist anti-war campaigners, first raised the issue of UK involvement in Iraq to justify widespread Muslim discontent with UK and US policies and attitudes.[115] Salim Lone argued that anti-terrorist measures would 'only succeed if accompanied by steps to address intense Muslim grievances, including curbing wars of aggression and occupation, which are among the central causes of the exponential growth in terror'.[116]

Academic experts concurred, thereby affording further legitimation to the jihadist doctrine of 'paying the price'. Chatham

House early afforded support for the external cause thesis. Its briefing paper concluded that, 'Riding pillion with a powerful ally has proved costly in terms of British and US military lives, Iraqi lives, military expenditure, and the damage caused to the counter-terrorism campaign.'[117] *The Guardian* opined that it was 'self-evident' that 'riding pillion on George Bush's motorbike, as Chatham House put it, has exposed Britain more than before to al-Qaeda's fanatical enmity'.[118] Meanwhile, Tariq Ali observed, 'on 7 July the murderous chaos of Blair's war on Iraq came home to London in a lethal series of suicide bombings'.[119]

The view that the bombings responded to the Iraq insurgency rapidly found support from members of all political parties, and particularly from anti-war campaigners, like Jeremy Corbyn from the then ruling Labour Party, between 2005–10.[120] If involvement in the Iraq war made Britain vulnerable to suicide bomb assaults, it followed that troop withdrawal 'would curb terrorism'.[121]

This was the logic of appeasement. In an increasingly interconnected but by no means integrated global order, appeasement, in fact, went to the heart of the progressive response to the threat of Euro-Islamism. Before the July 2005 bombings, informed academic and media comment considered the danger of Islamist militancy exaggerated. To the extent a threat existed, it responded to the insensitive prosecution of British and American foreign policy – the prime motive for one-off attacks on New York, Bali and Madrid. Even after the July 2005 attack, this misconception assumed that suicide bombing was a passing 'craze',[122] the product of a specific and resoluble grievance, namely Iraq. Consequently, the response to the problem required a swift and 'orderly withdrawal' from Iraq.[123]

Somewhat perplexingly, however, the overthrow of Saddam Hussein's regime also saw Islamist groups carrying out attacks in France, the Netherlands, Russia, Canada, Germany and Turkey, whose governments had criticized American policy and studiously avoided participating in any coalition of the willing.[124] Ultimately, the belief that foreign policy caused Islamist rage ignored the fact that violent Islamists displayed an equal contempt for the pluralism, secularism, and moral degeneracy that they believed rendered all Western democracies *jahiliyya*.[125]

While the progressive commentariat considered terror as a form of communicative reasoning and hence negotiable, the Islamist's conception, by contrast, was total. It was always likely that Western interventions in the Middle East would constitute another source of Islamist grievance. Yet, the Iraq cause and the London bombing effect was actually a case of the logical fallacy *post hoc ergo propter hoc*, as the coalition of the willing's unwillingness to intervene in Syria's civil war after 2012 subsequently demonstrated. The Syrian civil war merely served as yet another source of grievance and recruitment for disaffected British, European, American and Australian youth into jihadism.[126] In the Salafist version, Western foreign policy, as Abu Bakr Naji had cogently explained, was damned whatever it did.

Euro-Islam and the Progressive Predicament

The developing new liberal consensus on the motivation of homegrown jihadism refused to countenance the positive conditions that fostered the evolution of a de-territorialized and radicalized Islamist identity across Europe. This distinctively European Islamist identity had actively sought, at least from the 1980s, not only to purify the Middle East but also, given its diasporic location, Europe as well.[127] The Iraq case merely gave additional impetus to Euro-Islam's already violent antagonism to the West and its secular values.[128]

The decision, after 2005, to ignore the distinctive European genealogy of an Islamist terror idiom testified to the deep hold that faith in state-sponsored diversity and minority rights socially engineering harmonic cultural convergence had established over the official mind. In the thrall of post-national cosmopolitanism, and international and European legal conventions, UK policy after 7 July was a capricious amalgam of despotism and anarchy. It was despotic in that the UK government, as elsewhere in the West, proposed draconian and invariably duplicative anti-terrorist legislation after a homegrown attack.[129] At the same time, the response bred anarchy, in that the government often lacked the legal means to enforce the anti-terrorist measures it announced, having contracted out the sovereign right to protect the United Kingdom's internal security and its borders to the European Convention on Human Rights and the European Commission.[130]

Policy conceived under such circumstances necessarily assumes an arbitrary and ad hoc character as the government response to resident Islamists granted asylum and the later recruitment to and return of foreign fighters and jihadi brides from IS between 2014–19 only served to confirm.[131] Thus in dealing with Omar Bakri Mohammed in 2005, the Home Office first suggested that he had been expelled from the country while on a visit to Lebanon, with no right of return. Subsequently, it emerged that the government was unsure whether Bakri had been allowed to leave the country of his own volition, or whether he would be barred from re-entering Britain.[132] A similar incoherence, adumbrated by interference from both the UK and European courts, affected the British government's decade-long attempt to constrain and, eventually, deport Abu Qatada, Osama bin Laden's 'right hand man in Europe'.[133] The by now familiar pattern repeated itself with the May government's uncertainty about repatriating, prosecuting or ignoring British foreign fighters, stranded in the wake of the Syrian war, or their abandoned brides and their jihadi offspring abandoned in Syrian refugee camps in the wake of the collapse of IS in 2018.

Such vacillation contrasted with the US and French homeland response to their experience of Islamist inspired bombings after 2001. These very different democracies adopted measures tightening the organization and control of mosques and targeting suspected hard line elements in the minority community.[134] By contrast, the UK government presented a mixture of diffidence and indifference to the 7/7 attack and later to lone actor attacks and foiled plots.[135] Only in early August 2005 did Blair eventually announce legislation to deport radical imams and restrict the activity of those committed to furthering the Euro-Islamist ideal by violent jihad.[136] But any such decision could still be referred to British and European courts, without ever reaching a clear conclusion.

'To govern means to choose', Pierre Mendès France, the socialist Prime Minister of the Fourth Republic, declared in 1954, as France struggled with post war de-colonization and insurgency. Successive British administrations, between 1997–2019, chose indecision. When, after 1997, New Labour sought to engineer a new third way for British politics, it also introduced a practice of homeland insecurity. Modernization along progressive, new liberal lines required the Departments of Education and Culture to observe an impartial neutrality toward the majority community. The BBC even eschewed the term 'Britain' except as a geographical expression. Yet, concurrently, the progressive establishment promoted the cultures of diasporic minorities and of the pre-industrialized tribal world more generally, as more authentic, deserving special rights, and certainly more exciting than the disenchanted condition enjoyed by the stale and pale majority.[137]

The unintended consequences of the official mind's neutrality towards different cultural values together with the migration polices pursued after 1997 diluted any sense of a shared British identity. Rather than achieving intercultural harmony, progressive modernization intensified an already deep pluralism. As Gray predicted, and with the best of new liberal intentions, it facilitated political fragmentation rather than integration and harmony. In fact, it only served to aggravate alienation amongst minority communities, cementing their sense of otherness, whilst deracinating the pale majority not committed to the progressive, post-national, European vision.

The white working class disappeared from public discourse in the course of the 1990s, written out of the multicultural script by their monocultural adherence.[138] At the same time, the neutral state's progressive commitment to recognizing neglected or oppressed cultural identities afforded the conditions for the emergence of a countervailing politics of ersatz certainty that addressed the alienation of those identifying as BAME.[139]

Multiculturalism, in other words, had the paradoxical consequence of providing the conditions for the re-Islamization of British Muslims and their commitment to a faux traditionalist, de-territorialized and potentially violent Islamism. Alienated from the bland pieties of multicultural faith in a shared, but diverse, community, the emerging Euro-Islamic identity recognized that 'hate is stronger than love, and that, therefore, the appropriate means for realizing common objectives is to disinhibit man's aggressiveness and to build up hate' of the Godless secular order.[140] Ironically, the politics of fear and its preferred policy option of indifference and grievance settlement manufactured the danger whilst simultaneously denying any danger really existed.

The disjuncture between the external and internal aspects of the progressive reaction to Islamism might be termed the paradox of liberal progressivism which translated into an indecisive politics of homeland insecurity. It held that, in domestic politics, minority difference must always be tolerated, or appeased. Such tolerance would erode majority white prejudice and enhance increasingly diverse yet communitarian democracies. Ironically, this liberal faith in an Enlightenment project that, in its Kantian form, embraces all mankind, is also 'a religious deformation' that replaced a Christian faith in 'a transcendent spirit of the community with an earthly condition of perfected humanity'.[141]

This progressive faith in a secular but cosmopolitan, liberal yet multicultural, pluralism assumed all values to be ultimately compatible, and that universal truth and justice would emerge eventually through tolerance and uncoerced interfaith dialogue. Further, since all values are equal from this relativist viewpoint, minority understandings must be afforded equivalent status and receive affirmative action in the shape of state or charitable subsidies, like those provided by the Charities Commission to mosques such as Finsbury Park in the 1990s.[142] Yet, at the same time, in practice, diversity, empowerment and pluralism also implied that cultural minorities possessed the communal right to their own separate and, if necessary, illiberal development, even at the expense of the polymorphous cosmopolitanism that enabled that identity to flourish.[143] To do, or even to think, otherwise would be at best intolerant, at worst racist.

Talking to terrorists, as Tony's Blair adviser Jonathan Powell[144] counselled, however, required ignoring or reinterpreting in a disingenuous way statements made by UK jihadist spokespersons like Omar Brooks (aka Abu Izzadeen) of *The Saviour Sect*. In 2005, Brooks announced, 'I am a terrorist. As a Muslim, of course, I am a terrorist'.[145] Meanwhile, the influential former *al-Muhajiroun* spokesman, Anjem Choudary, speaking at a public gathering after the 9/11 attacks, observed, 'Blair came out, George Bush came out at the same time. But what did he say? He said: "You're either with us or you're with the terrorists." And what did we Muslims say? We said, "we're not with you – we're with the terrorists! Allah Akbar!"'[146]

Such statements, which achieved a rhetorical consistency over the next decade, do not immediately suggest a basis for uncoerced communication leading to shared, universal norms at the end of history. Instead these and similar speech acts embrace the rhetoric of the closed fist and 'talking for victory'.[147] During an earlier, Cold War outbreak of liberal relativist histrionics, Leo Strauss had identified the ultimately illusory desire of liberal, value-neutral social scientists to engage sympathetically with the totalitarian Other. As Strauss observed:

> Is such an (empathetic) understanding dependent upon our own commitment or independent of it? If it is independent, I am committed as an actor and I am uncommitted in another compartment of myself, in my capacity as a social scientist... In that latter capacity I am completely empty and therefore completely open to the perception and appreciation of all commitments or value systems. I go through the process of empathetic understanding in order to reach clarity about my commitment for only part of me is engaged in my empathetic understanding. [This means, however, that] such understanding is not serious or genuine but histrionic.[148]

If Western democracies acted upon such empathy, Strauss warned, it would lead to chaos:

> For to say in the same breath that our sole protection against war between societies and within society is reason, and that according to reason 'those societies and individuals who find it congenial to their system of values to oppress and subjugate others' are as right as those who love peace and justice, means to appeal to reason in the very act of destroying reason.[149]

Only in an open society, one that questions the values it promotes, could the issue of empathy with and tolerance of radical cultural difference arise. As a consequence of the progressively histrionic attempt to recognize and cherish difference, there arose a curious disjuncture between what Islamists say, and have been saying for many years, and what analysts think they really mean; and between what the commentariat think they really mean and what Islamists actually do.

Interestingly, the progressive mind, for all its empathic engagement with the suffering other, inhabits a world that finds the proponents of Islamism incomprehensible. Third Way governance, the liberal media and academic commentariat, all function within successful, market-oriented, post-religious, plural societies characterized by a modular and disenchanted pursuit of reason. Their worldview further assumes the movement of history globally in the direction of a progressive, democratic, secular modernity. It considers violent disruption on the path to the end of history as temporary interruptions, caused either by local psychopathology, or structural inequality, to be addressed with empathy, equal opportunity, market opening and economic redistribution. It treats all political action in terms of cause and effect and assumes that if an actor's means appear limited, so too must the ends.

It also refuses to entertain the possibility that instead of normative convergence at the end of history, globalization might, in fact, have spawned a new dialectical conflict between progressive universalism and an anti-political, purificatory, exclusive and incorruptible faith. European, Enlightenment *philosophes*, it might be recalled, preached tolerance, not on the basis of radical relativism, but out of the ideological belief that reason, science and progress would ultimately prevail over outmoded custom and religious enthusiasm. The enlightenment state thus promoted secularism and a politics grounded in scientific rationalism, not multicultural diversity.

By contrast, the post-Cold War version of Enlightenment assumed an impartial, neutral state allocating rights that positively discriminated in favour of excluded minorities. Multicultural policies embraced the tolerance of difference. In so doing they paradoxically encouraged an intolerant enthusiasm of an Islamist hue. Toleration is a virtue appropriate to those who 'acknowledge their imperfectability'.[150] To Islamists, embracing a very different eschatology, tolerance was weakness, and secularism a form of spiritual death requiring salvation via the certainty of political religion. Simply put, while Western liberal tolerance posits a multi-sum game, Islamist assumptions are zero-sum. The difference is that traditional Muslims would not have even understood the multi-sum proposition, while today's Islamists understand it very well indeed – and take full advantage of it.

The Euro-Islamist thus finds liberal multiculturalism deracinating, but wonderfully helpful. The anomic character of the post-national, radically neutral, state container thus enhanced the strategic appeal of an emancipatory and apocalyptic fundamentalism, particularly attracted to global cities, especially those like London, Paris and New York, whose diversity and multiculturalism it defines itself against, but whose tolerance it finds highly congenial for organizational purposes.

The unpredictable character of de-territorialized ideological movements, promoted by those who, whatever their ideological preference, find the character and values of secular pluralism deeply suspect, presents a profound challenge to Western political democracy, and one that progressive thought has consistently denied since 2001. Islamism presents its most coherent manifestation, but as the emergence of a variety of non-negotiable identities appeared in Islamism's wake, it by no means constitutes the only challenge to a Western, democratic, pluralist conception of order.

The Islamist challenge, however, most obstinately questioned the progressive faith in the inevitability of a pluralist and secular end of history. When Osama bin Laden proclaimed on 9 December 2001 that 'the time has come when all the Muslims of the world, especially the youth, should unite and soar against the *kufr* and continue jihad till these forces are crushed to naught, all the anti-Islamic forces are wiped off the face of this earth and Islam takes over the whole world and all the other false religions', he clarified this rejection.[151]

The progressive mind cannot take rejection, ironically, because its own teleology denies Islamism's premise. A 2003 Islamist training manual clarified the issue:

> Islamic governments have never and will never be established through peaceful solutions and cooperative councils. They are established as they always have been…by pen and gun…by word and bullet…by tongue and teeth.[152]

Such statements do not obviously allow space for dialogue, discourse ethics or even political compromise.

Denying Islamism's non-negotiable faith encouraged instead an official tendency to mistake the terrorist's limited means for limited ends. Yet as Machiavelli cautioned, at the beginning of the modern state, 'You must never believe that the enemy does not know how to conduct his own affairs. Indeed, if you want to be deceived less and want to bear less danger, the more the enemy is weak or the less the enemy is cautious, so much more must you esteem him'.[153]

This was of course the kind of advice that progressive thought acknowledged only in the breach. The tendency of much official, political, legal, academic and media commentary either to dismiss these views as having nothing to do with Islam, or to offer their more articulate spokespersons grants, university appointments, or positions on commissions addressing diversity issues and ethnic and religious exclusion – in order to build bridges where none existed – merely enhanced their cachet.

In a similar spirit of wishfulness, international relations theorists and international lawyers regularly lamented the extension of powers of detention and pre-emption extended to police and security agencies, despite the fact that such powers were subject to parliamentary oversight and review. Indeed, without the powers of detention and surveillance granted, for example, under the UK Terrorism Act 2006, and extensions to the Australian Security Intelligence Organisation Act 1979 and the Australian Anti-Terrorism Act 2006, fifth column jihadist attacks like those planned *inter alia* for Melbourne in 2005, Heathrow airport in 2006, Holsworthy barracks in Sydney 2012, Birmingham (UK) in 2013, and on Anzac Day 2015, as well as the escalating number of planned attacks across Europe, groomed by social media after 2014, would have taken place.[154]

The denial of Islamism's global appeal thus became an enduring feature of the response to it. It accounted for the scale of official misapprehension before the assaults on New York and Washington DC, Bali in 2002, Madrid in 2004, London 2005, Paris 2015, and Berlin 2016. It continues to inform official counter-terrorism policy and informed commentary upon it. A government and media propensity to dismiss increasingly frequent leaderless attacks on Western targets after 2014 as the acts of 'small-time losers'[155] or psychologically disturbed 'lone wolves' reflected the incomprehension.

Yet rather than question their progressive faith in expanding social justice and inclusivity, Western governments instead doubled down on policies promoting and celebrating cultural and ethnic diversity, believing they would, temporary setbacks notwithstanding, speed the inexorable global movement to harmonic convergence at the end of history. Across the West, policy responses after the 9/11, London 7/7 and Paris 13/11 attacks opted for a bizarre amalgam of despotism, tolerance, anarchy and indifference.

The response distorted democratic self-understanding and corrupted the language of politics in which the West conventionally expressed its particular and contingent understanding of constitutional democratic practice and its relationship to the wider world. In particular, endorsing, even at second hand, the intolerant visions of distinct cultural communities, created an ethical tangle that distorted an already ambiguous political vocabulary concerning rights, liberty, justice and equality which governed political conduct. In order to silence any questioning of the direction of progress and the policies required, new liberalism disported an increasingly intolerant character. This became particularly apparent for those who ventured to question the prevailing progressive orthodoxy, its multicultural enthusiasm and its toleration of the intolerant.

5

THE LANGUAGE OF PROGRESS AND THE CLOSURE
OF THE EUROPEAN MIND

The slow-motion disintegration of British and, by extension, European political self-understanding began almost precisely at the moment the Cold War ended. It may be traced to the British Conservative government's inept response to the Rushdie affair in 1989. The affair began with the government's tolerant indifference to the leaders of the Barelvi community of British Pakistani Muslims' decision to burn Salman Rushdie's novel, *The Satanic Verses*, in public.[1] The Home Office's decision to ignore an intransigent minority censoring works it found offensive created a precedent. The Religious Hatred Act (2006) gave it effective legislative sanction.[2] The European Muslim response to Rushdie's *The Satanic Verses* had 'little to do with importing Islamic radicalization to Europe'.[3] On the contrary, it represented the first premonitory snuffling of the dialectical clash between a *sui generis* Euro-Islam with the secular, progressive universalism that ironically made it possible.[4]

For over a decade Rushdie required police protection. Christopher Hitchens presciently wrote at the time that the demonstrations and death threats represented 'the opening shots in a cultural war on freedom'.[5] This cultural war and the exclusive identities it upheld constituted what the radical French feminist Caroline Fourest identified as an assault on blasphemy, or the secular right to speak sacrilegiously of sacred things.[6] Endorsed after 9/11 by the progressive attempt to empathize with or cherish minority cultural understandings, it not only closed debate but also restricted the language in which any debate might be conducted. It is this evolution and its implications for political freedom that we shall explore in this chapter.

Radicalization, Islamophobia, and the War on Culture

The next shot in the evolving culture war was fired in 2004 when a Dutch Islamist of Moroccan descent gunned down filmmaker Theo Van Gogh as he cycled to work in Amsterdam. His blasphemy consisted in making, with Ayaan Hirsi Ali, a short film, *Submission*, questioning the Koran's treatment of women. The cultural war escalated dramatically the following year. After the 7/7 attacks in London, the Tate Gallery cancelled an exhibition that featured an installation depicting torn up copies of the Koran, the Bible, and the Talmud. In Denmark, a Danish children's writer complained that he could not find an illustrator for a children's book on the life of the Prophet, while Salafist-inspired Muslims assaulted a lecturer in Copenhagen for reading verses from the Koran to non-Muslim students.

In October 2005, Fleming Rose, the culture page editor of *Jyllands Posten*, a mass circulation Danish daily, responded to this self-censorship by commissioning twelve cartoons depicting 'The Face of Mohammad'. In 2006, the Organization of the Islamic Conference in Mecca condemned Denmark for using 'freedom of speech to defame religion'. Global demonstrations against the cartoons broke out. Jihadists attacked Danish, Austrian and Norwegian embassies in Syria and the Lebanon and burnt down churches in Nigeria. Following these attacks, Scandinavian, Swiss, German and Dutch newspapers published the Danish cartoons in a display of solidarity. The UK, US, and Australian media failed to follow suit.

In France, the satirical magazine *Charlie Hebdo* demonstrated its support not only by publishing the *Jyllands Posten* cartoons, but also displaying a cartoon of its own. It depicted the Prophet dismissing his fanatic adherents with the comment 'C'est dur d'être aimé par des cons' ('It's tough to be loved by these jerks').[7] The Paris Mosque subsequently prosecuted the magazine under France's hate speech laws.[8]

In November 2011, in the wake of the Arab Spring and the election of Islamist parties to power in Tunisia and Libya proposing to introduce a 'moderate' form of sharia law, the satirists published a special *Charia Hebdo* issue. It featured the Prophet as guest editor explaining what 'sharia light' might involve.[9] In 2013, al-Qaeda placed *Charlie Hebdo* on its most wanted list. On 7 January 2015, home grown jihadis attacked the journal's offices crying 'the Prophet is avenged'. On 11 January nearly four million people demonstrated in Paris to support freedom of speech, creating the 'Je Suis Charlie' effect.

In the weeks following the attack, however, the progressive mainstream media, academics and politicians began distancing themselves from the magazine's religious satire. *Je Suis Charlie* rapidly mutated into 'Je Suis Charlie, mais...' ('I am Charlie, but...'). Interviewed on Sky News (UK) about the post-massacre issue of the journal on 12 January 2015, Fourest, a former contributor, asked, 'How can I comment on the Charlie cover without showing it?'[10] which, of course, she did. The cameras panned away and the interviewer apologized 'to any of our viewers who may have been offended'. As Fourest commented, 'we are talking here about a news channel in a democratic country...thinking that people cannot be grown up enough to decide if a drawing is offensive or not'.[11]

The unquestioned official, progressive understanding of Islam being anything other than a peaceful religion reinforced a climate of media, academic and cultural self-censorship. In the aftermath of the *Charlie Hebdo* affair, the progressive media and the European political class effectively endorsed, in the name of diversity, a minority practice of religious intolerance. Tolerating intolerance on the grounds of blasphemy came to legitimate a growing and widespread condemnation of remarks that might cause offence on British and North American campuses. Hate speech, trigger warnings and no platforming campaigns were the inexorable consequence.

This illiberal outcome was quite a remarkable achievement of the post-Rawlsian liberal mind. After all, it had taken several centuries of confessional conflict to establish secularism and tolerance of religious difference in Europe and the West after 1517. In France, where secularism was part of its modern republican identity, the revolution had abolished the crime 'of speaking sacrilegiously about God or sacred things' in 1791.[12] Reforms of 1881 and 1905 established freedom of the press and removed the offence of 'moral and religious outrage' from the French legal code, guaranteeing a right to blasphemy.

However, the Rushdie affair and its aftermath witnessed academia, the law and the media throughout Europe condoning minority viewpoints that took violent exception to a particular verbal or artistic expression deemed blasphemous or disrespectful. A vocabulary of racism, Islamophobia, and empathy closed debate whilst accommodating a climate conducive to violence at the expense of secularism and individual freedom of expression. How did this curious political accommodation between what Fourest terms 'fanaticism' and the multicultural, progressive left evolve after 2005 and what are its implications for censorship, democratic freedom and an open society?

Closing the European Mind

The normative and critical thinking of the 1990s, rendered politically explicit in the third way style of government post 9/11, accounts for this development and its deleterious implications for an open secular society. In particular, the increasingly anti-capitalist wing of the transnational progressive movement in the West experienced what Nick Cohen identified as a 'dark liberation' after 2003.[13] Following the European demonstrations against the Iraq war in February 2003, critical progressive thought recognized that achieving global emancipatory transformation increasingly required opposing the 'civilised barbarism' and hegemonic universalism of the US and its allies.

This latest attempt at embedding utopia, as we have seen, regarded the recourse to jihad not as a violent attempt to impose Islamist values, but as a form of emancipatory 'resistance', perpetrated by a small but alienated Muslim minority.

It also considered home-grown terrorists victims of an oppressive capitalist social order.[14] Whether it was Michael Adebolajo and Michael Adobelawaye murdering Lee Rigby in Woolwich in May 2013 or the Kouachi brothers and Ahmedy Coulibaly attacking the offices of *Charlie Hebdo* in Paris in January 2015, transnational progressive idealism came to consider home-grown jihadism as the inevitable product of a fractured society and a capitalist global order. European proponents of this Olympian tendency in progressive thought, like the academic contributors to the journal *Critical Studies on Terrorism*, or the Parisian radical feminist and filmmaker, Rokhaya Diallo, or Seumas Milne, Jeremy Corbyn adviser and former *Guardian* columnist, considered Western foreign policy and millennial capital, not the Koran, as having given rise to Islamic State and jihadism in the West.

Advancing this transformative worldview required transvaluing, or radically re-describing secular, democratic, pluralist values like freedom of speech and opinion. It also required the active compliance of the West's progressive media and academia in the development of an attenuated political vocabulary to foreclose what might be expressed about particular cultures or identities. The evolution of this version of communicative reasoning increasingly favoured speech acts that limited debate by concealing and preventing thought. It labelled pejoratively those who attempted to disclose, for example, the totalitarianism explicit in Islamism's political religion or in other forms of minority social purificationism. The BBC's editorial guidelines that advised journalists to describe terrorists as 'militants' and qualified Islamic state with the adjective 'so-called' were perhaps the most obvious examples of official complicity with this rhetorical development.

The pejorative noun 'Islamophobia' proved particularly helpful in censoring any criticism not only of Muslim culture, but also, by extension, of Islamism. George Orwell would have recognised that such an abstract term inscribed a worldview and 'mental habits proper to the devotees', and, in the process, 'makes other forms of thought impossible'.[15]

Its adventure, as a word, is worth exploring. Shiite propagandists first coined the neologism in the wake of the Ayatollah Khomeini's 1979 Islamic Revolution in Iran. A decade later, in London, those campaigning against Salman Rushdie's *The Satanic Verses* realised they had more to gain by transforming their status from assassins implementing the Ayatollah's *fatwa* against Rushdie to that of victims of Islamophobia. In the 1990s, The Runnymede Trust and the Islamic Human Rights Commission (IHRC), a London based, UN recognised NGO, promoted the term's use. IHRC founder, Massoud Shadjareh, hands out annual awards for Islamophobe of the year.[16] Islamophobia treats any criticism of Islamic fanaticism as a form of racism against

Muslims in general. It elides racist attacks on mosques or Muslim cemeteries with criticisms of sharia law, the treatment of women or religious violence. It thus functions as a semantic signifier deterring any criticism of Islam or, by implication, Islamism.

European progressive thinkers and politicians embraced the term. The French government funded *Conseil Francais du Culte Musulman* (CFCM) encourages research into French Islamophobia. In 2014, the *Collectif Contre l'Islamophobie en France* (CCIF) somewhat predictably identified 'a wave of Islamophobia' sweeping the country.[17] Meanwhile, in the UK, both Islamists and critical political and international relations theorists found Islamophobia increasingly helpful for promoting their emancipatory ethics and their commitment to transforming world society. In a 1997 report, the Runnymede Trust adopted the term, and critical and progressive academic theorists applied it to Western foreign policy and its destructive international consequences both before and after 9/11. In 2018, an All-Party Parliamentary Group on British Muslims defined Islamophobia: 'rooted in racism and is a type of racism that targets expressions of Muslimness or perceived Muslimness'.[18]

The parliamentary group called upon the government to criminalize such expressions and impose penalties upon those who resorted to criticism that a Muslim might consider Islamophobic. In this way, the impeccably liberal, all party parliamentary group appeared willing to give official credence to Islamophobia and thereby prevent any exposure of the political dissimulation the term conceals. It would disallow criticism, for example, of the view advanced by prominent Muslim public intellectuals, like Oxford academic Tariq Ramadan,[19] and his fellow progressives, like the Trotskyite owner of the journal *Médiapart*, Edwy Plenel, that Islamism represents a legitimate response to colonialism and racism. 'If words are weapons', Fourest observed, Islamophobia 'is one designed to hurt secularists while feigning to target racists'.[20]

Those who detect Islamophobia in any secular criticism of Islamism's political religion also find the recourse to violence explicable in terms of a grievance culture and its root causes that breed alienation. Thus for Plenel and Ramadan, and critical and progressive thought generally, homegrown jihadis are 'the victims of a social order that already condemns' them.[21] Jihadists like the Kouachi brothers and Ahmedy Coulibaly were 'the fruit' of French social and political realities, 'the product of a fractured society'.[22] For the filmmaker, Rokhaya Diallo, French secular democracy, not the Koran, creates terrorists. Even President Obama, before the Bataclan massacre of November 2015, considered France, unlike the US or the UK, to have a 'problem' with integrating its Muslim population.

Given its progressive attachments, the western liberal media and academia proved eminently co-optable in this latest ideological endeavour to make 'lies sound truthful and murder respectable, and to give an appearance of solidity to pure wind'.[23] The mainstream media, allied to the wider post-Rawlsian, new liberal concerns with balance, impartiality, and cultural sensitivity, proved particularly helpful in disseminating this relativist perspective.

Thus in the wake of the massacre of *Charlie Hebdo* journalists in 2015, Sky News, the BBC, CNN, NBC, and ABC (Australia) refused to show the journal's cartoons. Taking 'responsibility' and neutrality to extremes further required that the opinions of those who supported the victims of the Paris attack had to be 'counterbalanced by those who support the killers' point of view'.[24] In February 2015, UK Channel 4 interviewed Abdullah al-Andalusi who compared the position of Muslims in contemporary Europe to that of the Jews in Nazi Germany, equating the murder of the *Charlie Hebdo* journalists with the 1936 assassination of the Nazi publisher William Gustlaff. The interviewer failed to challenge this 'equivalence between a drawing of Mahomet and a period when the Jews had their citizenship revoked'.[25]

By endorsing al-Andalusi's moral relativism, the neutral media failed to discriminate between a democratic opinion and a totalitarian practice. More worrying still, it is often only the apologists for politically motivated violence that are permitted a voice in the ethically responsible, progressive western press. Thus, in 2015, *The Guardian* refused to publish a piece it commissioned from Michael Goldfarb that exposed the equivocation and distortion in Tariq Ramadan's defence of Islamism. New global social media platforms like Facebook, YouTube, Google, and Twitter gave further credence to the anti-secular relativism *The Guardian* and Channel 4 promulgate, blocking videos mocking terrorists, whilst messages on social networks calling for the murder of apostates, or beating up Islamophobes, are rarely withdrawn.[26] Social media now licenses intimidation of secularists on a global scale.

As it evolved after 2003, a progressive academic, media and political orthodoxy came to absolve jihadists of responsibility for their actions, blaming it instead on contingent factors like colonialism, racism, poverty or, after a series of lone actor attacks across Europe between 2015–17, madness, generated by the anomie the perpetrator/victim experienced in his Western isolation. In this manner, the progressive mind came rationally to explain the murderous action, whilst at the same time empathising with it. In the process, it chose to ignore the somewhat inconvenient fact that most home grown terrorists did not turn to violence because of poverty, but out of choice, and, as we have seen in chapter 3, for politically religious reasons.[27]

'By naming things wrongly', Albert Camus observed, 'we add to the misfortunes of the world'.[28] The practice of state neutrality towards the self-development of minority communities means equality and social justice now 'consists in respecting the totems and taboos of each community to ensure peaceful co-existence'.[29] Such a perspective has evident authoritarian implications; if the purpose is always to avoid offence, then we end up, as Caroline Fourest contends, 'importing the laws of dictators and fanatics and placing their sensitivities' above the law.[30]

Moreover, the mainstream Western media decision to censor images that may give offence to a Muslim minority gives perverse credence to the assumption that satirical journals like *Charlie Hebdo* must have published unacceptable images. It implies that the offended have the right to be angry and, therefore, react violently. Self-censorship, allied to an anti-secular relativism, reinforces religious and cultural taboos, making it increasingly impossible to offer any criticism of a minority identity (except, of course, Christian, Jewish or white male) that might give offence and be considered 'hate speech'.[31]

You Can't Say That: The Arts After 9/11

Since the sixteenth century, European secularism and reasonable, as opposed to radical, scepticism, from Montaigne to Hume and later Camus and Orwell, questioned taboos in order to promote reflection and dialogue. This distinctively European philosophical style and practice accepted disagreement as a necessary condition of individual and political freedom. By contrast, the progressive model of official state neutrality accepts and respects non-negotiable identities and their taboos whilst seeking to manage rather than question their behavioural excesses. This constitutes the new liberal default response to an increasingly totalitarian 'other'.

The new liberal fear of being labelled Islamophobic and a progressive penchant for tolerating the intolerant, combined with the dread of provoking violence, silenced open debate about the rise of Euro-Islam and its impact upon the practice of secular democratic politics. Over the past decade, not only the mainstream media, but also literature, theatre and the art world have opted for moral equivalence and self-censorship.

After the *Charlie Hebdo* attack, 'shows, exhibitions and plays were cancelled' across Europe.[32] One event on *Art and Violence* that went ahead in Copenhagen featuring Lars Vilik, a Swedish cartoonist who had drawn an image of the prophet, closed on its opening night in February 2015, after a jihadist attack upon the event failed.

The progressive mind, rather than defending or celebrating the culture, secular values and the civilisation the West created, now actively participates in its censorship. The only art about terrorism that can be publicly exhibited displays an officially approved mixture of collusion and relativism, where artists 'offer a range of perspectives' questioning 'the War on Terror' and its impact.[33] Thus the Imperial War Museum's *Age of Terror Art since 9/11*, which opened in October 2017, shows how artists have responded to 'the perpetual state of emergency in which we now exist'. The artists explore not only personal reactions to 9/11, but also the manner in which Western civil liberties have been 'compromised and security and surveillance amplified'. The civil liberties compromised are those of Muslim minorities after 9/11, not those of cartoonists or film-makers assassinated for having an Islamophobic reaction that deviated from the prevailing progressive orthodoxy. Wandering through the three rooms devoted to *Art Since 9/11* the spectator will struggle to find a reference, even an ironic one, to Theo Van Gogh, *Jylands Posten* or *Charlie Hebdo*'s cartoons. Instead, the visitor will encounter Fabien Knecht's *Verachtung* (2014) offering a video of the artist walking around New York in a dust covered suit acquired, allegedly, from a dead suicide bomber in Iraq. Knecht's solipsistic exercise intends, like Islamic State, to draw the link between 9/11 and the Western way of war. Jenny Holzer, meanwhile, offers one of her 'redaction' paintings, featuring images of heavily censored accounts of the Iraq war acquired under the US Freedom of Information Act. Elsewhere Peter Kennard and Kat Phillips present a photo montage showing Tony Blair taking a selfie in front of a burning oil field. Jim Ricks' *Predator* (*Carpet Bombing*) depicts an image of a drone weaved into a carpet that Ricks commissioned from a Kabul rug maker. It makes a rather obvious visual pun. As too do Jake and Dinos Chapman, with their '*Nein! Eleven*' which features two mounds of corpses symbolizing the twin towers.

The artwork curated by the Imperial War Museum gives visual support to the radical pacifist and critical understanding of the war on terror, that Western interventions have created instability abroad and a surveillance state at home. The preoccupation with balance and moral equivalence extends to excluding from post-9/11 art any negative view of Islamically inspired censorship and iconoclasm, or any acknowledgement of the cartoons that al-Qaeda and IS used to justify homegrown terror attacks after 2012.

Artists like Kennard/Phillips and Jenny Holzer receive commissions and grants from multinational conglomerates for their exercises in radical pacifist agitprop. Meanwhile cartoonists like Lars Vilik, French academic Robert Redeker, who criticized the Koran in a 2006 article in *Le Figaro*, Ayaan Hirsi Ali, or Mohamed Sifaoui, who exposed al-Qaeda's network operating from London and across Europe in 2001, eke out their lives under permanent police protection.

The combination of state neutrality, the omnipresent threat of violence, and the fear of being labelled Islamophobic, means that it is now impossible to organize a conference on political Islam or freedom of expression on a UK, US or Australian campus. The preoccupation with 'safe' spaces on Western campuses, along with the fact that the Gulf States endow chairs in Islamic Studies at Oxford, Princeton, and Griffith University in Australia, further inhibits the discussion of uncomfortable secular values like the tolerance of blasphemy or sacrilege.[34] The UK National Union of Students considers any criticism of the imposition of sharia law upon some British communities to be Islamophobic. 94 of the 198 member states of the United Nations Assembly currently have blasphemy laws and the Organization of Islamic Cooperation regularly pushes for the UN Human Rights Council to recognize defamation of religion as a crime. The rising price of the freedom of expression, it seems, is too high for many Western governments to pay. The long war for cultural freedom that Hitchens foresaw in 1989 is thus in danger of being lost.

The evolution of an intolerant, non-negotiable Islamism reflects the fact that Western governments persist in treating it impartially and tolerating its right to be intolerant, addressing its excesses in the neutral vocabulary of 'radicalization' and 'violent extremism'. As a result, governments and the mainstream media engage in a practice of dissimulation replacing more accurate descriptions that might be deemed Islamophobic with euphemism and equivocation. To avoid naming the political religion that undermines the practice of secular pluralism, Western democracies and their security agencies insist on calling jihadism's proselytizing activity 'radicalization', enabling grant-funded agencies and academic experts to devise 'counter-extremism' strategies to contest the phenomenon it deliberately refuses to understand.

Curbing the Enthusiasm: How Deradicalization Programmes Get Fanaticism Wrong

After the massacre of concert goers at the Bataclan Concert Hall on Friday 13 November 2015, a predictable chorus of politicians, security and terror experts appeared in the mainstream media to announce that the attack had nothing to do with religion. The Australian Prime Minister set the chorus off on the right note, opining that the attackers were 'godless tyrants'...'completely at odds with the precepts of Islam'.[35] Joining in, Melbourne University professor and former UN official Andrew Macleod told the ABC that 'this is not a time for slogans'. Instead, what the political class must do, Macleod sloganized, 'is to determine who is the 'them' and who is the 'us'... Is it us Westerners, against them, all of Islam, or is it us, moderates of all religions, against them, radicals of all religions?'[36]

The official answer to Macleod's rhetorical question assumed a familiar pattern. After every attack since 9/11, Western governments, the mainstream media, and academic experts maintained that those attacking in the name of the Prophet misinterpreted his message. The consequence of official denial has led to domestic policies and programmes that treat the homegrown threat as a community relations problem, rather than an ideology that threatens the internal stability and integrity of secular politics.

It was after the 2005 bombings in London that the term 'radicalization' established itself firmly in the Western lexicon of criminology and counter-terror policing, to describe the process that leads jihadists along a path of violent extremism. Governments and their expert advisors therefore promoted programmes designed to preempt radicalization. Yet what exactly is the problem that de-radicalization supposedly addresses?

Somewhat problematically, radicalism or radicalization is not what Salafi-jihadist groups like Islamic State (IS)promote. They want to achieve something else, namely an ideological vision that is absolute, total and apocalyptic. Yet this fact, despite the evidence of almost two decades, continues to elude the official and progressive gaze. After the Paris attacks and despite an escalating pattern of IS linked assaults across Europe between 2015 and 2018, Western governments nevertheless continued to respond with tried and failed de-radicalization programmes to manage the phenomenon.

The New York Police Department (NYPD) was the first to commission a report into *Radicalization in the West* (2007). It defined it as a four-stage process: pre-radicalization, intensification, indoctrination and 'jihadization'.[37] On this basis, the report outlined a programme of intervention. Somewhat differently, the British government's *Prevent* programme for countering 'radicalization' among alienated, second-generation Muslim youth, begun in 2003, had developed by 2016 into a four part counter-terror strategy, *Contest*: to pursue; prevent; protect; and prepare the community against violence.[38] The strategy assumed, like the NYPD report, that 'radicalization is a social process particularly prevalent in small groups'. It was about 'who you know', 'group bonding, peer pressure and indoctrination' cultivating 'the view that violence is a legitimate response to perceived injustice'.[39]

These and similar programmes developed in Denmark, Australia and elsewhere to intervene in the radicalization process, however, did little to counter the third wave of global Salafist jihadists that turned to social media after 9/11. In February 2015, the Obama administration felt constrained to convene a summit of like-minded democracies in an attempt to counter the growing appeal of politically motivated violence to a new millennial generation. The summit discussed ways to 'prevent violent extremists and their supporters from radicalizing, recruiting, or inspiring individuals or groups in the United States and abroad to commit acts of violence'. Described as a 'strange and woolly affair', President Obama's summit only conveyed a sense of Western impotence. The president feebly observed that: 'We all know there is no one profile of a violent extremist or terrorist, so there's no way to predict who will become radicalized'.[40]

The default Western response to the growth of IS in the West was to introduce yet another tranche of counter-terror legislation and direct even more money into security agency budgets and counter-radicalization strategies. Despite an annual budget of £40 million dedicated to preventing it, the number of young, second and third generation British Muslim men and women leaving for Syria to join Islamic State rose dramatically in 2015.[41] The same pattern was true of other foreign fighters brought up in secular, Western, multicultural societies. The rising number of travellers to Iraq and Syria suggested that de-radicalization policies did very little to curb the appeal of jihadism.

Nevertheless, *Prevent* expanded after 2016 into *Contest*, an 'all-purpose government community programmes' policy to curb the appeal of political violence. Elsewhere in Western Europe, Denmark's de-radicalization programme focused increasingly on the reintegration of returnees from Syria rather than challenging their ideology. Denmark had the second highest number of foreign fighters with Islamic State after Belgium, the command-and-control centre for the Islamic State's attack on Paris in 2015.

In the United States, after 2007, and in response to the NYPD report, the US Justice Department funded de-radicalization initiatives aimed at understanding the motives of those who might be attracted to political violence. Similarly, the Australian federal government, shocked by the number of Australian foreign fighters departing for Iraq in 2015, devoted AUS $13.4 million to counter radicalization through programmes like 'Living Safe Together'. The programme stressed the need for 'social cohesion'. Yet in the same week in 2015 that state and federal governments announced enhanced de-radicalization initiatives, *Hizb ut-Tahrir*, the transnational Islamist party, which only established a presence in Australia after 2003, denounced both the Australian oath of allegiance and the 'forced assimilation' implied by singing the national anthem.[42]

Despite more than a decade funding de-radicalization policies, a worldwide survey of eighty-seven programmes found 'little independent evaluation or evidence based research to suggest that social cohesion or prevention initiatives have led to an actual reduction in extremism anywhere in the Western world'.[43] In other words, whilst ISIL offered jihadi cool messaging and sophisticated branding, Western authorities responded with official pieties about social cohesion and community bonding achieved through culturally sensitive de-radicalization programmes that proved expensive and ineffectual.

Western governments, academics, police and security agencies began to use the language of radicalization and violent extremism to describe home-grown attacks on Western targets after 2005. Subsequently radicalization and extremism became neutral abstract nouns used to present and rationally manage the internal security debate.[44] However, no government agency or counter-terror expert paused to consider whether the term adequately captured the process that converts a young Western Muslim to jihadism.

What's in a Name: Radical or Fanatic?

The language matters. An adequate response to those who find Islamic State's messaging seductive needs an accurate diagnosis. George Orwell observed in 1948 that 'the slovenliness of our language makes it easier to have foolish thoughts'. 'Political chaos', he argued, 'is connected with the decay of language', or, more precisely, with prevailing orthodoxies that 'conceal and prevent thought'.[45]

As with the neologism 'Islamophobia', the official misinterpretation of 'radical' and 'radicalization' both conceals and prevents analysis. Radicalism has a precise political etymology. It entered modern usage in the context of nineteenth-century political and economic reform and social progress. Jeremy Bentham, James Mill and their fellow 'philosophical radicals' devised the modern understanding of radicalism. They stood for a programme of utilitarian constitutional, social and economic reform. Radicalism, as a political science, dismissed religion as irrational superstition and sought reform along secular, scientific and utility-maximizing lines.[46] The one thing we know about Islamic State and its message is that it does not do scientific rationalism or secular modernity. It is, therefore, not radical, nor does it engage in radicalization. Distorting meaning, as Orwell wrote, 'distorts understanding'.[47]

Rather than being radicalized, young, Western Muslims are attracted to what a more religious age than our own recognized as 'enthusiasm', 'zealotry', or 'fanaticism'. This phenomenon has enjoyed a long history amongst the major monotheist religions, Judaism, Christianity and Islam. Seventeenth century Europe knew only too well the revived post-Reformation penchant for religious sectarian enthusiasm and its deracinating social consequences. Ben Jonson satirised this puritanical character in plays like *Bartholomew Fair* (1614) where Zeal-of-the-Land Busy tries to impress a sceptical populace with his religious enthusiasm. Later in the century, during the English Civil War (1642-49) millenarian sects like the Ranters and Fifth Monarchy Men considered their antinomian faith justified violating all social and political norms. Ranters like Abiezer Cope claimed that to 'the pure all things are pure,' including murder and rape, in order to bring about the apocalypse and the rule of Jesus Christ over England.

In the aftermath of sectarian chaos, a more sceptical age satirized the enthusiasm and character of the zealot. Writing in *The Spectator* in 1711, Joseph Addison noted that 'Zeal is...a great ease to a malicious man, by making him believe he does God service while he is gratifying the bent of a perverse revengeful temper. For this reason, we find that most massacres and devastations which have been in the world have taken their rise from a furious pretended zeal'. The preferred 'instruments' that the zealot 'works with are Racks and Gibbets, Gallies and Dungeons; when he Imprisons Men's Persons, Confiscates their Estates, Ruins their Families and Burns the Body to save the Soul,

I cannot stick to pronounce of such a one that…his Faith is vain, and his Religion unprofitable'.[48]

Alexander Pope found that 'graceless zealots' always fight for 'modes of faith'. Hence, 'his can't be wrong whose life is in the right'.[49] Hume, meanwhile, thought fanaticism and enthusiasm had produced 'the most cruel disorders in human society'.[50] Hume, Pope and Addison would recognize in the activity of today's jihadi zealotry and fanaticism not an anachronistic radicalism.

Salafism and Zealotry

In other words, any analysis of jihadism's self-confirming zealotry suggests that those labelled 'radicalized' are not really radical at all. Philosophical radicalism, properly understood, required a break with tradition and religion, of whatever faith, in order to achieve a pluralist, disenchanted, secular modernity. By contrast, a scriptural literalism based on the message of the Prophet and the example of his rightly guided seventh century (CE) successors, the Rashidun, fuels Islamic State's thought and practice. They look to past models purified by violence today to build tomorrow's utopia, via an apocalyptic conflict. Like seventeenth-century English sectaries they are fanatics who adapt the tenets of an ultra-traditional scriptural literalism to guide present action. Today's jihadi is an enthusiast as defined by the Oxford Shorter English Dictionary, namely one who is 'possessed by a god' or in 'receipt of divine communication'. No matter how implausible their motives appear to modern secular sensibilities, they consider themselves directly engaged in a divinely ordained mission to re-create the caliphate.

Prior to the Enlightenment, most of the world, including Europe, subscribed to exclusive religious identities often with a fanaticism similar to that motivating today's jihadis. Both medieval Christendom and, in its aftermath, the early modern confessional state saw battle as an instrument of divine will, a providential means to deliver God's judgement. Even after the Enlightenment and with the decline of religious enthusiasm, as well as the Christian faith across Europe, the rise of political religions that replaced divine ordinance with ideologically determined nations, races or proletariats remained the touchstone of purifying violence intimating utopia. They reached an apocalyptic apogee in the death cult of Nazi Germany during World War II.

Radicalism and Modernity

By contrast, the emergence of cosmopolitan, representative, liberal democratic forms of rule in the nineteenth century constituted the real 'radical', modern, structural break with the past and what Walter Bagehot termed the 'cake of custom'.[51] As a consequence, democratic pluralism in the West embraced secularism and, with it, as Max Weber observed, a condition of disenchantment. Soteriological order receded before a world increasingly governed by scientific reasoning. This secular rationalist worldview achieved spectacular and revolutionary change, but also narrowed the horizon of the good life, rendering citizenship modular and promising fulfilment through consumption and the joys of shopping for physical and material rewards.[52]

It also had a downside. From at least the late nineteenth century, sociologists, psychologists, and philosophers as different as Freud, Durkheim and Nietzsche recognized in modernity not only democratic opportunities for self-discovery and the revision of life choices, but also the anomie, anxiety and alienation associated with a complex, modern, mass society. By the late twentieth century writers as various as Herbert Marcuse, Tom Wolfe and Christopher Lasch identified a modern culture of narcissism and anxiety where the human potential for altruism dissolves into an atomised relativism, a condition that increasingly lends itself to rational techno-managerialism rather than autonomous individualism.[53]

In other words, secular modernity offers a radical and modular form of life against which the jihadi rages. Indeed, from the fanatic perspective, this *kufr* world order is weak and fragmented because it has lost the capacity to submit to a politically religious truth. Modernity also offers a stage upon which the modern zealot can disport his oppression, proselytize and strategize. The global Salafist-jihadist movement's appeal resides, then, in its ability to re-enchant the world through a Manichean worldview and a millenarian vision. Its style is not so dissimilar to the manner in which the seventeenth century sectaries anticipated a new heaven and a new earth or the Nazis offered a racially pure future as a means of overcoming the failings of depression-hit Weimar Germany in the 1930s. Contemporary Salafist fanatics transform the fears and anxieties of disaffected sections of the diasporic Muslim youth in the West into a fanatic enthusiasm via on-line as well as primary socialization.

What is to be Done?

The progressive refusal to acknowledge the attractions of zealotry, and not only amongst those drawn to Salafist jihadism, as we shall show in chapter 9, is itself the problem. The neutral language of radicalization and deradicalization reflects and reinforces a progressive secular rationalism that treats religious, or nationalist, worldviews as beyond belief, rather than coherent within their own politico-theological terms of reference. It persists in dismissing disaffected Muslims, inclined to travel to Syria, as 'clowns' and 'numbskulls', the pejoratives Australian politicians also applied to *Hizb ut-Tahrir*'s recruitment activity in 2015, rather than zealots that are willing to die and behead for the realization of the apocalyptic vision.

Western public policy thus discounts fanatic agency and responds instead with depoliticized programmes intended to manage grievance. Deakin University's terror expert Professor Greg Barton maintains this requires communities to 'befriend' their local jihadi. Islamic state, Barton claims, 'offers friendship. They're filling a void'. What 'we have to provide', with community initiatives, is 'alternative forms of friendship'.[54] Such an approach perceives the need only to de-programme those who have been 'radicalized' with a mixture of therapies offered by a small army of counsellors offering empathy and boosting self-esteem.

In effect, this therapeutic model treats the zealot not as a danger to the wider society but as a passive victim groomed by anonymous but unscrupulous online recruiters. Deradicalization presents the young jihadi as the gullible victim of brainwashing. The approach applies particularly in the case of young women seduced online who offer themselves as jihadi brides.

However, like the men they embrace, they too have found meaning in an enthusiasm which the wider society finds incomprehensible, but which inspires action. Neither radical nor victims, they are largely immune to the community-sensitive de-radicalization programs Western governments offer, because there is not much that is particularly radical in jihadist self-understanding.

Given that those who share Islamic State's version of religious conviction now move freely between Europe *sans frontières* and the Middle East, and derive support from Western diasporic communities, Western policy appears worryingly misconceived. Yet rather than abandon its faith in multiculturalism, state neutrality and tolerance, Western governments prefer to ignore the distinctly Islamist idiom of expression.

Arguably, it is the West that is deluded and should begin by 'de-radicalizing' its own progressive thinking. The difficulty with the prevailing new liberal orthodoxy is that Europe's problem is not with Christian evangelical, Buddhist, Jewish or Hindu Nationalist 'radicals', but with a literal interpretation of the Koran and what a modern form of zealotry abstracts from it.

It is this that a more prudent approach to a cultural *modus vivendi* between incommensurable values in a condition of deep pluralism would need to understand, because without understanding it we cannot comprehend its strategic thinking or devise an effective response. In order to address the prevailing progressive orthodoxy that we must tolerate and offer friendship to the intolerant, as current Western government programmes assume, it might be worth secular liberal multiculturalists attending to the thinking of a philosopher who understood the necessary conditions for maintaining an open society against its enemies. Karl Popper, another refugee from the Third Reich, identified the liberal paradox that 'unlimited tolerance must lead to the disappearance of tolerance'. In fact, he argued that 'if we are not prepared to defend a tolerant society against the onslaught of the intolerant, then the tolerant will be destroyed, and tolerance with them'. Popper further contended that we need not 'suppress the utterance of intolerant philosophies; as long as we can counter them by rational argument and keep them in check by public opinion'. Yet as Popper foresaw, 'it may easily turn out that they are not prepared to meet us on the level of rational argument', but begin, as Islamism does, by denouncing all argument. They may forbid their followers to listen to rational argument, because it is deceptive, and teach them to answer arguments with violence. In this context, Popper would advise that a pluralist democracy must claim 'in the name of tolerance, the right *not* to tolerate the intolerant'.[55] Indeed, a political democracy characterised by deep pluralism that does not comprehend this paradox cannot survive for long.

6

THE NETWORKED GLOBAL ORDER
MILLENNIAL CAPITAL AND THE MELTDOWN

The liberal progressive mind sought, as we have seen, to manage, rather than resolve, the problem of exclusive identities that resisted assimilation into its secular vision of a socially just, post-national global society. The response to the rise of a non-negotiable, Islamist identity exposed the inconsistencies at the core of new liberalism's inclusive, but diversity-sensitive secular agenda. Third way style social justice placed its progressive faith in 'using the power of society as a whole to bring opportunity, prosperity and hope to those without it; to do so not just within our own national boundaries but outside of them; to judge our societies by the condition of the weak as much as the strong'.[1] Tony Blair, one of the leading architects of this progressive political project, considered these values 'static, unmoveable, and not subject to the ravages of time'.[2]

The global financial crisis of 2008 and its aftermath eroded the economic foundations supporting these values and undermined the already fragile relationship between the nation state, the market, the media, international society and the ubiquitous cosmopolitan faith in a liberal democratic end of history. We observed in chapter 1 that the preconditions for economic redistribution, growth and equality, locally and globally, required an increasingly interconnected regional and global trading order, regulated through a golden straitjacket that *inter alia* removed restrictions on foreign investment, deregulated capital markets, opened industries to direct foreign ownership, deregulated economies and exposed banking and telecommunications systems to privatization and competition.[3] As Blair observed, 'for almost twenty years after 1989, the West set [this] agenda'.[4] Following the collapse of Soviet style communism, it was all too easy to believe 'that the West's model of liberal democracy and free-market capitalism, supported by a clear set of US-sponsored international rules, would spread to the four corners of the Earth'. Ultimately, however, as former HSBC chief economist Stephen King observed, 'this proved to be nonsense'.[5]

Summarizing the Washington consensus at the millennium, commentators steeped in this nonsense, like Thomas Friedman, claimed that the democratization of technology, finance and information drove the homogenizing processes of globalization and democratic progress. It also created a new power source in the world, the 'Electronic Herd'. The herd comprised 'the faceless stock, bond and currency traders' pioneering exciting new financial products like derivatives and collateralized debt obligations. It rewarded, with investment capital, countries that put on the Golden Straitjacket and 'kept it on'. Meanwhile, multinational corporations spread production around the world, shifting factories to the 'most efficient low-cost producers'. The late twentieth-century globalization story was about convergence. 'Western capital went in search of cheap emerging-market labour. Thanks to information technology, supply chains began to expand at a rate of knots'.[6] Asia, and China in particular, was the main beneficiary.

From Davos' magic mountain top,[7] however, China, like the Asian miracle economies of the 1990s, it was assumed, would come within the purview of the Electronic Herd and their credit rating enforcement agencies, ensuring market compliance and inevitable political liberalization. The global system at the millennium reflected a complex interaction between the Electronic Herd, nation states and the all-enveloping Golden Straitjacket.[8]

This world 'was governed by market forces', where 'the fast eat the slow'.[9] The best way to achieve rapid increases in living standards was to follow market liberalizing norms; low inflation and the great moderation would do the rest. This 'was the mantra' of the globalization era.[10] Rational governments, irrespective of the character of the regime, would embrace the free-market convention that ever-larger cross-border capital flows ensured a more efficient allocation of resources with gains for all. States either got on board the global expressway to a borderless, liberal democratic world order or found themselves consigned to an *ultima thule* of failed statehood, where only crime, terror and olive trees flourished.

The consequences were staggering, but not quite what the end of history scenario anticipated. The progressive visionaries of the great moderation had failed to spot an inconvenient anomaly, namely that 'if enough people believed that the world's fundamental economic problems had been solved, they would begin to take risks that, collectively, would make the world a much more dangerous place'.[11] Indeed, within a decade of the Davos Forum addressing 'the shifting power equation' shaping the global agenda,[12] Stephen D. King could observe that 'many of the values and beliefs that the Western world embraced following the end of the Second World War' were now crumbling. Western progressivism wildly overestimated the emancipating effects of trade and technology, 'lazily assuming that, with the Cold War at an end, the rest of the world would embrace supposedly universal truths associated with liberal democracy and free markets'. By the second decade of the twenty-first century many countries, notably China and Russia, had done 'no such thing'.[13] After September 2008, millennial capitalism and the borderless world, part of the 'end of history bedrock', found itself 'in the dock'.[14]

The golden straitjacket unravelled with extraordinary rapidity between 2007 and 2018, the decade of financial crises that, Adam Tooze argues, 'changed the world'.[15] Whatever else, it destroyed the fashionable meliorist assumption linking capitalism, globalization, and democracy. Outside of the cocoon of Western academia and a liberal commentariat, it rendered the international pursuit of universal emancipation, social justice, international norms and social perfection at best aspirational, at worst redundant. The political and geo-political consequences of the US sub-prime crisis of 2008–10, followed by the fiscal attrition the Eurozone crisis imposed on Southern Europe between 2010–18, indicated history had far from concluded whatever teleological journey it undertook after 1989. Indeed, despite the progressive pieties of the world economic forum, third way visionaries and the Washington consensus, it was already clear to some commentators, prior to the collapse of Lehman Brothers in September 2008, that globalization and the revolution in information technology had an uncomfortable and illiberal, dark side.

The Rise and Fall of Neo-Medievalism

In 2006, as we have seen, Philip Cerny characterized the emerging politico-economic structure of the post-Cold War period as 'neo-medieval': a condition distinguished by overlapping jurisdictions and cross-cutting allegiances where the transnational character of global exchanges undermined the traditional territoriality and allegiances of the nation state, de-concentrating loyalty as it deracinated identities.[16]

New communicatory media like the internet, and the speed of physical and virtual communication, altered the character of what Michael Oakeshott identified as political or 'civil association'. By civil association, Oakeshott understood a non-instrumental, political arrangement whose 'purpose was inherent and its rules authoritative by virtue of being recognized as such'. Acceptance of its authority constituted the only mutual bond that connected the members of such a conventionally political or civil association, whose guiding principle was individual liberty under the rule of law, within a sovereign, territorial, unit of rule.[17]

The market state that emerged at the end of history operated financially and economically both within and outside the boundaries of civil association. It also evolved a distinctive form of Anglo-Saxon risk capitalism much derided by Europeans. Yet equally conducive to the process of globalization were states that functioned as 'enterprise associations' managing their subjects, rather than citizens, towards rational goals.[18] In this context, Singapore, described by Danilo Zolo as a 'negative utopia',[19] offered a successful, non-liberal mode of organization where a techno-mandarinate organized all aspects of social and political life and distributed the economic product via an administrative apparatus of state-licensed, hierarchically ordered, ethno-religious community groups, without the need for politics based on autonomous groups freely articulating their interests in a public setting. Here, the state bureaucratically defined identities and entitlements and distributed them according to a consensually agreed but state-managed formula. This arrangement can be open to investment whilst severely curtailing the space for civil society and freedom of opinion. Despite the difficulties of exporting the model from the city-state of Singapore to more complex societies, this version of illiberal or karaoke democracy is a formula that increasingly appeals to an elite, transnational, technocratic mind generally, and affords the model to which the Communist Party of China (CPC) aspires.

Somewhat differently, but less successfully, the Russian Federation has also functioned as a state-led, inclusionary corporatist enterprise after Vladimir Putin's re-election to the Presidency in 2012. Such arrangements, as the Singapore, South Korean, Taiwanese and Chinese cases show, can be more effective in terms of infrastructure building, 'picking winners' and managing internal security than the relatively open market, liberal progressive alternative. In other words, the neo-medieval structure emerging at the millennium was both market state and administrative state-friendly.

At the same time, millennial capital, driven after the 'big bang' of the 1980s by the development of wide, deep and increasingly global financial markets, has undermined social democratic, state-based, or regionally focused, capitalism. The post-1945 Ford era contract with the nation state, which assumed that both workers and managers remained within a territorial state, no longer held. This upset the presumed harmonious convergence between capitalism and the social democratic state and fundamentally recast socio-economic relations, party behaviour, and political conduct across the Western democracies. The new mobility of capital and labour could no longer sustain a cradle-to-grave, state-based welfare blanket. Instead, millennial capital, crudely depicted in terms of globalization and deregulation, was actually about regulation to protect the purported efficiency of markets, and allow wider access to their benefits. As Walter Russell Mead explained:

> National regulation may be decreasing, but the rise of millennial capitalism is creating new forms of international regulation that simply did not exist in the past. Free trade agreements (notably bilateral

rather than multilateral or regional) are much more than trade agreements, they create new transnational forms of regulation.[20]

The demographic changes that redefined the social and political character of citizenship in the networked, market state after 1990 also affected millennial capitalism. As population growth shrank and went into reverse in many of the developed democratic West European states, the socio-economic arrangements of the consensus and convergence era no longer made sense: welfare, health, education, and pension schemes faced inexorable pressure to mutate into market-driven, yield-sensitive investments, rather than state entitlements.

The globalized division of labour and the death of the blue-collar working class in the developed world's rust belts also had significant implications for democratic citizenship with the emergence of a new, and insecure, 'precariat' class, increasingly drawn to a paranoid style of politics. Policies that assumed that diversity in modern cosmopolitan cities must be addressed by an elite-driven norm of multiculturalism only increased the difficulty of sustaining civil association in conditions of profound cultural fluidity. Bureaucratically engineered identities, as we have seen, did not liberate but instead imprisoned minorities and transformed them into an alienated resource for leaderless resistance, rather than facilitating the modular or civil character necessary to sustain civil democratic practice.

Prior to the financial crisis, millennial capital was already in the process of transforming the political economy, whilst alienating mass working class constituencies. Although the phenomenon promoted multiple, cross-cutting allegiances, it did not, however, undermine the state. Indeed, a particular variant of the nation state model – the semi-privatized, networked market state (sometimes described as the Anglo-Saxon model) – had, prior to 2008, driven the process.

One of the notable features of the evolving arrangement that dates from the Reagan and Thatcher epochs, and conducted in more emollient, Rawlsian and progressive fashion by Clinton, Blair, Cameron and Obama, was the manner in which the market state sought to integrate global trade. As Cerny observed, it was the market state that brought about the neo-medieval condition and was both enhanced, in terms of growth and wealth, and threatened, in terms of the migration and capital flows across the world it made possible.

More precisely, secular, modular, market-oriented modernity is dialectically challenged by those who seek to exploit its structures, notably the networked fast world that rendered its wealth maximization both tangible and vulnerable. Millennial capital, with its wide, deep, and globally interconnected financial markets by no means facilitated global economic or political integration. How Western democracies subsequently conceive both membership and security required a range of responses that have only come into focus since the Asian Financial Crisis of 1997, the attacks of 9/11 and 7/7, and the global financial crisis of 2008.

One obvious response to this millennial age of anger was heightened investment in security and enhanced government surveillance both locally and globally. Bradley Manning's Wiki Leaks, and Edward Snowden's revelation of the scale of National Security Agency electronic surveillance between 2008 and 2013, illustrated both the extent and the difficulty Western democracies faced in gathering covert information. At the same time, the propensity of bureaucratic organizations like ASIO in Australia,[21] MI5 in the UK, and the FBI in the US to respond managerially to the problem of increasingly networked violence proved both expensive and incoherent, as the failure to identify threats posed by al-Qaeda, or forestall a number of homeland attacks perpetrated by adherents of IS, demonstrated.

Despite these limitations, the progressive, managerial, proactive approach to internal security devoted higher levels of GDP to security infrastructure. This necessitated the privatization of social services and pension provisions, which further undermined civil association based on common participation in the *xynon* of a shared political culture. As Philip Bobbit observed in 2006, the modern democratic state legitimated its power on the grounds of 'enhancing your opportunity. What you do with it – that's up to you. We will not assure you of equality, and we will not ensure you steadily improving security, but the total wealth of society will be maximized'.[22]

Within nation states, it also became 'increasingly obvious that pre-financial crisis globalization was not a force for social cohesion'. The idea that international free-market capitalism delivered the best outcome for all was 'less than compelling'.[23] At the same time, the market state's global networking with like- and unlike-minded states assumed an essentially bilateral or trilateral structure in terms of agreements to maximize trade, wealth, and security. This trend, over time, eroded regional or multilateral arrangements, still considered by proponents of international norms and institutions as the harbinger of a post-state, liberal international order.[24] Since the Asian financial crisis of 1997, the spread of low intensity violence, the rise of China as the globe's major manufacturer and consumer of natural resources, and the financial meltdown of the West after 2008, largely caused by the 'light touch' regulation demanded by the Electronic Herd, Cold War arrangements like NATO, the UN, the EU, and ASEAN have all lost salience and credibility. The IMF, the WTO, and APEC have also declined in terms of their international significance, whilst Obama's proposed multilateral, Trans Pacific Trade Partnership (TPP) failed to survive the first weeks of the Trump presidency.

Before 2008, the financial sector earned thirty-five per cent of all profit in the US economy.[25] If the political impact of millennial capital had already diminished assumptions about the equitable and wealth enhancing character of globalized currency and trade flows leading to harmonious convergence in a borderless world, they were transformed, utterly, by the financial crisis and its aftermath, which reinforced the anomic character of this globally anxious and paranoia inducing condition.

The Collapse of the Market State Order, 2007–18

'In reading the history of nations', wrote Charles Mackay in 1852:

> we find that, like individuals, they have their whims and their peculiarities; their seasons of excitement and recklessness, when they care not what they do. We find that whole communities suddenly fix their minds upon one object, and go mad in its pursuit; that millions of people become simultaneously impressed with one delusion, and run after it, till their attention is caught by some new folly more captivating than the first.... At an early age in the annals of Europe its population lost their wits about the sepulchre of Jesus, and crowded in frenzied multitudes to the Holy Land.[26]

We might add that at a later age in the annals of the West, its political and financial elites lost their wits, and fiscal and economic credibility, over the illusion of the end of history, a borderless world and the great global moderation that had, they alleged, terminated the cycle of economic booms preceding inevitable busts.

Ironically, whilst the scale of the 2008 financial crisis was global in its synchronicity, a number of its key elements – an asset bubble, tight money, rising interest rates, a frothy stock market followed by a panic and a long depression – have been far from uncommon, as Mackay first noted, in economic history.[27] In fact, despite the millennial preoccupation of economists and governments with the market's rationality prior to the crash, what occurred in 2008 was far from unprecedented.

The great financial crisis resembled successive financial panics dating back to the Dutch tulip mania of the 1630s and the South Sea and Mississippi scheme bubbles of the 1720s in the UK and France. Even the international scale of the crisis was not new. The first use of the term 'financier' and 'financial capital' appeared in the *Pall Mall Gazette* in 1867. Speculators raised money by issuing stock on railroads running across the US and South America, opening up the continent for agriculture and resource exploitation. This was Mark Twain's *Gilded Age* (1873) and the world that Trollope described in *The Way We Live Now* (1875). International financial speculators like Trollope's Melmot exploited the mania for US railway stock. However, when it became apparent that there were too many railway companies and some roads were unlikely to be built, a panic on the New York, London and Paris exchanges ensued. The first international financial crisis saw depression follow the bust.

The UK and US economies only began to recover towards the end of the century. Some profited, notably the robber barons Vanderbilt, Carnegie, and J.P. Morgan's banking and industrial conglomerates, the Google, Amazon, Facebook and Apple of their day, before anti-trust legislation curtailed their monopolies.[28] And then there was 1929, the crash that happened in slow motion. Wall Street had not fallen too dramatically by December 1929. However, banks gradually came under pressure as their liquidity proved inadequate. By July 1932, the Dow Jones index, which had stood at 3,312 in June 1929, had dropped to

312. More than one fifth of US banks, holding ten per cent of deposits in 1929, went out of business. By 1933, the US net national product had fallen more than fifty per cent. All told, Milton Friedman showed, money income fell by fifty-three per cent and real income by thirty-six per cent. Friedman concluded that the depth and intensity of 'the great monetary contraction' of 1929–33 was a consequence of ineffective fiscal policy. 'Whatever its magnitude', he argued, 'the downward pressure on income produced by the effects of the stock market crash on expectations to spend…was strongly influenced by the stock of money' which contracted dramatically.[29] In other words, the reserve system and its failure to bail out the Bank of United States (the Lehman Brothers of 1930) amplified the crisis and created uncertainty, distrust and a catastrophic lack of confidence.

Friedman's monetary analysis influenced the Federal Reserve's response to the 2008 subprime crisis, with consequences that Friedman, and his erstwhile student, Ben Bernanke, had not fully anticipated. Instead, Hyman Minsky's less well known theory of financial instability appears to apply not only to 1929 but also to 2008.[30] A sustained economic expansion, Minsky maintained, leads eventually to euphoria, a point at which ever higher levels of debt finance excessive risk-taking. George Soros termed this process market reflexivity: 'the illusion that markets manage to be always right is caused by their ability to affect the fundamentals they are supposed to reflect.'[31] Market euphoria, however, turns inexorably to fear and panic. The crisis that follows witnesses a brutal process of liquidation.

Moreover, if, as Stephen King contends, 'a central bank steps in to prevent bankruptcies – via aggressive interest rate cuts and generous "lender of last resort" activities – the subsequent recovery will be even more financially fragile'. From Minsky's perspective, the 'Great Moderation' was always going to end badly.[32] To the extent that low and stable inflation encouraged excessive risk-taking, 'economies had become increasingly exposed to financial, rather than price, instability'.[33]

With the onset of the global financial crisis in September 2008, the disruption in world markets and the panic it caused amongst investors from New York to Sydney, politicians as various as Australian Prime Minister Kevin Rudd and German finance minister Peer Steinbruck claimed that the crisis was the consequence of 'extreme' or Anglo-

Saxon, free market capitalism. The first critic of extreme capitalism made a dramatic comeback: politicians as diverse as Nicholas Sarkozy, Dominique Strauss-Kahn, and Steinbruck himself, all confessed, without noticeable embarrassment, to dusting down their copies of *Das Kapital*. Economists like Thomas Piketty and Paul Mason who adapted Marx's analysis of the destructive impact of deregulated capital for contemporary consumption enjoyed a surprising popularity.[34] How 'extreme' was the millennial capital order and what effect did its implosion have upon the cosmopolitan pursuit of justice, equality and social perfection at the end of history?

Prior to Lehman Brothers' bankruptcy, (US) $2.5 trillion of collateral 'was posted on the triparty segment alone of the repo (repurchase) market on a daily basis'.[35] September and October 2008 witnessed not only Lehman Brothers, but banks from HBOS and RBS in the United Kingdom to Filma in Belgium either cease trading, or being forcibly merged into ostensibly more solvent entities. Even sovereign wealth funds, considered impervious to the crisis, encountered difficulties. Singapore's Government Investment Corporation and Saudi wealth funds found themselves out of pocket after 'prudently' assuming big stakes in Morgan Stanley, Lehman Brothers and Merrill Lynch in March 2008. Elsewhere, developing markets, once assumed immune from the US sub-prime crisis, also began to melt down. Latvia, Hungary, and the Ukraine, amongst other countries benefiting from cheap loans in dollars or euros, required lines of credit from an increasingly stretched International Monetary Fund (IMF). What made the collapse so severe was 'its extraordinary global synchronization'.[36] It was, as the US Federal Reserve chair, and former proponent of 'the great moderation', Ben Bernanke, observed, 'the worst financial crisis in global history, including the Great Depression'.[37]

If we were to offer a symbol of the crisis it might be an iconic American investment bank like Bear Stearns or Lehman Brothers or a national, but rusting, manufacturing marque like General Motors. It might also be the Viking economy of Iceland. Once a modest, but stable, economy based on its fishing fleets, the small North Atlantic island discovered the joys of investment banking and offshore financing in the course of the new millennium. The country's three leading banks lent globally, offering high rates on deposits lodged in the state's cash poor banks. When investors demanded their cash back in October 2008, the banks and the state went bankrupt – a situation not dissimilar to what happened with Lehman Brothers as it tried to roll over $20 billion of its Mortgage Backed Securities portfolio on the repurchase market without finding takers, or the Mississippi Scheme that destroyed the credibility of the French monarchy in 1720.

As the Iceland government froze accounts, it also caused a diplomatic rift with the UK where *Icesave* franchises of Landsbanki that operated on British high streets had offered term deposits at rates a point higher than United Kingdom lenders. British local councils, the police pension fund, and over a billion dollars of private investor capital were caught in the crisis. Gordon Brown's Labour government invoked Britain's anti-terror laws to freeze Icelandic assets. Without recourse to the European Central Bank (ECB) or the US Federal Reserve, and studiously ignored by neighbours that shared its Viking past (Norway and Denmark), Iceland had recourse to a $US 4 billion line of credit from Russia. The Iceland case, like those of Hungary, the Ukraine and, of course, Greece and Italy, which followed a not dissimilar path, was a harbinger of the unintended geopolitical consequences the global financial crisis unleashed.

The Myth of De-coupling

Meanwhile emerging economies, especially the BRICS (Brazil, Russia, India, China, and South Africa), that a number of analysts[38] thought had de-coupled from the US-driven global trading and financial order also saw their growth decline. The Russian, Brazilian, and Chinese economies slowed dramatically after the Beijing Olympics of 2008 that had symbolically announced China's emergence as a global power. The myth that the BRICS, and East Asia more generally, had grown a sufficient pool of domestic consumers to be immune from the meltdown in the US and Europe was *ex post facto* falsified. In fact, from 2002, and China's entry into the WTO, the BRICS and the Asian tiger economies of South and East Asia had become thirty per cent more dependent on export-oriented growth than they had been at the time of the Asian financial crisis of 1997.

It soon became clear that the US banking sector, the Federal Reserve and the greenback, as the global reserve currency, remained central to global growth and stability. Without US consumption and liquidity, growth rates declined. Meanwhile China and the other emerging market economies subsidized US debt as they held dollar reserves and US treasury bonds.[39] Rather than de-coupling, the global financial crisis showed that the world was financially interconnected, but by no means fiscally, monetarily or politically integrated.

The US, Europe and China were in fact locked in a Faustian pact where China exported its manufactures, saved its surpluses, protected its domestic markets, and maintained a cheap currency controlled by the People's Bank, whilst the West benefited from the effect of China's economic rise, enjoying cheap credit to fuel consumption, asset price inflation and debt. The deflationary impact of China on global growth after it opened up and began to grow at double digit pace, as well as suck in a vast proportion of the globe's foreign direct investment after 1998, meant that it effectively bankrolled western and more particularly US consumption and consumer debt. 'Chimerica', Niall Ferguson's term for this curious financial and trading hybrid, represented 'a balance of financial terror'.[40] Indeed, both before and after 2008 China and Southeast Asia subsidized a mountain of US and European debt, reflecting the dollar's continuing, but increasingly ambivalent, status as the world currency.

A Tale of Three Crises

The 2008 crisis was not a speculative frenzy like the tech wreck of 1999–2003, but a credit crisis where liquidity dried up and banks with low deposit bases, dependent for lending upon the international money market, went bust (as was the case with Northern Rock, the UK lender or, small, open economies, like Iceland and Ireland). The crisis bore similarities with what occurred in Japan and Asia after the *endaka* wave of Japanese investment generated by the Plaza Accord of 1987. After 1987, the strong yen saw the Nikkei soar to over 30,000 points in January 1990 and asset values rise. At one stage the fashionable Ginza district of Tokyo was worth more than Canada. The outcome for Japan, after its housing bubble began to deflate, was a continuing reliance on export-oriented growth and domestic savings, locking the country into low growth deflation, and generating a government debt to GDP ratio of 236 per cent by 2017. Interest on the Japanese currency turned negative for the best part of almost two decades.[41]

Somewhat differently, the period leading up to the Asian financial crisis, beginning in the summer of 1997, witnessed export-oriented growth and foreign direct investment fuelling short term borrowing on international markets to stimulate long term investment, especially in property. In Singapore, house prices only returned to their 1996 peaks in 2007. The assumption fuelling the miracle growth decade was that the relationship between the Singapore dollar, Thai baht or Indonesian rupiah would remain stable against both the yen and the greenback. When hedge funds questioned this assumption, foreign direct investment pulled out and South East Asian central banks needed recourse to the IMF as lender of last resort.[42]

The Asian crisis resembled the sub-prime and Eurozone crises: short-term borrowing funding highly leveraged, and inadequately securitized, long-term investment. The differences are also striking, however. The US, regardless of the financial meltdown, could maintain its financial credibility by printing US dollars. Thus, despite the roughly trillion dollars worth of loans handed out to banks and mortgage companies to ward off global financial collapse, the dollar continued to rise. Asia then, and China now, has no such recourse. This notwithstanding, the scale of what Stephen King terms the 'grave new world' of global trade and finance emerged courtesy of the stampeding, unregulated Electronic Herd that had so dramatically terminated the Soviet empire.

Debt and Discontent

Cheap interest rates, deliberately kept low by both the US Federal Reserve and Bank of England after the trauma of 9/11, had fuelled a consumption-driven asset price boom. It also made possible a new range of financial products designed to offset risk, notably the synthetic derivatives that mixed Collateralized Debt Obligations (CDOs) and Credit Default Swaps (CDSs) in an ultimately toxic blend. After 2002, investment banks like Merrill Lynch, Lehman and Bear Stearns became mortgage-based money machines vending leverage and securitization.

The New York Times reported that 'synthetic CDOs were the exemplar of a new type of modern financial engineering'.[43] They bundled mortgage related CDOs and CDSs in a complex amalgam ultimately linked to real world loans and debts. As the Fed raised interest rates after 2006, the housing market went sour and borrowers defaulted on their mortgages. Mortgage Backed Securities (MBS) contracts collapsed, exacerbating the meltdown, rather than defraying risk. In late 2008, after taking over Merrill Lynch, Bank of America found $71 billion of mortgage-related exotica decaying on its books. The fact that MBS received AAA ratings from Standards & Poor, Fitch and Moody's only added to the sense that the Electronic Herd's police had facilitated the electronic equivalent of Bovine Spongiform Encephalopathy.[44]

Moreover, this deregulated derivative practice was by no means confined to the United States. Canary Wharf generated many of these products, as London assumed the role of the 'capital of capital' after the US financial authorities restricted exotic, Enron-style accounting practices after 2001. In 2008, there was an estimated $US 684 trillion in debt-related, credit backed derivatives in the global market – some twelve times the size of total global gross domestic product.

The cumulative action of the US Federal Bank and the Bush and Obama administrations from 2008 to 2012 succeeded in stabilizing the financial system and recapitalizing mega banks like Citi group that were 'too big to fail'. The Troubled Asset Relief Program (TARP) and the American Renewal and Reinvestment Act (2009), followed by the three programmes of quantitative easing that Bernanke, the Federal Reserve board chair, initiated between 2010 and 2013 stabilized the US financial sector. The Fed, 'without public consultation of any kind' became the lender of last resort to the world.[45] In the process, it transformed the relationship between financial systems and national currencies. Far from withering away, the Fed's intervention between 2008–12 gave 'an entirely new dimension to the global dollar'.

The premise behind the provision of liquidity was, Tim Geithner, Obama's Treasury Secretary, averred, to uphold the stability of 'the financial system'.[46] From the liberal progressive perspective of Clinton-era globalizers like Larry Summers, the interests of America, global interdependence and the financial system necessarily converged. The US avoided bank nationalization by recapitalizing the banking sector. By 2013, J.P. Morgan, Goldman Sachs, Bank of America, Citigroup and Wells Fargo were thirty-seven per cent larger than they were in 2008. If, as Geithner insisted, the ultimate test of the policy of stabilization was the health of the banks, then the result was impressive. The eighteen biggest banks doubled their capital requirements whilst dramatically reducing their risky wholesale funding.[47] The bailout also came with a new regulatory framework, the Dodd-Frank legislation, that subjected the investment banking sector to Federal oversight. This re-regulation of the financial marketplace reflected the fact that, ironically, it had required all the resources of the state to save the deregulated global financial infrastructure, and the golden straitjacket, from 'systemic implosion'.[48]

The financial crisis revealed that national economic policy was ultimately subordinated to the needs of the financial system. However, saving that system came at the expense of the poorer and middling sorts in both America and Europe. The crisis also revealed a burgeoning gulf between the interests of financiers and those of taxpayers. To save the global financial system, national taxpayers paid 'to bail out what were, in some cases, global institutions. With much higher levels of government debt as a consequence of the financial crisis', they would 'continue to do so for many years to come'.[49]

The inequality debate that developed in Western democracies after 2011 exposed growing popular disillusion with the global, liberalizing progressivism of the Clinton, Blair, Schröder, Obama, and Cameron era. It was three years after the real estate bubble burst that the full effects of the credit crunch and mass unemployment made itself felt across the US economy. Between 2007–11 more than three million homes fell into foreclosure. Unemployment peaked at 10.9 per cent of the workforce in 2011.[50] The contrast between Wall Street, where top investment bankers netted $145 billion in bonuses in 2009, and Main Street could not have been starker. The 2011 *Occupy* movement slogan, 'The system isn't broken. It's rigged', captured the emerging popular mood.[51]

Since the early 1980s 'the top 1 per cent of US income earners received 41 per cent of the total increase in net worth'.[52] Beyond the top twenty per cent of income earners, 'there have been no gains to speak of whatsoever'. Middle-income earners in the US – those in the middle three income quintiles – 'got through much of this period only by upping their borrowing. Between 2001 and 2007, their debt equity ratio (mostly the level of their debt relative to the value of their house or apartment) rose from 46 to 61 per cent'.[53]

Middling and poorer black and Hispanic households found themselves particularly exposed to the US housing market crash. Even after the economic recovery began in 2012, middle-income earners continued to suffer. Even more egregiously, it was the wealthiest, both in the US and globally, that proved the major beneficiaries of the monetary policy of quantitative easing. This 'magical monetary medicine where, in effect, a central bank purchases financial assets in a bid to drive their price higher, in the hope that households and companies will spend more',[54] facilitated a bull run on equities between 2009–19. It disproportionately rewarded the top ten per cent of households that owned ninety per cent of the total value of financial assets in the US.

The most tangible consequence of the progressive liberal agenda that drove economic and political development in the three decades prior to 2008 was a burgeoning economic and social divide. J.D. Vance captured its character in his bestselling *Hillbilly Elegy. A Memoir of a Family and Culture in Crisis* (2016). He identified a rift between 'rich and poor; educated and uneducated; upper class and working class' who inhabited 'separate worlds'.[55]

Ironically, liberal progressive ideology, committed for the past thirty years to social justice and the idea that all social ills were 'amenable to technocratic remedy and that the state was a suitable instrument for making such change' had rationally managed this inegalitarian outcome.[56] The progressive mind had, by a fatal mixture of hubris and panic, inverted Rawls' second principle of social justice. After 2008, 'all social goods, liberty and opportunity, income and wealth and the basis of self-respect [were] to be distributed equally unless an unequal distribution of any or all of these goods is to the advantage of the *most* favoured'.[57]

Although the distribution of costs and benefits benefited the wealthiest, American crisis management nevertheless worked. After

2012 the US economy began to recover, but inequality was on the rise and the progressive political vision assumed an increasingly elitist and politically disconnected trajectory. Under such circumstances, Montesquieu observed, the spirit of inequality corrupts democracy. It 'arises when citizens no longer identify their interests with the interests of their country, and therefore seek both to advance their own private interests at the expense of their fellow citizens, and to acquire political power over them'.[58]

In particular, the post-crisis emergence of Silicon Valley, and the gig economy it sustained, promoted an increasingly inegalitarian, borderless, transnational and even transhuman vision. The new virtual economy was disruptive and politically destabilising. It embraced universal values, whilst undermining individual autonomy and advancing a democratically detached, big tech pursuit of indubitably progressive artificial intelligence driven social perfection.

AI and the Great Disruption[59]

Quantitatively easing the supply of money made it attractive for companies to borrow to buy out their competitors. After 2008, American capitalism refashioned itself in a more concentrated and monopolistic form. Information technology companies, with their growing global footprint, were the major beneficiaries, creating in the process a new, increasingly intangible, economy. The emergence of the GAFA (Google, Amazon, Facebook, and Apple) tetrarchy, which, in the wake of the crisis, escaped anti-trust, data protection and intrusive tax investigation, distorted the free market, corrupted the understanding of liberty and free speech, and fractured, perhaps irreparably, the relationship between individualism, property rights and political democracy. It also added a futuristic transhuman dimension to the increasingly Olympian pretensions of the progressive mind.

As recent scandals involving Facebook and Cambridge Analytica, Twitter and other networks demonstrate, the new media now surpasses the traditional media as a medium to influence voter behaviour and democratic outcomes. An unaccountable technocracy mines personal data and acts as the universal arbiter of political speech. Moreover, where governments have tried to constrain these platforms, subject them to anti-trust legislation or impose taxes, they have faced criticism and resistance. The little understood but increasingly ubiquitous impact of big tech upon the post-financial crisis global economy and what it entails for social justice, equitable redistribution and global convergence evidently requires consideration.

Artificial Intelligence or the fourth industrial revolution has already had transformative political and economic consequences. In practical terms, the new technology companies have acquired immense financial, social and virtual power. Amazon, PayPal and Google (restructured as Alphabet in 2015) launched after 1994; gmail first appeared in 2004, as too did Facebook. Twitter began tweeting in 2006; Airbnb, renting rooms in 2008; Tesla, making driverless cars in 2003; and Uber, ride hailing in 2009. Apple and Microsoft (1975) are pre-millennial. Apple launched in 1976 but its founder, Steve Jobs, rejuvenated it with the iMac (1996) the iPad (2004) and the iPhone (2007). Silicon Valley hosts the corporate headquarters of Apple, Google, Facebook, Twitter, Tesla, Uber, PayPal and Airbnb. The valley engineers the future and the future is algorithmic.

In 2017, eight of the world's most highly valued companies were technology businesses. Their combined market capitalization was $4.7tn. That was thirty per cent of the combined capitalization of the other ninety-two companies in the world's top hundred most valuable firms. Of these companies, five (Apple, Alphabet, Microsoft, Amazon and Facebook) are based in the US, two (Ali Baba and Tencent) in China and one (Samsung) in Korea. Europe is notable only by its absence. What are the social and political consequences of this remarkable dominance?

Google's slogan was 'don't be evil', subsequently changed to 'do the right thing'. Techtopians assume they are 'the solution, not the problem'. They also want 'one global community' that will 'reclaim our cities'. To build their new world order, they must first 'disrupt' the old.[60] But what does such disruption mean?

It is no accident that Silicon Valley evolved in California and imbibed the progressive, libertarian idealism of the late 1960s. Steve Jobs, the founding father, was a counter-culture dropout. A progressive, anti-establishment worldview shaped the valley's imagination as it mutated from counter-culture to cyber-culture.[61] At the same time, infant tech start-ups like Apple, from the 1980s onward, benefited from the Reagan era private sector reforms and the free market and minimal state thinking that underpinned a left coast version of Reaganomics. Sceptical of state economic power, both free marketers and counter-culture capitalists favoured market solutions and minimal taxation. Libertarians may diverge on the scope of their opposition to existing political and economic systems, but the libertarian precursors of the tech dream maintained that allowing the market free play would facilitate competition, economic and financial innovation, create employment and, as if by an invisible hand, generate greater wealth for all.

Robert Nozick, contra Rawls, argued in *Anarchy, State and Utopia* (1974) that only a minimal state that respects individual rights allows us 'to choose our life and to realize our ends and our conceptions of ourselves'.[62] This libertarian understanding formed the side constraints that nurtured the cyber-culture. In other words, libertarian in its foundations, the creators of the virtual world conceived it as an anarchy along hippie, communalist lines. The Internet Rights Charter holds the internet to be 'a global public space'... 'open, affordable and accessible to all'. Like the major US (but not Chinese) big tech companies, the charter upholds freedom of expression and rights to privacy.

Yet, despite its libertarian foundations, big tech behaviour came to disavow its libertarian roots. The economic strategy of the new media Leviathans is not competition but 'creative' monopoly. The difference between Apple's current book to share market value assumes the super normal profits that only a monopoly could deliver. Similar valuations apply to Amazon, Google and Facebook. They sustain their monopoly position by becoming an investment fund 'attached to a media machine'.[63]

Under monopolist conditions, the GAFA tetrarchy's impact on print and mainstream media has been both transformative and disruptive. Facebook, Google and Twitter are essentially media platforms that mine data and generate profits through advertising. In 2017, Google and Facebook received sixty-three per cent of all US digital advertising revenue.[64]

However, these enormously profitable businesses exist parasitically off 'the investments in collecting information' made by others. Despite weaponizing the first amendment, Twitter, Facebook and Google have become highly efficient disseminators of non-information. Paradoxically, the new anarchic space of virtual freedom offers the most valuable weapon for political control and manipulation. Used by 'people of ill-will', from Putin's Fancy Bears to Islamic State, it affords platforms 'for the deliberate dissemination of dangerous falsehoods'. These developments 'raise huge issues' for maintaining an open society from online enemies that neither Karl Popper nor Robert Nozick envisaged.[65]

The Intangible Economy

One consequence of this evolution is an increasingly intangible economic order. In *Capitalism without Capital* (2017) Jonathan Haskel and Stian Westlake show how major developed economies now invest in intangible assets – design, branding, R&D and software – rather than in tangible assets, such as physical machinery, or buildings. These intangible assets have determined the key economic changes of the last decade, from economic inequality to stagnating productivity. New technology drives this change. Apple, the world's most valuable company, owns no physical assets.

It is the intangible integration of software and design into a brand that creates value. The intangible economy is fundamentally different from the conventional, tangible one, as the boarded up former retail shops on the UK high street visibly illustrate. Its characteristics involve 'scalability' of the product design, especially through the new global communications environment, spill-overs into other products in the same domain and synergies where design and development hubs create dynamic environments where intangibles cluster, revitalising areas like Shoreditch in London, whilst, at the same time, generating greater inequalities in wealth and its distribution across the wider society. Whilst intangibility flourishes, the old economy, wages and employment stagnates.[66]

Yet investment in intangibles (the major source of investment in the UK, US, and Sweden in 2018) is risky because products are both scalable and mobile. Some estimates predict that by 2033, forty-seven per cent of jobs will be at high risk of disappearing. Robots will replace insurance writers, bus and truck drivers, waitresses, and carpenters.

An algorithm could soon outperform doctors, nurses, lawyers, accountants, architects, and artists.[67]

Intangibility also facilitates the rise of super dominant companies, removed from political or fiscal oversight. The oligopolist character of the new media and the intangible economy it has made possible means that since the 2008 financial crisis, the Gini coefficient has widened in all developed economies, fracturing a critical link between capitalism and democracy. Vilfredo Pareto showed, at the start of the modern democratic age, that society always reverts to a mean where twenty per cent of the population own eighty per cent of the wealth,[68] a social fact seemingly confirmed by the pattern of wealth distribution since the 2008 sub-prime crisis. Absent government oversight, intangible capitalism confirms the Pareto principle.

The structural implications of the intangible economy increasingly favour not global meliorism but what Robert Michels identified as an 'iron law of oligarchy' in a twenty-first century networked form.[69] It is estimated that in ten years there will be 150 billion networked measuring sensors. This will produce a mass of data about personal preferences which will enable those who own the data to disconnect the means of doing politics from its ends.[70] The new media platforms will increasingly gather data to produce information that influences decision-making, disrupting the political relationship between the autonomous individual, the constitutional order and the market. Social media companies like Facebook, Twitter and Google already offer platforms to target voter preferences and facilitate extremist ideologies that render democratic processes open to divisive manipulation by alien powers. Putin's subversive propaganda campaigns have been successful because all he needed 'was social media'.[71]

After 2008, the character of the US financial recovery promoted an unaccountable, technology-driven, transnational, progressive elitism, and burgeoning economic and political division. After graduating from Yale law school, J.D. Vance, the hillbilly elegist, worked for the Silicon Valley entrepreneur Peter Thiel, but later returned to the Midwest. San Francisco, he explained, represents a 'dystopian view of what middle America sees in the future. Two fundamental subsets of the population...completely separated by culture and wealth...[who] don't really interact with each other or feel any kinship'.[72]

By contrast, the European project, once envisaged as the harbinger of a more enlightened, socially just regional order, found, through more conventional managerial means, a route to inegalitarian and illiberal outcomes that divorced its cosmopolitan elites from its disenfranchised masses as it responded to its own rationally, self-induced, Eurozone crisis.

The European Train Wreck

The Eurozone crisis evolved later and differently from the subprime crash, but more damagingly, especially for the utopian prospect of the economic and political integration of 'core Europe' into a post national constellation. Millennial Wall Street was a North Atlantic, as well as a North American 'system'. By 2008, the European financial system functioned as a global hedge fund borrowing short and lending long.[73] Despite the jeremiads that core Europeans like Angela Merkel and Nicholas Sarkozy cast at 'extreme' Anglo-Saxon capitalism, Europe's financial system had itself become 'spectacularly overgrown' and it owed a large part of this growth to its 'deep entanglement in the American boom'.[74]

The City of London hosted 250 foreign banks prior to the crisis. RBS, Deutsche Bank, and BNP were the three largest banks in the world by assets. In 2007, the balance sheet of each came close to matching the GDP of its home country.[75] In Ireland, the banking sector was seven times greater than its GDP.[76] The eurozone crisis that began in 2010, and has yet to end, followed directly upon the Wall Street crash.

The fact that the zone was a bureaucratically designed work in progress dragged the crisis out interminably. The introduction of the ambitious political project to establish a single currency in 2001 rendered peripheral Europe particularly exposed to the destabilizing effects of global finance and its inegalitarian consequences. Between 1992 and 2001 the EU created a single market and a shared currency, but lacked the key resources that successful common currency areas (like the UK or US) take for granted, namely a common budget, fiscal transfers, a banking union and some form of political union.

As the global financial crisis evolved, many of the biggest deficits appeared in southern Europe. Yet, just as Asia discovered in 1997, private sector creditors from other states averted their gaze and withdrew their investments when markets panicked. As housing bubbles burst in Spain, Ireland, and Portugal, governments found themselves financially exposed. Despite their federal pretensions, European creditor states (most obviously Germany, but also the Netherlands and Finland) reinforced by the 'Troika', composed of the European Commission, the European Central Bank and the IMF, demanded that the 'borrower nations' shoulder the burden of adjustment. German Finance Minister Wolfgang Schäuble considered austerity imposed upon the debtors the best way of minimizing creditor losses and preserving the stability of the financial system, despite the fact that the creditors, notably German and French banks, constituted a major part of the problem.

The dominance of the German economy within the European Union, together with its constitutional commitment to fiscal austerity, dictated the course of the Eurozone crisis.[77] The unified Germany that emerged after the fall of the Berlin Wall had, during the chancellorship of Angela Merkel, become the Union's indispensable nation. A German penchant for fiscal rigidity, debt amortization, and a reluctance, prior to 2015, to let the European Central Bank's Director, Mario Draghi, 'do whatever it takes', through quantitative easing and operating as a lender of last resort to troubled southern European bond markets, exacerbated the crisis.

As the Eurozone unravelled,[78] Europe's economies diverged. Although intended to achieve economic integration, the single European currency and the austere monetary policy the ECB initially imposed actually achieved the opposite. It fragmented the union economically, socially and politically. The gap between northern and southern fiscal health and economic growth widened. Germany's export surpluses grew between 2010–18 while the PIGS (Portugal, Ireland, Greece and Spain) endured recession, deficits, mass unemployment and mounting political discontent.

Somewhat ironically, before the formation of the single currency, economic divergence between north and south had not been a significant problem for the union. Under-performing countries merely devalued against their stronger neighbours. Thus, over the period 1979–93 the Italian lira had fallen more than fifty per cent against the deutschmark. Italian exporters benefited, whilst German exporters lost out.

Within a single European currency, however, there was no equivalent burden-sharing mechanism. The post sub-prime crisis world of high debt and low inflation rendered the absence of a foreign exchange 'safety valve' even more fiscally challenging. Countries that once would have devalued had no alternative but to impose Troika-managed austerity programmes.[79] Ultra-low inflation meant ultra-low interest rates. Under these circumstances, a country within a single currency zone that remained uncompetitive had no alternative but to push prices and wages even lower. The outstanding nominal amount of debt to GDP, however, does not change.[80]

The tortuous European political process governing the Eurozone financial crisis created political, economic and social imbalances across the Union and mounting tensions between countries formally committed to the same progressive, post-national ideal of ever-closer union. Europe's largest economies, France, Germany and the United Kingdom, unlike the US, did not suffer the extreme inegalitarian distributional effects of the sub-prime crisis; instead the wealthier economies off-loaded them onto the weaker ones of southern Europe.

The Troika's bureaucratic management of the crisis between 2010–18 also involved a pronounced assault on the conduct of democratic politics in states within the Eurozone. Lending hard euros to weak states created unsustainable government deficits. The Greek experience exemplified the unintended consequences of fiscal managerialism in exposing, yet further, the democratic deficit at the heart of Euroland. Successive bailouts after 2010 bankrupted the Greek government, but the unelected Troika vetoed any attempt to restructure repayments. Not surprisingly, pro-European political parties lost support, and Greek voters found anti-European populism irresistible. Elected to government on a populist wave in 2015, the left socialist Syriza Party leader Alex Tsirpas appointed Yannis Varoufakis, an academic economist, as the new Greek finance minister tasked with restructuring Greek debt. Varoufakis' tenure lasted a mere 162 days.

In the process, however, Varoufakis secretly taped interviews with Europe's 'insiders', revealing how they intransigently sacrificed Greek democracy on the altar of fiscal discipline. The first two Greek bailouts between 2010–12, Varoufakis observes, actually served the interests of French and German banks as well as their, often corrupt, Greek counterparts, exposed to Greek debt. The mechanism bailed out bankers whilst heaping debt and austerity upon Greek taxpayers. Bankruptcy, repackaged as a liquidity problem, reduced Greece to 'a sad debtors' colony on the Mediterranean.[81]

In the period 2006-14, Greece's experience made the Great Depression look like a mild case of melancholy. The economy lost twenty-eight per cent of its national income, and unemployment rose from seven to twenty-one per cent. Negotiating with the Troika to restructure the debt demonstrated for Greece, as well as Portugal, Ireland, Spain and, more recently, Italy, that real financial power lay not with the European Commission, but with the Eurogroup, although the latter does not officially exist in European law.[82] Presided over in 2015 by Dutch Finance Minister, Jeroen Dijsselbloem, and comprising the ECB's Mario Draghi, the IMF's Christine Lagarde,[83] the EU economics Commissioner, Pierre Moscovici, and assorted finance ministers of smaller, East European states, Eurogroup power actually resided with the German Finance Minister, Wolfgang Schäuble.

At various times Christine Lagarde, Larry Summers, Pierre Moscovici, and then French Finance Minister, Emmanuel Macron, all considered Varoufakis' debt restructuring proposals reasonable. However, as Lagarde confessed, 'there was too much political capital at stake' for the Troika to admit any mistake. Instead Greece endured the equivalent of fiscal waterboarding until it 'agreed to the sick ritual of extend and pretend' loans. Greece either signed up to a third bailout and even more austerity or dropped out of the Eurozone, a fate Varoufakis contemplated, but Syriza could not.[84]

Schäuble's claim that 'elections cannot be allowed to change economic policy' illustrated the Eurogroup's indifference to democratic process. Of course, Varoufakis remarks, 'he had a point: democracy had indeed died the moment the Eurogroup acquired the authority to dictate economic policy to member states without anything resembling federal democratic sovereignty'.[85] In the bonfire of illusions that followed the euro crisis, 'Europe's deep establishment lost all sense of self-restraint'.[86] Had Germany and Greece been part of an integrated federal fiscal system, the European financial crisis would have required an automatic transfer of German tax revenues in order to support Greece. Instead, the crisis only served to highlight the economic and competitive gulf between the two states.[87]

The crisis revealed the single currency, like the European Union itself, to be a half-finished, if not half-baked, rationalist construct. The Eurozone possesses some aspects of nationhood: a single currency, a single monetary policy, a single (although incomplete) market and, for those who also happen to be members of Schengen, a common external border. Yet it lacks a common fiscal policy. It has no common border force. The European Parliament is a weak and distant institution; and a common European defence policy has proved, as in the Ukraine crisis of 2014, a matter of words rather than deeds. Summating the economic and fiscal 'train wreck' that the Troika engineered between 2010–18, Adam Tooze concludes that 'the botched management of the eurozone crisis...was damaging not only for millions of Europe's citizens. It had dramatic consequences for European business too... Far from being beneficiaries of EU crisis management, business was one of its casualties'. The European tech sector, unlike Asia or the United States, has no global or even regional marque. Post-crisis Europe, rather than being a progressive harbinger of a global ethical society, risks instead 'becoming the object of other people's corporatist capitalism'.[88]

The Political Consequences of Market Reflexivity

Fed policy from 2008-12 avoided the mistakes of 1929–33 by adopting an expansionary monetary policy to avoid an international financial collapse. Yet, as George Soros observed, a much larger boom-bust cycle had superimposed itself upon the local Western problem of a housing bubble in the Anglosphere and the related Eurozone crisis. It was the result of three factors: globalization, credit expansion and financial deregulation. Even monetarists like Milton Friedman supported the introduction of the Glass-Steagall Act in 1932 that required banks to maintain a clear demarcation between lending and deposit activities. The ending of Glass-Steagall in 1999, in a fit of premillennial market mania, now appears a 'shocking abdication of responsibility on the part of the regulators'.[89] The deregulation that followed made possible the easy credit and complex derivative products that engendered the animal spirits and subsequent panic from which the Eurozone has yet to recover.

Moreover, the return to boom and bust, or the creative destruction of capitalism, does not look good for the progressive future pursuit of social justice or the liberal democratic end of history.[90] The depth of the crash which hit the West has not led to a sustained recovery.

History, which may not repeat itself, but frequently rhymes, has witnessed similar modern crashes leading to illiberal, ideological outcomes before. Tracing the causes of the first great depression, Karl Polyani argued that the late nineteenth-century global market, created by European and US imperial expansion, witnessed the disembedding of the economy from a wider society and the nation state. The political consequences of the financial crisis of the 1930s resulted, Polanyi observed, in 'a double movement', firstly, the rise of special interests demanding protection, followed by the emergence of an aggressive nationalism demanding a retreat from internationalism and free trade and the return to a state-based corporatism and mercantilist autarchy.[91]

The great globalization crisis of the new millennium has also witnessed the premonitory snuffling of protectionism and nationalism (aka populism) in the West as well as in Asia. It has also simultaneously witnessed a semi-detached, transnational, big tech, hedge fund and investment banking elite developing an intangible capitalism, divorced from the concerns and values of their provisional and tangible nation state containers, in pursuit of an increasingly disruptive, emancipatory, virtual, but still progressive, global vision.

The Revenge of Politics

Stendhal's bewildered 'young hero', caught in the thick of the action at Waterloo, memorably enquired 'is this a real battle'?[92] In 2017 many pondered an ideological version of Fabrizio del Dongo's question. The European political elite and the certainties of Europe's most powerful head of state, Angela Merkel, whose desire to keep the Eurozone together whatever the cost engineered a nationalist backlash that ever closer union was intended to prevent ever happening again.

Not only in Greece, but also the UK, throughout Western Europe and in the US, an unanticipated and inchoate popular reaction to the financial crisis questioned the progressive assumptions that had informed the end of history project. Much to the bewilderment of the transnational liberal elites in politics, academia, finance and the mainstream media, the second decade of the twenty-first century witnessed a resurgence of nationalism, irredentism, and populism on both the left and right of the political spectrum and on both sides of the Atlantic.

The financial crisis of 2008 and the decade of bank bailouts and austerity that followed created a mounting sense of unease about the governance of Western Europe and the United States. It fed a loss of confidence in established political parties. In 2016, the Brexit referendum, the election of Donald Trump to the US presidency, and the rise of nativist and radical socialist political movements everywhere, announced a wave of angry populism crashing on the rapidly eroding shore of Western, progressive democracy. Trump and Brexit signalled a revolt of the masses[93] against the new liberal orthodoxy's commitment to the global and regional, rather than the national.

The new political movements that arose after 2008 represented, whatever else, an inchoate revolt against the liberal internationalism that dominated global politics from the end of the Cold War. Populism, of course, is no recent phenomenon. The American historian Richard Hofstadter identified in 1960s America a 'paranoid style' of politics that he linked to earlier, late nineteenth-century movements like the Mid-Western, agrarian, small farmers' revolt against Wall Street and the East Coast plutocracy. 'Politics', Hofstadter observed, 'has often been an arena for angry minds', identifying, in the populist style a 'heated mix of suspiciousness, exaggeration, and conspiratorial fantasy'.[94]

Financial crises since the 1870s have fed populism and its European cousin, nationalism. Across Europe, parties have either emerged from nowhere or chased electability from the political fringes – Podemos, Ciudadanos, Vox and the Junts per Catalunya separatists in Spain; Syriza and Golden Dawn in Greece; the Five Star Movement and the Northern League in Italy; the Finns Party, the Hungarian Jobbik party, the Dutch Party for Freedom; UKIP and the Brexit Party in the UK; the Alternative für Deutschland (AfD) and Pegida in Germany; and the French Front National, to name but a few.

Populism, like Euro-Islam, finds the new social media and the new liberal preoccupation with identity particularly congenial for transmitting its message, by-passing established party systems that once acted as filters to limit its appeal. Social media enabled previously fringe movements, such as Syriza in Greece, or the Five Star Movement in Italy, as well as facilitating the hijacking of mainstream parties. Donald Trump secured the Republican nomination for the 2016 US presidential election against the wishes of the party establishment, whilst Jeremy Corbyn's Labour Party leadership victory in 2015 lit a bonfire under Tony Blair's third way, progressive vanities.

The New Revolt of the Masses and the Decline of the West

The paranoid style might be the material form of contemporary nativist or socialist movements. However, it is by no means the efficient cause of Brexit, the *gilets jaunes* rebellion in France or the election of Donald Trump in 2016. Social commentators like J.D. Vance, David Goodhart, Paul Collier and Christophe Guilluy have identified instead a burgeoning divide between two 'subterranean value blocs' across the modern West.[95] Goodhart termed these blocs 'Anywhere' and 'Somewhere', whilst for Guilluy, the new Parisian hipster, urban, *bobo* class in the media, business and finance inhabit a different metropolitan world from those who live in 'lower France' on the '*périphérie*'.

It is the economic and cultural gulf between these worlds and worldviews that accounts for the rise of Western populism. Vance considers himself a rare 'cultural migrant' traversing the chasm between his white, Scots-Irish, working class, rustbelt, Midwest hometown and the Ivy League law school of the East Coast, where he discovers that 'the wealthy and powerful, are not just wealthy and powerful, they follow a different set of norms'.[96]

These progressive norms are the antithesis of the hillbilly, redneck, white trash culture of the Midwest. Vance's memoir traces how a white, working class culture disintegrated, as they watched manufacturing jobs that once supported stable family life disappear overseas.[97] A similar chasm accounts for the *gilets jaunes*, who like their hillbilly equivalents have looked on, powerless, 'as the implacable law of global markets has asserted its authority everywhere'.[98] Within a few decades 'France', Guilluy contends, 'has become an American society...inegalitarian and multicultural...polarised and seething with tension'.[99]

The Road to Nowhere

Similarly, and on the basis of survey data, Goodhart estimates that metropolitan elites represent twenty to twenty-five per cent of the UK population. Meanwhile, the periphery constitutes more than half the population. By wealth and education they correspond to a similar divide across the US and Western Europe. Peripheral 'somewheres' are socially conservative, political 'outsiders', uncomfortable with 'mass immigration, an achievement society in which they struggle to achieve, the reduced status of non-graduate employment and more fluid gender roles'.[100] Forty years ago, across the west, their values prevailed. Brexit in the UK, Trump in the US, the Lega Nord in Italy, the FN in France, the AfD in Germany and Vox in Spain, represent the reaction of this excluded middle, an instinctive response to the failure of the new liberal progressive agenda.

By contrast, the 'double liberalism' of the elites is market friendly and pro-globalization in economics, 'combined with state enforcement of greater racial and gender equality'.[101] This is a worldview for 'more or less successful individuals'. It places a high value on mobility and novelty and a much lower value on national social contracts, tradition and group identity, except those of abstract or excluded minorities.[102]

This cosmopolitan class, moreover, is comfortable with mass migration, European integration and the spread of universal human rights, all of which dilute the claims of national citizenship. Although meritocracy is their official creed, this new and increasingly non-domiciled elite are 'almost always born into the wealthy or professional classes'.[103] Education at elite universities and inter-marriage reinforce this transnational, multicultural oligarchy's shared values that 'bind and blind'. Before Brexit, and in the tortuous negotiations not to abandon entirely the post-national European constellation that followed, their viewpoint prevailed in the mainstream media, business and academia and set the agenda of the mainstream political parties across the West.

The baleful consequences of this agenda, however, were all too evident by the second decade of the twenty-first century. Before the Blair government's decision to open the country to mass immigration, Britain in the mid-1990s was a multi-racial society with a settled minority migrant population of around four million or seven per cent.[104] By 2016, eighteen per cent of the UK's working age population was born overseas and Britain's official immigrant and minority population had trebled to about twelve million or over twenty per cent.[105] After 2004, successive governments struggled to keep migration levels below 300,000 a year. As Goodhart emphasizes, migration, was not an 'unstoppable force of nature', but official European, New Labour and progressive Conservative policy.

However, as a consequence, middle income wages stagnated, the middle was squeezed and 'the fiscal contribution of newcomers' turned negative, placing additional pressure on already stretched state schools, housing, health and welfare services. An economic system which once had a place for those of middling and even lower abilities now privileged 'the cognitive elites and the educationally endowed'.[106]

The major group that has lost out from the most recent wave of migration and globalization are poorer people in rich countries. Thus, in the working class towns of the Midlands and North-East England, young white males aged 18-24 without education or training enter a twilight world of low status jobs. At the same time, 'hillbilly' Stoke-on-Trent witnessed a 200 per cent increase in its foreign born population between 2001 and 2014. Significantly, like the industrial North-East and South Wales, Stoke voted for Brexit in 2016 and for Corbyn's anti-market brand of left populism in the 2017 general election. Similar constituencies in the USA, Germany, Greece, Italy, Spain, Sweden and France support, *inter alia* Trump, the AfD, Syriza, the Lega Nord, Podemos, the Swedish Democrats and the Front National.

By contrast London, which dominates the UK economy, represents 'the apotheosis of the transactional, market society'.[107] Its attraction to migrants makes it the most economically, politically and ethnically polarized part of the UK. High end service magnets like London now contain caste systems based on extreme wealth and income stratification, where a largely migrant, menial class services a free spending, transnational oligarchy. As recently as 1971, white Britons comprised 86 per cent of the London population. By the 2011 census, London had become a 'majority minority city' – one where the largest ethnic group no longer constitutes more than half the population (44.9 per cent were White British).

Across Europe the move to ever closer union and the emphasis on the free movement of labour after 2004 has notably exacerbated the problem of national identity and the burgeoning gap between *bobo* cosmopolites and the peripheral precariat that mainstream political parties have ignored since history ended. Paradoxically, the educated and affluent bourgeoisie, which Marx assumed would be more nationalist than the urban proletariat, because they formed the 'executive committee' of the nineteenth-century constitutional state, have evolved into a new progressive *internationale*. By 2018, the intangible economy meant that this wealthy new class have more in common with 'each other – regardless of their respective national, racial or religious identities – than they have with everybody else'.[108]

The progressive identities and international legal practice of human rights, minority entitlement and social justice the new *internationale* class embraces serves, moreover, 'as a substitute for national identity'. The moral equality of all humans is taken to mean that national borders have become irrelevant and that partiality for fellow nationals is somehow flawed, even racist. Gus O'Donnell, at the time 'the most senior civil servant in the land', informed Goodhart at an Oxford college dinner in 2011, 'it's my job to maximize global welfare, not national welfare'.[109] His dinner companion, Mark Thompson, Director-General of the BBC, concurred.

The progressive *internationale* still passionately believe that European states must dissolve into some form of single political entity. Yet the pursuit of integration and immigration has since 2008 resulted in 'stagnant growth and high unemployment', the inability to secure Europe's borders and, of course, 'the horror' of Brexit. The free movement of labour, and the removal of borders following the Schengen Agreement of 1985, which meant that by 2008 twenty-six Eurozone countries had relinquished border controls, only exacerbated immigration flows, dramatically symbolized by the Syrian refugee crisis of 2015.

The European political class's migration fixation assumed three interlinked social facts. Firstly, that mass migration was an economic boon rather than a cost to the overstretched European welfare state; secondly, that the ageing of the northern European population desperately necessitated an influx of new (and culturally very different) workers from countries like Pakistan, sub-Saharan Africa or the Middle East. Thirdly, that this new population would somehow integrate or, alternatively, contribute a much needed diversity to an otherwise stale, male and pale European identity in urgent need of multicultural refreshment.

Sadly, these progressive assumptions proved largely illusory. The combined endeavour of the European Union managerial class and the impartially neutral state fashioned a new liberal politics that accorded special group rights to minority identities. In the process it fragmented any shared sense of national identity or attachment to a political community, whilst unintentionally facilitating the formation of minority ghettoes in cosmopolitan cities. Without any policy to integrate rather than celebrate these often very different minority cultural attachments, they developed separately, often freely exhibiting distinctly illiberal enthusiasms.

Failed liberal interventions in Libya and Syria after 2012 and the attacks of Islamic State on European civilian targets only exacerbated post-financial crisis popular anxiety and an increasingly bitter populist identity politics. The German Chancellor's arbitrary decision in 2015 to grant asylum to refugees from the civil war in Syria meant more than twice as many people entered the European Union as in the previous year. Of these, only roughly a quarter were Syrian. Others came from the Balkans (fifteen per cent), Afghanistan (thirteen per cent), Iraq (nine per cent) and Pakistan (four per cent). The numbers were larger 'than immediately after the fall of the Berlin Wall and larger, too, than in the various crises of the 1990s associated with the break-up of Yugoslavia'.[110]

Welfare, health and education services stretched to breaking point across Western Europe. Paradoxically, given its imposition of austerity on southern Europe after 2010, Germany relied on Greece, Italy and Spain to control a permeable European border. Southern Europe, faced with its own huge economic problems, lacked the resources — and perhaps the will — to provide the necessary controls. Leaky borders, however, created an obvious challenge for free movement across Europe.

Even after its disastrous failure to manage the 2015 refugee crisis, European Commission President Jean-Claude Juncker could still presume, in the manner of a Bourbon monarch, who learned nothing and forgot nothing, 'that borders are the worst invention ever made by politicians'.[111]

By contrast, Thomas Hobbes, observing the progress of the English civil war from Paris after 1642, argued that a social contract establishing an abstract, sovereign state, must afford its members peace and protection, otherwise 'solitary, poor, nasty (and) brutish' conditions necessarily prevail. Hobbes would have predicted European federalism and Schengen's open borders leading inexorably to well-meaning doom. The failure of the European project between 2010–18 saw nation states across Europe trying to reclaim their borders, undermining one of the four 'essential' freedoms on which the European Union uncertainly rested.[112]

Liberal democratic trading states, led by the US (and, in Europe, the Netherlands, Sweden, Denmark, France, Germany and the UK) were the foundations of the international architecture that governed globalization: the IMF; the World Trade Organization; and the European Union at the end of the Cold War. However, the unintended consequence of the huge increase in cross-border capital flows from the early 1980s rendered these institutions increasingly impotent. This shift also undermined the democratic legitimacy of globalization as well as its claims to advance emancipatory and shared universal norms. In particular, the 'turbulent and mighty continent' that Giddens celebrated looked both increasingly 'dark' and 'exhausted', whilst the European Union itself looked like it might become yet another 'vanished' European kingdom.[113] History had far from ended in Europe and realpolitik began to take its revenge in the form of the rise of revisionist powers on the other side of what Halford Mackinder described in 1919 as the 'world island'. It is to this development that we next attend.

7

ALL ROADS LEAD TO CHINA

Post-war international institutions worked well for a club of like-minded industrialized democracies. Yet, as if by an invisible hand, globalization and deregulation saw the West's share of global economic activity decline. In the 1980s when the West rediscovered its taste for liberal internationalism and the free or deregulated market, and China began to emerge from its Mao-era economic cocoon, the advanced economies enjoyed sixty-four per cent of the world's national income. China, India, Russia and a motley crew of emerging and developing nations made up the other thirty-six per cent.[1]

By 2015, the West's share of global national income had declined to forty per cent and the assortment of BRICS, tiger and dragon economies accounted for the rest. The economic decline of the West, particularly Western Europe, weakened economically by the euro zone crisis and politically by Brexit, is unlikely to be arrested. Yet the redistribution of global wealth has not advanced social justice, a Rawlsian 'law of peoples' or global emancipation, as progressive or critical international relations theory anticipated.

After 1945, the US and its NATO and Pacific Asian allies built and sustained the core international institutions. After Afghanistan, Iraq and the global financial crisis, however, this liberal order and its institutional structure appeared increasingly exhausted. Symptomatic of the fragmenting liberal economic order, the G7 of developed democracies founded in 1975[2] mutated at the millennium into a G20 of leading economies that included three authoritarian regimes and several heading in that direction. Unlike the G7, the G20 group, their interconnected interest in financial stability and economic growth apart, share little in common ideologically, politically or culturally.[3]

Whether it was the Asian Infrastructure Investment Bank (AIIB), Russia's growing assertiveness in Eastern Europe and Syria, the Shanghai Cooperation Organization (SCO)[4] of authoritarian regimes, or the ASEAN-led but China-dominated, Regional Comprehensive Economic Partnership (RCEP), revisionist powers have taken new, illiberal and potentially transformative, global pathways. In particular, arrangements like China's Belt and Road Initiative (BRI) and the SCO exhibit no enthusiasm for a progressive, multilateral, liberal order accountable to the shared norms of an increasingly otiose, post-Cold War 'international community'. Under China's leadership, the AIIB, together with the SCO (known as the Shanghai Five when it first assembled in 1996) has developed into a non-Western Silk Road organization. In the wake of the Asian Financial Crisis and particularly after joining the World Trade Organization (WTO) in 2002, China emerged as the dominant, authoritarian geopolitical presence, central to an unanticipated illiberal intervention into the borderless world of deregulated globalization. Whatever else the China model entails, it confutes the progressive faith in the triumph of liberal democracy and the end of ideology after 1991.[5]

The China Effect: Globalization with Neo-Confucian Characteristics

The ruins of the sixteenth-century St Paul's Church sit atop a hill above Malacca, the Malaysian port city and popular world heritage destination. At Christmas 2017, tour parties from mainland China – in pursuit of, as one tour operator announces, 'a new aristocratic demeanour' – swarmed up the hillside taking selfies beside the mute gravestones of seventeenth-century Dutch and English merchants. Local Muslim families allowed their children to clamber over the statue of St Francis Xavier, the Jesuit missionary who first brought Christianity to Southeast Asia. Merchants sold cold drinks, cheap batik prints and fake watches from pop-up stalls around the ruined church. From a corner of what remained of the nave a local singer belted out the chorus to the 4 Non Blondes 1992 hit *What's Up?*

And so I wake in the morning
And I step outside
And I take a deep breath and I get real high
And I scream from the top of my lungs
What's going on?

Well might he ask. Cultural dissonance is everywhere on display in Malacca. The site of a mythic Malay sultanate before its successive occupation by the Portuguese in 1511, the Dutch in 1641, and the British from 1819 until independence in 1957, the city is a fusion of Malay, Chinese and European influences that make up its distinctive Peranakan culture.

Malacca (Melaka) historically functioned as an entrepot for Asian trade, the source of its initial attraction to Portuguese and Dutch merchant adventurers in search of spices for the European palate. It also interested Ming dynasty China. The Yongle emperor commissioned seven tributary missions under the command of the eunuch Admiral Zheng He to the South China Sea and beyond from 1405–30. All these expeditions stopped at Malacca *en route* to the Indian Ocean and the east coast of Africa.

Today, it is not only Chinese tourists who descend upon Malacca. Xi Jinping envisages Malaysia as a key link in the Belt and Road (BRI) initiative and the 'string of pearls' (Chinese-built ports) stretching from the Bay of Bengal through the Straits of Malacca to Hong Kong and beyond. The BRI is the outward and visible sign of the 'China Dream' to restore China to its historic pre-colonial role as the Central Kingdom (中国 *Zhongguo*).

Chinapower, a state-linked conglomerate, funds the US $7.2 billion Melaka Gateway project constructing a deep-sea port and an entertainment hub. Chinese investment also funds the Carey Island port city development further up the Straits as well as an East Coast rail link ultimately intended to connect Malaysia via Laos and Thailand to Southern China. China is now Malaysia's major source of Foreign Direct Investment (FDI) and largest trading partner.

Given that the Straits of Malacca constitute a major choke point for world shipping, the symbolic and strategic impact of the investment has rung alarm bells in Singapore, already at odds with the PRC over Singapore's support for the Hague tribunal's 2016 ruling condemning China's island reclamation activity in the South China Sea. By contrast, Malaysia, like a number of ASEAN states, ignored the ruling in exchange for Chinese investment.

The PRC's economic and strategic ambition does not stop in Southeast Asia. It extends across the Eurasian continent. Demonstrating China's economic and financial reach, in January 2017 a freight train from the eastern Chinese city of Yiwu pulled into the container depot in Barking, London. The 12,000 km journey along the New Eurasian Land Bridge took 18 days – half the time it takes to ship containers by sea via the Suez Canal. The UK already perceives its post-Brexit future as a global commercial and financial hub linked to Beijing as much as the US.

Less well advertised is China's growing influence and investment in Central and Eastern Europe (CEE). Since 2012, China has established a '16+1' forum, where Chinese government officials meet with leaders from sixteen CEE and Balkan countries, eleven from the EU and five non-members.[6] In 2017, China invested $9.4 billion in the 16+1, more than fifty per cent of which went to the five non-EU Balkan economies.[7] A Chinese state-owned enterprise is also building a high-speed rail link between Belgrade and Budapest. President Orban's illiberal democratic government – which, like his fellow Visigrad group members, finds EU diktats on immigration increasingly exasperating – sees Hungary's future as a middle European gateway to Chinese investment.

Elsewhere in the Eurozone, the China Ocean Shipping Company has acquired fifty-one per cent of the Piraeus Port Authority in Athens, with the Belgrade-Budapest rail line envisaged as the first stage in a transport corridor that will eventually convey sea-borne trade from the Chinese-run Piraeus to the heart of Europe. Matteo Salvini's populist Italian government, frustrated by European austerity constraints on his budget and strictures on immigration, in a significant political gesture, announced a Memorandum of Understanding with China in March 2019.[8] Italy became the first member of the Group of Seven major economies, and founding member of the European Community to sign up to China's Belt and Road Initiative, advancing the PRC's vision of the new Silk Road.[9]

The China dream is more than a regional vision. It envisages Eurasian hegemony based on China's market heft and capital investment. European infrastructure projects follow a pattern road-tested in South East Asia. Beijing incentivizes Chinese state-owned enterprises and state-owned banks to fill gaps in EU funding and investment in southeastern Europe in return for political support for Chinese positions on issues like human rights, technology transfer, Tibet, or the South China Sea.[10] Significantly, China takes advantage of the EU's rule based procedures, whilst not affording similar access to the China market.

In particular, despite its membership of the WTO, China has successfully restricted the access of foreign capital, services and information technology to its domestic market.[11] In short, it enjoys an asymmetric relationship with the borderless world that has geopolitical repercussions. In 2018, Johannes Hahn, EU Commissioner responsible for countries negotiating to join the bloc, said that Europe had underestimated China's growing European influence and its propensity to pressure countries that don't repay their loans on infrastructure projects to relinquish them to China.[12]

Europe, which as a consequence of its progressive, bureaucratic addiction to communicative reason since 2003 evinces an idealist geopolitical innocence in its conduct of international relations, has consistently underestimated the influence of China and overestimated that of Russia in its near abroad.[13] Nevertheless, since 2014, Russia under Putin has also acquired a new international confidence exploiting the vacuum created by Obama's 'strategic patience' in Iraq and Syria and America's uncertain pivot to Asia after 2008.

NATO and the European Union's incompetent and uncertain expansion eastward at the end of the Cold War, which Moscow interpreted as a 'threat to national security',[14] reinforced Russian revanchism when opportunities arose with alluring regularity after the 2008 financial crash. Moscow's military and diplomatic efforts in Syria and the Ukraine gifted it the Crimea and stabilized the Assad regime. Moreover, with China recognizing that it needs to find new sources of economic growth, it is not impossible to imagine that the two main Eurasian revisionist powers could turn the Shanghai Cooperation Organization into something more than a simple sum of its parts.

Yet ultimately, it is China that would play the leading role in any global realignment. As the Trump administration's National Security Strategy (2017) contended, 'China is gaining a strategic foothold in Europe' through 'predatory' and 'unfair trade practices and investing in key industries, sensitive technologies and infrastructure'.[15] Meanwhile, Trump's antipathy to free trade agreements, graphically illustrated by the US withdrawal from Obama's Trans Pacific Partnership (TPP) in November 2017, indicates not only growing US disenchantment with the liberal order it created after 1945, but also the emergence of a 'contested world' as the 2017 Australian foreign policy white paper euphemistically observed.[16]

What then does the growing threat posed by 'revisionist powers that seek to create a world consistent with their authoritarian models'[17] mean, not only for the future of Southeast Asia, but also for the Eurasian continent more generally and the struggle to dominate what the founder of geopolitics, Sir Halford J. Mackinder, christened the 'world island'?[18]

The Geopolitical Foundations of the Liberal Order in Asia

Geopolitically, America is a large island off the larger landmass of Eurasia, a huge resource-rich area with some seventy per cent of the world's population. A great Eurasian 'heartland' power like China could press simultaneously and by internal lines of communication upon all the peninsulas of the world island.[19] After the Cold War, Henry Kissinger still thought that '[t]he domination by a single power of either of Eurasia's two principal spheres – Europe or Asia – remains a good definition of strategic danger for America... For such a grouping would have the capacity to outstrip America'.[20] This is the threat that Xi's China dream now presents.

US grand strategy during the Cold War largely adhered to Kissinger's twin anti-hegemony strategy in Europe and East Asia. The mode of implementation was forward deployment, with the US Navy and Air Force as the main instruments of that strategy allied to favourable access to the US market and US technology for those states in Eurasia that embraced the US strategic calculus.

Forward deployment and the open market were the ante that let the US play in regional politics on both sides of the Eurasian continent. The aim was to suppress regional security competitions so that potential hegemons could not exploit them. With the occasional exception, the strategy successfully contained and deterred the Soviet Union through to the end of the Cold War when the United States emerged, if only briefly, as the world's 'paramount power'.

But this era of unchallenged American supremacy and the progressive, liberal international order it sustained is now coming to an end. Today, whether in Europe – where the refugee crisis, Brexit and the revolt of the European masses together with Russia's Middle Eastern and Middle European ambitions exploits growing European disunion – or in Asia, where the emergence of the global giants China and India at the same historical moment threatens regional stability – a noodle bowl of security competitions haunts Eurasia. The rise of revisionist powers poised to take advantage of an interconnected, but increasingly disintegrated and durable world disorder, contests the post-Cold War liberal multilateral order.[21]

Porous borders have already eroded European unity and fragmented what the French poet-diplomat Paul Valéry termed the 'western appendix to Asia'.[22] It is, however, in East Asia where, as Hillary Clinton observed in 2011, 'the future of [Eurasian] politics will be decided'.[23] Echoing Clinton, in 2015 US Defence Secretary Ashton Carter observed that Asia 'is the part of the world of greatest consequence to the American future, and no President can take his eye off of this'.[24]

This claim assumes additional pertinence given President Trump's unilateralist 'America first' approach to trade and foreign policy after 2016.[25] Has the Trump Presidency unhinged not only the Obama pivot, but also the post-Cold War assumptions about US foreign policy in Asia and the international trading order it made possible? Given Trump's unpredictability and suspicion of multilateralism, will an increasingly assertive China now fill the apparent leadership vacuum, not only in Asia, but across the world island?

There is not only China and how it might cooperate, conflict or co-evolve with the US, but also new or newly empowered players in India and Japan whose national interests do not necessarily coincide with US foreign policy either of a Wilsonian or Jacksonian provenance. How will second order powers like Indonesia, South Korea and Australia adjust to this fluid strategic environment? More particularly how will the competing economic and security demands of this complex environment affect the fragile states of Southeast Asia and their mission to build regional good citizenship according to soft ASEAN norms of cooperation, consensus and non-confrontation? In this context of regional integration might South East Asia's recent economic experience be Europe's future, given the BRI's potential to be rolled out across Eastern and Southern Europe?

Pivot or Pirouette?

After 1945, the United States determined the regional order in the Asia Pacific. The San Francisco Conference (1951) and the alliances that emanated from it, linking Japan, South Korea, Thailand, the Philippines, Australia and New Zealand to the Washington hub, anchored that order. Unlike the North Atlantic system, it sustained no multilateral security organisation. Its Asian equivalent, SEATO (1954–77), disintegrated in the wake of Richard Nixon's 1972 rapprochement with China and the end of the Vietnam War.

What Nixon's 'strategic gamble' recognised, however, and the infant Association of Southeast Asian Nations (ASEAN) – formed in 1967 – inscribed in its Treaty of Amity and Cooperation (TAC 1976) was the centrality of the nation-state to regional and international order. All signatories to the Treaty recognised 'non-interference in the affairs of member states' as the basis for future cooperation.[26]

Indeed, the new postcolonial states of Southeast Asia emerged during the Cold War as the Westphalian system's most significant legatees, imbibing the necessity of *realpolitik* more completely than in Europe where, as we shall discuss in the following chapter, it first made an appearance. In Asia often 'historically antagonistic peoples' organised themselves as sovereign states and their states into regional groupings.[27] Commenting on this feature of Asian foreign relations in 1970, Singapore Foreign Minister S. Rajaratnam averred that any regional institution had, somewhat paradoxically, 'to reconcile the theory of regionalism with the practice of nationalism'.[28] Asian regionalism, unlike Europe's, assumes the nation-state order.

The Contested Indo-Pacific Order

It is this order that the rise of China and the emergence of India have shaken. Even as inter-Asian trade and investment increased exponentially after the Asian Financial Crisis (1997), the pursuit of national interests and secure borders, not international law, remains an enduring concern. China's current assertiveness in the South China and East China Seas, and the ambiguous response it evokes, has intensified these regional verities.

Japan has responded to China's increasing assertiveness in the East China Sea by seeking to normalise its constitution, permitting its self-defence force to 'assist foreign countries in close relationship with Japan' and intensifying its alliance ties with the United States – even sustaining Obama's Trans Pacific Partnership (TPP), despite Trump's decision to abandon it.[29] Japanese Prime Minister Shinzo Abe also promotes investment in Southeast Asia, maritime links with Vietnam and the Philippines, and economic and security dialogue with Australia and India. Closer to home, Japan holds trilateral summits with the Republic of Korea and the United States that affirm a shared interest in democracy and a peaceful resolution to the North Korean nuclear threat.

South Korea, meanwhile, distrusts both Japan and China, but holds irregular summits with them both.[30] These began in 2008, ceased in 2012, and resumed briefly in 2015 until the US deployed its THAAD anti-ballistic defence system along the South Korean border in 2016. Subsequently, Chinese sanctions damaged the South Korean economy. President Moon Jae-in's attempt to resolve the dispute in December 2017 resulted only in ritual humiliation during a brief diplomatic visit to Beijing.

Moreover, as the joint Korean participation in the Seoul winter Olympics demonstrates, South Korea considers its relationship with its northern counterpart 'special' and different from that of China, Japan, or the US. Elsewhere in Northeast Asia, the 2016 election of an independence-minded president of Taiwan, Tsai Ing-wen, further exacerbated tensions with the mainland over the 'one China principle' that Nixon's 1972 gamble somewhat impulsively acknowledged.

South Korea also seeks to leverage influence beyond its backyard. 'A shrimp among whales', it wants to build a quixotic middle power grouping within the G20 comprising Mexico, Indonesia, Turkey, and Australia (MIKTA). Japan, by contrast, conducts mini-lateral dialogues with Australia, India, and the US. China's rise has driven India and Japan to establish closer ties.[31] Since 2011, building a strategic alliance with its fellow Asian democracy has become a cornerstone of Japan's expanded defence strategy. It coincides with India's growing apprehension over China's naval incursions into the Indian Ocean and its burgeoning security and economic ties with Pakistan, India's traditional foe, and Sri Lanka. Meanwhile, in 2016, over a half century after their 1962 border war, Indian 'talks' with China entered their eighteenth round with no sign of a resolution.

China has effectively pushed formerly non-aligned India into the US sphere. In the process, it has extended the geographical and maritime scope of competition westward into South Asia, extending the regional contest into the Indo-Pacific. The Pacific and Indian Oceans carry the bulk of the world's trade, and the Malacca Straits, where China has a growing presence, link the two oceans.

In 2007, the PRC condemned quadrilateral military exercises proposed by India, the US, Australia, and Japan as a putative 'Asian NATO'. As China extended its presence in the Indian Ocean and South China Sea, and its political influence in Naypidaw and Lahore in 2011, India, Japan and the US began a trilateral dialogue. By 2017, this had evolved into a quadrilateral dialogue involving Australia. India's entry as 'a major defence partner' into an extended US alliance system that links Washington, Tokyo and Canberra with New Delhi, represents one enduring legacy of China's rise and the Obama pivot.[32]

At the same time as India embarked on its slow passage to Washington, it also looked east for economic growth. Since 2002, India has prioritised ties with Southeast Asia and in 2009 concluded an FTA with ASEAN, investing more in Southeast Asia than it does in China. It is in Southeast Asia that the hopes and fears of China's dream of regional, if not eventual Eurasian, hegemony converge. Japan, China and South Korea have each signed FTAs with ASEAN and belong to the

ASEAN plus 3 grouping that, after 2005, mutated into an East Asian summit mechanism.

An integrated ASEAN Economic Community (AEC) would have a population of 600 million and a combined GDP that would make it the seventh largest economy on the planet. However, the states that form ASEAN vary greatly in regime type and levels of economic and social development. Since the 1970s the US has nonetheless emphasised ASEAN's importance, whilst Trump's *National Security Strategy* considers it the centrepiece of 'the Indo-Pacific regional security architecture'.[33] But does ASEAN actually 'develop shared solutions to shared challenges…ensuring that collective multilateral operations are the norm rather than the exception'[34] in the region, as US Defence Secretary Chuck Hagel claimed in June 2014 at the aptly-named Shangri-La security dialogue in Singapore?

Chinese Power and Soft Regionalism's False Promise

In November 2015, the Singapore National Gallery re-opened in the specially converted colonial era Supreme Court Building. Its collection of Southeast Asian art formed the focus of its first exhibition. *Between Declarations and Dreams* traced the development of art in the region during the colonial and postcolonial eras. The title referred to Indonesian poet Chairil Anwar's poem, *Karawang Besaki*. Written by fighters who fell in the independence struggle against the Dutch in 1948, they prosopopoeically implore: 'We who are now dead/give us significance/ Keep watch over the line between declarations and dreams'.[35]

As in Europe, the gap between declarations and dreams haunts the political imagination of the ten Southeast Asian states that comprise ASEAN as they come to terms with the competing economic and political realities of a rapidly changing region that is once again the focus of great power competition for territory and resources.

Unusually in the history of international relations, and an enduring source of its appeal to constructivist international relations theorists, the weak states of Southeast Asia established the only meaningful architecture for the multilateral resolution of regional disputes. How this arrangement has come to influence regional discourse is curious given that, since its inception in 1967, it has largely ignored long standing intra-mural territorial disputes. Such disregard reflects ASEAN's normative commitment to internal resilience and non-interference.

Bilateral disputes, however, frequently disturb inter-ASEAN relations and hinder effective cooperation. China's rise and the uncertainty of US regional commitments renders ASEAN's ability either to continue ignoring these issues or shape the economic and political relations of its more powerful Northeast Asian neighbours increasingly open to question.

Since the AFC (1997), ASEAN has relied on China for both investment capital and as its primary export market. Its capacity to counter China's geopolitical advance is, therefore, likely to erode. Over the decade since 2003, China-ASEAN trade increased twenty-four per cent year on year from US$78 billion to US$444 billion. By 2018, China was ASEAN's largest trading partner for the ninth consecutive year, with trade reaching US$514.8 billion in 2017.[36] Moreover, the return of FDI to Southeast Asia after the AFC reflected Chinese rather than Western, Japanese, and South Korean investment. 'Chinese FDI into ASEAN increased 11 times' between 2003 and 2008.[37] Meanwhile, ASEAN exports to China offset their losses in Western market share.

Trade between ASEAN and China will reach US$1 trillion by 2020, as China continues to deepen capacity building and promotes, in the PRC's estimation, 'win-win' development for all.[38] The ASEAN–China Free Trade Area (ACFTA) signed in 2002 and implemented in 2010 stimulates this growth. Since 2012, ASEAN and China have promoted an extension of their bilateral FTA to include Australia, India, Japan and South Korea as well. This is the basis for what China envisages as 'the maritime silk road' through the formation of an ostensibly ASEAN-led RCEP. Reflecting and informing this partnership is China's AIIB with fifty, primarily Asian, members, but also including the UK and Germany.[39] The AIIB complements the BRI's land transportation corridors connecting China to Europe, and South Asia as well as Southeast Asia, whilst the Maritime Silk Road promotes port development, 'a string of pearls', to enhance trade from the Bay of Bengal to Hong Kong.[40]

Yet the 'Belt and Road' model not only complements ASEAN's Master Plan for ASEAN Connectivity (MPAC),[41] it also cements China's strategic foothold in the region. Ultimately the BRI integrates the smaller ASEAN economies into 'China-centric regional production networks'.[42] In other words, the AIIB and the BRI also create intra-ASEAN competition for infrastructure funding rather than enhancing inter-ASEAN cooperation. In fact, China's increasingly proactive economic diplomacy in Southeast Asia reflects a broader strategy that seeks to bind its neighbours in 'a web of incentives that increase their reliance on China and raise the cost to them of adopting a confrontational policy towards China on either territorial or economic disputes'.[43]

Creating asymmetrical economic dependence among weaker states enables the PRC to influence their foreign policies in ways congenial to China's interests, as the shifting alignments of founding ASEAN member states Indonesia, Malaysia and the Philippines demonstrates. Indonesia receives the largest share of China's BRI funding to the region. In April 2018, president Joko 'Jokowi' Widodo signed five infrastructure contracts with Beijing. They include the construction of a US$17.8 billion hydropower plant on the Kayan River, in Kalimantan.[44] Meanwhile China Railway Corp (CRC) is building the first high-speed railway in Southeast Asia, connecting Jakarta and Bandung.

Indonesia urgently needs this investment, amounting to US$87 billion in repayable loans, to achieve nationwide access to electricity and service a rapidly increasing urban population. But economic 'benevolence' comes at a price. Beijing's economic diplomacy imposes unwritten obligations that recipients of its largesse reciprocate in the political sphere.[45] Thus while Indonesia – the largest Muslim country in the world – condemns the treatment of Muslim communities in Israel, Palestine or Myanmar, it is notably silent about the treatment of the Uighur minority in Xinjiang. Similarly, Indonesia, despite its legal sovereignty under the United Nations Convention on the Law of the Sea, eschews exerting its control over the resource-rich Natuna Islands which lie in an area of the South China Sea claimed by China.

As EU commissioner Hahn observed, inability to repay infrastructure loans and their accumulated interest renders the recipient's ports, railways and power networks vulnerable to takeover. The BRI eerily resembles the *Vereenigde Oostindische Compagnie*'s (VOC, the Dutch East India Company) similar promise of trade and investment that led to 350 years of Dutch colonization of Indonesia.[46] As one local scholar observed *'penjajah kulit kuning'* (yellow-skinned colonialism) has already reduced Angola and Zimbabwe to Chinese dependencies.[47]

However, in the absence of an economic counterweight, it seems inevitable that China will extend its geopolitical reach not only to Indonesia but across Southeast Asia. The Philippine case is suggestive. A former colony and traditional US ally, under the Presidency of Rodrigo Duterte (2016–) the Philippines has openly courted China, spectacularly jettisoning its sovereignty over islands in the South China Sea, established by the Hague ruling of 2016, in return for infrastructure investment. To achieve a 'Golden Age of Infrastructure', and alleviate poverty, Duterte's populist government required Chinese FDI.[48] Manila relies on Chinese capital to achieve an ambitious 'Build, Build, Build' programme. China pledged US$7.34 billion in soft loans to facilitate Duterte's *Ambisyon Natin 2040* ('our vision').[49]

Duterte's pivot to China occurred after President Obama and Western human rights activists criticised his aggressive prosecution of a domestic war on drugs that featured a penchant for extra judicial killing. Duterte told foreign companies worried about his human rights record to 'pack up and leave', observing that Chinese businesses would take their place.[50]

Malaysia meanwhile offers an interesting case study of how asymmetric dependence can produce unintended political consequences. In 2009 Prime Minister Najib Razak, in response to the global financial crisis, announced 1 Malaysia Development Berhad (1MDB), a sovereign wealth fund, to boost economic growth. However, the fund quickly amassed US$11 billion in debt. At the same time, close to US$700 million found its way into Najib's personal accounts.[51] In a bid to rescue the state investment fund, and allay suspicions over financial impropriety, Najib's government, regarded by the international community as a model of a moderate Muslim polity, cultivated close links with China. In November 2015, the government sold 1MDB's power assets, Edra Global Energy Berhad, to China General Nuclear Power Corporation (CGN) for RM 9.83 billion (US$2.3 billion). In return, CGN assumed the gross debt that Edra Global Energy Berhad and its operating companies had accumulated.[52]

This bailout guaranteed Malaysia's silence on China's increasingly assertive stance in the South China Sea and the brutal treatment of its Uighur Muslim minorities. In an increasingly fiscally challenged environment, Malaysia's economic dependence translated into a shift from a non-partisan foreign policy to a pro-China stance. Following an official state visit to Beijing in 2016, Prime Minister Najib Razak stated that 'we believe it is incumbent upon larger countries to treat smaller ones fairly. And this includes former colonial powers. It is not for them to lecture countries they once exploited on how to conduct their own internal affairs today'.[53] Najib made this statement shortly after the US Department of Justice issued a lawsuit implicating 'Malaysian Official 1' with money-laundering, a charge Najib considered interfered in Malaysia's internal affairs.

China's indifference to Najib's kleptocracy, and to sultanic regimes and human rights abuses globally, prompts corrupt and illiberal regimes to deal with Beijing, rather than face the scrutiny that rule-governed international organizations like the IMF might cast over their financial conduct. Najib's 2016 state visit to China resulted in loans to fund eleven high-profile projects. They included the US$15 billion East Coast Rail Link (ECRL), connecting Malaysia's underdeveloped east coast with Kuala Lumpur, as well as a controversial luxury real estate project in Johor.

Failure to repay these BRI loans, however, would render Malaysia, like Indonesia and the Philippines, exposed to the fate of Sri Lanka, forced to cede Hambantota Port and 15,000 acres of land to China for ninety-nine years, to erase US$1 billion worth of China denominated debt.[54] The Chinese built port now affords China a strategically critical foothold in the Indian Ocean. In this context, the Chinese construction of Forest City on four artificial islands off the coast of Johor raised concerns that Najib was ceding Malaysian territory to a foreign power.[55]

Only after the unanticipated fall of Najib's government in the general election of May 2018 could questions about China linked investment be openly raised. Assuming office, following a victory that unseated the *Barisan Nasional* coalition after sixty-one years of uninterrupted rule, new Prime Minister Dr Mahathir Mohamad cancelled the China-backed East Coast Rail Link. Mahathir described these projects as 'unequal treaties',[56] a term deliberately used to invoke the Chinese Communist Party's frequent reference to the agreements the Qing dynasty made with Western powers in the nineteenth century that eroded China's sovereignty and exposed it to Western colonialism.

Nevertheless, despite the new administration's attempt to modify the Najib strategy, China remains Malaysia's second largest export trading partner and largest source of imports.[57] Reduced reliance on BRI does not equate to diminished dependency on China, and in the absence of a counterweight, Malaysia, like all the ASEAN economies, depends on the China trade and Beijing's financial largesse.

Moreover, Donald Trump's decision to abandon the TPP in 2017 and launch a trade war with China over breaches of WTO rules has only enhanced China's regional cachet. TPP, a US initiative to determine the rules for Asian trade had briefly posited an alternative to the China-backed RCEP. A cornerstone of Obama's 'Pivot to Asia', the TPP involved twelve countries (four from ASEAN) together with Japan, New Zealand, Australia, Canada and three South American states.[58] Whilst Australian Trade Minister Craig Emerson asserted that the two trading arrangements meant two pathways to the same destination, this was disingenuous.[59] China promotes the former; the US, under Obama, the latter. China belongs to the former and not the latter, and the US, before Trump, to the latter and not the former.

The now emasculated TPP envisaged a comprehensive, robust and rule-binding trade agreement, which a number of ASEAN states, as well as China, resisted. By contrast, the ASEAN-led, but China-backed, RCEP brings under one umbrella the various bilateral and trilateral preferential trade deals concluded between China, ASEAN and a number of regional states. However, the 'free' in these trade agreements is notional. Key agricultural and manufacturing sectors remain protected. The RCEP comprises sixteen countries: ten ASEAN nations, China, India, Japan, South Korea, Australia and New Zealand. On 13 October 2018, the Sixth RCEP Inter-Sessional Ministerial Meeting held in Singapore witnessed all participating members reaffirming their resolve to conclude the region-wide trade pact.

When concluded, the RCEP will be the largest trade deal in the world, accounting for forty-five per cent of the world's population (3.4 billion people), a third of global GDP (US$20 trillion) and global total trade (US$10 trillion).[60] Although an ASEAN initiative, the grouping of weak states, despite its norm-driven, post-national identity, is incapable of driving the process.[61] The emerging economic bloc instead reflects the interests of China and the larger economic players in the 'partnership'.

However, territorial disputes over the South China Sea between China and ASEAN; territorial issues between China, Japan and South Korea; and historically challenging China-India and China-Japan relations complicate the conclusion of the trade deal. In particular, India fears the RCEP would increase its already burgeoning trade deficit with China.[62] The RCEP is thus contingent on whether it suits the political and economic will of more powerful players.

These caveats notwithstanding, China is busily rewriting the rules for international trade, gradually constructing a Sinocentric regional order. The China-ASEAN Free Trade Area and 'Belt and Road' countries could over time form a One Belt, One Road Eurasian market,[63] giving substance to China's hegemonic, neo-Confucian conception of harmonious world order. How might this evolution affect the prospect of norms, even those culturally attuned to Asian sensibilities, informing a post-national, socially just, global society?

China's ASEAN

At the 31st ASEAN summit held in Manila in November 2017, the grouping turned a predictable blind eye to the massacre of the Rohingya Muslim minority in Burma/Myanmar. ASEAN and China did agree, however, to a framework to negotiate a code of conduct in the South China Sea. It was non-binding, which suited China. At the same time, Australia and the US recited the now familiar mantra calling on all parties in the dispute to abide by international law.

China's proactive ASEAN economic diplomacy forms part of a broader strategy that imbricates its neighbours in a web of incentives and raises the ante for calling China out over 'either territorial or economic disputes'.[64] As one Vietnamese academic observed, China refers to itself in meetings with ASEAN representatives as 'big brother' guiding its 'little' Southeast Asian 'brothers'. And big brother increasingly determines the regional security agenda. Significantly, China finds ASEAN-style norms hugely conducive to promoting its national interest. This is most apparent on the South China Sea, the region's 'major fault line'.[65]

The dispute dates from the 1951 San Francisco Treaty, which failed to stipulate possession of the Spratly island chain after Japan lost its title in 1945. It developed into a regional conflict when a number of claimants began extracting resources from the seabed contiguous to their Exclusive Economic Zones. China, Taiwan (which holds the largest Spratly island), and four ASEAN states – Brunei, Malaysia, the Philippines and Vietnam – all claim or occupy islands and reefs in the South China Sea.

The dispute assumed its current form in February 1992 when China laid claim to the entire South China Sea on the basis of its alleged pre-colonial hegemony. It subsequently became becalmed in ASEAN's non-binding process of dialogue. China's engagement in processes like the ASEAN Regional Forum post-1994 that sought to inculcate China in the 'norms of regional good citizenship' has been a cost-free investment in public relations.[66] Thus no progress had been made on resolving China's 'uncontestable' claim to the South China Sea.[67]

The shift from a soft to a hard line or from 'smile' to 'frown' diplomacy, moreover, always remains a Chinese option. A standoff between Chinese and Philippine naval vessels near the Scarborough shoals in the Spratly island chain in 2012 first announced a harder line. In response, the ASEAN members divided, failing for the first time to agree on a post-summit communiqué at the annual Foreign Ministers' Summit in June 2012. Shortly afterwards, former Philippine President Aquino abandoned the ASEAN process, referring the dispute with China instead to the Hague's International Tribunal for the Law of the Sea.[68] In July 2016 the Tribunal found that China's claim to eighty-five per cent of the South China Sea had 'no legal basis'. China dismissed the decision as 'preposterous'.[69]

Policymakers and academics in second track forums nevertheless continue to assert their confidence in ASEAN's normative processes. As the dispute developed between 2012 and 2018, China applied a compelling mixture of smile and frown diplomacy. At the Brunei Summit in October 2013, the PRC proposed a new treaty of friendship, ushering in a 'diamond decade'. As The Straits Times (Singapore) editorialised, 'the implicit message was that China had sufficiently deep pockets' to offer a 'slew of sweeteners in the form of billions of dollars of development projects'.[70] These deep pockets, as we have seen, persuaded the new Philippine President, Duterte, in a stunning about-face executed after his election in 2016, to consider the Hague ruling 'as nothing more than a piece of paper', in return for the promise of Chinese investment.[71]

China's diplomacy has thus effected a sea change in the regional strategic balance. Hence, although Chinese premier Li Keqiang envisages a 'common destiny', it is also one of asymmetric dependence. China's understanding of regionalism assumes a Chinese core operating across its Southeast Asian periphery. The relationship is one of reciprocity, but failure to respect China invokes the frown. Thus, when either the Philippines or Vietnam reject China's interpretation of its history and territory, they suffer in terms of investment and market access.

Chinese statecraft has fragmented ASEAN, sucking Cambodia, Laos and Myanmar, and more recently Indonesia and the Philippines into its orbit. Vietnam gravitates to the US, whilst Singapore, Thailand, Brunei and, more recently, post-Mahathir, Malaysia hedge between the US and China. Meanwhile, Indonesia's foreign policy oscillates between indifference and ambiguity. Rather than advancing regional norms, ASEAN now finds itself between a rock and a hard place. As former ASEAN Secretary General Ong Keng Yong observed, 'in crude terms', China was 'doing divide and rule'.[72]

The South China Sea dispute demonstrates how a more powerful actor, China – unconstrained by ASEAN's norms – advances its grand strategic design, gaining control of both the maritime and economic space in a manner familiar to players of *Weiqi* (Go), where each side tries to achieve relative advantage through strategic encirclement. A talented player moves into the 'empty' spaces on the board, gradually mitigating the strategic potential of the adversary.[73]

Realism or Regionalism?

The incoherence of ASEAN's response to a range of security and economic issues falsifies the Wendtian idealist, constructivist and multilateral IR theory that progressively shared norms can transform interests to bring about a regional or post-national identity. It has also given the PRC a taste for multilateralism *à la Chine*, manipulating international institutions to its own purposes and exploiting the Trump administration's growing dissatisfaction with the international regime that the US established after 1945.

In Southeast Asia – as is also becoming apparent to Europeans – second order and weaker states are having to recognize diplomatic first principles, namely that a great power can only be balanced by a great power. The smaller and weaker ASEAN states, as the South China Sea dispute demonstrates, cannot balance China alone. ASEAN states therefore need the US.

The US, moreover, after the end of the Cold War, never tried to contain China's rise. What should concern the US, however, is regional balance. With North Korea, Hong Kong, and maritime and trade tensions making the headlines, the US presence remains necessary to protect regional freedoms that China's actions potentially jeopardize. The US has a stake both in reassuring its allies and protecting its trade with the most vibrant region of the world economy. However, Trump's unpredictability worries its regional allies, even, it would seem, in Australia.

Proactive diplomacy, statecraft and principled but realist US engagement – as the National Security Strategy suggested – are now needed more than ever.[74] This could prompt a more prudent version of the 'China dream', in order to contain regional conflict rather than exacerbate it. The alternative, as Nixon worried shortly before he died, was that opening to China had unleashed 'a Frankenstein['s monster]'.[75]

Paradoxically, the Chinese also have an interest, at least in the short term, in a US that prudently engages with and balances their rising power, rather than asserts universal norms, abstract rights and global justice. Indeed, if the US disengaged from Asia, regional tensions would rapidly escalate. Japan would necessarily acquire nuclear weapons, particularly against a proven North Korean threat. In such circumstances, Chinese confrontation with Japan would intensify, and India and Pakistan would be drawn into the conflict. Rising nationalism would see South Korea hedge between China, Japan, and an emboldened North Korea. Meanwhile hedging states in Southeast Asia and the Pacific – from Thailand and Singapore to Australia – would have to make some hard choices, facing a version of the dilemma that Thucydides described in the Peloponnesian war where smaller states were engulfed in the conflict caused by the 'growth of Athenian power and the fear which this caused in Sparta'.[76]

Significantly, former Singaporean ambassador to the US and former Dean of the Lee Kuan Yew School of Public Policy, Kishore Mahbubani, drew 'big lessons for a small state' from such classically realist lucubrations. The most important was that, irrespective of their wealth, 'small states must always behave like small states'. Singapore in the post-Lee Kuan Yew era, Mahbubani wrote, 'would have been wiser to be more circumspect…on the arbitration which the Philippines instituted against China concerning the South China Sea dispute'. Significantly, he drew the lesson for small state discretion not from the structure of regional order but from Thucydides' account of the dilemma that the neutral, small state of Melos faced during the twentieth year of the Peloponnesian War.

Mahbubani cited approvingly the Athenian delegation's response to the Melian question about the justice of Athenian behaviour. 'Right', they replied, 'as the world goes, is only in question between equals in power, while the strong do what they can and the weak suffer what they must'.[77] Mahbubani further contended that a small state 'needs to be truly Machiavellian in international affairs' and concluded that the hard truth of geopolitics is 'that sometimes, principle and ethics must take a back seat to the pragmatic path of prudence'.[78]

The classical and early modern understanding of prudence has been notably absent not only in Asia, as Mahbubani observed, but also from the understanding and practice of Western foreign policy since the end of the Cold War. States have prioritized economic growth and the promotion of progressive universal norms, suitable to an embedded utopian global society, over strategy and politics. Yet as a Mao-era aphorism maintained, the people have to concern themselves with politics because even if they don't care about politics, politics cares about them. The principle still applies. Politics is alive and well on the world island. Mao's maxim also has important ramifications for the conduct of Western diplomacy and the understanding of international order in a world of power politics, dissimulation and national interest more familiar to students of Machiavelli than Kant and his modern adherents in schools devoted to international relations theory.

8

MAXIMS OR AXIOMS?
NORMS, POLITICAL PRUDENCE, AND THE RETURN OF GEOPOLITICS

The idea that history ended with the fall of the Berlin Wall in 1989 and the dissolution of the Soviet Union in 1992 cast an enduring pall over Western domestic and foreign policy thinking for more than two decades. Its influence reached its apogee in the period leading up to the Iraq War of 2003. Francis Fukuyama argued that Western liberal democracy constituted the 'final form of human government'. One consequence of this 'ideological evolution' was the progressive assumption that large-scale conflict between the great powers was 'passing from the scene'.[1] Fukuyama's vision of the future complemented fellow neo-conservative Charles Krauthammer's contention that the US should 'lead a unipolar world, unashamedly laying down the rules of world order and being prepared to enforce them'.[2] As John Mearsheimer observed in 2011, 'US grand strategy has followed this basic prescription for the past twenty years, mainly because most policy makers inside the Beltway have agreed with the thrust of Fukuyama's and Krauthammer's (and, we might add, Thomas Friedman's) early analyses'.[3]

The attempt to impose a liberal, democratic, secular, progressive, norm-based global order appealed across mainstream party political lines and across the West. As we have seen, progressive leaders from Bill Clinton and Tony Blair to David Cameron, Angela Merkel, Kevin Rudd, and Barack Obama all embraced the 'unstoppable force' of 'an interdependent global community'.[4] Whether they adopted, with Blair and Bush, a more aggressive neo-conservative stance or, like some of their critics, a more emollient 'Liberal Imperialist' posture, one that maintained 'that running the world requires the United States to work closely with allies and international institutions',[5] Western political elites, democratic governments, and normative, liberal institutionalist, critical and constructivist international relations theorists all subscribed to some version of this progressive worldview. This grand theory of a global interdependent society premised on secular values of equality and social justice that transcended left and right prompted interventions, humanitarian or otherwise, in Asia, Africa, and the Middle East in support of what was assumed to be an ultimately shared, universal, normative orientation.

As the West boldly set off to re-make the world after the fall of the Berlin Wall, these progressive values set the global agenda. Even though the long wars in Iraq and Afghanistan exposed the limits of imposing the end of history by military means, its intimation nevertheless lingered on in the wake of the assassination of Osama bin Laden (2011), the UN-sanctioned overthrow of the Gaddafi regime under the post-2005 rubric of the Responsibility to Protect doctrine,[6] and the brief Arab Spring. Indeed, it remains an entrenched progressive elite and academic avocation to build an integrated world governed by rational, new liberal and ethically just values.

The results of this strategy have proved disastrous. The United States was at war 'for a startling two out of every three years' between 1989 and 2012.[7] In these circumstances of struggle and flight, is it possible to recuperate a more circumscribed international vision that recognizes that 'universal moral principles cannot be applied to the actions of states in their abstract universal formulation, but…must be filtered through the concrete circumstances of time and place'?[8]

In order to consider this counsel, we shall first elucidate the limitations of the liberal, normative, rationalist approach to war and peace and its unintended fragmentation of the global order since 2008. We shall then consider how European theorizing at the inception of the modern state about the nature of interest and the 'supreme virtue in politics', prudence, a virtue that weighs 'the consequences of alternative political actions'[9] might more usefully inform the conduct of statecraft today.

History Restarted

At the millennium, the victory of liberal market capitalism over rival economic models and alternative ideologies confirmed the Enlightenment faith in universal progress towards equality, human rights and social justice.[10] Following the collapse of communism in Europe, liberal market democracy appeared the 'only game in town'.[11] As a universal moral understanding, Enlightenment values also afforded the impulse for reforming capitalism's more unjust and inegalitarian outcomes, whilst compensating those who suffered from the unfair distributional effects of scientific progress. History, in this secular, rationalist recension, would witness capitalist democratic states ineluctably transformed into a Kantian universal state combining morality with politics through participation in cosmopolitan, post-national constellations like the United Nations, the European Union, ASEAN and the East Asian Community (EAC).[12] These state-transcending organizations and their norm entrepreneurs would facilitate human rights, transnational justice and economic re-distribution throughout the international system, 'as all politics must bend the knee before right'.[13]

In the aftermath of Iraq and Afghanistan, however, this teleology yielded some unintended, perverse and countervailing consequences. Unforeseen but intractable obstacles appeared on the path to a socially just emancipatory transformation of the interstate system. The recrudescence of nationalism everywhere, Russian irredentism in the Caucasus, and the civil war in Ukraine; China's emergence as a great, but authoritarian, power on the world island, together with the continued turmoil in the Middle East, intimate not the end of history, but the 'revenge of the revisionist powers' and the 'return of geopolitics'.[14] 'History', after a brief, but troubled, slumber, awoke in a belligerent mood asking states and international institutions how they might conduct themselves in an uncertain, anarchical, international economic and political world where only the realist verities of diplomacy, alliances, and war prevailed.[15]

Faced with a changed reality, Western powers and regional institutions appeared, in the second decade of the twenty-first century, 'distracted [and] weak'.[16] Russia and China, states with a realistic appreciation of their national purpose, consistently out-manoeuvred putatively more advanced and ethical international regimes on the world stage.[17]

During the Ukraine crisis of 2013–18, European policymakers clung to the 'false hope' that dialogue, law and judicious sanctions could achieve a solution. The EU's attempt to extend its Association Agreements into what had once been the western Soviet Union inevitably clashed with Putin's interest in creating a Eurasian Customs Union. The fault line ran through the Ukraine. Under its 'anodyne labels of association, cooperation and convergence' the European Union imposed a 'heavy geopolitical weight on a fragile region under considerable economic and political stress'.[18] In February 2014, Russia seized the Crimean peninsula and supported a separatist insurgency in Donbas, the eastern region of the Ukraine. By March 2019, with presidential elections approaching, the situation in the eastern Ukrainian cities of Donetsk and Luhansk remained unresolved and open to further Russian manipulation and *kompromat*.[19] Europe's 'diplomacy without arms', as Frederick the Great observed, was 'like music without instruments'.[20] Charles Powell, former foreign policy adviser to Prime Minister Margaret Thatcher, contended, the 'false doctrine of soft power' and 'creeping legalism' made it increasingly 'hard to galvanise democratic societies to meet new threats'.[21]

Consequently, while the EU naively dismissed 'the whole notion of geopolitics' as old-fashioned and unappealing, geopolitics happened on its doorstep.[22] As Russia violated the 'integrity of the Ukraine, and thus the entire legal order that governed Europe'[23] with growing impunity, the fallout from the Iraq and Syrian civil wars raised the problem of the internal and external security of European democracies in a more acute form, not evidently amenable to the application of abstract norms or internationally mediated legal solutions.

A cursory examination of new threats to the international order, like the rise of Islamic State and the geopolitical consequences of its demise, requires a reassessment of the utility of pursuing abstract norms, strategic patience and 'not doing geopolitics'.[24] Given recent tectonic shifts in global power, we might, then, reconsider how the realist contention that 'the concept of interest defined in terms of power' might save us 'from both…moral excess and political folly'.[25] Policy from this perspective requires the systematic pursuit of objectives that reconcile economic and military means with a reasoned appreciation of what is feasible in a dangerous world.[26] As Hans Morgenthau argued, 'there can be no political morality without prudence; that is, without consideration of the political consequences of seemingly moral action. Ethics in the abstract judges action by its conformity with the moral law; political ethics judges action by its political consequences'.[27]

The Return of the Nation State

'This is not the first border we will break, we will break other borders', declared a jihadist fighter (in English) in a well-produced video that announced the resurrection of a Sunni caliphate in June 2014.[28] Running south from Syria through the Sunni provinces of Iraq, the grouping formerly known as the Islamic State in Iraq and the Levant (ISIL) declared the formation of the Islamic State (IS). Abu Bakr al-Baghdadi, aka Caliph Ibrahim,[29] whom an IS document proclaimed the 'shaykh (sheikh), the mujāhid [fighter], the scholar who practices what he preaches, the worshipper, the leader, the warrior, the reviver, descendant from the family of the Prophet, the slave of Allah', presided over this entity.[30] Celebrating the restoration with a commemorative poem, the proclamation concluded:

> Our khilāfah has indeed returned with certainty
> And likewise our state, becoming a firm structure.
> And the breasts of the believers have been healed,
> While the hearts of kufr have been filled with terror.[31]

According to Abu Mohammed al-Adnani, an Islamic State spokesman: 'The legality of all emirates, groups, states and organisations becomes null by the expansion of the caliph's authority and the arrival of its troops to their areas'.[32]

An unintended consequence of the internal war against the Assad regime in Syria, IS emerged from the even more nebulous parastate of Iraq and al-Sham via a merger of Iraqi Islamists with elements of the Syrian al-Nusra Front.[33] The new entity briefly controlled key cities such as Mosul and the oil plains stretching from Mosul to the fields of Syria's Euphrates Oil Company. For the first time since the announcement of the war on terror in 2001, jihadists directly administered territory and resources.[34] Rather than relying on the tolerance of friendly states, like the Taliban regime in Afghanistan before 2001, or weak ones, like Yemen or Somalia, to afford them a base, the jihadist *internationale* met, if only briefly, the Weberian definition of a state exercising the monopoly of violence in a territorial unit of rule.[35]

This development presented profound problems for Western foreign policy and strategic thinking, as it also did for the various states of the Middle East itself. After Kemal Atatürk's modernizing regime dissolved it in 1924, the Caliphate remained an Islamist aspiration, representing a transnational ideological and religious alternative to the secular nation state. As the Islamic State journal, *Dabiq*, observed, Sunni militancy sought the 'demolition' of the post-Ottoman world as it came to be defined by the secret Anglo-French Sykes-Picot Agreement of 1916, the Anglo-French Agreement (1918), the Treaty of Sevres (1920) and the Treaty of Lausanne (1923).[36] Moreover, as a consequence of its territorial unity and its promulgation of a political religion with a global reach via social media, IS attracted recruits from Pakistan to Indonesia, as well as from an alienated diaspora of young Muslims located in the West. As *Dabiq* announced, 'it is a Khilafah that gathered the Caucasian, Indian, Chinese, Shami, Iraqi, Yemeni, Egyptian, Maghribi (North African), American, French, German, and Australian.'[37]

Foreign fighters swelled the ranks of the Islamist equivalent of the Spanish civil war international brigades: 'Their blood mixed and became one, under a single flag and goal, in one pavilion, enjoying this blessing, the blessing of faithful brotherhood'.[38]

This mutation of an Islamist utopian fantasy into a temporal political reality threatened to falsify the ruling academic, political, and media assumptions that determined post-Cold War Western thinking about the evolving new world order and its progressive faith in the abstract authority of an international community overseeing a secular, liberal, democratic end of history.

In its Middle Eastern manifestation, liberal progressivism assumed, *inter alia*, that the US-orchestrated Coalition had, by 2012, ensured, as President Barack Obama asserted, that the 'core of al-Qaeda in Pakistan and Afghanistan is on a path to defeat', while the broader global movement was 'on its heels'.[39] With the significant degrading of both the threat and organizational infrastructure of transnational Islamism, this perspective further assumed that the Arab Spring movements that questioned authoritarian rule in Tunisia, Libya, Syria, Bahrain, and Egypt after 2011 had set the Middle East on a path toward greater openness, regular elections and democratic transition.[40] This progressive consensus even assumed that Iraq had achieved some degree of political stability.[41] The subsequent exit of Western forces in 2011 had, President Obama claimed, left behind 'a sovereign, stable and self-reliant Iraq, with a representative government that was elected by its people'.[42]

Somewhat inconveniently for this progressive teleology, events across the Middle East after 2014 indicated something rougher, more unpredictable and unstable, slouching towards Bethlehem and beyond. Along with the evident return of great power politics, these developments portend an era of durable disorder marked by internal and even inter-state war. The Middle East evinced the character of this disorder in a particularly volatile configuration. The Syrian civil war that began in 2012, the disintegration of 'liberated' Libya since 2013, the Israeli intervention in Gaza in August 2014, and the fragmentation of Iraq after 2011 announced significant challenges not only to the wider region, but also for European states not directly involved in the crisis. These threats arose from the migration of displaced peoples after 2015, the terror threat posed by returning jihadis trained in the arts of bomb making and decapitation, 'home-grown' attacks by 'lone wolf' terrorists, the ubiquitous problem of energy security and the unpredictable consequences of major power conflict whether in the Ukraine or the East and South China Seas. In order to clarify the nature of the disorder, we shall proceed to explore the foreign and domestic policy implications of the crises in Syria and Iraq for Western diplomacy. Subsequently, we shall contend that state-interested, historically particularist, and prudentially calculated policy might better inform the thinking of Western democracies rather than the prevailing predilection for abstract, universal, and axiomatic norms.

Durable, Endurable or Unendurable Disorder?

The dissolution of any prospect for enduring stability in the Middle East happened after 2011. It occurred when Western involvement in the region was notable only for its absence. Western forces had largely departed Iraq by 2008. Support for anti-Gaddafi forces in Libya, delivered via air power in 2011, only taught Western states to be wary of any further Middle Eastern interventions, humanitarian or otherwise. Libya descended into tribal and religious factionalism despite the United Nations authorization, under the 2005 Responsibility to Protect mandate, of the overthrow of the Gaddafi regime.[43] Subsequently, European national parliaments explicitly rejected intervention in the far more strategically important Syrian civil war.[44] Meanwhile, US foreign policy after 2008 appeared increasingly indifferent to shaping the international order in general and the Middle East in particular. The fracking revolution, that gifted the US resource independence and facilitated Obama's somewhat uncertain pivot to Asia after 2008, permitted the US to downgrade the threat posed by the Middle East.[45]

The cost in both personnel and matériel of Coalition and NATO interventions in Iraq and Afghanistan further rendered it unlikely that the US, let alone British or European governments, would embark again on costly and largely futile state-building exercises in the world of state dissolution. As the US military prepared to leave an uncertainly pacified Afghanistan, the cost to the American taxpayer of these long wars amounted to $4 trillion,[46] while the cost to the UK exchequer approached £30 billion.[47]

The West's attempted disengagement from the Middle East and the wider Islamic world,[48] together with the widespread rejection of engaging in large-scale counter-insurgency operations, demonstrated the failure of the neo-conservative doctrine of pre-emption. At the same time, the emergence of the Islamic State and its affiliates in North Africa also indicated that Western non–intervention or the more radical transformative and emancipatory agenda that tried to empathize with Islamist demands also proved less than optimal. In other words, a cursory examination of the politics of intervention, with or without UN or humanitarian sanction, or for that matter non-intervention, in order to achieve regional transformation since 1990 fails to demonstrate a formal Western cause of the jihadist effect. Instead it reveals a condition of great complexity. What does this complexity disclose not only about Islamist strategic thinking but, more importantly, about how European states and the US might respond?

Grand Historical Narratives and Cosmopolitan Norms

The complexity, whatever else it did, exposed the deficiencies in the progressive desire to find the root causes of Islamist disaffection. Even a superficial examination of the intense sectarian and tribal divisions and rivalries affecting very different societies in the Middle East or across the wider and more diffuse 'Muslim world' exposes the practical limitations of root cause explanations.[49] The diversity of Islam, both in its heartlands and its diaspora, further demonstrated the limitations of an abstract rationalism or an empathetic reflexivity revealing the purportedly hidden connection between very different issues and conflicts.

Moreover, the fact that the dominant normative and cosmopolitan approach to political and international relations theory 'does not do war' reinforced this misunderstanding. As Cécile Fabre noted, 'cosmopolitans...have tended to focus on defending principles of distributive justice, as well as normative guidelines for world governance, but have not devoted much attention to articulating norms for the use of military force'.[50] In this sense contemporary international and critical security studies as well as much European policy making assumed that all violence was a form of distorted communication, the solution to which was uncoerced conversation.[51] Consequently, international relations scholars deliberately sought to 'extricate, not selectively but completely, all aspects of *realpolitik* from its conceptualizations of social conflict'.[52] Instead, they 'expended their energies on postulating the basic processes of tension reduction to prevent...war and revolution from breaking out'.[53]

To correct this misunderstanding, which engendered a faux naïve European innocence concerning geopolitics,[54] requires a return to a more pragmatic, historically minded and politically realist appreciation of the need for balance in world order. A prudent, rather than a cosmopolitan and ethicist, foreign policy requires case-based assessments of the merits of intervention, calculating their practical and moral limitations, informed by some appreciation of the Machiavellian doctrine of the lesser evil.

In this context, in 2014, General Sir David Richards adventurously speculated whether it might not be 'better to back a victory for President Assad in Syria's civil war' if the international community was not prepared to act in concert, 'because the alternative is chaos... [and] Assad poses no threat to the UK's national interest'.[55] The former Chief of the Defence Staff further contended that the national interest, properly understood, 'cuts through muddle'. Analogously, Paddy Ashdown thought that the obsession with 'kinetics rather than context' meant that the West had forgotten the doctrine that 'war is the continuation of politics by other means'. In the Middle East, this might require, Ashdown pondered heretically, bringing Russia into the coalition against Islamic State.[56] What might an interest-based, context-driven approach to foreign policy entail and how might it differ from the progressive project of social perfection fashioning a universal normative regime to transform the world into a morally acceptable, cosmopolitan and ethically just global order?

Politics, Statecraft and the Art of War

Only cases of extreme human rights violation meeting the normative criteria established by the United Nations Charter, subsequently refined into its responsibility to protect doctrine (R2P, 2009), legitimate the progressive use of force.[57] Preoccupied with this legal model, adjudicated by an abstract international community that takes the mundane form of a regime of international lawyers and a media chorus of liberal opinion makers, Western foreign policy at the end of history lost sight of the contingent factors that condition political action.

Yet ambiguity sits at the heart of the international legal regime. Interventions, especially in conditions of internal or external war, frequently fail to meet abstract, normative criteria. As former diplomats and soldiers like Charles Powell, Paddy Ashdown or David Richards appreciated, this created policy confusion during the Afghanistan and Iraq campaigns and ill-timed or ill-considered responses to IS, Russian irredentism and China's assertiveness in the South China Sea and beyond.

It might, therefore, be worth reappraising the rationalist, cosmopolitan legalism that the West embraced at the end of the Cold War, and revisit instead a practice of statecraft that eschews universal panaceas.[58] The political realism that Richards and Ashdown evince is, as Hans Morgenthau perceived, 'not unaware of the existence and relevance of standards of thought other than political ones'. It necessarily parts company with abstract, universal norms when the latter impose standards of thought and practice upon the political sphere appropriate 'to other forms of life'. Indeed, it is at this point that political prudence takes issue with the 'legalistic-moralistic' Kantian, critical and constructivist approaches to international politics.[59]

A return to a prudent rhetoric of reasonableness, especially in foreign policy debates, could restore the balance which the preoccupation with certain rules and systems has disturbed. In a world of uncertainty and complexity, abstract rationalist rigour is less appropriate than the early modern scepticism of those like Michel de Montaigne, who exhorted his readers to live with ambiguity without judgment. Indeed, as Stephen Toulmin argued, an updated practical case ethics, or casuistry, may still have value in resolving doubtful moral dilemmas ranging from war to euthanasia and knife crime in the twenty-first century.[60]

Such reasoning assumes no system or strategic script. Therein lies its merit. It possesses both classical and Christian antecedents but it is by nature ambivalent, historically conditioned, and somewhat elusive. Nor is its exercise something that sits easily with the character of modern democracy. It was Alexis de Tocqueville, in *Democracy in America*, who first observed that the democratic system seemed resistant to the traditional requirements of statecraft. He warned that 'foreign politics demand scarcely any of those qualities which a democracy possesses; and they require on the contrary the perfect use of almost all of those faculties in which it is deficient'. When it came to their dealings with other states, democracies 'cannot combine measures with secrecy, and it will not await their consequences with patience... [They] obey the impulse of passion rather than the suggestions of prudence and...abandon a mature design for the gratification of a momentary caprice'.[61]

Such concerns about imprudence weighed heavily on the minds of American strategists during the Cold War. One of the greatest challenges faced by the United States was always assumed to be the management of its passions and its budget. In the 1950s, Dwight Eisenhower's 'New Look' emphasised cautious containment and long-term sustainability as the best means of outlasting the Soviet Union. This further required caution in fiscal, temperamental, and military terms, as a counter-balance to the irrationalism and emotionalism that led to idealistic foreign policy misadventures.

It was in this context that Cold War prudence was often taken to denote 'frugality' or 'restraint', with which it was situationally connected. Prudence was seen as the antidote to unwieldly idealism or democratic excitability, and thus was assumed to be the handmaiden of realism writ large. In foreign policy terms, therefore, it came to connote never exceeding the pragmatic bounds set by the national interest. This was how it lived on in much academic literature on realism thereafter, notably in the work of Hans Morgenthau. In *The Tragedy of Great Power Politics*, John Mearsheimer wrote that 'prudence dictates that they behave according to realist logic'. Prudence certainly has a significant role to play in the realist story. And yet the point of prudence is that it rarely dictates.

Indeed, the Protestant theologian Reinhold Niebuhr objected to what he saw as too attenuated an understanding of prudence, as some sort of 'procedural standard' for foreign policy decisions in the work of Morgenthau and George Kennan. As a virtue with both classical and Christian antecedents, prudence could never be reduced to a formula to keep the national interest paramount at all times. Human beings could not escape 'loyalties and responsibilities to a wider system of values than that of the national interest – to a civilization for instance, to a system of justice, and to a community of free nations'. This sensibility, Niebuhr suggested, 'must prevent prudence from becoming too prudential in defining interest'. The real work of prudence was not simply to check democratic excitability, but to 'safeguard against both sentimentality and moral cynicism'.[62]

190

The key point here is that prudence and the ethics that accompany it are contingent and situational. It assumes no pre-determined rule for action and evolves experientially through quotidian practices rather than abstractly by decree or axiomatically according to norms. Most of all, it offers a pre-scientific and anti-rationalist approach to practical reasoning. This arises from prudence's rich heritage that long predates the Enlightenment rationalism that sought to replace it as a guide to moral and political conduct.

Prudence: A Brief History

The origins of prudence may be traced to the Athenian understanding of politics, as it developed in the aftermath of the city state's unexpected defeat in the Peloponnesian Wars. Aristotle distinguished between three 'virtues of thought': *episteme* (scientific knowledge), *techne* (craft knowledge) and *phronesis* (prudence, or practical wisdom). As he explained in the *Nicomachean Ethics*, *phronesis* derived from experience. It was 'concerned with particulars as well as universals, and particulars become known from experience'.[63] Its main business was 'to determine not ends but means to ends, i.e. what is most useful to do'.[64]

More than that, however, *phronesis* also demanded powers of persuasion and rhetorical skill to persuade citizens of the most expedient course of action. The Latin word *prudentia* is one possible translation of *phronesis* and conveys its journey from Athens to Rome. For Roman politicians, like Cicero, concerned with preserving the *res publica* ('the public thing'), it was the most important virtue for senators engaged in governing a citizen body (*civitas*).

Later, in the hands of medieval Christian thinkers, prudence was deemed to be a virtue in itself, precisely because it provided an assessment of both ends and means. For Thomas Aquinas, 'rightness of choice necessarily involves two factors, namely a due end and something suitably ordained to that end...consequently, an intellectual virtue is needed in reason to complement it and make it well adjusted to these things. This virtue is prudence'.[65] Aquinas's *Secunda Secundae* of the *Summa Theologiae* was largely devoted to finding a synthesis of classical and Christian thinking on prudence. Following Aristotle, he considered prudence a form of practical reason, based on experience and shrewdness. It was intimately concerned with *euboulia* (deliberating well), and *synesis* (judging well).

Doing God's will on earth remained the priority of Thomist theology. But Aquinas understood that political prudence also addressed practical concerns where 'even as the false is found with the true, so is evil mingled with good'.[66]

It was partly in response to the excesses of religious enthusiasm that prudence moved from the domain of personal ethics to assuming a greater role in the affairs of the early modern state. Difficult politico-theological choices encouraged the practice of prudent counsel. A wise prince would make use of experienced counsellors, informed by the classical, particularly Roman past, affording insight into how the maxims of practical reasoning might apply to the contingent circumstances of present statecraft. In the course of the sixteenth century, writers and counsellors as various as Niccolò Machiavelli, Franceso Guiccardini, Jean Bodin, Giovanni Botero, and the Dutch humanist Justus Lipsius sought to offer more than abstract moral injunctions when it came to questions of religion, morality, war and peace. Instead they offered a distinctive counsel of practical morality. This was based on their reading of historical, usually classical precedents, informed by a neo-Stoic *ataraxia* that valued calmness of mind as the antidote to religious enthusiasm, passion and zealotry.

Tiziano Vecelli (Titian's) *The Allegory of Time Governed by Prudence* (1565) portrayed this understanding of political wisdom.[67] His painting depicts a man with three faces: a mature adult faces the viewer, flanked on one side by the wizened profile of an old man and on the other by the callow features of a youth. Beneath the three-faced figure sits a three-faced beast, a lion facing, profiled by a wolf on one side and a dog on the other. Across the top of the painting runs the maxim: 'Ex praeterito praesens prudenter agit, ni futuram actionem deturpet' (From the experience of the past, the present acts prudently, lest it spoil the future). The painting may be read both as a depiction of the three ages of man and, symbolically, as a wolf devouring the memory of the past, a lion depicting the fortitude necessary in the present and a dog bounding into the future.

In recognizing the many-sided faces of knowledge and experience, prudence found itself confronted by the rationalist and revolutionary understanding associated with the later Enlightenment, one that sought to apply abstract universal rules and scientific methods to the political domain. Contra the scientific rationalism that sought to replace it, this earlier understanding of reasoning stressed the role of experience, history and tradition. It also demanded a deeper appreciation of contingency and circumstance, as well as the importance of self-understanding and political *virtù*, rather than abstract, legalistic moralizing as a guide to decision making.

In this respect, it is worth recalling how early modern European thinkers understood what prudence entailed in terms of politics and the strategic use of force. To do this, they first developed a distinctive modern vocabulary of statecraft, sovereignty, social contract and political conduct that might circumscribe recourse to abstract, universal, moral dicta. Progressive normative and critical schools of international relations ignore or dismiss this idiom of political understanding. Yet this neglected reason of state genre, which framed the ambiguous terms of our modern political vocabulary, discloses a practical form of reasoning still relevant to modern western democratic practice as well as its internal and external defence.

Prudent Counsel

Between 1550 and 1648, early modern Europe suffered divisive internal as well as external war. The period saw the often brutal severing of traditional political and religious allegiances from Prague to Edinburgh. Religious, dynastic and civil war destroyed European Christendom. In particular, the Thirty Years War (1618–48) affected all Europe 'and the course of the continent's history'.[68] Although the war's impact varied across time and space, the most informed recent assessment notes that its impact was 'overwhelmingly negative'.[69] As a result of war and pestilence, the population of Bavaria, for example, fell between twenty-three and sixty-nine per cent depending on the district, whilst the pre-1618 Nuremburg birth rate was not matched again before 1850.[70] 1621, moreover, marked the beginning of 'the Western world's first financial crisis'[71] as economic and financial collapse accompanied population decline.

The modern state form emerged ambiguously from the religious fundamentalism and internecine strife that eviscerated European Christendom. A sceptical view of morality that doubted sources of authority outside the territorial state, and came to be defined as *raison d'état,* accompanied it. The early modern philosophers, lawyers, dramatists, rhetoricians and historians who defined this perspective, termed 'realists' by today's idealists, offered a neglected, pragmatic political perspective. Beginning with diplomats and statesmen like Niccolò Machiavelli and Francesco Guicciardini in Florence in the first decades of the sixteenth century, to French jurists like Jean Bodin and Northern Humanists like Joost Lips (Justus Lipsius) in the last, this *politique* style dismissed ethical and theological abstractions when it came to addressing difficult political decisions in particular and contingent circumstances. Rather than universal religious moral standards, they offered instead advice grounded in practical reason (*phronesis* or *prudentia*) informed by historical example and experience when faced with hard cases and difficult moral and political choices.

What then was the character of this practical reasoning, and what implications does it have for statecraft and strategy? To recover this viewpoint, and what it means for contemporary political thought, requires that we first establish how a distinctive approach to difficult cases of obligation emerged in the sixteenth century, as a response to confessional fragmentation and the disintegration of a unitary, communitarian Christendom.[72] Faced with the dissolution of Christendom and the rise of the Ottoman Empire, humanist philosophers and statesmen looked to their classical past, to Aristotle's *Rhetorica* and *Nicomachean Ethics,* Cicero's *De Officiis,* and the histories of Tacitus, Polybius and Livy, to recover a practical case ethics and maxims or *sententiae* to address questions of politics, economy, moral conduct, war and peace. In the process of interrogating the classical world for advice on political conduct, they walked backwards into a new understanding of statecraft.

Revisiting the Machiavellian Moment

It was counsellors to the wealthy, but militarily weak, Renaissance Italian city states of the Cinquecento who first observed and criticized the burgeoning disparity between abstract Christian morals and the practical policies a republic, a principality or a tyrant might need to exercise in order to survive.[73] In the contingent circumstances of the invasion of the peninsula by 'barbarian' French, Spanish, and Imperial forces between 1494 and 1527, a distinctive school of humanist thought first identified the problem of the state (*lo stato*), a term devised by Machiavelli, and its requisite craft. As one of its leading proponents, Francesco Guicciardini, observed in his *Ricordi*:

> Before 1494 wars were long, battles involved very little bloodshed, and the method of besieging towns was slow and cumbersome... Hence it was practically impossible for anyone who had a state to lose it. The French came to Italy and introduced into warfare such speed of execution that...if one lost the surrounding country one lost the state.[74]

The idea of the state and how to maintain its external and internal relations has obvious, but invariably overlooked, contemporary ramifications. The Italian city states invented modern diplomacy.[75] As Guicciardini's more radical Florentine contemporary Niccolò Machiavelli observed, in order to preserve the state in a sea of insecurity, a ruler 'must learn how not to be virtuous, and to make use of this or not according to need'.[76] This was the capital with which a prince entered politics. More particularly, to ensure peace, a principality or republic must prepare for war; rulers 'must have no other object...nor acquire skill in anything, except war, its organization and its disciplines'.[77] J.R. Hale observed that war was Machiavelli's 'particular hobby horse'.[78] Machiavelli contended that 'without good military organization, there can neither be good laws or anything else good'.[79] Effective rule, and the stability of a republic, in other words, demanded a particular type of *virtù*, to use Machiavelli's technical term for this skill.[80]

Machiavelli's frankness was often too shocking for contemporary consumption. Nevertheless, the understanding of statecraft that he and his humanist contemporaries pioneered came to influence a later generation of European rulers and advisers facing analogous problems of civil and religious disorder.[81] They adopted the perspective, but modified its tone to render it more palatable. This modified

Machiavellianism reconciled the need for ethically dubious actions, while also acknowledging the moral virtue in sustaining peace and the public good.[82]

At the start of the seventeenth century, it was the pliable Jesuit philologist Justus Lipsius who crystallized this understanding for an elite European audience that included statesmen as various as the Earl of Leicester in England, Cardinal Richelieu in France, and the Duke of Alba in Spain.[83] By the mid-seventeenth century Lipsius' *Politica* (1589), a digest of maxims or *sententiae* taken from classical authors and woven together in the distinctive form of a *Cento*, had gone through ninety editions and had been translated into the English, French, Spanish and Italian vernacular languages.

The *Politica* constituted the statecraft primer for counsellors or ministers to rulers in early modern Europe. As with Machiavelli's *Prince* and *Discourses* it was principally concerned with the state, political reasoning, and the character of internal and external war. Lipsius, in other words, instructed the early modern political elite of Europe on how to address the problem of conflicted allegiance and what we might term today religious and populist violent extremism. Significantly, despite their religious differences, both Protestant and Catholic monarchs, and their counsellors, valued Lipsius' redaction of classical maxims largely drawn from the Roman historian Tacitus and the Stoic moralist, Seneca.[84] What did prudent counsel involve and how might it apply to contemporary statecraft?

State Right Trumps Human Rights

From the early modern period in Europe, statecraft taught rulers their interest, the dangers attendant upon religious and political fanaticism, and how such zealotry might be curtailed. These concerns and their remedy interestingly resemble the internal and external ideological dilemmas that confront European democracies in the second decade of the twenty-first century. In order to address them, prudent counsel acknowledged the importance of rhetoric in the new media age that Gutenberg's printing press announced,[85] and the need to persuade subjects to view a controversial political policy in the most favourable light.

This practice of justification, to a local or international audience, might be described as a presentational art. To be effective, it deployed the prevailing ethical and legal vocabulary that included a range of positive terms like *ius, lex, auctoritas, pax, conscientia, virtus, salus populi suprema lex esto* or *bonum publicum.*[86] The rhetoric of presentation drew upon this vocabulary to give credence to the policies needed to address political or religious conflict, as well as justify the use of force to achieve legitimate ends.

At the same time, the skilful rhetorician distinguished this presentational discourse from the related but very different practice of deliberative reflection. In the deliberative phase, counsellors and advisers to the prince or republic came to arrive in cabinet at particular decisions like, for example, declaring war, negotiating peace, burning heretics or raising taxes.

The justificatory presentation that followed upon deliberation was successful when its auditors, the political nation, accepted it. Somewhat problematically, however, this presentation opened itself to a counter-presentation drawing upon the same lexicon but rearranging its terms to offer an alternative interpretation. A failure in effective messaging occurred, then as now, when a particular policy, presented in an axiomatic or normative language of moral rightness and self-righteousness might be countered with charges of self-interestedness, contradictoriness or hypocrisy, 'the tribute', as La Rochefoucauld later reflected, 'that vice paid to virtue'.[87]

In the religious and dynastic wars that announced the struggle for supremacy in Europe after 1580, statesmen who depicted their policies in too abstract or ideal a form risked exposure from a counter-presentation that subverted its legitimacy. As Lipsius remarked of the times, 'O better part of the world, which fires of strife has religion (or the pursuit of moral theological truth) not ignited in thee!'[88]

The problem of contested presentational exposition, moreover, created a polemical context for additional and different responses. Firstly, those whose ethical rectitude was questioned may reply by more forcefully asserting their purity of purpose and denounce their interlocutors as corrupt or misled. The radically alternative, and political, rejoinder instead differentiated dimensions of human intercourse, permitting them distinct and often dissimilar standards of behaviour. Machiavelli was, as Hannah Arendt observed, 'the first to visualize the rise of a purely secular realm whose laws and principles of action were independent of the teachings of the Church in particular and of moral standards, transcending the sphere of human affairs, in general'.[89] It was, however 'state casuists',[90] following Machiavelli and working within the reason of state idiom, who, through a synthesis of early modern canon law case ethics or casuistry, and drawing upon examples drawn from the Roman historians, developed a practical method for addressing particular political and moral dilemmas.

In this developing practice, actions of a political character could be persuasively promoted, not in terms of their justness or rightness, but because they were necessary, timely or prudent.[91] Indeed, 'You must decide separately on every occasion, if it is not better to close an eye than *to provoke offences by untimely remedies*'.[92] This new emphasis on the contingent and the practical in matters of policy acknowledged the problem that abstract ethical claims to justice frequently dissolved into alternative and often conflicting choices when confronted by the facts of a contingent situation.

However, because of its later pejorative characterization as cynically obsessed with power at the expense of morality, such prudent statecraft was often maligned, notably by modern scholars of ethics and foreign policy. This misunderstanding reflects, in part, the fact that the English term 'reason of state' inadequately translates the French *raison d'état* and the Italian *ragion di stato*. This is unfortunate. In the French and Italian understanding the term implies not only the reason of state but the right that the non-neutral state has to preserve itself in order to sustain the public good.[93]

The right of the state, moreover, may be expressed in terms of both its right to survive as well as sustain its political order or constitution. In sum, a reason of state infused prudential realism addresses two aspects of policy making: the presentational dimension, which draws upon the prevailing moral and political vocabulary available to make a plausible case for a particular policy; and the deliberative justification for a policy that occurs in the counsel chamber, or cabinet, not in public. Material used in deliberation, moreover, might often be suppressed in the subsequent public presentation.

198

The Casuist Idiom and the Practice of Mixed Prudence

Lipsius, his humanist contemporaries and the prudential tradition they established, framed the right of the state in the context of the interplay between the implacable force of Providence, 'that great Mind of the world', 'Necessity' that 'overcomes all things' and the requisite prudential response.[94] As in the Graeco-Roman world,[95] effective counsel acknowledged prudence or practical reason as the ruling principle in politics. Political *virtù* could not exist without it.[96] Lipsius defined prudence as how to understand and choose what should be looked for or evaded in both the public and private sphere.[97] It was 'useful in all human affairs, but most of all in government'.[98]

Prudent counsel also drew upon the casuistry that the Jesuit Order evolved, and Protestant divines adapted, in the course of the Counter-Reformation. This style of ethical reasoning had evolved in the medieval church as the branch of moral theology that addressed cases of conscience. It constituted the technical method for resolving cases 'when conscience is in a strait between two or more courses' of action.[99] In this, it exhibited a concern with practical reasoning that also had implications for the practice of reason of state. Responding to the moral 'variety of persons and situations',[100] the state casuist attended not only to the general rule that, for example, 'thou shalt not kill' but also to the extenuating circumstances that might affect a particular case of homicide.[101]

Thus, rhetoric, prudence and casuistry came together in a compelling ethico-political amalgam in the course of the sixteenth and seventeenth centuries. Under Jesuit influence, casuistry 'applied the general principles of natural and divine law to specific cases, and merged seamlessly with...controversies'.[102] Problems of statecraft, resistance and allegiance, like any other practice or activity, fell within its burgeoning grasp. Moreover, despite the polemical tone of political debate, which saw casuistry 'deplored in name and deployed in spirit', the denominational divide between Catholic and Protestant case divinity 'was deceptively negotiable'. Indeed, for Catholic and Protestant alike, 'the rules and criteria, the meta-language used to appraise ordinary and extraordinary cases, were likely to lead to probably right and (possibly) wrong courses of action'.[103]

In political terms, adjusting policy to the times, then as now, necessitated a probabilism that assumed that doubt regarding the correct answer to a moral or political dilemma permitted a course of action that allowed that one particular course was probably right. It facilitated a situational ethics that 'pays closest attention to the specific details of particular...cases and circumstances'.[104]

More particularly, political probabilism required a distinct type of mixed prudence (*prudentia mixta*). The ruler practiced this in order to 'bridle' or manipulate an otherwise wilful populace.[105] Such prudence necessarily fluctuated in response to circumstances. It selected and combined 'things which relate to each other now in this way, then in that way... It takes time, place, and people into consideration and changes with the slightest change in them'.[106] Political prudence involved 'two parts: Civil and Military', the first concerned with 'everyday government when things are peaceful' and the other 'applied in war and times of unrest'.[107] The first branch divided naturally into religious and secular categories, the latter into foreign and internal civil war.

It was here that princely counsel adjusted rules to the requirements of the times and the people. The people were unpredictable, unruly and 'affected by emotions'.[108] They 'ignored the interest of the Commonwealth'. Hence to persuade them to a course of action, the prince and his advisers in securing the common interest and the public good had to use a prudence that mixed 'the honourable and the useful'. Indeed, if the harbour of good government could not be reached 'by sailing straight, you do it by a different course'. Shifting metaphors, Lipsius contended 'wine does not stop being wine when it is mixed with water, nor does Prudence cease being Prudence when it is mixed with a little drop of deceit'.[109] Thus, in conducting affairs of state, Lipsius, acknowledging Machiavelli, observed that there is something honourable and praiseworthy in cunning.[110]

In this context, 'civil planning' might depart 'from virtue or the laws in the interest of' political order.[111] This applied to military even more than civil prudence, which required a recourse to dissimulation and 'stratagems'. Lipsius thought this 'necessary for a Prince before everything else'.[112] As with Machiavelli, all military prudence concerned 'foreign and civil' war. Lipsius identified three aspects of warfare:

Starting it, Waging it, and Ending it. If you neglect any of these or execute it wrongly, you are most unlikely ever to celebrate a good outcome. In starting a war, I urgently admonish you to take these two things to heart: that it happens without all Injustice and all Rashness.[113]

Ultimately, war was 'safer than an unreliable peace' and peace could be 'made stronger by war'.[114] In this context, moreover, effective command achieves more 'by strategy than by force'. More particularly, 'nothing is more useful in war than deceit'.[115] Lipsius developed his guidance not for a gullible public, but for political advisers 'experienced of men and human affairs' who offer government 'beneficial insights in peace and war'.[116] Timely advice leads to wise decisions. A prudent ruler thus requires deliberative counsel that adjusts morality to political circumstances. This political flexibility contrasted with the loyalty required of the state's subjects, which also sustained the practice of prudent governance.

Prudence, Casuistry, and Modern Diplomatic Ethics

In the seventeenth century Europe's political elite came to understand, through bitter experience, that sustaining the state's interest might require a prudent adjustment to general rules of political conduct. Wary of popular emotion and fashionable enthusiasm, they looked to careful deliberation to effect long-term policy goals. How might such mixed prudence deal with current dilemmas in international politics?

Early modern statecraft of a non-neutral, *politique* character, like contemporary European diplomacy, confronted the moral difficulty of framing policy in an unstable milieu of contingency and mutability. The prudential view was acutely aware of the difficulty of applying impartial, abstract rules to the moral ambiguity of political experience and the human condition. Early modern political advice books, unlike modern, post-Kantian handbooks of international ethics thus considered maxims, like those that Lipsius, or later, the Duc du Rochefoucauld compiled, rather than abstract norms or axioms, a better guide for rulers confronting dilemmas not amenable to clear-cut moral decisions.

Whilst an axiom is a proposition derived from science and abstract reason, a maxim is distilled from experience and offers a practical guide to conduct. Practical reasoning, not abstract rationalism, shaped by experience, example and historical awareness should thus inform the counsel offered to princes and republics in difficult cases concerning public morality or the use of force in contingent circumstances. The prudential approach is founded on practical experience, emphasizing statements that are concrete, limited in time and presume a specific and particular knowledge.[117]

Foreign and domestic policy, unlike the abstract sciences, are more amenable to a practical reason that treats particular and often anomalous world events via a mixture of deliberative judgment combined with presentational acumen. Such counsel contrasts vividly with the contemporary legalistic-moralistic approach that, from the perspective of international law and cosmopolitan justice, requires axioms that apply to all cases, like the violation of human rights, in an abstract theoretical manner, applying rules as theorems.

Cosmopolitan Ethics, Casuistry, and Just War

The practical difficulty of applying abstract norms to modern warfare prompted some cosmopolitan and critical international relations scholars, like Cécile Fabre, to reconsider the norms determining the theory and practice of just war.[118] In this context, David Fisher, in particular, tried to show how a just cosmopolitan foreign policy might benefit from a greater appreciation of classical and Christian ethical and political thinking, and especially the sixteenth century Jesuit scholarship on just war theory. Fisher adapted Thomist and Jesuit theological constraints on warfare to his own 'virtue consequentialism' when dealing with contemporary hard cases.[119] By so doing, Fisher sought 'to make war just' and to engage only in 'just war'.[120]

Fisher's virtue consequentialism assumed, following the established Rawlsian normative tenets of IR scholarship, that a just or ethical approach to intervention forbids, or should exclude, realist, or reason of state thinking, as immoral and unjustifiable.[121] Instead, Fisher, and cosmopolitan scholarship generally, contended that the contemporary practice of just war must meet criteria that only expanded upon the principles first outlined in the late thirteenth century by St Thomas Aquinas in the *Summa Theologiae*.[122] All recourse to war, therefore, requires a just cause, the correct intention, and must be legitimated by a competent authority. It may only be undertaken as a last resort and with the probability that more good than harm will result from its successful prosecution. Meanwhile conduct *in bello* should be discriminate and proportional, minimizing casualties to non-combatants. Finally, it should conclude with a just peace.[123]

The problem with such modified Thomism, like the counsel offered by the medieval church, is that it could never be fully realized in an imperfect world.[124] It demands universal ethical consistency, captured most recently in the R2P doctrine, which 'assumes that intervention can and should be applied universally, regardless of the weight of circumstantial evidence against such a strategy'.[125]

Yet such virtuous consequentialism might prompt a course of inaction, regardless of whether the matter is urgent, because policymakers have to ensure their interventions satisfy abstract tests of legal competence, last resort and just cause (by which time the humanitarian tragedy it may have averted has transpired). Alternatively, the axiom may require a too precipitate rush to action, regardless of circumstance and timing, 'brushing aside the sovereignty of the offending state when confronted with gross abuses of human rights'.[126] Acting axiomatically, then, ignores the complex, contingent realities of a particular case with inevitable sub-optimal consequences.

Contemporary IR scholarship's anachronistic treatment of reason of state and its dismissal of classical prudential realism as amoral misunderstands the character of its situational ethics. Such practical counsel assumes a mixed prudential stance to address the predicament of rule in a contingent and uncertain world. An updated prudential manual of advice would provide not virtuous consequential axioms, like Fisher's, but general rules and examples addressing specific cases.

In this context, Edmund Burke's political writings, rather than cosmopolitan ethics, offer a more interesting attempt to apply classical and early modern prudence to a modern, revolutionary age pregnant with danger as well as progressive possibility. In his *Reflections on the Revolution in France* (1790), Burke considered scientific theories of government 'an affront to the practice of prudence'. Rationalism in government was 'a computing principle; adding, subcontracting, multiplying, and dividing, more and not metaphysically or mathematically, true moral denominations'.[127]

In 1796, he condemned the government of William Pitt when it countenanced a peace treaty with revolutionary France after three years of war. Burke argued 'the rules and definitions of prudence can rarely be exact; never universal'. In his view, the idea of seeking a settlement with a regime that had murdered its king was an example of 'false' or 'narrow' prudence. His *Letters on a Regicide Peace* (1796) bemoaned what he saw as a desperation for peace that came from a 'false reptile prudence, the result not of caution but of fear', the result of 'abject distrust of ourselves' and 'an extravagant admiration of the enemy'.[128]

Burke, following earlier writing in the reason of state idiom, recognized no set rules in international politics. Decisions had to be made on the basis of the situation at hand. 'Matters of prudence are under the dominion of circumstances, and not of logical analogies', he wrote, 'It is absurd to take it otherwise'. 'There are many things which men do not approve, that they must do to avoid a greater evil', he also observed. 'To argue from thence, that they are to act in the same manner in all cases, is turning necessity into a law'.[129]

Among the circumstances in which Britain found itself in the late eighteenth century was that it was a great power. Among the contingent factors that states had to consider when choosing between peace and war was their status and prestige among their peers and competitors. Burke understood that small states would often be forced to compromise when presented with superior force. But a great state also had a reputation to maintain which meant that excessive caution could damage its long-term security.

Prudence required an awareness of how others perceived you. Burke differentiated between great powers and second order ones, 'small truckling states' where:

> a timely compromise with power has often been the means, and the only means, of drawing out their puny existence. But a great state is too much envied, too much dreaded, to find safety in humiliation. To be secure, it must be respected. Power, and eminence, and consideration, are things not to be begged. They must be commanded: and they who supplicate for mercy from others can never hope for justice thro' themselves.[130]

Rationalist and virtue consequentialist calculations would stress the costs of war and the moral dangers therein. A truly prudent counsel, Burke argued, following Thucydides and Machiavelli, should not enfeeble pre-existing power. After Burke, those who emphasized the importance of prudence in British diplomacy saw it mediating between sentimentalism and passion in international affairs and a too rationalist calculation that stressed the paramountcy of self-interest. Henry Temple, Viscount Palmerston, argued that the policy of Britain – 'apart from questions which involve her own particular interests, political or commercial' – should also be 'the champion of justice and right'. But his counsel was that it was necessary to pursue that course 'with moderation and prudence, not becoming the Quixote of the world'.[131]

As Michael Oakeshott later wrote, political virtues such as prudence are best understood as 'historic compounds' rather than time-bound absolutes. Unlike the language of science, ambiguity permeates the modern vocabulary of politics as these compound words adapted over the last five hundred years to changing political and economic fortunes.[132]

Ambiguity particularly affects the realm of statecraft where a historic compound like 'prudence' assumes different forms in mutable conditions. It requires an awareness of political status, as well as power and circumstance. Part of the modern Western political predicament now, as it was in seventeenth century Europe, stems from the fact 'that it would be difficult to find a single word that is not double tongued or a single conception which is not double edged'.[133] This is particularly the case with keywords in our political vocabulary like 'justice', 'democracy', 'equality', 'freedom', 'rights', and, of course, prudence.

As Thucydides observed, prudence for the Melians was very different to that of Athens. Small 'truckling' states like Singapore hedging against a rising China must necessarily, as Mahbubani contends, adopt a prudent practice that focuses on modest goals such as limited order, tranquillity and accommodation. Its inward logic is an instrumental conception of international morality coupled with reasonable scepticism toward any radical, transformational design of world politics. In this mood prudence is primarily about restraint.

However, depending on circumstances, a statesman animated by *virtù* might not attend to 'the benefits of time' or strategic patience.[134]

When such political actors 'make mistakes they are of ambition and not of sloth. Develop the strength to do bold things', Machiavelli cautioned those virtuous republics seeking to maintain their status in the world. [135]

Prudent counsel then, might be adapted and applied differently to cases that trouble the conscience of the international community whether it involves Putin's assertiveness in Eastern Europe, the rise of China or the ethical and political implications of intervening or not in Syria's internal war. In an era of political turmoil, a contemporary version of Lipsius' *Politica* would advise leaders of Western democracies that prudential statecraft requires a situational morality that directs action to 'the public good'.[136] Ethical flexibility applies particularly in the international sphere where unstable emotions and distorted images often shape global public opinion. Prudent counsel would also recognize the gullibility and fecklessness of the masses in an age of social and mass media. This constrains the modern democratic state's ability to conduct international relations. To sustain the national interest, the non-neutral state, in these circumstances, requires a *prudentia mixta* that responds to the power shifts in an interconnected but fragmented global order. 'Because what we call Prudence [here] is in reality…changeable in every respect',[137] it has to be, to cope with the instability in international politics where to practice 'strict moral correctness' may actually harm the common interest.

Prudent policy instead requires a mixture of expedience and dissimulation to maintain peace and stability. Indeed, political leaders who do not know how to dissimulate do not know how to rule. In the 'troubled sea' of politics, keeping the ship of state afloat requires 'clever planning' and must occasionally depart 'from virtue or the laws'.[138] In difficult cases, therefore, prudent policy necessarily deviates from international norms.[139]

Whilst political action requires both virtue and prudence, it is prudence that must direct conduct.[140] It is prudence that offers insight into the statecraft necessary to adjudicate cases of war or peace. In this, a knowledge of international and political history, together with diplomatic experience, rather than the prevailing legal-ethicist approach, leads to practical outcomes. Prudence 'regulates the present, foresees the future, and remembers the past'.[141] History was the source or resource from which 'political and prudential choosing flows'.[142]

Somewhat problematically, however, in the post-Cold War era western democracies, political elites and international organizations have studiously neglected political and diplomatic history, with predictable consequences.[143] Inattention to history leads to a failure to appreciate, for example, the long term strategic interests of rival powers in a condition of anarchy, like Russia and China, and their mutual spheres of regional interest.

By contrast, the historically conscious statesmen of early modern and Cold War Europe were conscious of the fact that framing policies in terms of abstract ideals could lead to a disastrous loss of authority. The 'pretence' of moral absolutism in such cases may only reignite 'the fires of strife'.[144] In this vein, prudent statecraft would be acutely aware of the historic difficulty in achieving a balance of power in Europe and might have advised restraint before expanding the North Atlantic Treaty Organization into Eastern Europe after the fall of the Berlin Wall, as well as caution in addressing Russia's geopolitical interest in the Crimea and the Black Sea.

Prudent counsel to a president or prime minister faced with difficult policy decisions in the Middle East, Eastern Europe or Pacific Asia would recognize that statecraft requires what is 'necessary in practice'. In such circumstances Western statesmen should avoid hyperbole or 'what is beautiful to say'.[145] In troubled and conflicted times, moreover, the ignorance of the conduct of war, exhibited by Western political elites and their advisers, would astonish prudent state counsellors from Machiavelli to Burke. Neglecting military prudence could only lead to the inept use of force and inevitable political failure.

Ultimately the democratic conduct of foreign policy requires far greater sensitivity to the particular character of hard cases and the need to adjust policy casuistically to changing circumstances. Such an approach, as writers from Tacitus to Machiavelli and Burke observed, recognizes the mystery or 'arcana' of statecraft and its distinctive and differential ethical practice. A mixed prudential combination of reason of state with the Roman disposition to active political morality that defends the common interest, rather than Fisher's abstract virtue consequentialism, might more fruitfully address the issues raised by our 'troubled condition of confusion and change'.[146]

From a contemporary prudential perspective, a democratic state, founded on the political consent of its diverse citizenry, conceives domestic and foreign policy in terms of advancing the national interest. This may, in certain circumstances, require strategically necessary, but not necessarily morally virtuous, interventions overseas. At the same time, it may require precaution, avoiding questionable entanglements in wars of choice. Given that early modern (and modern)[147] political realism eschews an abstract rationalist approach to foreign policy and instead prefers historically grounded and prudential counsel, how should it address a case like the rise and fall of an Islamic State which continues to threaten the stability of a region close to Europe, but which increasingly seems less strategically relevant to the United States?

Reason of State and the Middle East, Europe's New, Old Problem

The Islamic State's strategic theorist Abu Bakr Naji observed that the West, like Islam, is not a monolith. The *kufr* West is 'vitiated by self-interest'. In *The Management of Savagery: The Most Critical Stage Through Which the Umma Will Pass* (2006),[148] Naji quotes Palmerston's dictum that states have no permanent friends, only permanent interests, to support his contention that the West is friable. The purpose of violence, whether in Europe or in Raqqa, as Naji explained, was both to facilitate this fragmentation and secure the borders of the Islamic State.

A prudent statesman would recognize, and take seriously, rather than dismiss the tactics and strategic vision that the Islamic State advanced between 2014 and 2018, and develop the means to contain and defeat it, and not just on the battlefield. IS strategy was, in many respects, realist and not in the least amenable to those European policy elites who promoted abstract norms via a communicatory, cosmopolitan global public sphere. The prudent state and its diplomatic corps would evolve a tactical and strategic response to countermand Islamism that would necessarily differ from those devised to contain a revisionist Russia or a rising China.

In the context of the Middle East, a cursory acquaintance with post-Ottoman history and the bitter experience of failed interventions since 1990 would counsel against intervention to advance Western ideological preferences. With the rise of Islamic State, Western policy underwent something of a *volte face*, briefly making common cause with Iran. This also seemed imprudent given that Iran seeks regional hegemony, antagonizing, in the process, the Sunni majority states of Turkey, Saudi Arabia and the Gulf, who although inimical to IS considered it a useful buffer against Iranian expansion.

Treaties with Iran intensified religious and regional cleavages rather than resolving them. Furthering the regional ambitions of a potentially nuclear-armed Iran is thus inimical to the interests of the West. Both the US and European interest in the Middle East is perhaps best served by stability rather than democracy promotion. In retrospect, and somewhat paradoxically, this is precisely what an autocratic Baathist Iraq under Saddam achieved, balancing, as it did, Iran's expansionist, post-1979 revolutionary theocracy.

The recreation of balance in the Middle East will require both patience, fortune and involve some strange bedfellows as well as a practiced dissimulation. Moreover, given the regional ambitions of Iran, Turkey, and Russia, a counsel of prudence would also recognize that instability in the Middle East raises Europe-wide security concerns that cannot be mitigated by a policy of indifference.[149] IS attracted jihadist recruits from Europe. Generation jihad in the diaspora communities of the West found in the new caliphate the equivalent of the utopian counter-culture movement of the late 1960s that radicalized a generation of Western students. In the jihadist case it possesses the added attraction of licensing transgressive violence that not only contributes to regional instability, but also threatens the integrity of open societies like France and the United Kingdom, in the form of homegrown or returning jihadist fighters. A prudent counsel would recognize that external conditions affect civil peace.

Prudent thinkers like Machiavelli and Thomas Hobbes considered peace and stability – today we would say national security – a primary political concern. In this regard, minorities who reject the state's foreign policy have, in democracies, the right to dissent, but not the right to decapitate fellow citizens in the name of a transnational ideocracy. Moreover, if citizens of a democracy commit themselves to an enemy entity like the Islamic State by joining its jihad, they necessarily forfeit the rights of political citizenship that assumes consent to a social contract as the condition for enjoying those rights in a democracy and the security that it affords.

In the late sixteenth century, the early modern English state faced a transnational politico-religious threat and a fifth column within, not dissimilar to that facing the modern state. Confronting foreign invasion and internal dissent, privy counsellors to the crown like Francis Walsingham, Robert Cecil, and Robert Dudley, Earl of Leicester, who studied Tacitus, read Machiavelli and briefly employed Lipsius, expanded the treason statute and imposed tests of allegiance on those subjects whose loyalty to the Elizabethan political settlement seemed questionable.[150] Only as IS's strategy and that of its Western adherents became transparent did the UK government announce measures to close extremist mosques and require those seeking a visa to enter the UK 'to sign a declaration that they will respect British values'.

The Muslim Council of Britain and the Islamic Human Rights Commission considered even these limited measures aimed at promoting internal stability 'a shameless expression of hate and bigotry'.[151] Yet, in an anxiety-prone, durable disorder where global interconnectedness by no means presages a greater sense of international community, a secular political democracy minimally requires a shared public morality to sustain the national interest expressed through domestic legislation. The rules of civil association must bind all citizens equally.

Modern democracies may also require an active foreign policy to secure their interests and values over time. Neither indifference, nor an abstract international legal regime that, while theoretically open to intervention, sets unrealistic abstract standards of consistency, addresses the complexity of the Western democracies' besetting predicament.

A return to prudential calculation adapted to increasingly volatile inter-state relations, not evidently amenable to international legal axioms, by no means guarantees order. In real time, as Lawrence Freedman observes, policy makers function in a fallible realm full of vicissitudes, where '[c]onsistently high strategic performance is extremely hard' to attain, let alone maintain.[152] The search for a grand master strategy is therefore as elusive as the quest for grand utopian schemes of cosmopolitan justice. Unlike normative grand theorizing, however, prudent statecraft adjusts morality and law as circumstance and interest dictates.

As a consequence, the state's right to self-defence determines any strategic appreciation of what constitutes the national interest and how it can be maintained. In the disordered, neo-medieval world of states, regions, para-states, failed states and transnational networks, policies based on an abstract ideal of an international community promoting supposedly universal norms of conduct cannot achieve coherence, let alone order. Inter-state political diplomacy requires instead a greater appreciation of history, experience and past precedent rather than abstract, rationalist commitments to a historicist teleology. As the Anglo-Australian political philosopher Kenneth Minogue once observed, 'reflection on prudence reveals that all virtues do not constitute a single coherent system of the moral life'. In fact, 'exhibiting some virtues can be incompatible with acting on others'. The man of honour, for instance, cannot always be prudent. 'Prudence is a joker in the moral pack and its business on occasions, is to trump its fellow virtues'.[153]

Trump, Prudence and the End of Liberal Order

Echoing this view, the liberal commentator David Brooks asked in early 2017, 'If you could give Donald Trump the gift of a single trait to help his presidency, what would it be'? Brooks' thoughts initially turned to prudence. 'Prudence is the ability to govern oneself with the use of reason. It is the ability to suppress one's impulses for the sake of long-term goals', he explained, 'my basic thought was that a prudent President Trump wouldn't spend his mornings angrily tweeting his resentments'.[154] The French philosopher André Comte-Sponville, Brooks noted, wrote that 'Prudence is what differentiates action from impulse and heroes from hotheads'.[155]

Prudence does not immediately spring to mind when assessing Trump's foreign policy since 2016. This notwithstanding, one notable feature of his arrival in the Oval Office was a situational awareness that America's international status had declined. He told *Playboy* in

1990 that 'People need ego, whole nations need ego. I think our country needs more ego, because it is being ripped off so badly by our so-called allies'.[156]

Ultimately, those looking for prudence in the Trump administration are probably better served not by looking to the Prince himself, but those whose role it is to offer counsel. The history of prudence suggests that the challenges posed by such a role are both practical and ethical. Within the Trump national security team, prior to their departure, officials as various as former National Security Advisor H.R. McMaster, and former Secretary of State Rex Tillerson all advised the need for greater prudence in addressing issues as various as Obama's approval of the Iran nuclear framework treaty, addressing North Korea, and responding to China's growing economic and geopolitical assertiveness. Michael Anton, the director of strategic communications at the National Security Council, also used the term. Acknowledging that military action against North Korea was unlikely, and would have dire consequences, he told *Politico* that 'For reasons of prudence, it can't be taken off the table at a juncture like this'.

Anton questioned what he considered the Washington national security establishment's uncritical fidelity to the idea of liberal international order. In a Burkean vein, he argued that powerful nations had to strike a balance between 'contempt' and 'prestige'. Being held in contempt damaged a great power's ability to influence. The antidote was to be respected and 'even a little bit feared'. Too much could be a problem too, he warned, which was why prudence should be the handmaid of prestige. 'A delicate balance is therefore always required, which means prudence is always required'.[157]

Unlikely as it may sound, then, prudence circulated, albeit somewhat briefly, as a working concept amongst the various factions within the Trump White House. In revisionist times that require flexibility, prudence appeals to those vying for influence and seeking to make America, if not great, then at least worthy of respect. In world politics, as Machiavelli observed, this requires fear, rather than love. Given that prudence is a term that can be used with considerable flexibility, moreover, one suspects its precise definition is, like red lines and much else besides, open to interpretation as well as skilful presentation.

'To know that nations are subject to the moral law is one thing', but to pretend to know with certainty, as progressive enthusiasts for global justice do, 'what is good and evil in the relations among nations is quite another'.[158] As the accuracy of Hans Morgenthau's observation becomes daily more apparent, it might also be worth considering how the political democratic state should prudently conduct itself in uncertain times. It is to this that we now turn.

9

THE REVENGE OF POLITICS AND THE SEARCH FOR ORDER

As we saw in chapter 5, the creative destruction that the financial crisis and big tech unleashed created a political and economic climate increasingly inimical to liberal, secular, progressive, or socially just outcomes. The financial crisis and its aftermath witnessed an inversion of Rawlsian new liberal principles and a redistribution of wealth and other social goods justified, unintentionally or otherwise, by improving the position of those who were best off. Global interconnectedness only deepened an emerging divide between an elite *internationale* and the nation state bound masses. New liberal commitments to abstract social justice at home and humanitarian intervention abroad fuelled the problem of violent jihadism. The shibboleth of multiculturalism activated a non-negotiable politics of abstract group identity. *Soi-disant* victims demanding state compensation for their various, often historic, grievances replaced the classical and modern understanding of a civil association where citizens of a state enjoy equal rights.

The neutral, new liberal, techno-managerial, postmodern state now adjudicates oppressions according to a quotient of perceived suffering – a misery, as opposed to a felicific, calculus – that requires not equal, but different treatment. State imposed formulae accord the victimized group 'privileges over the majority', as well as over other (less oppressed) minorities.[1] The juridical pursuit of social justice facilitated a despotism of the minorities in areas of public policy and a condition of clientelist dependence for the rest. Tutelary authoritarianism was not what the third way intended to be the final state at the end of history. But the obsessive concern with social justice and the suffering situation over time eroded the concepts of prudential politics, individual liberty, and the acceptance of incompatible values without judgment. In its place, mainstream political parties, in accordance with new liberal and post-national fashion, oligarchically managed the servile masses in depth and detail according to their own progressively intrusive iron laws.

Attempts to give legal force to incommensurable values and cultures in circumstances of deep pluralism were always likely to provoke fragmentation and evoke both more intolerance and more violent responses. As Ortega y Gasset wrote in the 1930s, 'the desertion of the directing minorities is always found on the reverse side of the rebellion of the masses'.[2] This is what has happened in terms of the emergence of populism and the growing fanaticism of the alternative or 'alt' right, and what Bernard-Henri Lévy termed the post-progressive 'zombie left'.[3] The inchoate revolt of the masses, driven by social media and the fallout from the financial crisis, has encouraged an ideological return to race-based and primitive socialist visions of utopia achieved, if necessary, through emancipatory violence.[4] The economic and geopolitical exposure of the illusion of progress, its subsequent dissolution, and the legacy it has bequeathed in terms of the decline of the nation state and its traditional political institutions created a climate where new ideologies emerged and old ones that had never lost a subterranean presence in Europe's dark heart flourished once more.

Providence, Progress, Political Religion and the Rise of Transnational Social Movements

Eric Voegelin, the Austrian philosopher who fled the Third Reich in the wake of the *Anschluss* in 1938, argued that the ideological fanaticism of the Nazis was not only a moral and political mistake, but also a spiritual deformation. More precisely, so far as the political religions of the twentieth century — Fascism, Stalinism, Maoism and Islamism —

are concerned, the meaning or substance of religious phenomena moved from a spiritual concern with transcending the mundane world towards the realization of imaginary fantasies of immanent apocalypse. This was evidently the case with IS's recent chiliastic pursuit of the millennial caliphate.

However, in the secular West similar fantasies are not 'always recognized for what they are because the image of an earthly condition of perfected humanity'[5] was, in Europe before 1990, expressed in rational, scientific, or pseudo-scientific language. Only the West, which ironically now seems embarked on a suicide mission, killed God, and did it twice for good measure, once symbolically and on the cross, and more recently via the Enlightenment project to transform the world through progress, secularism and science, rendering religion either reasonable or irrelevant.

This evolution of European rationalist thought from the nineteenth century has a long history. Voegelin traced its origins to earlier Christian hermetic and medieval Gnostic heresies. In Voegelin's treatment, modern progress, and its basis in Kantian, Hegelian, Whig or Marxist philosophies of history, is really a rationalized version of God's providence. Whereas Augustine in *The City of God Against the Pagans*[6] and later Thomist thought recognised an eschatological purpose to world history, God's foreknowledge of its direction, its teleology, was not revealed to man.

This truth was unsatisfactory to the more adventurous mind. Gnostic thinkers like the Cistercian monk Joachim of Fiore (c. 1135–1202), the Anthony Giddens of the twelfth century, proposed instead three ages of developing spiritual growth: the Old Testament era; the revelation of Christ; and an anticipated third age, which would realize the kingdom of the Holy Spirit. Joachimite thinking subsequently influenced a variety of medieval and early modern chiliastic movements[7] seeking to realize the *teleion* of the age of perfection, or the rule of Christ over the kingdom of the blessed.[8]

These early attempts to 'immanentize the eschaton', in other words, to bring the 'beyond' into the here and now, assumed a secular, progressive and philosophic clothing at the Enlightenment, and Kant, Hegel and later, Marxist and twentieth century post-Rawlsian liberal progressive thought, explored its implications. Secularized, historicist thought assumed that the past was unenlightened, the present confused and corrupt, and that what Kant termed the 'eschatological hope' of enlightenment would be achieved through the blessings of scientific rationalism.

In Voegelin's view, this style of thinking deformed the Christian pursuit of salvation and accounts for many ideological forms of contemporary political religion and intellectual deformation. In doing so it disguised the quest for meaning or the urge to find alternative ways of satisfying this existential human need.[9] Translated into an ideology, the Gnostic impulse is inherently Manichean, and sometimes violent. Moreover, the end community to which the ideologist aspires has natural enemies, notably those who accept the world as it is, with all its messy pluralism.

It was a version of this sensibility and the potential for the realization of global social justice at the end of history in 1989 that preoccupied the progressive third way version of the Joachimite three ages. The fact that this vision was frustrated post-Iraq and after the financial crisis of 2008 accounts for the current crisis in progressive thinking. Yet the desire for an emancipatory epiphany remains.

Consequently, the populist social movements of both left and right that have emerged since 9/11 promulgate political religions that, whilst renouncing God, nevertheless pursue the immanentization of a perfected utopia. This is the case with both race-based and anti-capitalist social movements that pursue what Ernest Sternberg terms 'world purificationism'.[10] In this chapter, we shall discuss the commonalities between the return of these repressed or obscured political religions, as history and the search for order recommenced, after 2016, before examining the possible range of Western responses and their implications for the future of a limited, secular, liberal order.

The Extreme or Alt Right after 9/11: Cultural Nationalism and Political Activism

Emilio Gentile observed that totalitarian ideologies of a Marxist-Leninist or a National Socialist provenance attribute 'sacred status to an earthly concept', whether that concept is the race, the nation, the proletariat or, in recent radical environmental extinction literature, the planet itself.[11] This sacralization of the political provides the space for an apocalyptic clash between the world waiting to be born and the doomed, decadent quotidian order that resists it. The ideology unmasks a decadent past, a divided present about to perish that reveals the opportunity for emancipatory change, and the immanent realization of a purified third age.[12] The cosmic melodrama further legitimates those possessing the ideological key to history to use force to instantiate it. The politically religious mind considers violence, as we saw in chapter 4, both purgative and purificatory.

Since the nineteenth century, all modern revolutionary creeds have scripted some version of this violent melodrama. The secular political religions, Leninism, Maoism, and, in its more intransigently empathetic transnational moods, Olympian progressivism, focus their ideological gaze on human emancipation. By contrast, fascist and race-based ideologies emphasize the *palingenesis* or rebirth of the nation or race through a purgative process of ethnic cleansing. Exemplified in Third Reich ideology and practice, fascist political religions also share the sense of living at an imminent turning point in history when the dominance of the bankrupt forces of an old order, then, as now, a messy, pluralist, liberal democratic one, give way to a new era where an activist national identity triumphantly reasserts itself.[13]

From this perspective, violence is necessary to overcome national degeneracy and eliminate the parasitic and decadent liberal and financial elites who have betrayed the nation. This apocalyptic, racial vision informs white supremacist thought. Despite the collapse of European fascism in 1945, it exercised a minority appeal in Western democracies in the early decades of the Cold War, the era of European decolonization and widespread fear of international communism.

After 9/11, however, palingenetic ideologies have proved increasingly attractive to an alienated, working class, white male demographic in Europe, Australasia, and the US. As the era of post-war social democratic consensus in the West[14] gave way to speculative, millennial capitalism without capital, the ideology offered a seductive solution to the alienation experienced by white male millennials. This inchoate new precariat 'class', in low paid, semi-skilled work on short-term contracts exposed to the vagaries of the Electronic Herd, immigration, and the gig economy of the global marketplace, derived comfort from ancient and not so ancient eugenic fantasies.

The precariat was the human residue left by the decline of traditional, blue-collar industries, as multinational corporations moved offshore and reshaped the global economy after 1990. In developed Western democracies this alienated demographic became more evident as the financial crisis deepened between 2008 and 2016. As unemployment levels, especially amongst young, male workers in Europe and the US, reached historic heights, the white male population in declining hillbilly manufacturing towns from Ohio to the North of England and the French *périphérie* offered a fertile breeding ground for ethno-nationalist extremism.[15] Networks, movements and parties committed to this white nationalist or white supremacist alt right ideology claim that the cosmopolitan, liberal ruling elites have abandoned their national cultures and the white race in favour of international or regional arrangements like the United Nations or the European Union. At the same time, from this paranoid perspective, a transnational business and political elite, the 'Davoisie', exploit the machinery of managerial bureaucracies, constitutions and courts to enslave a once free, Aryan nation.[16]

In the US, this racial paranoia assumed material form in movements like the Ku Klux Klan (KKK), whose origins date from the era of Reconstruction in the southern United States after 1865, but whose clan organizational structure revived in the 1960s to oppose the movement for civil rights. KKK members shared links with the Aryan Nations Church of Jesus Christ – Christians who felt that the government 'no longer represents the White Race in this Nation'.[17] RAND Corporation described the Aryan Nations churches of the 1980s as 'the first truly nationwide terrorist organization' in the United States.[18] The 1960s also witnessed the foundation of Lincoln Rockwell's American Nazi Party. After Rockwell's assassination in 1967, the party mutated into the National Socialist White People's Party, before settling on its current title, the National Alliance, in 1974.

Alongside such outright racist groups, there also emerged in the 1980s various state-based militia movements, associated with the right-wing *Posse Comitatus*, that treated attempts to restrict gun ownership and the imposition of federal law at the expense of states' rights as evidence of an international conspiracy against the values of the American revolution and the 1776 Declaration of Independence.

Prior to 9/11, anti-Semitism defined these movements. They termed the tyranny they confronted the Zionist Occupied Government (ZOG).[19] It was the role of the various state militias to resist this federally imposed, Zionist tyranny. Militias adopted both a libertarian and a Christian, white fundamentalist rhetoric and were organized and trained for the prospect of an imminent Armageddon.[20]

National Alliance leader William Luther Pierce outlined the vision of the coming, final, race war in *The Turner Diaries* (1978). Set in 2099, the diaries recount Earl Turner's guerrilla insurgency to overthrow the US federal government and exterminate inferior races, first in America and then across the globe. In 1993, the Southern Poverty Law Center described the diaries as 'the bible of the racist right'.[21]

The fictional Turner inspired Robert Jay Mathews to form *The Order* or *Silent Brotherhood*, which undertook a series of robberies and bombings between 1983 and 1984, culminating in the murder of talk show host Alan Berg. Mathews died in a shoot-out with the FBI in December 1984. Pierce drew on these events to develop the character of *Hunter* (1989). In this work, Oscar Yeager represented the first fictional evocation of a distinctive, new, postmodern terrorist type – the lone wolf.[22]

The paranoid style informing US right-wing extremism meant that white supremacist and militia groups interpreted all federal responses to their activities as part of an international conspiracy to eliminate the white race. Thus the FBI's siege of Christian Identity survivalist Randy Weaver's farm at Ruby Ridge, North Idaho in 1992, followed by that of David Koresh's Branch Dravidian compound in Waco, Texas, between February and April 1993, which culminated in the death of seventy-six sect members, afforded further proof, if proof were needed, of ZOG tyranny.

From the white supremacist perspective these events necessitated and justified a strategy of asymmetric leaderless resistance and lone wolf attacks on federal agencies to counter its evolving despotism. In the 1980s, Louis Beam, a Vietnam veteran, emerged as the leading extreme or alt right strategic thinker. He served as both a state leader of David Duke's Knights of the Ku Klux Klan and as the Aryan Nation's

Ambassador at Large. His thinking influenced the actions of lone actor terrorists like Timothy McVeigh, a veteran of the first Iraq war. It was Beam who creatively linked clean skin, lone actor violence to a wider strategy. Beam's 'concept of leaderless resistance' was 'a fundamental departure in theories of organization'. Based upon the guerrilla cell organization, it:

> doesnothaveany central control or direction... Utilizing the Leaderless Resistance concept, all individuals and groups operate independently of each other, and never report to a central headquarters or single leader for direction or instruction, as would those who belong to a typical pyramid organization.[23]

This thinking inspired McVeigh to bomb the Alfred. P. Murrah Federal Building in Oklahoma City in 1995. McVeigh's action claimed 165 lives. It was the most serious terrorist attack on US soil prior to 9/11. McVeigh and his associates sympathized with the militia and patriot movements, but acted outside any formal cell structure.

In the course of the 1990s, websites like *stormfront.org* promulgated the race mythology and the strategic thinking of the US white right to an international audience. Started by Klan leader David Duke in 1990, by 2000 it was the most visited hate site on the Internet. As with IS, the new social media, somewhat serendipitously, offered a critical networked organizing and propaganda tool for promulgating the post-9/11 proliferation of white supremacist purificatory ideas and Beam's phantom cell structure of leaderless resistance both in the US and across Europe and Australasia.

European Disunion and 'Patriotic' Extremism

Although identity and race-based nationalism never died out in Western Europe after 1945, right-wing nationalist and neo-fascist social movements have seen a surge in popular support across Western Europe since the mid-1990s and particularly since the 2008 financial crisis and its Eurozone aftermath. Germany, Austria, Italy, and Spain, states that experienced fascist regimes between the 1920s and 1970s, have, since the 1990s, witnessed the re-emergence of extreme nationalist political parties informed by myths of racial supremacy.

Whilst the German *Strafgesetzbuch* (criminal code) forbade neo-Nazi material and the 'use of symbols of unconstitutional organizations', this failed to prevent the emergence of the extreme right Nationalist Party (NPD), which captured 9.2 per cent of the vote in the Saxony state elections in 2004. Attempts to ban the party have thus far failed.[24] Meanwhile, Germany has also witnessed the emergence of an illegal neo-Nazi movement, the National Socialist Underground (NSU), allegedly responsible for a number of murders of migrant workers and gay men since the mid-1990s.[25]

The tentative European Union reaction to the migrant and refugee crisis in a Europe without borders in 2015, combined with the convoluted response to the financial crisis, created conditions ripe for a revival of apocalyptic nativist and 'identitarian' movements. After 2014, the rise of Islamic State in the Middle East and the civil war in Syria, which dramatically increased migrant flows into Europe, along with IS inspired jihadist attacks in Paris in January and November 2015, in Berlin in December 2016 and in Brussels in 2016, boosted far right nationalist and anti-immigration social movements across Europe.

These protean white supremacist social movements with their palingenetic zealotry should be distinguished from the illiberal populist parties that sought to revive, by constitutional means, nation states founded in a common, but particular, culture that the progressive universalism of the ever closer European Union project works to dissolve.

Since 2015, however, this distinction has often been difficult to maintain in practice as the burgeoning populist reaction to the European post-national project gave electoral ballast to new parties seeking, legitimately, to undo the pan-European progressive orthodoxy. By 2016, the populist nationalist, anti-European, Alternative für Deutschland (AfD) party, founded in 2013, had established a significant electoral presence in Landtag elections in Saxony-Anhalt (where it polled 24.2 per cent of the vote), Baden-Württemberg, and Rhineland-Palatinate. In 2017 federal elections, AfD achieved 12.6 per cent of the vote and ninety-four seats in the Bundestag. It had rapidly established itself as the largest opposition party to Merkel's increasingly fragile, grand coalition government. The AfD also established links with the Austrian Freedom Party and the anti-European UK Independence Party (UKIP), which shared versions of its nationalist ideology.

At the same time, the ethno-nationalist and anti-Muslim social movement *Patriotische Europäer Gegen die Islamisierung des Abenlandes* (PEGIDA – Patriotic Europeans against the Islamization of the West), founded in Dresden in 2014, was an openly racist movement, prepared to engage in violent street demonstrations to assert its anti-migrant and anti-Muslim stance. Its appeal grew in the wake of assaults on German women perpetrated, it appeared, by North African migrants, in Cologne on New Year's Eve 2015. By 2016, PEGIDA had established a presence in the Netherlands, Belgium, Denmark, and the UK.

The period from the end of the Cold War also saw rising electoral support for nationalist political parties in Austria. In the 1999 general election, the Austrian Freedom Party (FPO, *Freiheitliche Partei Österreichs*), which emphasized the primordial bond of *Heimat* (homeland), captured twenty-seven per cent of the vote and briefly shared government with the Conservative People's Party. Like 'patriotic' parties elsewhere in Europe, the FPO reaped an electoral boost from the chaotic European Union response to the Syrian refugee crisis. The FPO polled 20.5 per cent of the legislative vote in 2013, and in the presidential election of 2016 its candidate, Norbert Hofer, led the first round of polling. In 2017, the FPO took twenty-six per cent of the electoral vote and entered into a coalition government with the Conservative Austrian People's party (OVP, *Österreichische Volks Partei*). After a corruption scandal in 2019, the FPO left the coalition but its electoral support has seemingly not substantially diminished.[26]

Meanwhile, in Italy, after the fall of Benito Mussolini's Fascist regime in 1944, far-right parties were never absent from the political scene. The neo-fascist Italian Social Movement (MSI) dates from 1946. Constitutional changes after 1995 saw the formation of parties canvassing a return to Mussolini-era, fascist-style politics. These included the Northern League (*Lega Nord per l'Independenza della Padania*, branded simply as *Lega* from 2018) formed in 1991, the National Alliance formed in 1995, and the *Forza Nuova* or New Force party, founded in 1997. These faction-prone parties periodically formed alliances, and participated in coalition governments of the right with Silvio Berlusconi's *Forza Italia* and, after 2008, with Berlusconi's

People of Freedom Party (*Il Popolo della Libertà*) (PdL). Mussolini's granddaughter, Alessandra, sits in the Italian parliament as a PdL representative, whilst National Alliance leader Gianfranco Fini served as President of the Chamber of Deputies between 2008 and 2011.

After 2014, the combined effect of the migration and financial crises has, as elsewhere, boosted right wing populism along with rehabilitating Benito Mussolini's reputation and palingenetic ideas of national rebirth, now promoted by his granddaughter Alessandra, 'the mouth from the South'. After 2009, Italy also witnessed the rise of a new purely anti-establishment social movement, founded by a former comedian, Beppe Grillo, the Five Star Movement (*Movimento 5 Stelle*). In the 2018 general election, the Eurosceptic, 'antipartytocracy' Five Star movement received thirty-seven per cent of the popular vote and entered into a coalition government with the anti-migrant League led by Matteo Salvini. Salvini's government took a populist stand against immigration, turning back boats crossing the Mediterranean and resisting European Union pressure to adopt austerity programmes to deal with bank debt to restore Italy's fragile finances. Despite being a founder member of the European Community in 1956, the new government demonstrated Italy's growing alienation from the Union, establishing close ties with Russia and, in a move fraught with geopolitical significance, signing a memorandum of understanding with China in March 2019. The coalition collapsed in August 2019. Salvini resigned and, in September, the Five Star Movement formed a new and equally unstable government with the centre left Democrats (PD Partito Democratico).

Spain, which experienced Europe's longest fascist dictatorship – the Franco regime lasted from 1936 to 1975 – also played host to a distinctive variety of populism. As in Italy, populism, of both the left and right, responded to the devastating effects of the Eurozone crisis. The depth of the financial crisis reopened constitutional, class, and identity questions that dated back to the Civil War of the 1930s. In 2012, Spain's unemployment rate of 24.4 per cent stood at twice the Eurozone average. The experience of the Madrid train attack (2004) and the inept European and mainstream political response both to the decade long 'great Spanish depression' and the movement for Catalan independence witnessed the erosion of Spain's fragile democracy.

The 'illegal' referendum on Catalan independence in 2017 led to the banning of separatist parties and the trial and imprisonment of their leaders.

The potential for the further fragmentation of Spain also saw new populist parties demanding the reassertion of a centralized, strong Spanish state after decades of democratic decentralization. Deemed responsible for the economic and constitutional crisis, both the centre-left Socialist Party and conservative People's Party lost support and political credibility. The emergence of new populist parties like the socialist *Podemos*, dating from 2014, and the right-wing *Ciudadanos* party threatened the established two-party system that had dominated Spain's democratic politics after Franco's demise. In general elections held in 2015 and 2016, *Podemos* secured over 20 per cent of the vote. Meanwhile, the anti-Islamic *Vox* party, formed in 2013 to revive a fascist understanding of Spanish integrity, won twelve seats in Andalusia's regional elections and ten per cent of the popular vote in the April 2019 general election. Indicative of the new European electoral volatility in the era of the great recession, the election of April 2019, the third held since 2016, also saw the Socialist Party reviving its electoral credibility under the leadership of Pedro Sanchez. The Socialist Party secured the most number of seats in the *Cortes Generales*, but remained unable to form a coalition government in the politically fragmented parliament. In November 2019, Spain went to the polls for the fourth time in four years. The result merely confirmed Spain's deepening political divide. Vox emerged as the third largest party with 15 per cent of the vote and the parties of the left entered into an uncertain coalition.

Elsewhere in Europe, Jean-Marie Le Pen's *Front National* (National Front) (FN) dates from 1972 and emerged from a number of militant right-wing groups opposed to the decolonization of Algeria and the inauguration of the Fifth Republic (1958). Le Pen's party initially attracted former Poujadists, the *Ordre Nouveau* (ON), and alienated former servicemen with links to the right-wing terror group the OAS (*Organisation de l'Armée Secrète*) that attempted to assassinate President De Gaulle in 1965. Over time, Le Pen's anti-immigration and anti-European Union policies proved popular electorally. By the 1990s, the FN emerged as the third force in French politics, and under the leadership of daughter Marine Le Pen since 2012, the FN has enjoyed more popular support than the two mainstream French political parties.[27] Islamist attacks on the *Charlie Hebdo* office in January 2015 and on the Bataclan theatre and Stade de France in November 2015 further boosted the appeal of the FN. In regional elections in 2015 it polled over twenty-seven per cent of the vote. Le Pen has attempted to broaden the FN's appeal by distancing the party from its anti-Semitic and Poujadist roots. In 2017, Le Pen contested the second round of the Presidential election, and received thirty-two per cent of the vote, but lost to the charismatic former socialist Emmanuel Macron's *France En Marche*. Macron's movement also surfed a populist wave, but wants, somewhat against the tide, to channel it into a revitalized European project.

Greece, as we have seen, witnessed a surge in left-wing populism in the form of Tsipras' Syriza party, which led coalition governments between 2012 and 2019. In order to sustain its authority after it had failed to restructure Greece's debt in 2015, Syriza even formed a somewhat unstable coalition with the equally populist, but anti-immigration, Independent Greek party. The 2015 general election also saw the violently anti-Semitic and anti-Muslim national socialist Golden Dawn become the third largest party in the Greek parliament. Golden Dawn, like Syriza, grew in popular appeal as the Eurozone financial crisis devastated the Greek economy. Led by Greek nationalist Nikolaos Michaloliakos, Golden Dawn first registered as a political party in 1993. In the 2012 national elections it gained seven per cent of the popular vote and twenty-one parliamentary seats. By 2015, in the wake of the Greek immigration and financial crises, it had established itself as a political force. The party has a violent paramilitary wing, the *Stormarbeitung*, responsible for attacks on migrants and synagogues. Golden Dawn has links with the FN, the Italian *Forza Nuova*, the German NDP and the ethno-nationalist Hungarian *Jobbik* Party which in 2015 polled twenty per cent of the popular vote in a country where Victor Orban's ruling *Fidesz* Party has, since 2010, already successfully promoted a populist, anti-European, ideology of illiberal democracy.

Yet when Greece eventually stabilized its finances in 2018, albeit with a GDP twenty per cent less than in 2010, the Greek electorate, after the brutal years of austerity, turned its back on both Syriza and

Golden Dawn in the European parliamentary and the Greek general elections held between May and June 2019.[28] The election of Kyriakos Mitsokakis' pro-European, centre-right New Democracy party to government may prove only a temporary return to the political mainstream, but the result suggests that the populist mood, whatever else, is fragile and capricious and its enthusiasms unstable.

By 2016, extreme nationalist and anti-immigrant parties had also achieved a significant, if volatile, electoral presence in Sweden, the Netherlands, Norway, Denmark and Finland. In Finland, the True Finn party, like the FN in France, had, by 2013, more popular support than the traditional mainstream parties. In the Netherlands, anti-immigration libertarian parties like Pim Fortuyn's List (*Lijst Pim Fortuyn*) briefly shared government in 2002, whilst Geert Wilder's anti-Islamic and anti-immigration Freedom Party commands thirteen per cent of the popular vote and, since elections in 2017, holds twenty parliamentary seats. Dutch politics has also seen the rapid rise of Thierry Baudet's Forum for Democracy (FvD) which claims 'the country is being destroyed by the people who should be protecting us'.[29] Founded in 2016, this Eurosceptic, Dutch-first party won the most seats in provincial elections held in 2019, and currently holds a majority in the upper house of the Dutch parliament.

Meanwhile, in Sweden the anti-migrant and anti-European Sweden Democrats (*Sverigedemokraterna*) formed in 1988 has seen its electoral support rise, particularly in rural areas, in every election since its formation. In the 2018 general election the party received nearly twenty per cent of the vote and became the third largest party in the *Riksdag*. Similarly, in Denmark, the populist, nativist and anti-immigrant Danish People's Party (*Dansk Folkeparti*) formed in 1995 became the second largest party in the Danish parliament after the 2015 general election. However, the passage of new laws limiting migration and integrating minorities saw the nativist vote collapse in the June 2019 election to the *Folketing*.

Thus the new European populist parties have a propensity to charismatic leadership, factionalism, the pursuit of single issues, and fragmentation, with a highly volatile political base. The UK Independence Party (UKIP), like the Danish People's Party, is a good example. UKIP evolved from an anti-federalist party, founded in 1991, into an anti-European and anti-migration party under the leadership of Nigel Farage. Between 2014–16, UKIP enjoyed considerable success in local and European elections and received 12.6 per cent of the popular vote in the 2015 general election.

After the Brexit referendum, however, the single-issue party fragmented and factionalized as its post-Farage leadership embraced an increasingly xenophobic political agenda. In this context, it came to share membership with, and some of the thinking of, British alt-right figures like Tommy Robinson (a.k.a. Stephen Yaxley-Lennon) and the British National Party (BNP) (a party with links to the US National Alliance) which also saw its fluctuating electoral appeal improve during the 1990s.

Formed in 1982 from the dissolution of the white, extremist, National Front party, the BNP attracted alienated, young, white, working class members, especially in areas of high Asian migration in London and in northern cities like Rochdale and Bradford. The aftermath of 9/11, and the London bombings of 2005, saw a further surge in support amongst the British white precariat. Under the leadership of Nick Griffin, the BNP won 6.2 per cent of the vote and two seats in the European parliament elections in 2009. In 2009, the BNP joined the French FN and the Hungarian *Jobbik* party to form an Alliance of European National Movements.

Although it formally eschews violence, the party's stance attracts a violent fringe. David Copeland, who carried out a series of nail bomb attacks in London in 1999, belonged to both the BNP and the National Socialist Movement. Some of its membership subsequently joined the now banned white supremacist party, National Action, one of whose more unstable members assassinated the Labour MP, Jo Cox, shortly before the Brexit Referendum of June 2016.

These openly palingenetic movements[30] share an ideology of ethnic purity and promote economic protectionism and hostility to migration and open borders. They seek the dissolution of the EU and oppose the political elitism and Euro-federalism that, they claim, characterizes the mainstream European conservative, liberal and social democrat political parties. Extreme right movements support programmes of either repatriation or coercive integration for legal migrants from non-European or Muslim backgrounds.

Populist parties generally and nativist movements particularly, as we have seen, responded to the European financial crisis after 2010 and the austerity measures European Commissioners imposed upon national economies, creating high levels of unemployment across the Eurozone, Germany apart. The emergence of Islamic State in 2014, and the migration crisis that followed the Syrian Civil War, accelerated their latent appeal. Meanwhile, the contempt in which the European political class and the mainstream media holds them has only intensified their appeal to a precariat class conscious of its political and economic marginalization.

Like the US alt-right, European white supremacist movements traditionally embraced an anti-Semitism that reflected their national socialist ideology. Jean-Marie Le Pen, for example, is a Holocaust denier, and Zionism constituted the focus of both alt right conspiracy theories as well as political violence prior to 9/11. These openly racialist movements, as opposed to the populist parties that share some of their concerns about migration and national identity, also embrace a race mythology that assumes, in its more extreme manifestations, that only violence and an apocalyptic race war can abate national decline.

After 9/11, this palingenetic ideology, somewhat opportunistically, substituted Islam for Zionism as its main adversary in the Manichean struggle to abate decline. In some versions of this race-based political religion, both Zionism and Islam represent twin cancers incubated within the decadent liberal body politic that require surgical removal. However, the rising membership of right-wing extremist social movements correlates directly with the emergence of leaderless jihadism across Europe. Indeed, it was only as this threat became increasingly homegrown after 2005 that these white extremist groups came to identify Islam, rather than Zionism, as the root cause of national decline.

Thus, the latest ebullition of pan European right-wing extremism (RWE) responded to IS extremism, and the apparent absence of any coherent European policy to preempt leaderless jihadist attacks on soft European targets between 2014–18. It saw the emergence, within the RWE, of a European Counter-Jihad Movement (ECJM) comprised of English, Dutch, Norwegian, Danish, and Swedish Defence Leagues. After 2009, the leagues shared a commitment to white supremacy combined with a willingness for street combat. The ECJM 'is a loosely organized, decentralized network of sympathetic groups'.[31] Like Islamic State's leaderless jihadism, social media plays a crucial role in maintaining ECJM's networked structure, facilitating a pan-Western Stop the Islamization of Nations (SION) movement with similarly minded groups in the US, Australia and New Zealand.

In this protean, networked, form, the anti-Islamic English Defence League (EDL), founded in 2009, has no formal membership. It evolved from like-minded football fans opposed to the recruitment activities of *al-Muhajiroun* in Luton. The EDL's *de facto* leader, Tommy Robinson once belonged to the BNP.[32] At various street protests organized between 2009 and 2013, Robinson stated he was 'a hundred per cent certain that there will be civil wars within Europe between Muslims and non-Muslims'. This is a position Robinson shares with like-minded zealots on websites like Robert Spencer's *Jihad Watch* and Pamela Geller's *Atlas Shrugged*. As Alexander Meleagrou-Hitchens and Hans Brun explain:

> The ECJM's activism is inspired by an ideology which presents the current jihadist terrorist threat to the West as part of a centuries-long effort by Muslims to dominate Western civilization. The ideology also insists on the existence of a conspiracy to 'Islamize' Europe through the stealthy implementation of Islamic Sharia, and holds that many of Europe's Muslims are actively engaged in this conspiracy in various ways... The other main protagonists in this conspiracy...are found within a European liberal elite that refuses to resist the attack.[33]

From this totalizing perspective, all European Muslims, whatever their beliefs, are participants in a sustained assault on European cultural identity. *Génération Identitaire* (GI), formed in France in 2012, shares the ECJM ideology, but further identifies an organized, international, elite conspiracy to replace the European population with Muslim migrants from North Africa. The French post-structuralist author and gay rights activist Renaud Camus has notably influenced identitarian theory. Camus' theory of white genocide outlined in *Le Grand Replacement* (2012) makes chilling inferences from two unrelated facts, namely: the decline of the white European birthrate; and the growth of the Muslim population of Western Europe.[34] With its slickly produced YouTube videos, GI has rapidly evolved into a pan-European movement with branches across Northern Europe and Australasia. Its thinking influenced Australian Brenton Tarrant's *The Great Replacement Manifesto* released shortly before his attack on the Al-Noor Mosque in Christchurch, New Zealand, in March 2019.

GI, like the ECJM, functions as part of a global alt right network. The network consists of online blogs like *Defend Europe*, or Niccolai Sennels' *The Gates of Vienna*, which contends that 'Islamization is a phenomenon that has existed since the Muslim prophet Mohammed lived 1,400 years ago'. The website continues, 'We are now in a phase of a very old war'. In a similar vein, Bat Ye'or in *Eurabia* (2005) promoted an influential conspiracy theory that showed how European political elites accommodated Middle Eastern states after the 1973 oil crisis, facilitating the Arab world's desire to eliminate Israel and mount a cultural conquest of Europe. Contemporary Muslim migrants to Europe, Bat Ye'or explains, represent the latest phase in a historical mission dating from the seventh century to eliminate Europe and subsume it into the greater caliphate.[35]

On the basis of such reasoning, the ECJM believes that Europe is on the brink of a racial civil war, along the lines postulated in William Pierce's *The Turner Diaries*, but now fought between indigenous European nativists and a Muslim migrant population. This is the inexorable outcome of the European political class's betrayal of ethnic, Europeans, evidenced by the increase in the Muslim population of Europe and the fact that Islam is, from this perspective, a religion immune to reform and secularization.

In March 2012, the various defence leagues from Norway, Denmark, Sweden, Finland, Germany, and the UK met in Copenhagen, where Mimosa Koiranen of the Finnish Defence League condemned the creeping Islamization of Europe. The EDL similarly considers Islam an existential threat and responds with violent demonstrations against jihadi inspired attacks. Thus, when Michael Adebolajo and Michael Adebowale murdered off-duty soldier Lee Rigby in Southeast London in May 2013, the EDL and BNP organized protest marches in Woolwich and Whitehall. Elements connected with these groups were also responsible for an increase in attacks on mosques and cultural centres in the weeks following the murder.[36]

The case of Norwegian white supremacist and Norwegian Defence League member Anders Breivik (another key influence on the thought and practice of Australian Brenton Tarrant in 2019) further demonstrates the growing attraction of ideologically motivated white supremacist, lone actors, to leaderless asymmetric attacks. Breivik's July 2011 attack on Oslo and a youth league camp on the island of Utøya resulted in seventy-seven deaths. The purpose of his killing spree, Breivik subsequently maintained, was to draw attention to his 500-page compendium, *2083: A European Declaration of Independence*. The work alludes to the EDL and was published online under the pseudonym Andrew Berwick, Justiciar Knight Commander for Knights Templar Europe and the pan-European Patriotic Resistance. The Knights Templar, of course, were a medieval, European crusading order dedicated to expelling Islam from Europe and retaking Jerusalem (1129–1312).

Breivik, predictably, presented his modern crusade in terms of a Manichean civilizational clash between good and evil.[37] In this evolving context of white identitarian resistance, in June 2016 Thomas Mair assassinated Labour MP Jo Cox, shouting 'Britain First', the slogan of the BNP breakaway faction National Action. Mair also had links to the US National Alliance.[38] In the same month, a Royal United Services Institute report claimed that right-wing, neo-Nazi extremists like Mair and Breivik had conducted more lone actor attacks than their 'religiously motivated' (i.e. Islamist) equivalents across Europe.[39]

Extreme right leaderless resistance obviously represents an emerging threat to European liberal democracy and the institutions it evolved after 1945, as well as the progressive, post political, third way faith in Tony Blair's 'unmovable values' of global and regional integration that Islamism and the financial crisis devastated, but by no means destroyed.

This 'patriotic' extremism finds mainstream, secular, democratic politics corrupt, hypocritical and tyrannical. The EU's failure to deliver higher living standards, the economic recession caused by locking different European economies into a single currency, together with its open border policy, has fuelled the xenophobia upon which ethno-nationalist identity politics thrives.

Nationalism and populism evidently respond, as Ernest Gellner demonstrated in a number of books and articles, to the complex social and political predicament that modern capitalism's capacity for creative destruction engendered.[40] Although it might look to historic, mythic and folkloric roots, modern nationalism, in its many varieties, ranging from an understanding of a shared culture to its more extreme, fascist, xenophobic, and ethno-nationalist manifestations, responds directly to the needs of a centrally administered, modern industrialized state. Mobile, anonymous, atomized modernity, the semantic nature of work and its promise of growth and affluence, required a homogenous high culture or nation as its basis. At least this was the case prior to the era of the borderless world, millennial capital, and the Golden Straitjacket. The transition across the big ditch from tradition to industrial modernity meant the transition to a world in which literacy and education linked to a uniform high 'national' culture became the pervasive culture of society as a whole. It also led to the modern preoccupation with roots.

The cultural and linguistic separateness that nineteenth century German Romantics like Herder first celebrated, and national movements across nineteenth and twentieth-century Europe and the globe demanded, however, affords no reasonable, or prudently achievable, political solution. The right to self-determination might sound like a principle which could be implemented universally, and generate unique and hence uniquely binding solutions in diverse concrete situations. But demographic, historic or geographic measures to establish it cut across each other, as the case of the former Yugoslavia in the course of the 1990s tragically illustrated. Ultimately, Gellner observed, 'we may be doomed to a painful compromise between the longing for a meaningful order and the demands of rationalism and scepticism'.[41]

In this context, stability, continuity, affluence and economic growth should be recognized as political goods that soften manners and such supposedly primordial attachments. Moreover, although the nation state order is not sacrosanct, it should, Gellner maintained, be treated with respect. Significantly, Gellner observed in 1997 that 'people who are affluent and who believe themselves to be in an improving situation are much less likely to be tempted into violent conduct which will disrupt their world, than people whose situation is deteriorating'.[42] As the optimism of the great moderation turned to financial panic a sense of economic as well as moral and political deterioration accompanied it. It is this feeling that contemporary populism with its overtones of demagoguery and palingenetic renewal mobilizes and exploits.

By a curious irony, an analogously apocalyptic vision informs the anti-capitalist movement of post-democratic radicals and internet-linked anarchist groups like *Anonymous*. It also informs the worldview of social movements for global peace, justice and emancipation, that by a further irony evolved from, and were facilitated by, the post-political vision of the third way with its avowed intent to make capitalism socially just and globally accountable. We shall next consider the dark liberation anticipated by a transnational, but increasingly anti-capitalist, new left, alter-globalization movement that emerged from the contradictions of the progressive third way after 2003,[43] before considering why Western democracies have struggled to contain these millenarian and apocalyptic threats to secular political order and how, if at all, that order might be restored.

The Zombie Left and World Purificationism Post-9/11

An anti-anti-Islamism characterizes new left transnational thinking about post-9/11 jihadism. Since the 1990s, leading European and North American university departments promulgated, as we saw in chapter 2, a progressive critical international theory about world politics that afforded ideological support to non-governmental organizations (NGOs) and legal elites that questioned the politics of fear and the discourses of danger that, they argued, Western democratic governments and their security agencies promoted. These opinion-forming, transnational elites share a common suspicion of Western government responses to al-Qaeda and, more recently, Islamic State, both at home and abroad.

Emerging from the decaying chrysalis of third way progressivism, but assuming a purer, anti-political form, a new Olympian critical idealism after 2003 promised a socially perfected, emancipatory finale, not only to the end of history, but also of the West. Like the new liberalism it transcends, the Olympian project prefers an imperial form of rule through supranational structures and unaccountable global forums advancing world government by judicializing political conflicts. 'Its central instrument is in expanding treaty commitment to human rights and in creating international criminal law'.[44] In its imperial detachment, the transnational Olympian mode deplores the violence of non-state actors like Islamic State, but empathizes with their grievances, whilst condemning capitalism and Western liberal democratic states for hypocritically perpetuating the global injustices that induce their resistance.

This critique informs an emerging global movement, ironically funded by Western eleemosynary institutions that also sustain its intellectual credibility, against a Western imposed security order and its state-based, democratically accountable, institutions. As a millenarian transnational movement, it also assumes the character of a political religion.[45] Like the rise of palingenetic ethno-nationalism, the Olympian variety of transnational progressivism emerged at the end of the Cold War as a radical rejection of a liberal democratic market state order, advocating instead cosmopolitan, post-national constellations like the United Nations and the EU.[46] After 2003, this evolution of progressive ideology into a more idealistic, neo-Kantian, constructivist and culturally Marxist idiom, disclosed an increasingly Manichean struggle between redemptive social movements[47] and their allies in transnational NGOs (TNGOs), locked in combat with global capitalism, the nation state, and the US-inspired 'neo-liberal' Empire that sustained an oppressive and unjust global hegemony.[48] Just as Marxist-Leninist thought found in the international proletariat a potentially revolutionary class to expose and confront the contradictions in industrial capitalism, so new social movements, like the World Social Forum, play an analogous role in revealing the current contradictions of global capitalism, and anticipating its coming crisis as a harbinger to the new liberation.[49]

Liberal critics of this non-negotiable transnational emancipatory movement such as Bernard-Henri Levy argue that it replaced the post-1968 libertarian left's commitment to personal freedoms with the assumption that we are living in dark times, where a world controlling state-military-corporate complex enforces an unjust global order.[50] In this context, the United States and its allies function as the concrete imperial enemy, whilst Israel plays a special role as its demonic accomplice.[51] Nick Cohen similarly argued that this new left, networked global movement experienced a 'dark liberation' after 2003, inspiring its adherents to 'spread the theories of Jewish-Zionist world conspiracy...and excuse even the most brutal theocratic-fascist regime, as long as they opposed the United States and the capitalist status quo'.[52] The UK Labour Party is perhaps the most striking illustration of the new left's dark liberation. Once home to the third way progressive vision of Tony Blair's New Labour, under the leadership of Jeremy Corbyn and his Director of Strategy, Seumas Milne, after 2016, the party embraced the gamut of purificatory and emancipatory enthusiasms. This includes an empathy with oppressed minorities and the ritualistic denunciation of Zionism that has led to a growth in Muslim support for its new emancipatory style.[53]

The new alt left, then, constitutes an inchoate 'non-religious chiliastic movement that preaches global human renewal and predicts apocalypse as its alternative'.[54] Its world 'purificationism', as with other political religions, contrasts past oppression and a degenerate present with a utopian future. As Ernst Sternberg explains:

> The world system that perpetuates oppression is known as Empire. It exercises domination through corporate tentacles, media manipulation, state power and military prowess. It is selfish, greedy, ruthless, racist and exploitative and heedlessly pollutes the earth... Under the thrall of Neo-liberal Empire, people live in poverty, food is contaminated, products are artificial, wasteful consumption is compelled, indigenous groups are dispossessed and nature itself is subverted.[55]

After 2008, the global financial crisis boosted this radical critique of the failings of new liberal, third way, democracy. From this transformative perspective, at the end of the Cold War, progressive Western elites had naively, or, some might say, cynically, assumed that the liberal market state order would reshape the globe through its soft cultural and commercial power. A quarter of a century later, a new liberal, socially just end of history appeared increasingly unlikely. Government bailouts of banks too big to fail revealed the limitations of the rational market, as well as the hubris of investment bankers. The crisis legitimated loose congeries of anarchist-inspired, direct action groups to promote the Occupy movement that disrupted Wall Street in September 2011.[56]

By 2014, *Anonymous*, the international collective of anarchist-inspired activist entities that spread this leaderless, anti-capitalist resistance, conducted denial of service attacks on government, religious and corporate web sites it deemed corrupt. It also issued a YouTube manifesto,[57] challenging the 'so-called' global capitalist elite, informing its fellow 'citizens of the world' that they spread a message of 'true love, peace and compassion' against the 'unsustainable' order based on 'murder, hate, oppression and disorder' that was 'killing the surface of the planet'. 'We are the new world order' they declared.[58]

This alternative or *alter*-globalization movement, consisting of transnational networks of NGOs, sympathetic academics, radical pacifists, indigenous peoples and environmental activists, seeks social justice and emancipation by overthrowing, rather than managing, the Western capitalist *imperium*. In the first decade of the twenty-first century, alt globalization activists moved from the political fringes to shape mainstream international political debate.[59] After 2011, those committed to this anti-capitalist, anti-Western, but emancipatory global worldview, 'lead hundreds of activist groups and NGOs, conduct seminars and hold marches at international conferences, receive support from governments and eleemosynary institutions, enjoy various despots as their cheerleaders, are woven into the workings of the UN and the EU…and subscribe to a coherent though not uniform doctrine'.[60]

To overthrow the global, neo-liberal order, activists form 'bunds' or affinities with like-minded groups networking across communities, borders and cultures.[61] This transnational network of purified victims seeks to instantiate an environmentally clean, culturally harmonious, politically just and sustainable world, liberated from both capitalism and carbon.[62] From this redemptive, Manichean perspective, the various networks and movements struggle for an international regime of peace and justice against the selfish national interests of Western democracies. International rules, in line with constructivist and critical International Relations theory, will replace the 'chauvinist laws bounded by nationality [and]…climate and energy flows will come under transnational management'.[63] As the nation state order weakens, a transnational cadre of NGOs will replace it and serve as the globe's humanitarian enforcers and equalizers.

This Olympian movement's ideology is, then, post-democratic. It considers mainstream political parties and representative democratic institutions corrupt and oppressive, unless like UK Labour they are transformed through tactics of radical entryism. The preferred style is direct, deliberative, participatory action where grassroots activists raise the consciousness of the alienated and expose the toxicity of the liberal international capitalist order. In local forums, dominated by radical visionaries, activist facilitators create conditions for the rectification of false consciousness, leading to the enforcement of global justice and non-instrumental, uncoerced, communicatory reason. This purified order, both locally and globally, will replace the partial will of self-interested states and build a transnational, therapeutic, participatory order. Such utopianism thus posits a world on the cusp of a globally just cosmopolitanism achieved through the activity of communities of like-minded idealists.

Ultimately, those who anticipate the new order waiting to be born possess the Gnostic key to history and serve as guides to social and political emancipation. From this perspective, the global evil that the US-led liberal capitalist system perpetuates justifies resistance to it. Moreover, although these loosely structured congeries of local groups embrace pacifism, they nevertheless empathize with the grievances that motivate the global resistance of the al-Qaeda or IS-inspired variety. 'Resistance', as opposed to the more pejorative term, 'terror', explains, for example, the insurgency in Iraq after 2003.[64] This demonization of Western influence, whether it was actively engaged in Afghanistan or Iraq, or passively indifferent to inter-tribal and sectarian civil war in Syria and North Africa, fuels a relativism that relates all 'subaltern'[65] violence to oppression and grievance settlement.

Thus, at the same time as the new homogenizing global project denounces Western hypocrisy, it minimizes the crimes that occur in regimes that its emancipatory worldview considers subaltern and non-Western. Such relativism annihilates, Bernard-Henri Levy writes, 'whole chapters of contemporary history, killing one more time, millions of men and women, whose whole crime was being born and whose second was in dying the wrong way'.[66] Disregard for historical accuracy, or, anachronistically, cherry picking the historical record of the Western colonial past, a feature it shares with critical international relations theory, feeds the corruption of political language and inquiry. Language corrupts thought, or, in the discourse of post-colonial emancipationists, humanitarian terms become weapons to attack the flaws of liberal democracies. Exposing hypocrisy in liberal democracies, somewhat perversely, entails excusing the crimes of despots.[67]

These contortions of the transnational Olympian mind stem from the discovery of victims everywhere and the need to implement abstract universal norms and compensation for harm to alleviate their suffering both locally and globally. After the Cold War, this ethical imperialism took particular umbrage at any Western nation charting a unilateral course that contravened internationally agreed rules.

Olympian moral judgment, however, appears, as Yoram Hazony argues, strangely prejudiced.[68] Thus, this latest mutation of Western progressivism considers Brexit or Trump's independent approach to international agreements deplorable, whilst it overlooks or ignores Russia, China or Iran's more flagrant breaches of international law. In a similar vein, Olympian opprobrium greets any Israeli action in the Gaza strip, or a white supremacist attack on a New Zealand mosque, whilst the savagery of Islamist terrorists or third world despots evokes only mild disapproval. What accounts for this otherwise curious double standard?

One plausible answer is that, as we have seen, all ideological grand narratives assume that world history follows an inexorable trajectory towards a realizable utopia. In its post-Cold War progressive manifestation, new liberalism assumed a teleological progression from barbarism to the triumph of reason culminating in a universal state and an ethically informed global society.

Before the Second World War, liberal idealism traded at a political discount. This all changed, however, after 1945. Post-war, and more particularly after the end of the Cold War, Western liberalism maintained that European peace and progress required a paradigm shift, 'dismantling the states in which they live for the rule of an international regime'.[69] Such a world state responded to pure reason advancing to the union of nations that Immanuel Kant first anticipated in his *Perpetual Peace: a Philosophical Sketch* (1795). Ignored for two centuries, an academically reinvigorated Kantianism, as we have seen,

THE REVENGE OF POLITICS AND THE SEARCH FOR ORDER

now pervades the progressive mind. Transnational elites have come to share Kant's *Idea for a Universal History with a Cosmopolitan Purpose* (1784). History, from this perspective, proceeds through three stages: from tribal barbarism, through the intermediary stage of the nation state, to the ultimate realization of Kant's 'eschatological hope' – a world state. During the intermediary nation state stage, more advanced states would 'renounce their savage and lawless freedom, adapt themselves to public coercive laws and thus form an international state, which would continue to grow until it embraced all the people of the earth'.[70] Those who advanced it formed an enlightened, morally mature, cosmopolitan vanguard.

The problem such an idealist version of the end of history encountered in practice was that nations and cultures moved along the path from barbarism to the rule of universal reason at different speeds. Whilst Western Europe and North America were well advanced on Fukuyama's wagon train to full moral and political Enlightenment, less developed peoples in the Middle East, Asia and Africa remained at a politically prepubescent stage.

Consequently, the moral and legal standards applied to the advanced West could not apply to Turkey, Syria, Iran, or IS whose murderous behavior indicated a state of childish savagery from which virtually nothing morally could be expected. Cosmopolitan progressives patronizingly assume these moral adolescents will eventually grow up, but the process may be long and require great tolerance. At the same time, this imperialist idealism evinces an uncomprehending intolerance for those it deems to have apostatized from its secular, new liberal faith in immanent global perfection. Thus, it excuses a Daesh style management of savagery in Raqqa, whilst condemning Israeli conduct for defending its political integrity against Hamas or Hizbullah. The fact that the cosmopolitan mind considers Israel nominally European and an Enlightenment product that has reneged upon the values that since 1945 have informed ethical, responsible global citizenship accounts for this otherwise hypocritical stance.

Cosmopolitanism, in this Olympian form, thus subjects Israel to a higher moral standard than 'more primitive Arabs and Palestinians, because they were (really) Europeans'. In 2014, the Danish ambassador to Jerusalem revealed the dissimulation in this moral posture when he informed his hosts, without irony, that Europe had the 'right to insist that we apply double standards' to Israel.[71]

A further consequence of this moral posture is the new left tolerance of anti-Semitism and the otherwise curious comparison of Israel with Hitler's Nazi regime. What the Israel case demonstrates is the capacity for tolerance to turn to intolerance of those who dissent from the transnational, emancipatory mission. From an Olympian Kantian perspective every backsliding 'dissident and every dissent looks the same'. Its intolerance is a 'direct consequence of the advance of their own aspiration of attaining universal order'.[72] Hence, whether it is Israel, Trump's unilateralism, or the UK's pursuit of Brexit, the latest ebullition of cosmopolitan idealism reserves an Olympian disdain for any movement with a nominal European heritage that severs its connection with this transformational, emancipatory ideal.

There is now a curious affinity, Alexander del Valle writes, between the new transnational 'red' alter left, 'brown' alt right, and green (the latter colour covering both Islamist and environmentalist) social movements, the anti-political paths they follow, and the politically religious certitudes they embrace and promote via phantom cells, social media and leaderless resistance.[73] The different components of this apocalyptic axis share a common Gnostic belief structure: a corrupt past; a decadent contemporary Western political order on the verge of disintegration; and the necessity for resistance and, if necessary, clarifying acts of violence, to bring about a harmonious new order or third age, the end of history and the end of the West.

Yet, the Kantian-inspired purificationism of the new Olympians, like the new liberal progressivism it considers it has taken to its final stage, has no philosophical or epistemological justification to imagine the end of history. That, however, is the only justification for the sacrifices demanded of humanity in its name. It has no other basis than a *petitio principii* which introduces into history a value foreign to history. As Albert Camus wrote:

> Since that value is, at the same time, foreign to ethics, it is not, properly speaking, a value upon which one can base one's conduct, it is a dogma without foundation that can be adopted only as the desperate effort to escape of a mind which is being stifled by solitude

or by nihilism or a value which is going to be imposed by those whom dogma profits. The end of history is not an exemplary or perfectionist value: it is an arbitrary and terroristic principle.[74]

How, we might consider, has secular, political, democracy responded?

Pluralism, Democracy and Deracination

Examining the crisis that the West faced during the Cold War, when the idea of its decline and suicide first achieved wide circulation,[75] Leo Strauss argued that the first half of the twentieth century had undermined faith in the secular, rational, Enlightenment project. The crisis of the West then, as it has recurred again, after its all too brief, liberal, end of history epiphany, consists in the West having become uncertain of its universal purpose. The West, Strauss contended, 'once had a clear vision of its future'. As in the 1960s, despite the implacable, but increasingly desperate, progressive certitude, we find that we 'no longer have that certainty… Some of us even despair of the future and this despair explains many form of Western degradation'.[76] A society accustomed to understanding itself in terms of a universal and progressive purpose cannot lose faith in that purpose without becoming utterly bewildered. The particular political experience of liberal democracy and its failure to appreciate the threat of external and internal violence from state and non-state actors after 9/11, or absorb financial shock, has only amplified this sense of bewilderment.

Since the end of the Cold War, the pursuit of political and spiritual purification and an apocalyptic transformation of a corrupt world order was, as we have shown, by no means confined to Islamism. Al-Qaeda and Islamic State only represent the most obvious manifestation of this redemptive and apocalyptic style. The challenges posed by the world purificationist and ethno-nationalist versions of political redemption are the latest in a line of revolutionary activist assaults on the political systems of modern Europe that emerged in the course of the nineteenth century.[77] Those attracted to this activist style, and the utopian solutions they offer, pose a complex challenge for political rule and the secular order. At the core of the West's current difficulty is a need to take utopian ideologies seriously, whatever their provenance, whilst reaffirming the idea of politics as a distinct form of activity practiced within a limited, territorial unit of rule.

Problematically, however, Western governments have underestimated the role that political religion plays in both recruitment and the passage to the violent act. Instead, a secular and progressive commentariat has ignored or dismissed the ideological commitment, re-describing it instead as a response to poverty or social and economic grievance. Such progressive universalism was, as we saw in chapter 3, beset by illusion: the illusion of rational harmony; the illusion of ultimate agreement if speech conditions are regulated; and, most central of all, the idea 'that will and desire can ultimately be sovereign in human affairs': that things will ultimately pan out the way the progressive vision demands.[78]

In its transnational soteriological mood, progressivism heaped together a heterogeneous collection of impoverished victims in a manner that tempted it to treat this similarity as the most crucial fact about them. To justify this moral imperative, post-Rawlsian new liberalism attributed to the oppressed and the victimized a curious moral innocence. As a consequence, the wretched of the earth both require compassion and are set up to judge behaviour in a way that ultimately unravels the practice of both politics and political citizenship. Ultimately, not the citizen but the suffering speak and they, or their representatives, always communicate in an angry, subaltern demotic. Meanwhile a progressive elite in the media and government emotes, compassionately helping the voiceless articulate their pain. The discovery of victims everywhere ultimately induced what Pascal Bruckner termed a masochistic, new liberal 'tyranny of guilt' and the felt need, not for political liberty, but for redemption and social compensation.[79]

Radical democracy *sans frontières* where the oppressed reveal their suffering and receive recognition becomes the 'highest good'. It accepts that:

> The promise of multiethnic democracy, in which members of any creed or color are regarded as true equals, is nonnegotiable. Difficult though it may be for countries with a deeply monoethnic conception of themselves to embrace newcomers and minorities,

such a transformation is the only realistic alternative to tyranny and civil strife.[80]

The assumption begs the prudent question, why not introduce immigration policies that put the interests of existing citizens first? Democratization theory, it would seem, no longer even admits this possibility, demonstrating that political science itself has become ideological.

This multicultural, progressive absolutism became increasingly explicit in its response to minorities that transformed their oppression into violent forms of expression. Perplexed by their own post-colonial guilt, the progressive mind histrionically embraced the suffering 'other' in its various manifestations. Consequently, a liberal academic and media commentariat either dismissed, or sought to accommodate, the growing appeal of a politically religious identity, wrapped in Islamic guise, that exercised an increasingly fatal fascination for Western diasporic communities.

When governments responded, following the allocutory guidance of progressive theory, they adopted a policy mixture of engagement, co-option and pre-emption. In doing so they failed to recognize that a culture is a system of prejudgment. Social institutions, especially non-Western ones, are seldom chosen; 'they are our fate, not our choice'.[81] Consequently, multicultural policies promoting minority identity politics, cherishing difference, and addressing 'grievance' merely enhanced the appeal to cultic violence.

The progressive response, in other words, tolerated the intolerance of the subaltern other. It also fashioned a rationalist vocabulary that explained or, more precisely, explained away, the challenge to core understandings of secular pluralism founded upon a shared political or civic culture. It redefined zealotry as 'extremism', fanatic enthusiasm as 'radicalism', and cultic violence as 'resistance', whilst terms like 'Islamophobia' silenced those who questioned the new semantics.[82]

In order to recuperate a political understanding of the citizen and the nation state, or as Max Weber describes it, 'a compulsory political organisation with continuous operations (*politischer Anstaltsbetrieb*)' that successfully upholds 'the claim to the monopoly of the legitimate use of physical force in the enforcement of its order',[83] let us first turn to what political citizenship in a discrete and particular civil association entails, rather than its concept-stretched, distorted, cosmopolitan alternative.

The Citizen, the State and the Promise of Politics

In the last of *The Federalist Papers*, Alexander Hamilton averred that 'a nation without a national government is, in my view, an awful spectacle'.[84] Hamilton, one suspects, would be shocked by what is happening in Europe today, where nations without national governments are indeed making spectacles of themselves.

By 2016, the liberal progressive worldview premised on shared norms, open markets, open borders and an abstract commitment to social justice ameliorating global oppression left the West divided and fragmented, threatened internally by populist enthusiasms and externally by illiberal revisionist powers. How, we might wonder, might a return to a limited statecraft abroad and a prudent defence of a civic political order at home address the 'mid-life crisis' that now faces a distracted and confused, but still notionally democratic West?[85]

Modern democratic citizenship arose relatively recently. Of course, it had classical antecedents. Members of a Greek *polis* or the Roman *res publica* were *politeis* or *cives*, members of a *politeia, civitatis* or *res publica*, bound by the laws they made in the *agora* or *forum*. This understanding revived at the Renaissance and played its part in the Miltonic notion of an English revolutionary commonwealth or 'free state'.[86]

Its historically recent and updated formulation occurred primarily, however, in the context of the two political revolutions of the eighteenth century, the American and French. Citizenship became indelibly associated with the understanding and the integrity of the modern democratic polity. Indeed, it constituted a key word in the political vocabulary of modern, republican, democratic thought. Thus, the sceptical republican Tom Paine, who participated in both revolutions, considered a good American citizen 'an open and resolute friend and a virtuous supporter of the rights of mankind and the free and independent states of America'.[87] More precisely, James Madison believed that in a republic everything depends on a citizenry that understands the principles of freedom and the responsibilities that come with popular power. Citizens were entitled to the rights the Constitution guaranteed them. They do not merely submit to the government officials elected to positions of power. Instead 'public opinion sets bounds to every government, and is the real sovereign in every free one'.[88]

The American republican concept of the people further assumed independent citizens possessing and articulating a multiplicity of voices and interests. Thomas Jefferson considered it a principle 'to make us one nation as to foreign concerns, and keep us distinct in domestic ones'. Similarly, Madison could assert that popular regulation 'forms the principal task of legislation, and involves the spirit of party and faction in the operations of the government'. The positive accent, as Hannah Arendt observed, that the American founding fathers placed 'on party and faction is noteworthy, since it stands in flagrant contradiction' to the classical and early modern tradition of republican virtue, to which they 'otherwise paid the closest attention'.[89]

From a more radical contractual perspective, Rousseau defined the act of civil association creating a corporate body composed of as many members as the assembly contains voters. This public person formed by 'the union of all other persons formerly took the name of city and now takes that of republic or body politic'. It was called by its members:

> state when passive, sovereign when active and power when compared with others like itself. Those who associated in it take collectively the name of people and severally are called citizens as sharing in the sovereign authority and subjects as being under the laws of the state.

But, as Rousseau added, 'these things are often confused and taken one for another'.[90]

Rousseau and the American founding fathers, in their different ways, captured the essence of the modern notion of the citizen and the state. They arrived at it through a careful study of patriotism and politics in the ancient world. Thus Rousseau praised Lycurgus as a legislator because he kept the *patrie* before the eyes of the people in its laws, games, and festivals. He contrasted this with the indistinguishability of the eighteenth century enlightened cosmopolitan. 'There are today no longer Frenchmen, Germans, Spaniards, or even Englishmen', he wrote, 'there are only Europeans'. What Rousseau railed against became central not only to republican political theory, but also to the practice of the increasingly democratic state in the course of the nineteenth and twentieth centuries.

Implicit in understandings of modern, secular political thinking, reflecting its post-Machiavellian reinterpretation of classical republicanism, was the importance of citizenship as the criteria for membership of a civil association and the duties as well as rights associated with that status. It understood citizens, bound by the laws of an authentic authority, as the basis for the practice of political freedom. The true democrat distinguished the political *persona* of the citizen from that of a slave, a migrant, or a victim. The virtue of citizenship resided in loyalty to the polity, the practice of liberty and the mutual recognition of fellow members.

This public morality and the pursuit of what the American founding fathers termed 'public happiness' could, moreover, only be expressed within a bounded, or limited unit of rule. Genuinely political freedom, as opposed to progressive and abstract emancipation, 'wherever it existed as a tangible reality has always been spatially limited'. Hannah Arendt wrote, 'this is especially clear for the greatest and most elementary of all negative liberties, the freedom of movement'. It was the 'borders of national territory or the walls of the city state' that 'comprehended and protected a space in which men could move freely'. It was precisely this politically circumscribed liberty that the abstract rationalist and imperial project of Europe without borders dismissed. To be sure, later treaties and international agreements could provide an extension of this territorially bound freedom for citizens outside their own country, but even under these modern conditions, the European political class in their enthusiasm for ever closer union ignored 'the elementary coincidence of freedom and a limited space'.[91]

Conceptually stretched by recent developments in political and international relations theory, as well as government practice, citizenship has been either distorted or taken for granted. Yet, like the representative, catch-all party, vital to the expression of a multitude of voices in which citizens once freely participated, citizenship was central to the functioning of post-war political democracy. Even as late as the 1980s introductory undergraduate courses in politics or Western civilization explored its character and defended its constitutional role.[92] What might be done to recover this lost political understanding?

The Promise of Politics[93]

From the end of the Cold War, democratic governments, mainstream media and academia distorted the already ambiguous post-Enlightenment vocabulary of liberty, equality, rights and social justice that had evolved in the contingent and complex historical experience of the modern European secular state to suit the needs of an omnicompetent bureaucratic managerialism. Rejecting counsels of political prudence, Western governments ruling according to a rationalist technique fatally underestimated the role that nonnegotiable cultural understandings continued to play in non-Western cultures at the end of history. They preferred instead to characterize antithetical ideological commitments as either a self-inflicted problem of 'othering', or a somewhat extreme response to perceived social and economic grievance.[94]

In the light of the recent dramatic shifts in the character and conduct of international and domestic politics, we might do well to reconsider how the concept of national interest defined in prudential terms of limited power and constitutional or rule-based order might save us from recent moral and rationalist excess and political folly.

At the core of the West's democratic predicament, and the populist revolt against 'cherishing difference', is a need to reaffirm the idea of politics, the state and the citizenship that accompanies it, as a distinct form of activity practiced within the territorial bounds of a national state.

During the Cold War, political theorists, media commentators and politicians contrasted a prudent appreciation of limited political democracy with a variety of ideological alternatives. In what, in the recent past, passed for standard introductions to the undergraduate study of politics, written by, *inter alia*, Bernard Crick, Robert Dahl, Kenneth Minogue, Hannah Arendt, Leo Strauss, or Michael Oakeshott, the Western European and North American experience of political democracy assumed a 'common world in which we may talk to each other'.[95] A leading conservative journalist of the 1970s, asked what he had learnt as an undergraduate, replied, 'that the rule of law is more important than the vote'.[96]

More precisely, for those who attended to the political tradition and its contingent particularism, political philosophy was synonymous with the ancient Greek polis. The Greeks considered the tribe or *ethne* incapable of high civilization, whilst large, imperial arrangements could never experience the freedom of ruling and being ruled, by law.[97] Central to political or constitutional rule, therefore, was a limited government that separated the public from the private realm.[98] Recognizing this separation 'distinguishes politics, which we may loosely identify with freedom and democracy, from despotism'.[99] The overarching public world of the modern state sustained a structure of law appropriate to a self-determining association in order to maintain civil life. The mixture and balance of classes and interests the constitution reflected sustained the political condition and prevented *stasis* or stagnation leading to instability. As Aristotle observed, the chief cause of collapse in a state, then as now, was 'deviation from the principles of a constitution'.[100] It arose from the 'failure to secure a proper mixture of oligarchy and democracy'. Elaborating what transpired to be an enduring political insight, Aristotle considered that 'both oligarchy and democracy may be tolerably good...but if one carries either of them to excess, first the constitution will become worse and finally not even a constitution at all'.[101]

Political balance required the principle of the middle, or golden mean, rather than the third way. Just as virtuous conduct, and the good life, followed the mean between two extremes, the same principle also applied to 'the goodness and badness of cities and states'.[102] Consequently, democracies were safer and longer lasting where the middle class was strong. While the wealthy were full of superiority and hubris, the poor are weak or subservient. The excessive influence of either of these extremes tends to instability.

Political rule thus accepted the human condition for what it is, in all its fragility, variety and imperfectability. It was 'not ethics, law, science, history, or economics. It neither solves everything nor is present everywhere'.[103] Equally importantly, it 'is not religion, or, if it is, it is nothing but the inquisition'.[104] Crucially, the activity of politics, its actual practice, accepted and required difference and resisted the imposition of unity.

'There is a point', Aristotle recognized:

> at which a *polis* by advancing in unity will cease to be a *polis*: there is another point short of that at which it may still remain a *polis*, but will none the less come close to losing its essence and will become a worse *polis*. It is as if you were to turn a harmony into mere unison or reduce a theme to a single beat, the truth is that the *polis* is an aggregate of many members.[105]

This Aristotelian understanding of a mixed and balanced constitution, accommodating different interests and many members, influenced the medieval understanding of constitutionalism, the acknowledgment of different estates composing the body politic of the realm and the separation of the temporal from the spiritual jurisdiction. More particularly, it affected a distinctive English and, by extension, American and British Commonwealth understanding of common law. As the jurist John Fortescue wrote during the bitter dispute over the crown in the fifteenth century, England was a 'dominium politicum et regale' (a political as well as a monarchical form of rule).[106] Thomas Cromwell, who developed the understanding into the idea of parliamentary sovereignty in the sixteenth century, considered that the king at no time stood so highly in his 'estate royal' as 'in time of parliament'.[107] English as well as French and Dutch political counsel of the seventeenth century recognized the necessity of prudently mixing and balancing the kingly, aristocratic and popular elements in the constitution of the early modern state. Failure to secure the correct blend led to 'the confusions and revolutions of government'.[108]

In the evolving early modern language of political and constitutional thought both Locke and Montesquieu translated balance into the need for constitutional checks to sustain both political liberty and political stability. Montesquieu, following Aristotle, recognized that 'democracy has, therefore, two excesses to avoid – the spirit of inequality, which leads to aristocracy or monarchy, and the spirit of extreme equality, which leads to despotic power.'[109] To sustain public happiness, the properly constituted republic needed to avoid extremes of wealth and poverty:

The good sense and happiness of individuals depend greatly upon the mediocrity of their abilities and fortunes. Therefore, as a republic, where the laws have placed many in a middling station, is composed of wise men, it will be wisely governed; as it is composed of happy men, it will be extremely happy.[110]

Those who framed the most successful constitution for a *novus ordo saecularum*, the American founding fathers, deliberately set out to emulate the classical civic understanding of Rome and Greece. They not only evinced a very English 'distrust of philosophic generalities', but they were 'if anything more learned in the ways of ancient and modern prudence than their colleagues in the old world and more likely to consult books for guidance in action'.[111] John Adams notably 'ransacked the archives of ancient prudence' to help frame a 'system of powers that would check and balance in such a way that power neither of the union or its parts would decrease or destroy one another'.[112]

Sustaining such a balance in a complex modern society requires, Michael Oakeshott maintained, the 'prudent diffidence' of classical and early modern (but not radically nihilistic) scepticism to offset the growing modern predilection for an apolitical, rationalist, managerial, omnicompetence. To mediate the modern pursuit of universalist schemes of progressive perfection requires prudent correction to recall government to perform 'economically its perennial office of preserving order and balance relevant to the current conditions of society', restoring both 'a balance of attention and a balance of power'.[113]

In contrast with the ancient world, modern Western politics has, since the nineteenth century, oscillated between the poles of rationalist faith in the technique of managerial omnicompetence, and the politics of scepticism. To avoid the modern European propensity to oligarchy and progressive imperialism requires a dose of political prudence 'so that this pole of our politics can once more assert its pull'.[114]

Sustaining such political balance further requires 'the understanding of politics as a conversation in which past, present and future each has a voice; and while one or other of them may on occasion properly prevail, none is given exclusive attention'. To avoid a descent into an elite monologue, politics must also be a conversation 'between diverse interests'.[115]

In other words, 'the principle of the mean' should inhere in modern political practice. The 'principle' or the mean which 'this complex style of politics itself divulges' is not, moreover, 'a fixed' or 'central point of repose', but a middle region of movement in political activity. To be functional, political activity must sustain 'a habitable middle region in which we may escape the self-destructive extremes'. To be at home in this style then 'is to observe what may be called the mean in action'.[116]

European politics could be seen as once having been disposed towards this mean in action. To recall political activity to a middle region of movement, the prudent counsellor would question the progressive enthusiasm for a universal global order sanctified by neither God or history. Ultimately, politics, but not necessarily democracy, with which it is too easily conflated, can only occur in organized units of rule whose citizens accept themselves to be an aggregate of many members and not a single tribe, religion, interest, or tradition. It necessarily recognizes a plurality of contending interests and voices, but not non-negotiable identities, at its foundation. Political freedom is a result of this recognition of pluralism.

In this context, the economic Golden Straitjacket argument for liberty and free markets is as much a curse as a blessing. The rise of China amply demonstrates that economic growth neither leads to political freedom nor affords a 'proof of its growth'. The most important blessings of the political condition are, Arendt wrote, the 'truly political freedoms' of 'speech, of thought, of association and of assembly'.[117] Politics, under these conditions, becomes the public activity of free citizens, and freedom is the privacy of citizens from public action. Consequently, politics becomes a plausible response to the problem of governing a complex, modern state.

Only a particular state-based order, moreover, can sustain the practice of political freedom over time. The authority to make a common law through representative institutions and apply it equally to all citizens requires, as Thomas Hobbes observed, an enduring, Leviathan state. More recently, Steven Pinker has shown how 'a state and a judiciary with a monopoly on the legitimate use of force can... inhibit the impulse for revenge, and circumvent the self-serving biases that make all parties believe they are on the side of the angels'.[118] Hobbes' preoccupation with a lasting, abstract, sovereign authority represented an early modern version of the ancient quest for the perpetual state. The preoccupation with permanence and stability also runs 'like a red thread through the American constitutional debates', which were conducted in terms 'of the age old notion of a mixed form of government which combined the monarchic, aristocratic and the democratic elements in the same body politic', thereby 'arresting the cycle of sempiternal change'.[119]

Political theory, but not the international relations variety, represents, therefore, the historical attempt 'to rationalize the shelter-function of the *cosmion*, the little world of order, by what are commonly called political ideas'.[120] In other words, political thinking from Aristotle to Arendt, Oakeshott and Eric Voegelin rationalizes the territorially bounded shelter that gives meaning to human life against the external forces of 'disintegration and chaos, a shelter in the end that is maintained by force'.[121]

Equally significantly, in terms of the progressive apologetics of those committed to purging themselves of their post-colonial angst, this order, as with all political organization, has its origins in violence and crime. Cain slew Abel and Romulus Remus. As Hannah Arendt pointedly remarked, 'the conviction that in the beginning was a crime – for which the phrase 'state of nature' is only a theoretically purified paraphrase – has carried through the centuries'.[122]

Ultimately, the order that enables political activity and commerce to thrive must confine itself within a unit that exercises a monopoly on the legitimate use of violence within its boundary. It is neither transnational nor international. Politics requires a constitutionally limited authority for its practice. Maintaining borders and the terms of membership are matters of prudence rather than abstract norms of global justice or compassion. In the language of Miltonic republicanism, the free state maintained liberty and political virtue, not progressive universal values or minority group rights.

Yet it offers only one solution to the problem of order. Despotism, oligarchy and even democracy, in its majoritarian or minority, tyrannical and direct activist, radically deliberative, versions, are alternative, anti-political forms of rule. Against a limited political understanding, despotism considers everything in society its property.[123] Both the politically religious as well as the post-modern managerial versions of despotism see everything in society, and on the planet, as ripe for intervention and regulation. This imperial tendency in its latest modern form further assumes, as we have seen, the achievement of a post-democratic state of perfection via resistance, regulation and purification.

The governing elites of the West, fired by the new liberal enthusiasm for social justice, however, have become disenchanted with politics, its understanding of citizenship, order, mixture, and balance affording a condition of political liberty, together with the prudential statecraft it necessitates. Instead they capriciously engaged in post-national faith based projects of rational modernization and global justice. Consequently, a crisis of politics, and not, as Donald Trump's progressive critics claim, of democracy, now threatens the integrity, balance and constitutional order of Western democracies.

The Crisis of Politics

The contemporary crisis in politics takes the form of a crisis in representation and the radical disconnection between mainstream political parties and the people or demos that the UK parliament's failure to deliver Brexit most vividly illustrates. Over two centuries, the two party system that evolved in the US and the UK proved its viability as a stable and enduring form, whilst, at the same time, guaranteeing constitutional liberties. It is this system that is in profound difficulty. Unlike its more fissiparous, multi-party, European political cousin, the two party model effectively channelled popular sentiment, but the catch-all party was never a single issue popular organ. Rather, these parties were 'the very efficient instruments through which the power of the people is curtailed and controlled'.[124] Political scientists like Maurice Duverger and Otto Kirchheimer identified the modern party as the outstanding institution of democratic government, corresponding to one of the major trends of modernity, namely the equalization and political transformation of society.[125] The political party, then, was an institution that provides parliamentary government with the requisite popular support through voting, while political action remains the prerogative of an elected government. The deepest significance of political parties, historically, was in offering the necessary institutional framework to enable the masses to recruit from among themselves their own elites.

The most, however, the citizen could hope for in this process was to be represented. Actual participation increasingly became the activity of a detached and professional political class.[126] From the 1960s, politics evolved into a profession and career and an elite political class was increasingly chosen according to standards which were not political. By the 1990s, the third way vision that sought to transcend politics in order to instrumentalize universal progressive values profoundly distorted both the politics of balance that the party system sustained, and the mean in action that secured political freedoms. It further exacerbated the already burgeoning gap between a remote and, in Europe, an increasingly transnational governing elite and a state-based citizenry, a gap which new, but unstable, single issue populist parties exploited.

During the first wave of modern representative political democracy, catch-all parties served as the political vehicle for marshalling a collocation of social and political interests and organizing citizens for political engagement. However, in recent decades, mainstream political parties adapted 'themselves to declining levels of participation and involvement in party activities by not only turning to resources provided by the state, but by doing so in a collusive manner'.[127] They have become cartel parties. In the post-Cold War era, democratically elected governments increasingly functioned like 'a large media corporation'.[128] This fusion of the mainstream, but not the social, media and political domains intimated a managerial system of government, where 'techniques of manipulation, deception, smear and constitutional capture have taken power away from the ordinary voter and placed it in the hands of the political class'.[129] Such manipulative corporatism has fractured the constitutional relationship between elites and the people and led to a hollowing out of mainstream parties and the political democratic process.[130] Peter Mair even declared that:

> The age of democracy has passed. Although the parties themselves remain, they have become so disconnected from the wider society, and pursue a form of competition that is so lacking in meaning, that they no longer seem capable of sustaining democracy in its present form.[131]

The changing character of political parties affected their standing, legitimacy and effectiveness and, as a consequence, the legitimacy and effectiveness of political democracy, as the collapse of mainstream parties across Europe so amply demonstrates. Problematically, political leaders and the parties they serve no longer represent ordinary people, but function as emissaries of a centralized bureaucracy.

This is particularly the case in Europe, where mainstream party elites turned the EU into a 'protected sphere, safe from the demands of voters and their representatives'. Accordingly, a technocratic directorate has progressively taken decision-making away from national parliaments. From the currency and the economy, to counter-terrorism and immigration, decisions are made elsewhere. Mainstream politicians encouraged this process, as they sought 'to divest themselves of responsibility for potentially unpopular policy decisions and so cushion themselves against possible voter discontent'.[132] Brexit, followed by the House of Commons' arbitrary decision to seize control of the tortuous process of negotiating separation from European administration, in order to deny the will of the people expressed in a binding referendum, is only the most recent, if one of the more egregious, examples of this development.

Consequently, mainstream political parties are failing because 'the zone of engagement – the traditional world of party democracy where citizens interacted with and felt a sense of attachment to their political leaders – is being evacuated'.[133] This abandonment has led to a burgeoning popular indifference to politics and created a climate conducive to extremism and anti-political zealotry. The political class and the mainstream media appear increasingly remote from the quotidian concerns of the citizens they ostensibly reflect and represent. The rhetoric of manipulative corporatism reinforces this perception. Leaders like Tony Blair, David Cameron and Theresa May in the UK, Bill Clinton and Barack Obama in the US, Angela Merkel in Germany, Emmanuel Macron in France and Kevin Rudd and Malcolm Turnbull in Australia project images of themselves as above politics.[134] As a result, Mair noted:

> Citizens withdraw from parties and a conventional politics that no longer seem to be part of their own world... There is a world of the citizens – or a host of particular worlds of the citizens – and the world of the politicians and the parties and the interaction between them steadily diminishes.[135]

257

Arising out of this new alignment, European political and business elites have come very close to the abolition of 'what we have been brought up to regard as politics and have replaced it with rule by bureaucrats, bankers and various kinds of unelected expert'.[136]

Nor are things much better on the other side of the Atlantic. As David Runciman argues, during the financial crisis that overwhelmed the US economy after September 2008, 'no one could doubt that democracy was deeply implicated'.[137] The fact that Obama presented himself as a post-partisan and post-political redeemer only heightened the sense of political malaise. At the same time, the failure of the long wars in Iraq and Afghanistan seemed to confirm the fact that democracies have not learned how 'to avoid unwinnable wars'.[138]

It is no coincidence that the period after 1990 that witnessed the rise of manipulative corporatism also coincided with the rise of political religions that sought solutions to the disenchantment and hollowing out of political democracy in Islamist, right-wing populist, or transnationally post-political soteriologies. These versions of salvationism offer refuge from the disintegration of political practice properly understood in ways that the elites in government, business, the mainstream media and academia failed to acknowledge or appreciate. As the Liberal Democrat peer Lord Ashdown once observed, 'if this is the age of the collapse of [democratic] beliefs, the dissolution of institutions, then what you are going to find is people who find an appeal in answers that are simplistic'.[139] These simplistic answers range from a recourse to jihadism and the white supremacist reaction, to communities in the UK 'born under other skies [and]... from other cultures who would prefer to police themselves'.[140] When minority communities 'take the law into their own hands', the rule of law, integral to a political understanding of the mean in action, also dissolves and *stasis* inexorably ensues.[141]

Yet although a crisis of politics now threatens Western liberal democracy, it has survived similarly severe crises in the course of the twentieth century. The history of democracy in the modern age is both cumulative and cyclical. As David Runciman writes, 'the experience of crisis builds up over time, no crisis is quite like the one before, because the one before is always there to serve as a warning and a temptation'. Yet the 'repeated sequence of democratic crises over the past hundred years also describes a single over-arching narrative', namely, that twentieth century democracy was a success story. At the end of that short century (1914–90) liberal democracies emerged as the richest and most powerful states the world has ever seen. 'They had defeated their enemies and enabled their citizens to prosper. But success on that scale comes at a price'.[142] Ironically, it 'blinded democracies to the enduring threats they face'. Paradoxically, 'the cumulative success of democracy...created the conditions for systemic failure'.[143]

The elite abandonment of the idea of politics and the failure of established representative political parties exacerbated the paradox. Democracies, nevertheless, have in the past found a way of stumbling through. It is perhaps this capacity, along with the return to a more sceptical politics of balance, practiced by free citizens in their national states, that may still give them an edge over their politically religious, progressive transnational and illiberal authoritarian rivals.

10

CONCLUSION

The pursuit of enlightenment has been with us for a while. Our political understandings even longer. One of the themes we have pursued is how, at the end of history, progressive understanding reflected a new liberal version of an Enlightenment project to implement social justice, emancipation and equality universally. The project culminated in disaster. The inability to manipulate minorities, contain an implacable, apocalyptic, non-western ideology, or rationally manage disembedded financial markets, spawned unintended consequences and countervailing forces. These included a populist reaction to globalization, the rise of illiberal threats to the liberal international order, as well as a new, intensified, post democratic version of Olympian transnational emancipation.

The French poet René Char wrote, 'our heritage is preceded by no precedent'.[1] Both Camus and Arendt refer to Char's maxim in evaluating how plausible it is for modern democracy to lose its contingently achieved 'treasure' of political freedom. If the treasure is indeed irrecoverable and any return to the politics of prudent diffidence impotent to restore balance, civil association, and limited constitutional rule, what alternative dispositions might mould the contours of our post historical future?

Management and the Body Politic

Since 2016, if not before, the liberal mood music in the West changed from Beethoven's *Ode to Joy*, which had earlier achieved victory over all its ideological competitors, to Ravel's *Pavane pour une infante défunte*, indicative of the West's failure to impose its universal vision on a recalcitrant globe. Brexit and the election of Donald Trump suggested that the rough beast of populism was lurching towards Brussels and Washington, and its coming appeared far from progressive. Certainly the populist movements that have emerged across Europe and the United States after the financial crash threaten any liberal consensus based on multiculturalism at home and the promotion of globalization, social justice, and human rights abroad.

This *bouleversement* surprised mainstream political commentators. Douglas Murray's study of *The Strange Death of Europe* revealed a continent exhausted, bored, and self-loathing. David Goodhart's *The Road to Somewhere: The Populist Revolt and the Future of Politics* identified a 'great divide' between value blocs that had appeared in modern Britain. Across the Atlantic, liberal commentators like Steven Levitsky and Daniel Ziblatt contemplated the death of democracy and the re-emergence of the authoritarian personality, aka Donald Trump. Channelling the zeitgeist, Kevin Rudd, somewhat predictably, opined 'democratic capitalism is showing signs of deep, systemic sickness'.[2]

Western decline is on the political menu once more, and, not for the first time, it is the dish *du jour*.[3] Penning one of the longer suicide notes in history, Jonah Goldberg contends that 'the rebirth of tribalism, populism, nationalism, and identity politics' is killing Western democracy.[4] By contrast, Yoram Hazony, in *The Virtue of Nationalism*, finds in populism a welcome reassertion of national values, political freedom, and self-determination.[5] Does populism portend the suicide of the West, a welcome restatement of national identity, or something else, and what might that something else be?

The current wave of geopolitical and economic uncertainty troubling Europe and its political institutions both at the state and the regional level is, of course, nothing new. Historians like Norman Davies have shown how often European political arrangements either collapse or change into new forms. In *Vanished Kingdoms*, Davies traced the rise and fall of various European political arrangements from the end of the Roman Empire in the West to the 'ultimate vanishing act' the Soviet Union (USSR) performed in 1991.[6] Davies' history of half-forgotten Europe concludes with a chapter evaluating 'How States Die' and whether 'discernible patterns of causation can account for this demise'.

His analysis coincides with a developing field in comparative political science that identifies the 'independent variables' which affect how state 'systems' fail, endure 'breakdown', suffer 'mid-life crises' or 'die'.[7] After 2016, this field became increasingly crowded as populism swept the West.[8]

The current enthusiasm for comparing, measuring and categorizing failing or dying states draws, without acknowledgement, on a European tradition of political thought which, after Aristotle and Plato first contemplated Athenian decline, sought to identify the factors that limit the potential for state dissolution, *stasis* or disintegration.[9] Seventeenth century English political philosophers like Thomas Hobbes and John Locke, attempting to understand the course of the English Civil War and its aftermath, diagnosed, from different perspectives, the internal 'diseases that tend to the dissolution of a commonwealth'.[10] The most common intestinal distempers they identified were civil (or internal) and external wars, leading to state disintegration – a central preoccupation, as we have shown, of early modern statecraft. In referring to the decay of commonwealths, Hobbes particularly drew upon and revised the most powerful analogy in Western political thought: that of the body politic.[11]

States and unions dissolve from a number of disorders. Apart from Hobbes, there is a large and varied body politic literature in both the Graeco-Roman and Christian, as well as the Abbasid and Ottoman, traditions of statecraft. After the fall of Christendom and the emergence of Europe as an idea, much was made of the image of the political body, the stages of its growth and development and the reasons for its decay and death. Abbasid and Ottoman scholar diplomats like Ibn Khaldun and Kâtip Çelebi devoted treatises to the relationship between the various organs in the political body and the means of correcting their dysfunction. For the most part, these treatises were concerned with identifying sources of corruption and decay and their remedies. Yet whatever 'physic' the commonwealth's 'doctors' might advise, they only delayed the state's inevitable progress through the stages of growth, civilization, maturity and luxury, senility and death.[12]

Considering the current Western predicament, from this analogical perspective it is evident that imperial body politics like the European Union, or nation states like Germany or the United Kingdom, come and go, and with far more frequency than we like to admit. Apart from the internal and external factors affecting state development and decay, involuntary and voluntary factors also play their part. In Europe's recent history, Davies identifies a typology, or five 'mechanisms' – implosion, conquest, merger, liquidation, and infant mortality – accounting for state death.

Thus, in the eighteenth century, the Polish-Lithuanian commonwealth, founded in the fifteenth century, 'died' from unnatural causes at the hands of its neighbours and their brutal partitionary wars. By contrast, other political arrangements begin life through the amalgamation of pre-existing units. The degree of amalgamation differs widely. Spain and the UK are good examples – best described in either the corporate language of merger and demerger, or that of civil union, marriage and divorce. The European Union was in this sense a merger, meaning that those who, like the United Kingdom, seek to demerge, suffer seemingly endless and destabilising divorce proceedings administered according to arcane, legal, and bureaucratic formulae. Meanwhile, other mergers like those leading to the Soviet Union after 1945 were brutally coercive shotgun marriages. In this context of political bodies merging and demerging, it is evident that the USSR imploded. The party state had the equivalent of a heart attack and died from natural causes. By contrast a modern example of successful demerger or divorce would be Czechoslovakia.

The terms of membership by which one more successful body incorporates another is always a source of tension. It is no wonder perhaps that the remarkable document signed at Horodlo that created a Polish-Lithuanian state endured far longer than the Treaty of Lisbon. The preamble to the Act of Horodlo 1413 noted that:

> Whoever is unsupported by the mystery of love shall not achieve the grace of salvation... For by love laws are made, kingdoms governed, cities ordered, and the state is brought to its proper goal. Whoever casts love aside shall lose everything.[13]

Compare this with the bureaucratese of the Lisbon Treaty of the European Union that came into force in 2008:

> Determined to promote economic and social progress for their peoples, taking into account the principle of sustainable development and within the context of the accomplishment of the internal market and of reinforced cohesion and environmental protection, and to implement policies ensuring that advances in economic integration are accompanied by parallel progress in other fields.[14]

Moreover, the current lack of love displayed between the European Commission in its dealings with dissident members like Poland and Hungary or defectors like the UK, or the Eurogroup and the ECB's indifference to Italy, Spain and Greece's financial difficulties, does not bode well for the union's future happiness. The UK has given the European Union an acute case of indigestion. Evidently, unless a more agreeable remedy is found to address this particular distemper, the UK might suffer a heart attack and the EU expire from natural causes.

Myth and Statecraft, or Highway 61 Revisited

Despite its current penchant and potential for decline, suicide or death from natural causes, it is also worth recalling Europe and the West's Promethean capacity to reinvent itself. When Western states are not contemplating their decline, they can often be found anticipating their renaissance. Considering Europe's descent into barbarism and the revolt of its masses in the 1930s, Ortega y Gasset thought the remedy lay in greater European elite cooperation leading to a 'United States of Europe'.[15]

Whilst some anticipate the West's suicide, others envisage making America and even the UK great again. The fates of Prometheus and Icarus are distinctively Western myths. Yet perhaps the myth that most informs hubristic projects of growth, regeneration, and greater integration is that of the Tower of Babel, which expresses an unchanging, but distinctively Western, 'predicament'.[16] In its Old Testament version, after the flood God, man, and nature were reconciled, in a covenant made between God and Abraham. Abraham's grand-nephew, Nimrod, however, found its terms unacceptable and launched his followers on a project to conquer heaven, building a tower to reach it. Rather than let loose another flood, Abraham persuaded God to solve the threat by 'confounding the tongues' of Nimrod and his fellows. Not by a flood, but in a deluge of meaningless words, was Nimrod's empire destroyed. Babel, which originally meant the city of liberation, acquired mythic significance as the city of confusion.

Significantly, two major thinkers of and writers about the twentieth century Western predicament, the Austro-Hungarian, Jewish novelist Stefan Zweig and the English philosopher Michael Oakeshott, adapted the Babel myth to the political dilemmas confronting modern Europe. Interestingly, they addressed the myth in very different, and from the perspective of ever closer Union, prescient ways.

Zweig observed that the symbols in originary myths harbour a 'wonderful poetic force' suggesting, as they do, 'great moments of a later history in which peoples renew themselves' and in which the most significant epochs have their roots.[17] For Zweig, the Babel myth intimates a desire for unity – humans finding themselves in a foreign place with no means of escape, a place that seemed to them uncertain and filled with danger; high above them they see the sky and pool their resources in an attempt to reach it. This 'communal work brings them together'.[18] Their endeavours are remarkably successful, but a cruel and fearful God concerned by this human drive for unity, one only the Godhead can achieve, sows dissension. The Babel of different languages ensures they cannot understand each other. God's 'dark resolution' smote 'the spirit of unity and dedication'.[19] The project collapses, 'centuries…passed and men lived in the isolation of their languages', but the dream did not die. The lost project of community and the desire to come together again reasserts itself, after millennia.[20] As a result, the Tower of Babel once more 'began to rise gradually from the soil of Europe, the monument…to mankind's solidarity. But it was no longer raw materials that went into this tower's construction… The new tower was built with a more delicate and yet more indestructible substance which they discovered on earth' in the long era of division and separation, 'that of spirituality and experience, the most sublime material of the soul'.[21] However, a cruel God, horrified at their endeavour, caused confusion to break out amongst them once more. 'This is the monstrous moment we are living through today', Zweig wrote in 1916.[22] He returned to the theme again in 1930 and 1932, observing that 'The new Tower of Babel, the great monument to the spiritual unity of Europe, lies in decay, its workers have lost their way'. Zweig would no doubt see contemporary Europe's predicament as the latest response of a vengeful God who has sown dissension amongst European populists and Brexiteers who, indifferent to the union's collapse, 'believe that their contribution can be withdrawn from the magnificent construction'. Nevertheless, Zweig would maintain Babel's 'battlements stand, still its invisible blocks loom over a world in disarray'.[23] Moreover, 'some exist who believe that never can a single people, a single nation achieve what a collective of European nations' could, and 'must be brought to completion in our Europe'.[24]

Zweig's paean to the 'heroic' European 'endeavour' to overcome national attachments contrasts with Oakeshott's pessimism towards what he would deem an exercise in rationalist faith. In Oakeshott's telling, the modern day Nimrod inspires his Babelian subjects with a vision of 'forcing open the gates of heaven, dislodging' the 'miserly deity from his estate and appropriating for the enjoyment of all Babelians the limitless profusion of paradise'.[25] Ultimately, the motivation for such an endeavour stemmed from greed and a 'profound feeling of being alike deprived: allowed to have wishes but denied their immediate satisfaction'.[26] As a consequence of the joint endeavour, the city of freedom acquired over time 'a new communal identity in place of their former distinct individualities'.[27] All conduct was recognized only in relation to the enterprise. Proverbial gaiety gave way to spurious gravity.

Moreover, as the endeavour proceeded with no apparent end in sight, supported only by a precarious vision of limitless, progressive satisfaction, and marked by no interim satisfactions to break the monotony, it took its toll in terms of emotional stress. Suspicion and distrust concerning Nimrod and his managerial elite's intentions leads to a catastrophic populist storming of the tower, precipitating its collapse. 'What had been designed as a stairway to paradise' became 'the tomb of an entire people, not perished in a confusion of tongues, but the victims of a delusion and confounded by the distrust which dogs those who engage in titanic exploits'. Ultimately, those 'who in Elysian fields would dwell, do but extend the boundaries of hell'.[28] In the current European case, but not yet in the US, these boundaries are set by a Commission pursuing ever closer Union.

The conscious endeavour to instrumentalize a morality of ideals, in this case a European ideal, is, for Oakeshott, hubristic. It substitutes the illusions of affairs for self-understanding. Like the attempt to build a tower to heaven, post-Cold war progressivism mistakenly believed that the difficulties of life could be avoided by engaging in a project in which the ends have been determined for them by history. They are, indeed, history's fools.

Babel-17?[29] AI and the Pursuit of The Singularity

Nevertheless, as President Obama suggested at the time, the populist insurgency of 2016 might only be a blip on the road to the realisation of the rationalist dream of a universal, progressive, harmonious international order. New liberal and illiberal progressive futures may take the form of a digitally administered party state like China or Singapore or what Silicon Valley envisages as an algorithmically managed, digital oligarchy. Both envisage a technocratically managed brave new world where robots cater to and define the needs of a dependent population eking out their days in either a distracted or opiated stupor.[30]

The New Utopians, or Thomas More Meets Big Data

It was the European Renaissance that formed much of what became the West's ambivalent political vocabulary of individualism, liberty, equality, right, justice, and contract. It also advanced the idea of scientific inquiry freed from religious supervision or customary oversight. It gave rise, amongst other things, to speculation about the possibility of social perfection. Neo-Platonists like Pico della Mirandola wondered where man's release from a determinist chain of being might lead. 'What a great miracle is man', Pico wrote, 'the intermediary between creatures…familiar with the gods above him, as he is lord of the creatures beneath him'.[31]

In this spirit, later humanists like Thomas More imagined utopia, 'no place', where 'there's never any excuse for idleness'. More's society of perfect happiness was also one of complete surveillance where 'everyone has his eye on you'.[32] More's utopia was a Menippean satire. In the mode of the new scientific inquiry he did much to promulgate, Francis Bacon conceived a New Atlantis where Salomon's house, or the scientific College of the Six Days Work, would find 'out the true nature of all things'. He added, parenthetically, and, as a sop to ruling theological opinion, 'whereby God might have the more glory in the workmanship of them, and men the more fruit in the use of them'.[33]

The scientific revolution and the eighteenth-century Enlightenment reinforced this quest. Mary Shelley's *Frankenstein or the Modern Prometheus* (1816) captured the boundary-freeing dream of science, which also came to address the growing irrelevance of God. Atheism, scientific or social, saw God and by extension religion as a delusion. Marx considered it the opium of the masses. 'How low has Christianity sunk, how powerless and miserable it has become. It is reason that has conquered', Kierkegaard confided to his *Journals* in 1849.[34] Matthew Arnold heard the sea of faith's melancholy, withdrawing roar on Dover Beach. By the end of the century, Nietzsche, Dostoevsky, and Thomas Hardy were all preoccupied by what the death of God might mean.

And who or what shall fill his place?
Whither will wanderers turn distracted eyes
For some fixed star to stimulate their pace
Towards the goal of their enterprise?[35]

Thus it was that the Promethean West killed God in its rationalist and increasingly ideological quest for worldly truth, enlightenment and the end of history. In God's place it put a rational faith in an Enlightenment project that embraced all mankind. How different to Hindu and Buddhist religions, where the notion of killing God makes no sense. Meanwhile the idea of killing Allah, or even caricaturing His prophet, invokes a fatwa for blasphemy like those received by Salman Rushdie in 1988, Theo van Gogh in 2004, and *Charlie Hebdo* in 2011.

What we in the West are left with, it seems, is a religious deformation. The West's enlightenment quest replaced Christian faith 'with an earthly condition of perfected humanity'. It assumed an ecumenical universalism leading to the end of history premised on secularism, tolerance and freedom of speech.[36] It is in Silicon Valley, however, that we find big tech offering us the ultimate universal, rational form of perfected humanity and the latest answer to Hardy's question concerning 'the goal of their enterprise'.

Big Tech Meets Big Bro

In the *Myth of Sisyphus* Albert Camus identified what he considered the central question facing the West, in a post-religious and post-Holocaust world, namely, 'why don't we commit suicide?'[37] The big tech companies that have come, over the last two decades, to define a new, virtual world economic order answer the existential question with another and older one that the existentialists of the first half of the twentieth century never factored into their calculations: 'why don't we abolish, not just God, but death and disease too?'[38]

Fictional tales of conscious machines have been science fiction themes frequently referenced by internet pioneers like Elon Musk. *I Robot, Blade Runner* and *Ex Machina* evince an obsessive desire to replicate human cognition. Silicon Valley transcends existential angst, ignores mythic warnings like the Faust or Babel myths,[39] and pursues instead 'the singularity' where man and machine become one.

We are in the grip of a technological revolution which, like its nineteenth-century industrial precursor, challenges our moral values, social cohesion and political identity. Smart and interactive habitats, machine learning, data mining, and domain specific intelligence are new realities that disrupt conventional economic, political and moral understanding and in unanticipated ways. The Techtopian vision, which embraces and extends the Enlightenment belief in progress, requires transhumanism and artificial intelligence, leading to what Yuval Harari terms the new rational religion of dataism.[40]

Social media has given Silicon Valley immense power to shape identity and influence choices. Rapidly acquired wealth means that the new big tech elite form a transnational plutocracy, temporarily housed in the San Francisco Bay Area, that has little interest, as we saw in chapter 6, in the nation state or democracy unless it suits their disruptive but unimpeachably progressive vision. The new technologies and the way the Techtopians implement them, therefore, have profound but little understood implications, both for democratic and moral self-understanding, and the prospect of progressive emancipation by virtual means. As recent scandals involving Facebook, YouTube, Cambridge Analytica, Twitter and other networks demonstrate, the new media now surpasses the traditional print and televisual media as a tool to influence voter behaviour and democratic outcomes. Unaccountable, monopolistic big tech companies mine personal data and act as the universal arbiter of free speech.

After Gutenberg

Political and social organization has always reflected the state of technological knowledge. The invention of the stirrup created feudalism. The printing press enabled the emergence of the Gutenberg galaxy, which gave us the reformation of religion, the modern secular state, humanism, and scientific rationalism.[41] It liberated the individual from the cocoon of medieval order and made political liberty and individual character a possibility.

The computer age, by contrast, made possible the global village, world society and borderless, millennial capital. 'The computer is', Marshall McLuhan wrote, 'the most extraordinary of all the technological clothing ever devised by man, since it is the extension of our central nervous system'.[42] New technologies create new environments.[43] Any evaluation of the social impact of these 'new modes of experience' must recognize, McLuhan thought, that these technologies are already 'generations ahead of our thinking'.[44]

We might wonder what the social media revolution and its preoccupation with big data mean for our ruling Western political and economic assumptions post-9/11, post-2008, and post-the potentially brief, and inchoate, populist rebellions of 2016. More precisely, how will the latest technological clothing and the fourth industrial revolution it announced alter our enlightenment secular, liberal or prudently conservative modes of self-understanding and self-disclosure?

Pursuing the death of death is undoubtedly hubristic, but it has already had transformative political and economic consequences. Current debate concerning social media focuses primarily on its effects on economic and social infrastructure, the job market, personal privacy, or democratic transparency and the manipulation of the electorate through 'fake news' and disinformation. However, merely addressing AI's external impact on society neglects the existential question: how will intelligent algorithms affect the liberal humanist fiction of the autonomous, individual self, central to the understanding and the practice of political liberty?

The Great Disruption and the Progressive Loss of Liberty

Conceptions of social contract, natural right, and liberty that shaped Western secular political understanding from the seventeenth century assumed the existence of a rational, autonomous individual. Despite developments in neuroscience that dispute the understanding of the self as a 'single essence',[45] these advances did not necessarily have moral or political implications. I still have every reason to value and protect my seemingly free choices.[46]

Artificial Intelligence (AI) and data mining, however, alter the equation. AI will soon be able to analyze individuals in such intimate detail that it will know them better than they know themselves. The reasons for listening to the inner voice of conscience may well be extinguished. AI will know better what we really want. In *Anarchy, State and Utopia* (1974), the libertarian philosopher Robert Nozick assumed that no reasonable individual would choose a pleasure or experience machine if it became a possibility. AI suggests otherwise.[47] This has implications for the self-owning, autonomous individual central to liberal political thought, and republican and democratic theory and practice since the seventeenth century.

As the utility of preserving individual autonomy collapses, the political and social structures and values that reflect it may also dissolve. Governments will increasingly use algorithms to predict policy outcomes and manage smart cities.[48] If machines show that they can provide consistent and correct policy decisions, they may progressively replace democratic checks. Once a ruling elite, indifferent to individual liberty, the rule of law and constitutional accountability, accepts that intelligent machines can arrive at correct solutions to policy problems, whilst their electorates enjoy the benefits of those solutions, we will, as if by an invisible machine, enter a condition of techno-tutelage. 'AI could attain a level of intelligence vastly greater than humanity's combined intellectual wherewithal',[49] rendering the psychological utility and the rationality of voting redundant.

AI will not be a tool to make human life easier; it will instead construct intelligent systems capable of participating in a feedback loop with humans. It will present us with answers about our nature, needs, and desires that we did not know we wanted. It will force us to question what it means to exist with dignity, and what values should be preserved in order to live the good life. AI thus challenges the values that shape our social and political order and renders abstract philosophical arguments in defence of freedom and individual liberty obsolete.[50]

AI meets Homo Deus

AI dataism thus assumes a morally deforming, politically religious character. Ray Kurzwiel, director of engineering at Google, a media platform mutating into an AI business, predicted the coming of *The Age of Spiritual Machines* (2006). Kurzwiel anticipates that 'the human species, together with the computational age technology it has devised, will be able to solve age old problems…in a post-biological future'.

From Kurzwiel's transhumanist perspective, we have entered the fifth evolutionary epoch where human intelligence merges with technology to reach the 'singularity' at which point we (or at least an elite) would 'be transformed into spiritual machines'.[51] This is the 'rapture' when the demise of death will fulfil the enlightenment dream of *Homo Deus*. Oxford philosopher Nick Bostrom argues that it's probable that we already inhabit a matrix-like simulation of the past created by our post-human descendants.[52] Bostrom's followers embrace 'simulation theology'. They include big tech pioneers like Google's Larry Page, as well as Peter Thiel of Palantir and Pay Pal, and Elon Musk of Space-X and Tesla, who have founded the Singularity University and the Future of Humanity Institute.

Socrates maintained that to philosophise is to learn how to die. Whether one believes the soul is eternal or perishes with the body, Western civilization historically recognized this natural order of things. Big tech transhumanism, by contrast, seeks life everlasting. Beyond criticising what he calls 'the ideology of the inevitability of the death of every individual',[53] Peter Thiel also finances the SENS (Strategically

Engineered Negligible Senescence) Research Foundation, devoted to 'curing' death.[54]

The Zuckerbergs, Tim Cooks and Larry Pages call the shots on America's Left Coast. Although they maintain similar professional profiles as investors and entrepreneurs, Peter Thiel's endorsement of Donald Trump stands out against big tech's overwhelming new liberal, progressive, globalizing sympathies. Yet what unifies Zuckerberg, Kurzwiel, Musk and Thiel may be more decisive than the traditional and perhaps increasingly redundant Republican/Democrat political divide.

All big tech entrepreneurs embrace the ideology of 'technologism', or more accurately an abstract scientific rationalism, one that transcends conventional left-right partisanship. All questions recede before the task of technological progress. In the first decades of the new millennium, the techno-rationalist dream triumphed. Even economists today are essentially technologists, locating the demand-side 'real' factors behind our chronically low interest rates, which in turn account for contemporary secular stagnation.

Elon Musk, channelling Francis Bacon, explains that big tech applies the scientific method both to engineering and society. 'It's really helpful', he maintains, 'for figuring out the tricky things'.[55] Techtopians possess an unprecedented belief in building new worlds by promulgating a technological ideal untrammelled by the threat of competition or social discontent, which new big data insights will in future repress before they even emerge. Visionary entrepreneurs like Musk, Thiel and Zuckerberg have, in the process, acquired the status of philosopher-CEOs. Unlike the classical world, where philosophy was a stoic and contemplative affair, the new philosopher-CEO augments his wealth and scale in the service of 'realising' a utopia based on incessant innovation. Like Bacon before them, Zuckerberg, Page, Thiel and Musk pursue a New Atlantis.

Technology, Transhumanism and Rationalism in Politics

More precisely, the techtopian vision represents the latest version of what Michael Oakeshott identified as 'rationalism in politics'. This style first emerged in the early modern period of European politics.[56] It emphasized reason, not as Aristotle or Thomas Aquinas prudentially understood it, as a faculty of the practical understanding, but as Bacon, and, subsequently, Descartes and Kant came to reinvent it, in rationalist, axiomatic, abstract scientific terms. Since the Enlightenment, rationalism has promoted the sovereignty of technique that affords the prospect of scientific certainty. AI represents the latest and most hubristic version of this Enlightenment project.

The possibility of certain knowledge, which a scientific method applied to the realm of politics or society intimates, provides a technique which not only 'ends with certainty but begins with certainty and is certain throughout'.[57] Already by the early decades of the twentieth century, the extent to which particular traditions and cultures had given way to the abstract, scientific ideologies of Marxism, liberalism, and nationalism illustrates how deeply the rationalist disposition had penetrated modern political thought and practice.[58] In the case of Techtopia, the new ideology is AI-determined dataism.

Since the nineteenth century, the rationalist concern with technique assumed a politics of social perfection. In its twentieth century form, it welcomed the growing bureaucratic power of government to make the people conform to its politics of rational faith.[59] The rationalist endeavour reduces 'the tangle and variety of experience' to a set of universal principles.[60] Cutting itself off 'from the traditional knowledge of society', rationalism, or, what Musk terms the 'scientific method', combines the politics of perfection with the politics of uniformity. Under Techtopian guidance, political activity will increasingly 'consist in bringing the social, political, legal and institutional inheritance of society before the tribunal' of artificial intelligence. 'The rest', as those who experience the roll-out of the intelligence gathering, Chinese social credit system know, 'is rational administration'.[61]

What will be Done?

The Silicon Valley giants of technology, therefore, do not crave monopoly merely as a matter of profit. Instead, as Franklin Foer argues, 'big tech considers the concentration of power in its companies – in the networks they control – an urgent social good, the precursor to global harmony, a necessary condition for undoing the alienation of humankind'.[62] Under conditions of internet oligopoly, techno-managerialism through the manipulation of choices, fears and desires, undermines and replaces the free individual of classical liberal thought with a servile dependent. It renders democracy potentially malleable and obsolete. It creates conditions for oligarchical rule based on the control of and access to technology and big data. This has already occurred in China, where the ruling party, in collaboration with big data gathering companies like Ali Baba, and a universal social credit system, is busily constructing a virtual, digital despotism.[63]

Somewhat differently, across the splinternet, we can identify in Silicon Valley utopianism the lineaments of a new techno-guardian class building transnational processes and networks and evolving a theory of political and social organization that seemingly confirms Vilfredo Pareto's thesis of elite circulation.[64] The recent eruption of populism against this trend, represented by Trump, Brexit, and the victories of PIS in Poland or Orban's Fidesz in Hungary, might only be a temporary revolt, susceptible to long-term data management and big nudging by a Machiavellian, fox-like, elite.[65]

The potential for political manipulation reflects the fact that the new media technologies have rapidly turned into compulsions. This is as their designers intended.[66] Facebook's first president, Sean Parker, even acknowledges that the platform was designed to act like a drug, by '[giving] you a little dopamine hit every once in a while, because someone liked or commented on a photo or a post or whatever'. Similarly, Google's business model, as former executive Tristan Harris observes, fracks 'for human beings' attention'.[67] Social media platforms maximize their advertising revenue by competing for the interest of the more than two billion people 'jacked into a technology owned by five or six companies'.[68] As well as addicting their users, social media contributes to 'continuous partial attention', limiting people's ability to focus.[69] Everyone is now distracted all of the time.

The human brain 'has no chance against a supercomputer... calculating human weaknesses'. Becoming stupid and inattentive, big tech undermines political democracy with the despotism of big data. AI can alter voters' beliefs and behaviour 'by intentionally and precisely targeting their unconscious cognitive processes'.[70] As Harris acknowledges, ruefully, 'it's a race to the bottom of the brain stem to get attention, which means I have to go lower into fear, outrage and anxiety'. Two billion people use Google's YouTube. Widely criticised for its failure to crack down on fake news, harassment and extremism, it has evolved into a 'digital Frankenstein', a 'huge ideological influence' spreading outrage, fear and anxiety. [71]

Silicon Valley has thus created a God-like technology to play with our Palaeolithic emotions. Somewhat belatedly, Western governments have woken up to the problem of regulating big tech. Facebook's Head of Global Affairs, Nick Clegg, acknowledged the need for government to exercise some oversight over 'the sensitive decisions we have to make'. [72] The European Union has imposed fines of €1.49 billion on Google and €100 million on Facebook for anti-trust violations. [73] Closer to home, the US government has started to pursue the tech monopolists under anti-trust laws as well as render them accountable for the material they post. The Senate joint committee hearing into 'Facebook, social media privacy and the use and abuse of data' that began in 2018 could lead to the media platform's break-up. [74] Meanwhile the US Department of Justice is currently exploring a competition investigation against Google.

The End

However, it could already be too late. Silicon Valley's craving for monopoly stretches back to the counterculture of the 1960s, where it emerged 'from the most lyrical of visions of peace and love'. [75] The hippie counter-culture of Haight-Ashbury dreamt from the outset of subverting the 'straight', conservative, traditional order. A utopian vision, grounded in anarchic idealism, but leading to a society of permanent surveillance, offers little prospect for a balanced or prudentially diffident political solution. Analogously, a European Union post-national constellation represents the antithesis of a creative, moral, or prudent, political project.

Both forms of rationalism in politics represent the antithesis of the conservative understanding of civil society as a local and contingent compact between the dead, the living, and the yet to be born. As the English conservative philosopher Roger Scruton wrote of the great disruption, the tech world of virtual networks erodes places and erases:

...the hierarchies that settle there. They replace space by time, and time by a succession of crowded instants in which nothing really happens since everything only happens on screen... The web is an unspecified nowhere, a Hobbesian state of nature in cyberspace. But for that reason it cannot compete with the trustworthy somewhere for which most people yearn. It is a release from place but not a replacement.[76]

Properly understood, the situations of a normal life are met, 'not by consciously applying to ourselves a rule of behaviour, nor by conduct recognized as the expression of a moral ideal, but by acting in accordance with a certain habit of behaviour'. The moral life, or, for that matter, a political condition, in this traditional form does not 'spring from the consciousness of possible alternative ways of behaving and a choice, determined by an opinion, a rule or an ideal, from among these alternatives'.[77] Conduct should instead be as nearly as possible without reflection. Most of the current situations of life should not appear as occasions calling for judgment, or as problems requiring a solution. There should instead be nothing more than 'the unreflective following of a tradition of conduct in which we have been educated or more precisely habituated'.[78]

For the big tech entrepreneur or the European bureaucrat to engage in their rationalist quests are gambles which may have not insubstantial rewards. However, 'when undertaken in a society not itself engaged in the gamble, it is mere folly'.[79] The project of finding a short cut to heaven, as we have seen, is as old as the human race, and conduct that orients itself by big data, the scientific method, post-nationalist constellations and axiomatic rules is precisely an attempt at this kind of shortcut.

Such projects assume that they may avoid the difficulties of life by engaging in a scheme in which the ends have been determined for them. They explicitly pursue a future state of perfection, all the while neglecting the joys and sorrows of our present temporality. The truth is that a morality and a political project in this form, whatever the quality of its ideals, breeds nothing but distraction and moral and ultimately political instability.[80] Chagrin ultimately awaits all those who embark upon such an enterprise.

AFTERWORD

THE STUDY OF INTERNATIONAL RELATIONS AND THE EROSION OF ACADEMIC INTEGRITY[1]

There has been, as Stefan Collini observes, 'a general erosion in academic integrity' over the last thirty years, that is, the period covered by *History's Fools*.[2] Moreover, this erosion has had an impact on the scholarship of international relations and a practice of large grants 'aligning with progressive, normative, transnational ideas and theories'. There is quantitative and qualitative evidence to show that this statement is no polemical exaggeration, but based on data available both in surveys of the current state of the university, mainly in the English speaking world, and in the disbursement of grants by large grant-giving bodies like the European Research Council (ERC) and the Australian Research Council (ARC). A number of interrelated factors account for the decline in academic standards and the consequent research bias towards progressive normativity, and a default position critical of Western democratic states and their traditional institutions. In sociological terms, the changes in higher education have been systemic and have created a functional framework for the activity of agents or academic entrepreneurs that the structural changes in the character of universities, particularly in the United Kingdom, the United States and Australia have facilitated.

279

The scientific and business performance models applied to the university sector from the 1980s changed the system. They undermined academic freedom and repressed heterodox viewpoints in a number of key ways: an evolving managerialism preoccupied with branding; conformity and uniformity; an obsession with large research grants, research metrics and student satisfaction; and a progressive ideological preoccupation with diversity and identity. This overarching structure has had, we shall further show, a particularly perverse outcome on the study of the human sciences in general and most notably on the theory of international relations.

The Management of Knowledge

Managerial and business models that emphasized raising productivity, increasing enrolments and winning large grant funding from state and non-state sources has determined university ranking since the 1990s. This evolving, utility-maximizing educational model dates back to the Thatcher/Reagan era in the UK and United States and the Dawkins era in Australia. The borderless market in students that came into being in the 1990s gave the model a powerful boost during the Blair-Brown era in the UK (1997–2010), the Clinton, Bush and Obama presidencies in the US (1992–2016), and under the Howard and Rudd governments in Australia (1996–2007).[3]

That this structural change occurred is beyond dispute. In 1990 the UK had forty universities catering to 350,000 students. In 2016, there were 140 universities and two million students. A similar dramatic change occurred in Australia over the same period.[4] This, as Stefan Collini points out, has radically revised the traditional purpose of the university. Its new purpose has a number of distinctive characteristics.[5]

As Collini and a number of other sociologists of higher education, including Alvin Gouldner and Frank Furedi, have shown, one consequence of this dramatic change has been the emergence of a new academic managerial class.[6] Alvin Gouldner first documented the emergence of this new conventionally liberal, intellectual, managerial class in the late 1970s.[7]

In the 1990s, animated by state interest in increasing student numbers and state investment in university funding, the managerial rationalization of the university took off. It has had a number of little appreciated consequences. After thirty years, these can be identified as lower entrance requirements, plummeting academic standards, and more students achieving degrees in subjects that offer little prospect of future employment. It has also spawned the rise of an academic bureaucracy, presided over by a managerial vice-chancellery, dedicated to cutting unfashionable or difficult subjects in the Arts and Sciences, from Chemistry and Physics[8] to Philosophy, Modern Languages and Classics.[9] In its place, academics are encouraged to produce practical 'research' and pursue industrial, governmental, or charitable sources of funding both at home and abroad.

The increase in student numbers led not only to a decline in standards and grade inflation. It also fundamentally altered the character of the university as it increasingly assumed the role of socialization in values or norms, a duty once provided by the family and the secondary school. Universities are now doing what high schools used to do, that is offer socialization through the validation of progressive norms and diverse identities. As Frank Furedi has shown, in a number of studies, the university's new *in loco parentis* role has facilitated 'paternalistic practices and a tendency towards [the] infantilization' of the campus.[10] Instead of treating students as 'young adults', encouraged to think freely, in an atmosphere of tolerance, they are 'offered protection and support by the administration'.[11]

As Furedi argues, 'the paternalist turn took off in the US' in the 1990s. Actually, as Allan Bloom and Saul Bellow showed, it had been closing the American mind since the 1980s.[12] Globalized, it introduced a climate of moral regulation and conformism onto the Western campus. Conformity with the ruling progressive campus ideology has had the practical consequence of estranging a millennial generation of students from notions of freedom of expression and tolerance.[13] Recent surveys of opinion indicate 'that a significant proportion of students support the banning of speakers whose views offend them'.[14] Regulation, conformity, and uniformity of practices have progressively undermined academic freedom on campus. A survey commissioned by the UK University and College Union in 2018 demonstrates that the UK university, in terms of freedom of opinion, is now 'the sick man of Europe'.[15] As Collini explains, 'genuine academic freedom in British universities is in a parlous condition'. It reflects 'the daily erosion of intellectual integrity, the relentless commodification of scholarly values, and the tightening grip of a managerialist autocracy'.[16]

Grant-Getting and Research-Only Academics

The expansion of the university sector, therefore, encouraged a pervasive managerialism and a growing but certainly progressive paternalism that undermined freedom of speech and encouraged conformity in ideas and uniformity in behaviour. The growing administrative preoccupation with grant funding teams of researchers, as opposed to independent scholars, reinforced the predisposition to ideological and disciplinary orthodoxy. Applying for large grants and success in getting grants has become the key criterion measuring early career academic performance, on the basis of which university committees assess suitability for promotion up a steeply hierarchical career ladder. The increasingly segmented profession of university teacher runs the gamut from lumpen sessional academics on zero hours, teaching-only contracts, to grant-receiving research-only academics *en route* to the status of professor and head of department, sitting on various academic and industry linked boards.[17]

In this academic structure, key performance indicators designed by management consultancy companies like Deloitte Touche and KPMG count success in achieving large grants as a key measure. From the 1990s, as the universities expanded, Commonwealth governments required the sector to run research and teaching quality exercises every three to five years as the basis for additional state funding. Success in applying for and achieving research grants is double counted, measured as not only as an academic 'input', but also, bizarrely, as a research 'outcome'.[18] This fetishizing of funding has become the academic norm, so much so that:

> All academics in British universities will immediately recognise that nothing they do as scholars and teachers wins anywhere near as much commendation and support from their university's 'senior management team' (older readers may still refer to them as 'administrators') as the securing of some kind of external funding. Such funding may

range from a project grant from a research council or charity, to the sponsorship of a post or studentship by a local business, and then on to the murkier regions of whole courses and centres being paid for by some overseas government or large corporation.[19]

The central importance of grants from both state and non-state sectors means the university administration tries to ensure that sources of funding are not jeopardized. The university administration consequently supports the imposition of disciplinary orthodoxy at the expense of academic freedom.[20] The most obviously egregious effect is university funding from overseas governments of an authoritarian disposition, or their state licensed bodies, that seek academic validation for political or religious practices not subject to open, critical or free inquiry. This has been the case most notably with large donations by Middle Eastern regimes endowing Chairs in Islamic Studies which take an 'empathetic' approach to Islamic fundamentalism and questionable regimes. The LSE's involvement in the Gaddafi funding scandal in 2011 was only the most notable, and press worthy, example of a widespread practice; the LSE was not the only university imbricated in the murky world of questionable donations. Nor were UK universities the only beneficiaries.[21] The scandal, however, drew attention to the scale of Middle Eastern patronage of British universities that between 1996–2011 amounted to nearly £750m.[22] It has since increased.

As Middle East scholar Christopher Davidson observed, this patronage paid for good public relations, presenting the autocrat as a '"good guy" to a Western audience'.[23] These gifts come with strings attached. '[T]here is generally no follow-up control, but this does not mean that self-censorship does not take root in the recipient institutions.' Davidson argued that staff or students:

> may feel uncomfortable pursuing sensitive topics relating to these countries. Imagine, for example, writing a negative critique of a regime that has paid for your salary, your scholarship or the building you sit in. In many UK universities, this is not only a possible scenario but now rather likely. What it may lead to (and in some cases it already has led to) is a field that carefully skirts around the key 'red line' subjects, such as political reform, corruption, human rights and revolution.[24]

There is, also, a growing corpus of international evidence that demonstrates British, US and Australian universities compete for questionable funding from authoritarian regimes and celebrate ties with tertiary institutions in China and Southeast Asia, as well as the Middle East, regimes that have no pretence to the rule of law or political accountability. The role of Confucius Institutes on Western campuses, advancing and supporting an uncritical view of the PRC and its role in the South China Sea, has only recently been questioned in the Australian media. Grants linked to the Chinese Academy of Social Sciences and the Party School in Beijing are unlikely to express a critical view of Xi Jinping's China dream, as recent events at the University of Queensland demonstrate. This again affects the quality of independent minded scholarship on single party dominant regimes in Asia. Such dependence on overseas funding particularly affects the manner in which International Relations departments teach, research and depict authoritarian regimes.[25]

At the same time, but somewhat differently, progressive normative and critical theory orthodoxies concerning international relations and the promotion of post-national constellations, social justice, and human rights dominate the list of those who receive the large grants dispensed by bodies like the ERC and the ARC. Jean Monnet Chairs in European Studies and other European Commission and ERC-sponsored awards promulgate a view of its study domain that reflect its patrons' interest in ever closer European union. The grant machinery promulgates the virtue of post-national European institutions and the necessity and inevitability of greater political, economic and financial integration.[26] The grants moreover are very large, often of up to ten million euros over a period of five years.[27] Such grants support, *inter alia*, Professor Christine Chinkin's team's €2,000,000 per annum grant (2018–22) to develop the theoretical foundations of 'a gendered international law of peace'.[28] A recent survey of forty-four large ERC grants of over €1million awarded between 2015–18 indicates that over ninety per cent go to research advancing a normative, human rights, critical theory approach to world politics.[29]

A similar survey of the ARC website on grants given to International Relations and Peace Studies research between 2002 and 2018 indicates that 79.8 per cent went to topics addressing a normative, radical pacifist, or idealist understanding of international politics.[30] Although the money dispersed by the Australian funding body is on a smaller scale than the ERC, grants made include AUS$2.6 million for a project examining 'Deliberative Worlds, Democracy Justice, and a Changing World',[31] $553,000 to assess 'inclusive peace',[32] $260,000 to question the Eurocentric assumptions governing the international state system,[33] $500,000 to question the uncertain, postmodern, Australian self,[34] and $145,000 to 'experience space' and sensory encounters 'from Baroque Rome to neo-Baroque Las Vegas'.[35]

More particularly, in the context of state sponsorship for international legal and UN-endorsed understandings of normative ideals and practices, both the ARC and the Australian Department of Foreign Affairs and Trade have devoted over four million dollars to the University of Queensland's Responsibility to Protect Centre, which take a notably soft line on the treatment of the Rohingyas in Myanmar and Uighurs in Xinjiang, China, whilst condemning the activity of the Australian government towards its aboriginal minorities or its dealings with states in the Pacific Island Forum.[36]

Diversity, Identity and Progressive Ideology

It is no mere coincidence that the change in the character of the university coincided with the rise of the social justice agenda and reflects the close ties between progressive politics, academia, and the media that social scientists like Richard Katz and Peter Mair first identified in the 1990s.[37] Western state research funding bodies, dispensing large grants to promote an international normative and legislative agenda, are in fact a disciplinary extension of the enlightened paternalistic bureaucracy that regulates the modern campus. This is hardly surprising. As John Gray and Brian Barry argued at the time, and Furedi and Collini's recent sociologies of the university confirm, it was out of normative political philosophy departments that the new liberal concern with identity and recognition emerged in the course of the 1990s.[38] This progressive new liberal orthodoxy became inscribed in the philosophy of the university and fashioned its commitment to the recognition and cherishing of diversity as it engaged in the process of large-scale structural change.

The consequences of this evolution now affect who can speak and what can be spoken of on campus. Commenting on an article in Columbia University's student newspaper, the *Columbia Spectator,* by 'a queer, multiracial woman of colour, survivor of sexual assault and sufferer from multiple mental illnesses', Furedi observes that 'the crucial facts relating to identity serve to endow the writer with moral authority'.[39] As James Allan writes of the Australian campus, 'initiatives (not to mention employees) trumpeting diversity proliferate. All sorts of group-based, head-counting and characteristic-counting, tied to attempts to re-balance things in favour of groups deemed statistically deprived, take place. Think of it as an entrenched mandate in favour of diversity'.[40]

However, it's not 'all sorts' of diversity that universities target. Given the fact that universities are actually in the business of thinking, what should really be mandated is a diversity of ideas, including of course alternative political perspectives. This, however, is not the case. The progressive campus has stifled the classical liberal, conservative or sceptical voice. A survey of grants awarded by the ERC or ARC in International Relations show very few going to studies that adopt a realist or state-centric perspective.[41] In the US, Allan finds that 'surveys and analyses of political donations show law professors identify themselves overwhelmingly as Democrat voters (at least 7 to 1)'.[42] US surveys conducted by the Carnegie Foundation since 1990 show an even more dramatic collapse in the conservative perspective on the US campus. Jon Shield writes that:

> ...conservative voices on college campuses began to diminish sharply in the late 1980s and early 1990s. When the Carnegie Foundation conducted its faculty survey in 1999, it found that a mere 12% of professors were conservatives, down from 27% in 1969. Conservative representation is even worse today in the social sciences and humanities, where they have practically disappeared from many areas of inquiry. Nearly every recent survey of the university places the percentage of conservative and Republican professors in these fields in the single digits. Conservatives also tend to cluster in economics departments, leaving other disciplines with hardly any center-right thinkers. By some prominent measures Republicans make up 4% of historians, 3% of sociologists, and a mere 2% of literature professors.[43]

286

Similar estimates would also apply to conservative political science and international relations professors on Australian and British campuses, which further buttresses the entrenched bias towards appointments and research funding that in turn reinforces the prevailing progressive university brand orthodoxy.

Structural Functionalism and the Academic Entrepreneur

The managerial rationalism that has pervaded the university sector since the 1980s has had intended and unintended consequences for funding, the quality and quantity of scholarship and education, hiring, firing, and promotion. Not all academics have suffered from the prevailing managerial orthodoxy. There have been winners and losers. The new dispensation has particularly suited the academic entrepreneur who identifies with the prevailing progressive mood and adapts to the managerial ethos, business model, and paternalistic intimations of the progressive campus.

Particularly successful from the standpoint of the social sciences, and advancing the progressive paradigm by aligning its norms with the university management model, were those who did most to advance the restructuring of the university along third way principles, like Lord Giddens of Southgate or Sir Steve Smith, former chair of the Russell Group of leading UK universities. The new cadre of 'university leaders' validates Thorstein Veblen's prediction that they would be 'plausible speakers with a large gift of assurance, [and] an urbane pillar of society'. Usually 'some astute veteran of the scientific [or social science] *demi-monde* will meet all reasonable requirements'.[44]

The professional structures introduced from the 1980s to rationalize standards, quantify 'impact' in terms of grants received, journal citations gained and publication outputs achieved with academic presses opened the academy to a distinctive type of conduct, manipulation, and bureaucratic guidance. It created the conditions for what their peers referred to in admiring terms as 'operators' or, more accurately, norm entrepreneurs. These new men (they were mainly men) learnt quickly how to play the evolving academic game. Indeed, they wrote its rulebook. An academic entrepreneur might not be a particularly accomplished scholar, conventionally understood.

In fact, it was better if he was not. His skill was that he knew how to identify the normative wave and surf it for journal articles, edited book collections and, most importantly, grants and networks that involved government departments, non-governmental organisations and relevant industrial partners. The entrepreneur also knows how to found new 'cutting-edge' journals, usually published by Taylor Francis, to address a demand that few people knew existed, sit on their boards, become referees on peer-reviewed journals and assess (always anonymously) grant applications to large government grant-giving bodies like the European Research Council (ERC) or the Australian Research Council (ARC).

Giddens epitomized this new breed of progressive academic entrepreneur, evolving on the radical new university campuses of the late 1960s to pioneer a critical, sociological and ethically activist worldview. He was by no means alone. A similar, if somewhat less glittering trajectory can be found in the careers of political scientists and IR scholars of comparable vintage. Professor Richard Higgott at Warwick University earned international fame for winning a multi-million pound grant from the ERC to establish a centre to study globalization in 1997. A dozen years later, its entrepreneurial founder moved on to a vice-chancellery in Western Australia where his academic career came to an undignified end in a corruption scandal. Elsewhere, Steve Smith's prescient embrace of the 'emancipatory' and 'transformative' potential of international relations transformed him over time into Sir Steve Smith, vice-chancellor of Exeter University (where one of his first acts was to close down the chemistry department),[45] and subsequently the chair of the Russell Group of university vice-chancellors. Networks associated with these scholar-entrepreneurs now dominate the senior echelons of international relations departments across the UK and Australia, reinforcing the progressive and critical theoretical viewpoint first announced in an introduction to *International Relations Theory Today* in 1995.

Utility and Conformity in Higher Education

Paradoxically, for all its market-oriented rhetoric, the academic policy paradigm that emerged in the course of the 1990s constrained both

288

innovation and differentiation. A concern with productivity both in terms of students processed and knowledge applied for industrial benefit or cherishing abstract group identities trumped any commitment to academic freedom or educational diversity. This pursuit of efficiency, conformity and uniformity undermined creativity and independence. It confirmed what the Nobel Prize winning economist and philosopher FA Hayek had argued, namely that the bureaucratic desire to plan markets was incoherent. As Hayek wrote in 1978, 'the halfway house between a completely planned system and a free market would indeed be the worst of all possible worlds', since the 'ability to make changes would become critically dependent on the red tape, delay and unpredictability that are characteristic of bureaucratic decisions'.[46]

Hayek's assessment accurately captures the contemporary state of higher education. Hayek further warned against the danger that the modern Western government's penchant for planning and industrial performance and the attendant coordination and centralization of research represented for *The Constitution of Liberty*.[47] 'Danger lies', Hayek warned, 'in the increased control which the growing financial needs of research give to those who hold the purse strings'. Belief in the superiority of directed research reflected 'the somewhat exaggerated conception of the extent to which modern industry owes its progress to the organized teamwork of the great industrial laboratories', rather than individual effort.

To facilitate both liberty and economic growth, Hayek averred, 'the prospects of advance would be most favourable if instead of the control of funds being in the hands of a single authority proceeding according to a unitary plan, there were a multiplicity of independent sources so that even the unorthodox thinker would have a chance of finding a sympathetic ear'.[48] The prospects of sustaining as 'many independent centres of work as possible' and thereby sustaining the intellectual diversity critical to liberty and tolerance is something the modern campus honours only in the breach. The propensity of modern democratic governments in general to conceive education as an instrument for advancing egalitarian aims rather than promoting excellence further eroded academic independence and subjected the higher education sector to 'the cruder kinds of interference by political or economic interests', kinds that Hayek could hardly have imagined.[49]

NOTES

1 INTRODUCTION

1. Francis Fukuyama, *The End of History and The Last Man* (London, Penguin,1992).
2. Tony Blair, *A Journey* (London, Hutchinson, 2010), p. 664.
3. Francis Fukuyama, 'The end of history?' *The National Interest*, Spring, 1989; *The End of History and the Last Man*; Samuel Huntington, 'Democracy's third wave', *Journal of Democracy*, Spring, 1991, and *The Third Wave Democratization in the Late Twentieth Century* (Norman, OK, University of Oklahoma, 1991).
4. In this context, see David Runciman, *How Democracy Ends* (London, Profile, 2018); Steven Levitsky and Daniel Ziblatt, *How Democracies Die. What History Reveals about our Future* (London, Penguin, 2018). Freedom House identified 'the twelfth consecutive year of decline in global freedom' in its survey, 'Freedom in the World 2018: Democracy in Crisis', https://freedomhouse.org/report/freedom-world/freedom-world-2018. Even more alarmingly The Economist Intelligence Unit's Democracy Index found that less than five per cent of the world's population enjoyed 'full democracy', whilst thirty per cent 'endured authoritarian rule'. *The Economist*, 31 January 2018, https://www.economist.com/blogs/graphicdetail/2018/01/daily-chart21?cid1=cust/ddnew/email/n/n/20180131n/owned/n/n/ddnew/n/n/n/nap/Daily_Dispatch/email&etear=dailydispatch
5. Fukuyama, *The End of History*, p. 276.

6. The title of one of David Held's many works on the subject. See his *Democracy and the Global Order: from the Modern State to Cosmopolitan Governance* (Cambridge, Polity Press, 1995).
7. Michael Oakeshott, 'Rational Conduct,' in *Rationalism in Politics and Other Essays* (London, Methuen, 1981), p. 88.
8. Michael Oakeshott, *The Politics of Faith and the Politics of Scepticism* (New Haven, CT, Yale University Press, 1996), p. 67.
9. *Prometheus Bound* and *Agamemnon* (453 BC), the first plays in the Oresteia cycle, come to mind. The latter play's concern with 'the ancient blinded vengeance and the wrong that amendeth wrong' seem particularly pertinent to the Western spirit of nescience at the end of history. See *The Agamemnon of Aeschylus*, Gilbert Murray (ed.), (London, Floating Press, 2008), p. 6.
10. Augustine of Hippo, *The City of God Against the Pagans*, R.W. Dyson (ed.), (Cambridge, Cambridge University Press, 2002).
11. Oswald Spengler, *The Decline of the West*, 2 vols. (New York, Alfred A. Knopf, 1939); Arnold Toynbee, *A Study of History,* 12 vols. (Oxford, Oxford University Press, 1948–61); see also W.H. McNeill, *Arnold Toynbee. A Life* (Oxford, Oxford University Press, 1989), p. 165.
12. Samuel Huntington, *The Clash of Civilizations and the Remaking of World Order* (New York, Simon & Schuster, 1996), p. 20.
13. Jonah Goldberg, *The Suicide of the West and the Rebirth of Tribalism, Populism, Nationalism, and Identity Politics* (New York, Random House, 2018).
14. Leo Strauss, *The City and Man* (Chicago, Chicago University Press, 1964), p. 3.
15. Ibid p. 6.
16. Runciman, *How Democracy Ends*, p. 3.

2 THE END OF HISTORY AND THE KANTIAN MOMENT

1. Francis Fukuyama, *The End of History and The Last Man* (London, Penguin, 1992), p. xii-xiii.
2. Ibid. p. 91. Italics in the original.
3. p. 112.
4. Fukuyama opted for the larger number based on Michael Doyle's findings in 'Kant, Liberal Legacies and Foreign Affairs', *Philosophy and Public Affairs* 12, Summer, 1983, pp. 205-235. Samuel Huntington opted for the more conservative figure in his *The Third Wave: Democratization in the Late Twentieth Century* (Norman, University of Oklahoma Press, 1991), p. 26.
5. See G.A. Almond & J. Coleman, *The Politics of Developing Areas* (Princeton, Princeton University Press, 1960), pp. 20-24; see also David Martin

Jones *The Image of China in Western Social and Political Thought* (London, Palgrave, 2001), ch. 5.

6. See, for example, Samuel Huntington, *Political Order in Changing Societies* (New Haven, Yale University Press, 1968); and Raymond Grew (ed.), *Crises of Political Development in the United States and Europe* (Princeton, Princeton University Press), 1978.

7. W.W. Rostow, *The Stages of Economic Growth* (Cambridge, Cambridge University Press, 1978), p. 50.

8. *The Journal of Democracy*, https://www.journalofdemocracy.org/about

9. University of Warwick website *Democratization: The Journal*, https://warwick.ac.uk/fac/soc/pais/research/researchcentres/csd/pubs_csd/democratisation/

10. Fukuyama, *The End of History*, p. 96.

11. K. Akamatsu, 'Historical patterns of economic growth in developing countries', *Developing Economies*, 2, 1962.

12. Immanuel Wallerstein, *The Modern World System: Capitalist Agriculture and the Origin of the European World Economy* (New York, Academic Press, 1974); *The Modern World System, 2: Mercantilism and the Consolidation of the European World Economy* (New York, Academic Press, 1980); *The Capitalist World Economy* (Cambridge, Cambridge University Press, 1980).

13. Kenichi Ohmae, *The Borderless World: Power and Strategy in the Interlinked Economy* (London, HarperCollins, 1991), p. 240.

14. As opposed to the European Community, the European Union achieved greater federal authority after 1993 in a process culminating in the Lisbon Treaty of 2007. See *Consolidated Texts of the EU Treaties as Amended by The Lisbon Treaty* (CM 7310, Norwich, HMSO 2008).

15. Fukuyama *The End of History*, p. 134; Talcott Parsons, *The Social System* (New York, Free Press, 1951); *On Institutions and Social Evolution* (Chicago, Chicago University Press, 1982). See also Daniel Lerner, *The Passing of Traditional Society: Modernizing the Middle East* (New York, Free Press, 1958).

16. Ibid. p. 207.

17. Ibid. p. 206.

18. Ibid. pp. 338-9.

19. R. Dahl, *Polyarchy: Participation and Opposition* (New Haven, Yale University Press, 1971).

20. Ibid. p. 123.

21. See also David Martin Jones, 'Democratization, Civil Society and Middle Class Culture in Contemporary Pacific Asia', *Comparative Politics* 30, 1, 1998.

22. Fukuyama, *The End of History*, p. 124.

23. *The Economist,* 10 May 1986.

24. *The Economist,* 5 Jan 1996.

25. Fukuyama, *The End of History,* p. 125.

26. See H.C. Chan, 'Democracy Evolution and Implementation', in *Democracy and Capitalism: Asian and American Perspectives,* R. Bartley, H.C. Chan, S. Huntington, & S. Ogata (eds.), (Singapore, ISEAS, 1993); K. Mahbubani, 'The United States: Go East Young Man', *The Washington Quarterly* 17, 2, 1994, 5-23; K. Mahbubani, 'The Pacific Way', *Foreign Affairs,* 74, 1, 1995, 100-111. Tu Wei Ming (ed.), *The Triadic Chord: Confucian Ethics, Industrial East Asia and Max Weber* (Singapore, Institute of East Asian Philosophies, 1991).

27. Goh Chok Tong, 'National Day Rally', in *Straits Times,* 22 Aug 1994. See also Mahathir Mohamad and S. Ishihara, *The Voice of Asia: Two Leaders Discuss the Coming Century* (Tokyo, Kodansha International, 1995).

28. *The Economist,* 6 Oct 1994.

29. See E. Vogel & G. Lodge, *Ideology and National Competitiveness: A Comparison of Nine Different Countries* (Boston, Harvard Business School Press, 1987).

30. N. Sopiee, 'The New World Order: What Southeast Asia Should Strive For', in R. Mahmood and T. Ramnath (eds.), *Southeast Asia: The Way Forward* (Kuala Lumpur, Friedrich Ebert Stiftung, 1992), p. 21. See also *The Straits Times,* 11 Nov 1992.

31. K. Mahbubani, 'The Pacific Way', p. 107.

32. *Straits Times,* 2 May 1994.

33. Anwar Ibrahim, *The Asian Renaissance* (Kuala Lumpur, Pelanduk, 1996).

34. Ibid. p. 243.

35. Ibid. p. 244.

36. B. Barber, *Jihad versus McWorld* (New York, New York Times Books, 1995), p. 4.

37. The image that captures the relationship is that of a Serbian sniper tapping his Reeboks to Madonna on his Sony Walkman as he picks off Muslims in a Sarajevo marketplace. Ibid, p. 23.

38. Samuel Huntington, *The Clash of Civilizations and the Remaking of World Order* (New York, Simon & Schuster, 1996).

39. P.G. Cerny, 'Paradoxes of the Competition State: The Dynamics of Political Globalization', *Government and Opposition,* 32, 2, 1997, p. 253.

40. Ibid.

41. Corruption, Cronyism and Nepotism. For its impact on Malaysian politics, see Juo-yu Lin, *A Structural Analysis of the 1999 Malaysian General Election* (Washington, Brookings Institution, 1999), https://www.brookings.edu/wp-content/uploads/2016/06/lin20021219.pdf

42. See E.T. Gomez, *Political Business: Corporate Involvement of Malaysian Political Parties* (Townsville, James Cook University Press, 1994); and Joe Studwell, *Asian Godfathers. Money and Power in Hong Kong and South East Asia* (London, Profile Books, 2007).

43. D. Tsang. 'Asia Needs a Bond Market'. *Asia Wall Street Journal*, 17-18 Jul 1998; S. Davies and J. Grant, 'Capital Market Pariahs', *Financial Times*, 12 Aug 1998.

44. See Alwyn Young, 'A Tale of Two Cities: Factor Accumulation and Technical Change in Hong Kong and Singapore' in O. Blanchard and S. Fisher (eds.), *N.B.E.R. Macroeconomics Annual 1992* (Cambridge, MA, MIT Press, 1992); Alwyn Young, 'The Tyranny of Numbers: Confronting the Statistical Realities of the East Asian Growth Experience.' NBER Working Paper No. 4680, 1994; and Paul Krugman, 'The Myth of Asia's Miracle', *Foreign Affairs*, 73, 6, 1994, pp. 62-78.

45. Ibid. p. 266.

46. Fukuyama's endorsement on the back cover of the paperback edition of Thomas L. Friedman, *The Lexus and the Olive Tree* (London, HarperCollins, 2000).

47. Ibid. p. 85.

48. Ibid. p. 107.

49. Ibid. p. 109.

50. Ibid. p. 105.

51. Ibid. p. 104.

52. See in this context: Baogang He, *The Democratization of China* (London, Routledge, 1996) and *The Democratic Implications of Civil Society in China* (London, Routledge, 1997); also William H. Overholt, *The Rise of China: How Economic Reform is Creating a New China* (New York, Norton, 1994).

53. Friedman, *The Lexus*, p. 413.

54. Ibid. p. 141.

55. See World Government Forum, 'Speech by Klaus Schwab', Feb 2014, https://www.worldgovernmentsummit.org/press/news-press-releases/speech-by-klaus-schwab

56. Robert H. Frank and Phillip J. Cook, *The Winner Takes All Society. Why the Few at the Top Get So Much More than the Rest of Us* (London, Penguin, 1995).

57. Friedman, *The Lexus,* p. 308.

58. Ibid. p. 340.

59. Ibid. p. 401.

60. Ibid. p. 402.

61. Ibid. p. 404.

62. Ibid. p. 334.

63. Ibid. p. 442.

64. George Soros, *On Globalization* (Oxford, Public Affairs, 2002), p. 7.

65. Friedman, *The Lexus*, p. 451.

66. Ibid. p. 465.

67. Ibid. p. 466.

68. G. John Ikenberry, *After Victory: Institutions, Strategic Restraint and the Rebuilding of Order after Major Wars* (Princeton, Princeton University Press, 2000), p. 256.

69. Ibid. p. 466.

70. See Michael Hardt and Antonio Negri, *Empire* (Cambridge, MA, Harvard University Press, 2001).

71. Immanuel Kant, 'Perpetual Peace. A Philosophical Sketch' in Hans Reiss (ed.), *Kant's Political Writings* (Cambridge, Cambridge University Press, 1970), p. 98.

72. Friedman, 'Foreword', *The Lexus*.

73. Anthony Giddens, *The Third Way: The Renewal of Social Democracy* (Cambridge, Polity Press, 1998).

74. Paul Hirst and Grahame Thompson, *Globalization in Question* (Cambridge, Polity Press, 1997), p. 179.

75. John Baylis and Steve Smith (eds.) *The Globalization of World Politics. An Introduction to International Relations* (Oxford, Oxford University Press, 2001), p. 23.

76. Giddens, *The Third Way*, p. 140.

3 THE PROGRESSIVE MIND AND THE ISLAMIST CHALLENGE

1. Cited in Ralf Dahrendorf, 'The Third Way and Liberty: An Authoritarian Streak in Europe's New Center', *Foreign Affairs* 79, 5, 1999.

2. Ibid.

3. Blair claimed in a BBC interview in 2000 that he 'was never really in politics'. See Peter Mair, *Ruling the Void. The Hollowing of Western Democracy* (London, Verso, 2013), p. 3.

4. David Held, *Democracy and the Global Order, from the Modern State to Cosmopolitan Governance* (Cambridge, Polity Press, 1995), p. 286.

5. Robert S. Boynton, 'The Two Tony's', *The NewYorker*, 28 Sep 1997. https://www.newyorker.com/magazine/1997/10/06/the-two-tonys-2

6. Held, *Democracy*, p. 284.

7. Dahrendorf, 'The Third Way'.

8. Anthony Giddens, *The Third Way: The Renewal of Social Democracy* (Cambridge, Polity Press, 1998), p. 67.

9. Ibid., p. 67.

10. Ibid., p. 146.

11. Ibid., p. 138.

12. Held, *Democracy*, p. 286

13. Ibid., p. 233.

14. Andrew Linklater, *Critical Theory and World Politics. Citizenship, Sovereignty and Humanity* (London, Routledge, 2007), p. 124.

15. Ibid., p. 144.

16. Dahrendorff, 'The Third Way'.

17. See Michael Oakeshott, *Rationalism in Politics and Other Essays* (London, Methuen, 1981). As Oakeshott noted, 'Either of these characteristics without the other denotes a different style of politics', p. 5.

18. Charles Taylor, 'The Politics of Recognition', in Amy Gutman (ed.) *Multiculturalism. Examining the Politics of Recognition* (Princeton, Princeton University Press, 1994), p. 25.

19. See Kenneth Minogue, *The Liberal Mind* (London, Methuen, 1963), p. 67.

20. See on this evolution, *inter alia*, Mark Lilla, *The Reckless Mind* (New York, New York Review of Books, 2001); Sheldon Wolin, *The Seduction of Unreason* (Princeton, Princeton University Press, 2004); John Gray, *Enlightenment's Wake. Politics and Culture at the End of the Modern Age* (London, Routledge, 1995); Tony Judt, *Past Imperfect* (Stanford, University of California Press, 1992); Duncan Bell, 'What is Liberalism?', *Political Theory* 2, 6, 2014; Pascal Bruckner, *The Tyranny of Guilt. An Essay on Western Masochism* (Princeton, Princeton University Press, 2011); Roger Scruton, *Fools, Fraudsters and Firebrands* (London, Bloomsbury, 2016).

21. Minogue, *The Liberal Mind*, p. 11.

22. Linklater, *Critical Theory*, p. 72.

23. See Jolyon Jenkins, 'The Green Sheep in "Colonel Gadaffi Drive"', *New Statesman*, 8 Sep 1987, and Gray, *Enlightenment's Wake*, p. 3.

24. Kenneth Minogue, 'Ideology after the collapse of communism', *Political Studies* xli, 1993, p. 7. Italics in the original.

25. See *inter alia* John Rawls, *A Theory of Justice* (Oxford, Oxford University Press, 1971), and *Political Liberalism* (New York, Columbia University Press, 1993); Ronald Dworkin, *Taking Rights Seriously* (London, Duckworth, 1977); Charles Taylor, *Sources of the Self. The Making of the Modern Identity* (Cambridge, Cambridge University Press, 1989); Brian Barry, *Culture and Equality* (Cambridge, Cambridge University Press, 1991); Will Kymlicka, *Contemporary Political Philosophy* (Oxford, Oxford University Press, 2002); Richard Rorty, *Contingency, Irony and Solidarity* (Cambridge, Cambridge University Press, 1989).

26. Sayyid Qutb, *Islam: The Religion of the Future* (Kuwait, International Islamic Federation of Student Organizations, 1971), p. 121.

27. See Mark Jurgensmeyer, *Terror in the Mind of God. The Global Rise of Religious Violence* (Oakland, University of California Press, 2017).

28. Olivier Roy, *Jihad and Death. The Global Appeal of Islamic State* (London, Hurst, 2017).

29. Raymond Aron, *On War* (London, Secker and Warburg, 1958), p. 2.

30. Al-Qaeda training manual recovered by police in Manchester following the search of a suspect's home in 1998 and translated from Arabic into English, Translation UK/BM-7. United States District Court: District of Massachusetts, United States of America vs. Richard Colvin Reid, 17 January 2003, p. 5.

31. 'Those who serve masters besides God may be compared to the spider which builds a cobweb for itself. Surely the spider's is the frailest of all dwellings, if they knew it.' *The Koran* (trans. N.J. Dawood) (London, Penguin, 1990), 29:39-42, p. 400.

32. Olivier Roy, 'The Jihad Within', *The National Interest* 71, Spring, 2003, p. 70.

33. See Robert Hefner, *Civil Islam* (Princeton, Princeton University Press, 2000), Ch. 1.

34. See David Martin Jones and Mike Lawrence Smith, "From *Konfrontasi* to *Disintegrasi*: ASEAN and the Rise of Islamism in Southeast Asia", *Studies in Conflict and Terrorism*, 25, 6, 2002, pp. 351–352.

35. See Bhikhu Parekh, "The Cultural Particularity of Liberal Democracy", in David Held (ed.), *Prospects for Democracy* (Cambridge, Polity Press, 1993), pp. 156–175.

36. "Relations with the Muslim Community" (Briefing on British Muslims: Socio-Economic Data and Attitudes, Updated, Cabinet Office, 10 May 2004), pp. 1–5. See also "Young Muslims and Extremism," p. 4.

37. James C. Davies, "Toward a Theory of Revolution", *American Sociological Review*, 27, 1962, pp. 5-18; James C. Davies, "The J-curve of Rising and Declining Satisfaction as a Source of Some Great Revolutions and a Contained Rebellion", in Hugh Davis Graham and Ted Robert Gurr (eds.), *The History of Violence in America* (New York, Bantam, 1969). Also see in this context Ted Robert Gurr, *Why Men Rebel* (Princeton, NJ, Princeton University Press, 1970).

38. 'Building Bridges with Mainstream Islam' (Foreign and Commonwealth Office, FCO Update, 5 Nov 2003), pp. 29–30.

39. Fred Halliday, 'The Politics of Islamic Fundamentalism', in Akbar S. Ahmed and Hastings Donnan (eds.), *Islam, Globalization and Postmodernity* (London, Routledge, 1996), p. 96.

40. "Profile: Omar Saeed Sheikh," BBC News, 16 Jul 2002, http://news.bbc.co.uk/1/hi/uk/1804710.stm, accessed 3 Sep 2005.

41. See Roy, "The Jihad Within", p. 67.

42. See David Cohen, "Terror on the Dole", *The Evening Standard*, 20 Apr 2004.

43. For this profile, see Roy, "The Jihad Within", pp. 67–68.

44. Ibid., p. 69.

45. Ibid., p. 67.

46. Ed Husain, *The Islamist. Why I Joined Radical Islam In Britain, What I Saw And Why I Left* (London, Penguin, 2007), p. 133.

47. Ibid., pp. 145–146.

48. Ibid., p. 67.

49. Francis Fukyama, *The End of History and the Last Man* (London, Hamilton, 1992); Samuel Huntingdon, *The Clash of Civilizations and the Remaking of the World Order* (New York, Touchstone, 1998).

50. One might just as easily, and more interestingly, throw Huntington against Huntington: The Huntington of the "clash" against the Huntington of the "Third Wave", or, better, the Huntington who wrote *Political Order in Changing Societies* (New Haven, Yale University Press, 1968).

51. Oswald Spengler, *The Decline of the West* (London, Allen & Unwin, 1922); Arnold Toynbee, *A Study of History* (Oxford, Oxford University Press, 1961).

52. Pieter Geyl, 'From Ranke to Toynbee: Five Lectures on Historians and Historiographical Problems', *Studies in History*, 39 (Northampton, MA, Smith College History Department, 1952).

53. Benjamin Barber, *Jihad vs McWorld* (New York, Ballantine, 1996); Thomas Friedman, *The Lexus and the Olive Tree* (London, HarperCollins, 1999).

54. Edward Gibbon, 'General Observations on the Fall of the Roman Empire in the West', *The History of the Decline and Fall of the Roman Empire*, 12 vols (New York, Fred de Fau & Co., 1902), vol. 6, p. 161.

55. "Cool Britannia" was the title of a Bonzo Dog Doo Dah Band song of 1967, penned by Viv Stanshall-Smith. Subsequently Ben and Gerry gave the soubriquet to one of their varieties of ice cream, and Stryker McGuire in a *Newsweek* 1996 article described London as the 'coolest city on the planet'. The term coincided with Tony Blair's election as Prime Minister in 1997, promising to re-make Britain as a "modern society." New Labour rhetoric implicitly endorsed the image of "Cool Britannia" which became identified with Blair's first term in office, although he never publicly used the phrase. See "Cooling Towards Britannia, Not Blair", *The Observer*, 12 October 2003.

56. Gibbon, *Decline and Fall*, vol. 6, p. 169.

57. 'The Miracle…is the product of a bourgeois revolution, an eighteenth-century middle-class ideology of merit, industriousness, innovation, contracts, and rights'. Jonah Goldberg, *The Suicide of the West: How the Rebirth of Tribalism, Populism, Nationalism, and Identity Politics* (New York, Random House, 2018) (all citations from the i-book edition), p. 29.

58. Karl Popper, *The Open Society and Its Enemies* (London, Routledge & Kegan Paul, 1962).

59. Ernest Gellner, *Conditions of Liberty: Civil Society and its Rivals* (London, Hamish Hamilton, 1994), p. 199.

60. See particularly Ernest Gellner, *Muslim Society* (Cambridge, Cambridge University Press, 1981).

61. See Kemal H. Karpat, *The Politicization of Islam: Reconstructing Faith, State and Community in the Late Ottoman Empire* (Oxford, Oxford University Press, 2001), p. 18.

62. See Natana J. Delong-Bas, *Wahhabi Islam: From Revival to Reform to Global Jihad* (London, IB Tauris, 2004).

63. See Elie Kedourie, *Afghani and Abduh: An Essay on Religious Unbelief and Political Activism in Modern Islam* (London, Frank Cass, 1966); Nikki R. Keddie, *An Islamic Response to Imperialism: Political and Religious Writings of Sayyid Jamal al-Din "al-Afghani"* (Berkeley, CA, University of California Press, 1968).

64. Wael Hallaq, "Was the Gate of Ijtihad Closed?" *International Journal of Middle East Studies*, 16, 1, 1984, pp. 3–11.

65. See Kedourie, *Afghani and Abduh*; Keddie, *An Islamic Response to Imperialism*; Natana J. Delong-Bas, *Wahhabi Islam: From Revival to Reform to Global Jihad* (London, I.B. Tauris, 2004).

66. See Shaykh Ibn Taymiyah, *Al-'Ubudiyyah: Being a True Slave of Allah* (trans. Nasiruddin al-Khattab) (London, Ta-Ha, 1999).

67. See Nazih N. Ayubi, *Political Islam: Religion and Politics in the Arab World* (London, Routledge, 1991), pp. 60–63; Hasan al-Banna, *Five Tracts of Hasan al-Banna* (trans. Charles Wendell) (Berkeley, CA, University of California Press, 1988); and Elie Kedourie, *Democracy and Arab Political Culture* (London, Frank Cass, 1994), chapter 6.

68. See Rudolph Peters, *Jihad in Classical and Modern Islam: A Reader* (Princeton, NJ, Marcus Wiener, 1996), p. 128.

69. Ayubi, *Political Islam*, p. 139.

70. Sayyid Qutb, *Milestones (Ma'alim fi al-tariq)* (Damascus, 1985), pp. 21-22.

71. See Sayyid Qutb, *Islam: The Misunderstood Religion* (Kuwait, Ministry of Awqaf and Islamic Affairs, 1967).

72. For this curious development, see Paul Berman *Terror and Liberalism* (New York, Norton, 2003), pp. 190–195; Barry Cooper, *New Political Religions, or An Analysis of Modern Terror* (Columbia, MO, University of Missouri Press, 2004), Chapter 4; Eric Voegelin, *Modernity Without Restraint: The Political Religions; The New Science of Politics; and Science, Politics and Gnosticism*, in Manfred Henningsen (ed.), *The Collected Works of Eric Voegelin*, Vol. 5 (Columbia, MO, University of Missouri Press, 2000).

73. Eric Voegelin, "Science, Politics and Gnosticism", in *Modernity Without Restraint*, p. 298.

74. Cited in Ed Husain, *The Islamist*, p. 83.

75. Ibid., p. 90.

76. Johannes J.G. Jansen, *The Neglected Duty: The Creed of Sadat's Assassins and Islamic Resurgence in the Middle East*, with a translation of Muhammad Abdal-Salam Faraj, *al-Faridahal-Gha'ibah* (London, Macmillan, 1986).

77. Nimrod Raphaeli, *Radical Islamist Profiles (3). Ayman Muhammad Rabi al-Zawahiri: The Making of an Arch Terrorist*, Middle East Research Institute Inquiry and Analysis Series, 127, 2003, p. 10.

78. See Montasser al-Zayyyat, *The Road to al-Qaeda: The Story of Bin Laden's Right-Hand Man* (London, Pluto Press, 2004).

79. See Ernest Gellner, *Postmodernism, Reason and Religion* (London, Routledge, 2001), pp. 13-16. See also Gellner, *Muslim Society*, especially chapter 3.

80. See Gellner, *Postmodernism*.

81. *Salafiya*, or salafism, refers to the honour due to the supposedly untainted Islamic beliefs and practices of the first four caliphs, the Rashidun. It thus becomes clear that fundamentalism in Islam equates more or less to radical Christian forms of Protestantism, a desire to "return" to a pure, unmediated and uncorrupted personal relationship with God.

82. See William E. Shepard, *Sayyid Qutb and Islamic Activism* (Leyden, E.J. Brill, 1996), pp. xxxix-xl.

83. Craig Whitlock, 'Briton Used Internet as His Bully Pulpit', *The Washington Post*, 8 Aug 2005.

84. Charlie Winter, 'Inside the Collapse of Islamic State's Propaganda Machine', *Wired*, 20 Dec 2017, https://www.wired.co.uk/article/isis-islamic-state-propaganda-content-strategy

85. Sayyid Qutb, *The Religion of the Future* (Kuwait, International Islamic Federation of Student Organizations, 1971), p. 121.

86. Ernest Gellner, *Conditions of Liberty: Civil Society and its Rivals* (Hamish Hamilton, London, 1994), p. 31.

87. Ibid., p. 27.

88.. David Martin Jones and M.L.R. Smith, 'Franchising Terror', *World Today*, 57, 10, Oct 2001, p. 10.

89. With the discovery of a plot in Britain, and clear links between the plotters and Abu Hamza's Finsbury Park Mosque, the mosque was belatedly raided by Scotland Yard on 20 January 2003. But in deference to Muslim sensibilities, police wore Islamically-appropriate footwear. See 'Anti-Terror Police Raid London Mosque', BBC News, 20 January 2003, http://news.bbc.co.uk/2/hi/uk_news/england/2675223.stm, accessed 19 Aug 2005.

90. Quoted in Robert Mendick, 'Now Bakri Attacks "Hypocrite Muslims"', *The Evening Standard*, 21 Jul 2005. Al-Muhajiroun dissolved itself in 2004. It was later banned in 2005, although it continues to flourish and propagate the ideology under a variety of aliases.

91. Olivier Roy's term. See 'EuroIslam: The Jihad Within?' *The National Interest*, 71, 2003.

92. Eric Voegelin, 'The Eclipse of Reality', in *What is History and Other Late Unpublished Writings*, in Thomas A. Holweck and Paul Caringella (eds.), vol. 28 of *The Collected Works of Eric Voegelin* (Baton Rouge, Louisiana State University Press, 1975), p. 112. See also Barry Cooper, *New Political Religions,* chapter 3.

93. Eric Voegelin, *The New Science of Politics* (Chicago, University of Chicago Press, 1952), p. 167.

94. Ibid., p.169.

95. London mayor Ken Livingstone, far from discouraging Islamist activism, publicly welcomed Sheikh Yusuf al-Qaradawi on a visit to London as an honoured guest, despite the cleric's endorsement of suicide bombing in Israel. In January 2005, Livingstone published a twenty-six page justification of his meeting, claiming: 'I regard it as my responsibility to welcome a leader of any great religion, such as Dr al-Qaradawi.' Mayor of London, *Why the Mayor Will Maintain Dialogues With All of London's Faiths and Communities* (London, Greater London Authority, 2005), p. 2.

96. See in this context, Amir Tahiri, 'Beards and Scarves aren't Muslim, They're Simply Adverts for al-Qaeda', *The Times*, 27 Jul 2005.

97. Collected by the author at the meeting, 25 Aug 2002.

98. See Roy, 'The Jihad Within', p. 69.

99. Voegelin, 'Science, Politics, and Gnosticism', p. 313.

100. British Foreign Secretary Jack Straw has maintained that many of the world's crises 'are a consequence of our colonial past', *New Statesman*, 15 Nov 2002.

101. *Asian Wall Street Journal*, 2–4 Aug 2002.

102. See Mohamed Sifaoui, *Inside al-Qaeda: How I Infiltrated the World's Deadliest Terror Organization* (London, Granta, 2003), pp. 129-131.

103. Ibid., p. 129.

104. Alexander Meleagrou-Hitchens, *The Global Jihadist Movement in the West. A Study of Anwar al-Awlaki and His Followers in the Context of Homegrown Radicalisation and the Global Jihadist Western Recruitment Strategy*, (London University, unpublished PhD thesis, 2015). See part 3 for Al-Awlaki's biography and his role in recruiting Western adherents to the cause.

105. Al-Awlaki was killed in Yemen in 2011.

106. Al-Suri is still wanted in connection with the Madrid attack of 2004.

107. See in this context, Shiraz Maher, *Salafi-Jihadism. The History of an Idea* (London, Hurst, 2016).

108. Meleagrou-Hitchens, *Global Jihadist Movement*, p. 114.

109. Abu Bakr Naji, *The Management of Savagery. The Most Critical Stage Through Which the Umma Will Pass* (trans. Will McCants) (Cambridge MA, Institute of Strategic Studies, Harvard University, 2006), p. 6.

110. Naji argued it was 'permissible' to read the revolutionary warfare theories of Mao or Che Guevara as long as their religious 'mistakes are corrected'. Ibid., p. 15.

111. Ibid., p. 23.

112. Ibid., p. 31.

113. The Islamist 'plot' to take over state funded Birmingham schools to advance political religion was revealed by *The Birmingham Mail* in March 2014, although some reservations were later expressed about the motivation for the takeover. See 'The Birmingham Trojan Horse Affair', *Open Democracy*, 2 Oct 2018, https://www.opendemocracy.net/en/investigate-birmingham-trojan-horse-affair/

114. Naji, *Management of Savagery*, p. 37.

115. The subtitle of *Dabiq* was *The Return of the Khilaffah*. See https://jamestown.org/program/hot-issue-dabiq-what-islamic-states-new-magazine-tells-us-about-their-strategic-direction-recruitment-patterns-and-guerrilla-doctrine/#.VpdTW5OLQ9c

116. The aspiration, for example, of International Relations theory idealists exemplified in Ken Booth, Tim Dunne & Michael Cox (eds.), *How Might We Live? Global Ethics in a New Century* (Cambridge, Cambridge University Press, 2001).

117. Umberto Eco, 'Ur Fascism', *The New York Review of Books*, 22 Jun 1995, https://www.nybooks.com/articles/1995/06/22/ur-fascism/

118. Richard Rorty, *Contingency, Irony and Solidarity* (New York, Cambridge University Press, 1989), p. 6.

119. Zawahiri's letter to Zarqawi: https://ctc.usma.edu/harmony-program/zawahiris-letter-to-zarqawi-original-language-2/

120. Naji, *Management of Savagery*, p. 57.

121. See Erich Ludendorff, *The Nation at War* [Der Totale Krieg], trans. A.S. Rappoport (London, Hutchinson, 1938).

122. See James M. Lutz and Brenda J. Lutz, *Global Terrorism* (London, Routledge, 2013), p. 277.

123. Further facilitated by the largely unsupervised activities of radical imams at mosques like Finsbury Park in London before 2005 or the community centre mosque in Plumstead, South London, where the radical cleric Usman Ali recruited Lambeth born jihadist Michael Adebolajo to fight for 'our Muslim land'. See Ayaan Hirsi Ali, 'The Problem of Muslim Leadership', *The Wall Street Journal*, 27 May 2013.

124. Both the Tsarnaev brothers in Boston and Michael Adebolojo and Michael Adebowale in London responded in this unpredictable way.

125. Beam based his strategy for liberating the American fatherland from decadent pluralism and socialism on what he termed 'the Phantom Cell', an arrangement derived from the Correspondence Societies of the American Revolution. The strategy assumes that 'the purpose of leaderless resistance is to defeat state tyranny, [in this] all members of phantom cells will react to objective events in the same way.' Louis Beam, *Leaderless Resistance* at http: www.crusader.net/texts/bt/bt04. html, p. 4.

126. Jonathan Powell, *Talking to Terrorists; How to End Armed Conflicts* (London, Bodley Head, 2014).

4 THE INCOHERENCE OF THE PHILOSOPHERS

1. The reference is to the title of al-Ghazali, *The Incoherence of the Philosophers (Tahafut al-Falasifa)* (Baghdad, circa 1091). See also Averroes (ibn Rushd), *The Incoherence of the Incoherence* (Cordoba, circa 1196).

2. See 'The Executive Summary', *The 9/11 Commission Report. Final Report of the National Commission on Terrorist Attacks on the United States* (Washington, 2004), p. 2.

3. Francis Fukuyama, 'History and September 11' in K. Booth and T. Dunne (eds.), *Worlds in Collision. Terror and the Future of Global Order* (London, Palgrave, 2002), p. 35.

4. Jean Marie Colombani, 'Nous sommes tous Americains', *Le Monde* 12 Sep 2001. The headline was perhaps more revealing: 'L'Amérique frappée, Le monde saisi d'effroi' (America attacked, the world takes fright).

5. President George W. Bush, *Address to a Joint Session of Congress and the American People* (Washington DC, Office of the Press Secretary), 20 Sep 2001.

6. Bush, *Address to a Joint Session,* https://www.washingtonpost.com/wp-srv/nation/specials/attacked/transcripts/bushaddress_092001.html

7. John Hooper, 'Anger at Rumsfeld attack on Old Europe', *The Guardian*, 24 Jan 2003. Accessed 1 Aug 2019, https://www.theguardian.com/world/2003/jan/24/germany.france

8. See Walter A. McDougall, *Promised Land, Crusader State. The American Encounter with the World since 1776* (New York, Houghton Mifflin, 1997); and Walter Russell Mead, *Special Providence. American Foreign Policy and How it Changed the World* (London, Routledge, 2002).

9. To use Walter Russell Mead's term in ibid.

10. McDougall, *Promised Land,* pp. 46-47.

11. Habermas in Giovanna Borradori, *Philosophy in a Time of Terror. Dialogues with Jürgen Habermas and Jacques Derrida* (Chicago, University of Chicago Press, 2003), p. 40.

12. Ken Booth and Tim Dunne (eds.), *Worlds in Collision* (London, Routledge, 2002).

13. Steve Smith, 'Unanswered Questions' in Booth and Dunne, *Worlds in Collision*, p. 58.

14. Ken Booth and Tim Dunne, 'Worlds in Collision' in Booth and Dunne, *Worlds in Collision,* p. 6.

15. Noam Chomsky, 'Who are the global terrorists?' in Booth and Dunne, *Worlds in Collision*, p. 128.

16. Jürgen Habermas and Jacques Derrida, 'February 15, Or What Binds Europeans Together: a Plea for a Common Foreign Policy, Beginning in the Core Europe', *Constellations* 10, 3, 2003, p. 289.

17. Ibid., p. 294.

18. Jürgen Habermas, 'Why Europe needs a Constitution', *New Left Review* 11, September/October 2001, p. 13.

19. As Tony Blair understood it. See Tony Blair, *A Journey* (London, Hutchinson, 2010), p. 430.

20. Cited in Owen Harries, 'An End to Nonsense', *The National Interest*, 65, 5, Thanksgiving 2001.

21. Richard Shapcott, *Justice, Dialogue and the Cosmopolitan Project* (Cambridge, Polity, 2002).

22. Charles Taylor, 'The Politics of Recognition', in *Multiculturalism,* A. Gutman (ed.), (Princeton, Princeton University Press, 1995).

23. Acheson was President Truman's Secretary of State, 1949–53. See Douglas Brinkley, 'Dean Acheson and the Special Relationship: The

West Point Speech of December 1962', *The Historical Journal*, 33, 3, Sep 1990, p. 599.

24. Irwin Steltzer, 'Letter from Londonistan', *Weekly Standard*, 1 August 2005.

25. Tony Blair, 'Speech to the House of Commons', 18 Mar 2003, quoted in *A Journey*, pp. 436-8.

26. David Rose, 'Flashy tactics won't defeat the terrorists', *Observer*, 24 July 2005.

27. John Gray, *Enlightenment's Wake*, p. 21.

28. Ibid., p. 30.

29. Blair, *A Journey* (London, Hutchinson, 2010), p. 287. It also encouraged a new and oxymoronic practice of 'progressive conservatism'. See David Cameron, *For the Record* (London, William Collins, 2019), chapter 17.

30. Quoted in Rose, 'Flashy tactics'. It should be noted that the quote attributed to the MI5 official stands in direct contrast to the view of the President of the Special Immigration Appeals Commission, Mr Justice Collins, who described Qatada as a 'truly dangerous individual (as opposed to just a loud-mouth)' who was 'at the centre of terrorist activities in the United Kingdom.' Quoted in Sam Knight, '"Al-Qaeda" cleric among ten detained for deportation', *The Times*, 11 Aug 2005.

31. Quoted in Richard Woods and David Leppard, 'Focus: How liberal Britain let hate flourish,' *Sunday Times*, 12 February 2006. Hossein was an Algerian journalist who reported on Abu Hamza.

32. Quoted in Rose, 'Flashy tactics.'

33. See Jamie Campbell, 'Why Terrorists Love Britain', *New Statesman*, 9 Aug 2004.

34. Interestingly this is a notion given implicit recognition in official documents: see Foreign and Commonwealth/Home Office Paper, 'Young Muslims and Extremism', p. 22. It was also given inadvertent acknowledgment by Tony Blair in his statement on 5 August that the 'rules of the game are changing.' See 'Rules of The Game', *The Times*, 10 Aug 2005.

35. A fact that led Bakri to assume his activities had immunity in the UK. See Yolam Fakner, 'Radical Islamist Profiles: Omar Bakri Mohammed', *Middle East Media Research Institute*, No. 24, October 2001.

36. Audrey Gillan, 'Detained Muslim Cleric is Spiritual Leader to Militants, Hearing Told', *The Guardian*, 20 Nov 2003.

37. See James Corbett, 'London's New Villains', *Al-Ahram Weekly*, 31 October–6 November 2002.

38. The stated aim of *Hizb ut-Tahrir* is 'to resume the Islamic way of life and to convey the Islamic *da'wah* [call: refers to the call to the 'Truth'] to

the world. This objective means bringing the Muslims back to living an Islamic way of life in *Dar al-Islam* [realm of Islam/sphere of faith] and in an Islamic society such that all of life's affairs in society are administered according to the Shari'ah [Islamic law] rules, and the viewpoint in it is the *halal* [that which is lawful and permitted in Islam] and the *haram* [that which is unlawful and not permitted in Islam] under the shade of the Islamic State, which is the Khilafah [Caliphate] State... The Party, as well, aims at the correct revival of the Ummah [community of Muslims] through enlightened thought. It also strives to bring her back to her previous might and glory such that she wrests the reins of initiative away from other states and nations, and returns to her rightful place as the first state in the world, as she was in the past, when she governs the world according to the laws of Islam. It also aims to bring back the Islamic guidance for mankind and to lead the Ummah into a struggle with *Kufr* [unbelief in Allah], its systems and its thoughts so that Islam encapsulates the world.' http://www.hizb-ut-tahrir.org/english/english.html, accessed 22 Aug 2005.

39. 'Muslim Cleric Says Groups Plan to Strike London', *The Boston Globe*, 19 Apr 2004.

40. Tony Blair, 'Work Together to a Brave New World', speech to Labour Party Conference, *The Times*, 3 Oct 2001.

41. Jonathan Guthrie and Chris Tighe, 'The eerily ordinary extremists', *Financial Times*, 15 Jul 2005.

42. See Libby Purves, 'The land that lost its pride', *Times*, 26 Jul 2005; Minnette Marin, 'Confronted with our own decadence', *Sunday Times*, 31 Jul 2005.

43. See the *Future of Multi-Ethnic Britain – The Parekh Report* (London, Profile Books/The Runnymede Trust, 2000). The Runnymede Trust set up a Commission on the Future of Multi-ethnic Britain in 1997. According to the Trust's summary, the 'Commission's remit was to analyse the current state of multi-ethnic Britain and propose ways of countering racial discrimination and disadvantage and making Britain a confident and vibrant multicultural society at ease with its rich diversity.' The degree to which the Commission received official recognition and endorsement is indicated by the fact that the report was formally launched by then Home Secretary Jack Straw on 11 October 2000.

44. Brian Brady, 'Hooked at Last', *Scotland on Sunday*, 30 May 2004.

45. See Richard Willing, 'Radical Cleric Fighting Extradition to USA on Terror Charges', *USA Today*, 27 May 2004.

46. Foreign and Commonwealth/Home Office Paper, 'Young Muslims and Extremism', submitted as part of a report into a study conducted by

the Cabinet Office, 'Relations with the Muslim Community', Cabinet Office, 6 Apr 2004, pp. 10–11. See also Steve Coll and Susan B. Glasser, 'Islamic radicals found a haven', *The Washington Post*, 10 Jul 2005, p. A01.

47. See Olivier Roy, 'EuroIslam: The Jihad Within?' *The National Interest*, 71, Spring, 2003, pp. 63-74.

48. Richard Beeston and Michael Binyon, 'Blair "Repeatedly Failed to Tackle Radical Muslims in his Backyard"', *The Times*, 10 Aug 2005.

49. Part of the statement claimed: 'The heroic mujahideen have carried out a blessed raid in London. Britain is now burning with fear, terror and panic in its northern, southern, eastern, and western quarters.' BBC News, 'Statement Claiming London Attacks', 7 Jul 2005, http://news. bbc.co.uk/1/hi/uk/4660391.stm.

50. Ramadan's words were: 'Des banlieues françaises aux sociétés musulmanes, vous ne trouverez pas de soutiens, sauf infimes, aux interventions de New York, Bali ou Madrid.' [From the French suburbs to Muslim societies, you won't find any support, except minute amounts, for the interventions in New York, Bali, or Madrid]. 'Islam et Occident: Interview Tariq Ramadan', *Le Point*, 22 Apr 2004, p. 68.

51. 'Major Incident—Travel Update', leaflet produced by the Mayor of London and Transport for London, July 2005.

52. According to the Russian anarchist writer Peter Kropotkin, a violent political action 'does more propagandizing in a few days than do thousands of pamphlets.' Peter Kropotkin, *Paroles d'un Revolté* (Paris, Marpon and Flammarion, 1885), p. 286.

53. 'Terror Attack "A Matter of Time"', BBC News, 17 Jun 2003, http:// news.bbc.co.uk/1/hi/uk/2997146.stm, accessed 21 November 2005.

54. Rosie Cowan, 'Attack on London is Inevitable', *The Guardian*, 17 Mar 2004.

55. David Cameron, 'State Multiculturalism has failed', http//www.bbc. co.uk/news/uk-politics-12371994

56. Oliver Wright and Jerome Taylor, 'Cameron: My War on Multiculturalism', *The Independent*, 5 Feb 2011, http://www.independent. co.uk/news/uk/politics/cameron-my-war-on-multiculturalism-2205074.html

57. See Anthony Heath and David Sanders, *Ethnic Minority British Electoral Survey* (Oxford, Oxford University Press, 2012) and Anthony Heath, 'Has Multiculturalism failed in the UK? Not Really', *The Guardian*, 10 Aug 2012, http://www.theguardian.com/commentisfree/2012/aug/10/multiculturalism-uk-research

58. Quoted in Charles Moore, 'Where is the Gandhi of Islam?' *The Daily Telegraph*, 9 Jul 2005.

59. Quoted in 'Rise in Hate Crimes Against Muslims After Attacks', Reuters Report, 11 Jul 2005.

60. 'Blair Pays Tribute to Resilience', BBC News, 9 Jul 2005, http://news. bbc.co.uk/1/hi/uk_politics/4666311.stm, accessed 24 Aug 2005.

61. See 'In Full: Blair on Bomb Blasts', BBC News, 7 Jul 2005, http:// news.bbc.co.uk/1/hi/uk/4659953.stm, accessed 24 Aug 2005.

62. BBC Newsnight, 8 Jul 2005.

63. Richard Ford, 'Two communities that hardly ever mix', The Times, 13 Jul 2005. See also Andrew Norfolk and Russell Jenkins, 'A laughing lad from the chippie and his mate', The Times, 13 July 2005; 'A legacy of deprivation', The Guardian, 15 Jul 2005.

64. Mick Hume, 'The age of intolerant tolerance', Spiked.com, 19 Aug 2005 at http://www.spiked-online.com/Articles/0000000CAD0A.htm.

65. Simon Jenkins, 'Panic in the face of fanatics is making Britain dangerous', Sunday Times, 31 Jul 2005. Jenkins contended, somewhat hysterically, that 'three weeks since the attacks…a howling mob has clambered aboard the terrorists' bandwagon… They are taking the opportunity to beat their political pectorals, roar abuse at all and sundry, and cloak prejudice in the dogma of necessity.'

66. See Christopher Adams, 'Growing fears of backlash as BNP seeks to make capital', Financial Times, 14 Jul 2005; Tom Baldwin, 'BNP fans flames with "sick" by-election leaflet', Times, 14 Jul 2005.

67. See for example, Karen Armstrong, 'The label Catholic terror was never used about the IRA', Guardian, 11 Jul 2005.

68. See Cathy Newman and James Blitz, 'MPs urge fellow Muslims to drive out "evil"', Financial Times, 14 Jul 2005; Burhan Wazier, 'People look at me on the tube', Metro, 14 Jul 2005.

69. Quoted in Nick Britten, 'Leading cleric rails at injustice of "Muslim" bashing', Daily Telegraph, 28 Jul 2005. Naseem also argued that the suspects closed circuit television cameras identified as the bombers on 7 July could simply have been 'innocent passengers.'

70. David Goodhart, 'It's paranoia, not Islamophobia', The Guardian, 15 Jul 2005.

71. Shiv Malik, 'The Muslim community', The Independent, 24 Jul 2005.

72. Michael Adebolajo's letter, 'Why carnage is hitting our towns', in The Times 4 Dec 2013, p. 7.

73. 'Hundreds of UK jihadists in Syria', The Daily Telegraph, 4 Dec 2013, p. 1.

74. Ernest Gellner, Relativism in the Social Sciences (Cambridge, Cambridge University Press, 1985), pp. 83-84.

75. This remained the default position of Blairism. Thus in August 2006, Blair called for a rethink on the war on terror strategy and called for

an 'alliance of moderation' to combat the growing arc of extremism. This was in fact not a rethink but a return to the muddled multicultural approach to the 'war' that Blair announced in September 2001. See *The Australian*, 3 Aug 2006.

76. Louise Richardson, *What Terrorists Want* (London, Random House, 2006); Louise Richardson (ed.), *The Root Causes of Terrorism* (London, Routledge, 2006); Robert Pape, *Dying to Win* (London, Penguin, 2005); David Kilcullen, *The Accidental Guerilla* (London, Routledge, 2004).

77. For a survey of this area see Karin Von Hippel, 'The roots of terrorism: probing the myths', in Lawrence Freedman (ed.), *Superterrorism: Policy Responses* (Oxford, Blackwell, 2002), pp. 225-39; Neil J. Smelser and Faith Mitchell (eds.), *Terrorism: Perspectives from the Behavioral and Social Sciences* (Washington, DC, National Academies Press, 2002), pp. 18-36; Dilip Hiro, *War Without End: The Rise of Islamist Terrorism and the Global Response* (London, Routledge, 2002), p. 409. The journal *Critical Studies on Terrorism* launched in 2008 summated and developed these views in a distinctly emancipatory and anti-capitalist idiom. See *inter alia* Ken Booth, 'The Human Faces of Terror: Reflections in a Cracked Looking Glass', in *Critical Studies on Terrorism* 1, 1, 2008, pp. 65-79.

78. Richard Jackson et al., 'Introduction', *Critical Studies on Terrorism* 1, 1, 2008, pp. 1-3. See also Rama Mani, 'The root causes of terrorism and conflict prevention', in Jane Boulden and Thomas G. Weiss (eds.), *Terrorism and the UN: Before and After September 11* (Bloomington, Indiana University Press, 2004), pp. 219-243; Susanne Karstadt, 'Terrorism and "new wars"', in Bülent Gökay and R.B.J. Walker (eds.), *11 September: War, Terror and Judgement* (London, Frank Cass, 2003), p. 140; Thomas G. Weiss, Margaret E. Crahern, and John Goering, 'Whither human rights, unilateralism, and US foreign policy?' in Thomas G. Weiss, Margaret E. Crahern and John Goering (eds.), *Wars on Terrorism and Iraq: Human Rights, Unilateralism and U.S. Foreign Policy* (London, Routledge, 2004), pp. 231-241; Tom H. Hastings, *Nonviolent Response to Terrorism* (Jefferson, NC, McFarland, 2004), p. 160; Pippa Norris and Ronald Inglehart, 'Public opinion among Muslims and the West', in Pippa Norris, Montague Kern, Marion Just (eds.), *Framing Terrorism: The News Media, the Government and Terrorism* (London, Routledge, 2003), p. 206.

79. Pape, *Dying to Win*; Richardson, *What Terrorists Want*; Richardson (ed.), *The Root Causes of Terrorism*.

80. Edward Said identified the ideology of *Orientalism* (New York, Pantheon, 1978). See also Edward Said, 'A Window on the World', *The Guardian*, 2 Aug 2003. Said was a Christian Palestinian, but was educated in Egypt

before his father 'Al' Said emigrated to the United States. See Edward Said, *Out of Place* (New York, Vintage, 1999).

81. Ziauddin Sardar and Merryl Wynn Davies, *Why Do People Hate America?* (London, Icon Books, 2003).

82. Tariq Ramadan is Professor of Contemporary Islamic Studies, St Antony's College, Oxford University. He is the grandson of Hasan al-Banna, the Egyptian schoolteacher who founded al-Ikhwan, the Muslim Brotherhood.

83. Tariq Ali, an editor of *The New Left Review* and author of *Rough Music: Blair, Bombs, Baghdad, London, Terror* (London, Verso, 2005) is a Trotskyite public intellectual.

84. Mohammad Yunus, 'Commonwealth lecture 2003: Halving poverty by 2015', *The Commonwealth Yearbook* (London, Commonwealth Secretariat, 2004), p. 58; Jody Williams in Irwin Abrams and Wang Gungwu (eds.), *The War in Iraq and Its Consequences: Thoughts of Nobel Laureates and Eminent Scholars* (Singapore, World Scientific, 2004), p. 31.

85. Tarak Barkawi, 'On the pedagogy of "small wars"', *International Affairs*, 80, 1, 2004, p. 228.

86. Barkawi, 'Pedagogy', p. 22.

87. Ibid., p. 22.

88. Ibid., referencing the destruction of the UN headquarters in Baghdad, 19 Aug 2003 by suicide bombers.

89. Ken Booth, 'The Human Faces of Terror', *Critical Studies on Terrorism*, 1, 1, 2008, p. 76.

90. Anthony Burke, 'The End of Terrorism Studies', *Critical Studies on Terrorism* 1, 1, 2008, p. 44.

91. See in this context, John Gray, *False Dawn: The Delusions of Global Capitalism* (London, Granta, 2002) and Manfred Steger, *Globalism: The New Market Ideology* (Lanham, MD, Rowman, 2002).

92. Ken Booth, 'The Human Faces of Terror', p. 75.

93. See Greg Bankoff, 'Regions of Risk: Western discourse on terrorism and the significance of political Islam', *Studies in Conflict and Terrorism*, 26, 6, 2003, pp. 413-428; see Seng Tan, 'An enemy of their making: US security discourse on the September 11 terror problematique', in Kumar Ramakrishnan and See Seng Tan (eds.), *After Bali: The Threat of Terrorism* (Singapore, IDSS/World Scientific Publishing, 2003), pp. 281-304; John Esposito, *The Islamic Threat: Myth or Reality?* (Oxford, Oxford University Press, 1992), p. 231; Meaghan Morris, 'White panic or Mad Max and the sublime', in Chen Kuan-Hsing (ed.), *Trajectories: Inter-Asian Cultural Studies* (London, Routledge, 1998), p. 246.

94. David Campbell, *Writing Security: United States Foreign Policy and the Politics of Identity* (Manchester, Manchester University Press, 1998), p. 68.

95. Azza Karram, 'Islamisms, globalisation, religion and power', in Ronaldo Munck and Purnaka de Silva (eds.), *Postmodern Insurgencies: Political Violence, Identity Formation and Peacemaking in Comparative Perspective* (London, Macmillan, 2000), p. 217.

96. See Richard Jackson, *Writing the War on Terror: Language, Politics and Counter-terrorism* (Manchester, Manchester University Press, 2005).

97. Michael Moore, *Dude, Where's My Country?* (New York, Warner Books, 2003), p. 101.

98. Anthony Burke, *Beyond Security, Ethics and Violence: War against the Other* (London, Routledge, 2007), p. 212.

99. Anthony Burke, 'Against The New Internationalism', *Ethics & International Affairs*, 19, 2, 2005, pp. 73-89.

100. The NSA operation PRISM and the GCHQ operation Tempora conducted the electronic eavesdropping.

101. Ed Weissman, 'The vote Ed Snowden needs to turn back the surveillance state', *Oped News*, 27 Nov 2013. See also 'MI5 chief Andrew Parker says Edward Snowden's leaks are a gift to terrorists', *The Huffington Post* 14 Oct 2013 and 'Edward Snowden's revelations prompt UN investigation of surveillance', *The Guardian* 2 Dec 2013.

102. Andrew Parker, 'Address on the evolving security threat', Royal United Services Institute, London, 8 Oct 2013, http://www.rusi.org/events/past/ref:E5254359BB8F44.

103. 'Edward Snowden Revelations prompt UN investigation of Surveillance', *The Guardian* 2 Dec 2013.

104. 'The Power of Nightmares: Baby It's Cold Outside', BBC News, 14 Jan 2005 at http://news.bbc.co.uk/go/pr/fr/-/1/hi/programmes/3755686/stm.

105. For example, King's College, London-Monash University Conference on The Roots of Terrorism, Florence, 7–8 July 2005.

106. 'The judiciary should not patrol our borders', *Daily Telegraph*, 30 Jul 2005.

107. Ibid.

108. Ibid.

109. Bill Durodié, 'Al-Qaeda: a conspiracy of dunces?' *Spiked.com*, 14 Apr 2005 at http://www.spiked-online.com/Articles/0000000CA90.htm.

110. See Anthony Giddens, 'Scaring people may be the only way to avoid the risks of new-style terrorism', *New Statesman*, 10 Jan 2005.

111. Sarah Oates, 'Selling fear? The framing of the terrorist threat in elections', *Security, Terrorism in the UK*, briefing paper 05/01 (London, Chatham House, July 2005), p. 9.

112. Bill Durodié, 'Terrorism and community resilience – a UK perspective', *Security, Terrorism in the UK*, briefing paper 05/01 (London, Chatham House, July 2005), p. 4.

113. Abu Hafs al-Masri Brigade, 'The Threats', *The Sunday Times*, 10 Jul 2005.

114. Ibid.

115. Clark, 'This terror will continue until we take Arab grievances seriously', *The Guardian*, 9 Jul 2005.

116. Salim Lone, 'Withdrawal would curb terrorism', *The Guardian*, 12 Jul 2005.

117. Frank Gregory and Paul Wilkinson, 'Riding pillion for tackling terrorism is a high risk policy', *Security, Terrorism in the UK*, briefing paper 05/01 (London, Chatham House, July 2005), p. 3.

118. 'The Iraq connection', *The Guardian*, 20 Jul 2005.

119. Tariq Ali, *Rough Music*, p. 53.

120. See for example, Peter Oborne, 'Don't be misled – the London bombs were a direct response to the Iraq war', *Spectator*, 30 Jul 2005.

121. Lone, 'Withdrawal would curb terrorism.'

122. Matthew Parris, 'Suicide bombings will pass – they are just a grisly terrorist fashion', *The Times*, 6 Aug 2005.

123. Rosemary Hollis, 'Isolating extremists', *World Today*, August/September 2004, p. 21.

124. David Aaronovitch, ' "If we don't provoke them, maybe they will leave us alone." You reckon so?' *Times*, 12 Jul 2005. Furthermore, the view that an aggressive and anti-Muslim foreign policy radicalized Islamic opinion ignored countervailing evidence of Western action in defence of Muslims in Kuwait, Kurdistan, Somalia, Bosnia and Kosovo.

125. Abu Hamza, for example, described Britain as a 'toilet', while according to a YouGov poll, thirty per cent of Muslims agreed with the statement that 'Western society is decadent and immoral and Muslims should seek to bring it to an end.' See Woods and Leppard, 'Focus: How liberal Britain let hate flourish'.

126. 'Hundreds of UK jihadists in Syria', *The Daily Telegraph*, 4 Dec 2013.

127. Suggestive of this was *Islam4UK,* one of the successor organizations of *al-Muhajiroun.*

128. See, in this context, Olivier Roy, *Jihad and Death. The Global Appeal of Islamic State* (London, Hurst, 2017).

129. 'We Have The Laws: Use Them', *The Sunday Telegraph*, 17 Jul 2005; David Leppard and Robert Winnet, 'Blair's Extremism Proposals Attacked as the Hunt Continues for Terror's New Breed', *The Sunday Times*, 7 Aug 2005.

130. See 'Who Will be Deported and Who Decides', *The Guardian*, 6 Aug 2005.

131. Duncan Gardham, 'Preachers of Hate Could be Charged with Treason', *The Daily Telegraph*, 8 Aug 2005; 'Calling Terrorist Traitors is No Answer', *The Daily Telegraph*, 9 Aug 2005.

132. 'Labour's Shambles', *The Daily Telegraph*, 10 Aug 2005.

133. See 'Abu Qatada Deported', *The Guardian*, 7 Jul 2013, http://www.theguardian.com/world/2013/jul/07/abu-qatada-deported-from-uk

134. Many of the Algerian GIA suspects implicated in the Paris Metro bombings of 1995 sought, and obtained, sanctuary in the UK. See Alan Travis, 'Judges Quash Extradition of Suspect', *The Guardian*, 28 Jun 2002.

135. See for example, David Clark, 'This Terror Will Continue Until We Take Arab Grievances Seriously', *The Guardian*, 9 Jul 2005; Simon Jenkins, 'Panic in the Face of Fanatics is Making Britain Dangerous', *The Sunday Times*, 31 Jul 2005.

136. 'Deporting Hatred', *The Times*, 6 Aug 2005.

137. See in this context Roger Sandall, *The Culture Cult: Designer Tribalism and Other Essays* (Boulder CO, Westview, 2001).

138. Michael Collins, *The Likes of Us: A Biography of the White Working Class* (London, Granta, 2004).

139. Black, Asian, Minority, Ethnic (BAME) became the official acronym that captured minorities potentially excluded from the mainstream and therefore entitled to special rights.

140. Eric Voegelin, 'The Political Religions', in *Modernity Without Restraint*, p. 63.

141. Eric Voegelin, 'The Political Religions', in *Modernity Without Restraint*, p. 61.

142. Philip Johnston, 'Hardline Cleric Faces Explusion from Finsbury Park Mosque', *The Daily Telegraph*, 17 Jan 2003.

143. The propensity of multiculturalism to lead to forms of cultural apartheid has long been noted by conservative and libertarian commentary. See for example, 'Multiculturalism: The New Racism', *Impact* (Ayn Rand Institute), November 2002. However, these kinds of criticisms were implicitly accepted by the 'Cantle Report' into the interracial riots in Bradford, Burnley and Oldham in the spring and summer of 2001, which pointed to the deeply segregated nature of Muslim and other communities in many urban areas in Northern England. See *Building Cohesive Communities: A Report of the Independent Review Team* (London, Home Office 2002), sections 2.13–2.19.

144. Jonathan Powell, *Talking to Terrorists; How to End Armed Conflicts* (London, Bodley Head, 2014).

145. Quoted in 'Inside the sect that loves terror', *Sunday Times*, 7 Aug 2005.

146. Quoted in report by Richard Watson, *Newsnight*, BBC, 1 Aug 2005.

147. See Bruce Lawrence (ed.), *Messages to the World: the Statements of Osama bin Laden* (London, Verso, 2005), p. xvi.

148. Leo Strauss, 'Social Science and Humanism', *The Rebirth of Classical Political Rationalism. An Introduction to the Thought of Leo Strauss* (Selected and introduced by Thomas. L. Pangle) (Chicago, Chicago University Press, 1989), p. 10.

149. Ibid., p. 12.

150. Gray, *Enlightenment's Wake*, p. 29.

151. 'Declaration of war against Americans occupying the land of the two holy places', in Yonah Alexander and Michael S. Swetnam (eds.), *Usama bin Laden's al-Qaeda: Profile of a Terrorist Network* (Ardsley, NY, Transnational Publishers, 2001), Appendix 1, A, p. 19.

152. Ibid., p. 3.

153. N. Machiavelli, *The Art of War* (1521) (Chicago, Chicago University Press, 2013).

154. As Australian Attorney General Mark Dreyfus observed, 'under Australia's [post-2001] terrorism framework, four major terrorist attacks on Australian soil have been disrupted.' Nino Bucci, 'Fine Tuning Push on Terror Laws', *Sydney Morning Herald*, 14 May 2013. In the UK, MI5 brought twenty-three major cases to court between 2002 and 2013 that would have otherwise led to a major terror attack in the UK. See MI5 Terrorist Attacks in the UK, http: www.mi5.gov. uk.home/

155. Anatole Kaletsky, 'The act of small-time losers', *The Times*, 14 Jul 2005.

5 THE LANGUAGE OF PROGRESS AND THE CLOSURE OF THE EUROPEAN MIND

1. See M.M. Ashan and A.R. Kidwai, *Sacrilege Versus Civility: Muslim Perspectives on the Satanic Verses Affair* (Markfield, UK, Islamic Foundation, 1993).

2. House of Commons, *Religious Hatred Bill* (Norwich, HMSO, 2005); *Racial and Religious Hatred Act*, 2006, Office of Public Sector Information, http://www.opsi.gov.uk/acts/acts2006/ukpga_20060001_en_1, accessed 25 Jun 2009.

3. Olivier Roy, 'EuroIslam: The Jihad Within?' *The National Interest*, 71, Spring, 2003, p. 67.

4. Kalim Siddiqui, head of the Muslim Institute, persuaded the Iranian authorities to issue the fatwa. See Dominic Kennedy, 'British Activist

was behind Iran's Fatwa on Salman Rushdie', *The Times*, 25 February 2019. https://www.thetimes.co.uk/article/british-activist-was-behind-iran-s-call-to-kill-salman-rushdie-7cd22753s, accessed 27 Jul 2019.

5. Christopher Hitchens, 'Assassins of the Mind', *Vanity Fair,* February 2009, p. 14.

6. Caroline Fourest, *In Praise of Blasphemy* (Paris, Grasset, 2015). All citations from the Kindle edition.

7. *Charlie Hebdo*, 9 Feb 2006.

8. The courts, however, found that the satirists had not insulted 'a group of people because of their religion'. Fourest, *In Praise*, Loc. 272.

9. *Charia Hebdo*, 3 Nov 2011.

10. It showed an image of Mohammad sporting a *Je Suis Charlie* headband.

11. Matthew Champion, 'What Happens When You Try to Show the Charlie Hebdo Cover on Sky News', 15 Jan 2015, http://indy100.independent.co.uk/article/what-happens-when-you-try-to-show-the-charlie-hebdo-cover-on-sky-news--lyJKbW0R5x

12. Fourest, *In Praise*, Loc. 71.

13. Nick Cohen, 'What has become of conservatism?', *The Observer*, 27 Nov 2016, https://www.theguardian.com/commentisfree/2016/nov/27/what-has-become-of-conservatism-trump-farage-le-pen-brexit, accessed 4 Sep 2019.

14. Caroline Fourest, *In Praise*. See also Edwy Plenel, *Pour Les Mussulmans* (Paris, Babelio, 2014).

15. George Orwell, *Nineteen Eighty Four* (London, Penguin, [1954] 2019), p. 237.

16. The 2015 ceremony, held less than two months after the Paris attack, awarded the international prize to *Charlie Hebdo*.

17. Fourest, *In Praise*, Loc. 401.

18. All Party Parliamentary group on British Muslims, *Islamophobia Defined,* 2018, p. 27.

19. Ramadan is the holder of the Saudi endowed Sheikh Hanafi bin Khalifa al Khari chair in Contemporary Islamic Studies at Oxford.

20. Fourest, *In Praise*, Loc. 315. See also Trevor Phillips, 'Foreword' in Sir John Jenkins, *Islamophobia. A Research Note*, Policy Exchange, London, 2019, p. 7.

21. See Plenel, *Pour Les Mussulmans*.

22. Fourest, *In Praise*, Loc. 463.

23. George Orwell, 'Politics and the English Language', in *Essays* (London, Penguin, 2000), p. 137.

24. Fourest, *In Praise*, Loc. 551.

25. Ibid., Loc. 586.

26. Ibid., Loc. 629. Unregulated social networks also propagate bigotry and provide platforms for fanatical violence of a white supremacist hue as we discuss in chapter 9.
27. Ibid., Loc. 512.
28. Albert Camus, *The Myth of Sisyphus* (New York, Alfred Knopf, 1955), p. 8.
29. Fourest, *In Praise*, Loc. 585.
30. Ibid., Loc. 599.
31. Ibid., Loc. 682.
32. Ibid., Loc. 718.
33. 'State Control', Official Brochure, *Age of Terror. Art Since 9/11*, Imperial War Museum, October 2017.
34. In October 2018, Professor Mike Rainsborough, Head of the Department of War Studies, King's College, London ran a series on 'Endangered Speeches'. The university received complaints and stopped the series after two events. Rainsborough lost his headship of the department the following year.
35. David Crowe, 'Paris Attacks, we'll never bend to godless tyrants', *The Weekend Australian*, 15 Nov 2015, tps://www.theaustralian.com.au/nation/nation/paris-attacks-well-never-bend-to-godless-tyrants-turnbull/news-story/0d9444b5e67417baab96b0d53694c804 Accessed 2 Aug 2019.
36. See 'Q&A Recap, Paris Attacks', *ABC News*, 17 November 2015, accessed 2 Aug 2019, https://www.news.com.au/entertainment/tv/tv-shows/qa-recap-paris-attacks-immigration-solutions-military-intervention/news-story/ea2a8a216c7858374b3d7f8d95847979?from=public_rss.

    See also Gerard Henderson, 'Paris Attack Apologists lose plot on Islamist threat', *The Australian*, 18 Nov 2019, https://www.theaustralian.com.au/subscribe/news/1/?sourceCode=TAWEB_WRE170_a_GGL&dest=https%3A%2F%2Fwww.theaustr
37. Mitchell D. Silber and Arvin Bhatt, *Radicalization in the West. The Homegrown Threat* (New York, NYPD, 2007), https://seths.blog/wp-content/uploads/2007/09/NYPD_Report-Radicalization_in_the_West.pdf
38. The Prevent strategy began in 2003.
39. https://esrc.ukri.org/public-engagement/social-science-forschools/resources/prevent-the-uk-s-counter-ter. It evolved into *CONTEST 3.0. The United Kingdom's strategy for countering terrorism* (CM 9608, Norwich, HMSO, 2018).
40. http://www.theaustralian.com.au/news/world/religion-a-dirty-word-at-white-house-summit-countering-violent-extremism/story-e6frg6so-1227224555123.

41. Between June and August 2015, 796 people were referred for de-radicalization in England and Wales, double the number of referrals for intervention in the first three months of 2015. Prevent did not deter an equal number engaging as foreign fighters.

42. Saffron Howden, 'Muslim children should not be forced to sing the national anthem says Hizb ut-Tahrir', *The Sydney Morning Herald*, 1 Nov 2015. https://www.smh.com.au/national/muslim-children-should-not-be-forced-to-sing-national-anthem-says-hizb-uttahrir-20151101-gknwy9.html

43. See Cale Horne and Samuel Bestvater, 'Assessing the effects of changes in British counterterrorism policy on radical Islamist networks in the UK 1999–2008', *Behavioural Science of Terrorism and Political Aggression* 8, 2, 2015, pp. 1-24.

44. Radicalization also, perhaps deliberately, played into street argot where to be 'radical' meant to be street smart.

45. George Orwell, 'Politics and the English language', in Bernard Crick (ed.), *Essays* (London, Penguin, 2000), ch. 31.

46. J.C.D. Clark, *Our Shadowed Present: Modernism, Postmodernism and History* (Stanford, Stanford University Press, 2003), p. 37.

47. Orwell, 'Politics and the English Language'.

48. Joseph Addison, *The Spectator*, 185, 2 Oct 1711. In *The Works of Joseph Addison*, 3 vols. New York, Harper, 1842, vol. 1, pp. 274-5.

49. Alexander Pope, *Essay on Man*, epistle iii, section vi, London, 1734.

50. David Hume, 'On Superstition and Enthusiasm'. In *Essays Moral, Political, and Literary, 1742–54* (Indianapolis, Liberty Fund, 1987).

51. Walter Bagehot, *Physics and Politics* (Cambridge, Cambridge University Press, [1873] 2011), p. 31.

52. See Ernest Gellner, *Conditions of Liberty. Civil Society and its Rivals* (London, Penguin, 1996), pp. 46-49.

53. See Herbert Marcuse, *One Dimensional Man. Studies in the Ideology of Advanced Industrial Society* (New York, Beacon Press, 1964); Tom Wolfe, 'The Me Decade', *New York Magazine*, 26 Aug 1973; Christopher Lasch, *The Culture of Narcissism. American Life in an Age of Diminishing Returns* (New York, Norton, 1979).

54. Quoted in 'State's 2.3 million dollars to divert Extremism', *The Australian* 3 Nov 2015.

55. My emphasis. See Karl Popper, *The Open Society and its Enemies* (London, Routledge and Kegan Paul, 2 vols. 1962), vol. 1, p. 302.

6 THE NETWORKED GLOBAL ORDER

1. Tony Blair, *A Journey* (London, Hutchinson, 2010), p. 683.
2. Ibid., p. 684.
3. Ibid., p. 104.
4. Ibid., p. 664.
5. Stephen D. King, *Grave New World. The End of Globalization and the Return of History* (New Haven, CT, Yale University Press, 2017), ibook, p. 295.
6. Ibid., p. 243.
7. Davos was the setting for Thomas Mann's health spa for tuberculosis patients in his novel *The Magic Mountain*.
8. King, *Grave New World*, p. 141.
9. As Klaus Schwab, the Davos World Economic Forum's *éminence grise*, observed on more than one occasion, 'we have moved from a world where the big eat the small to a world where the fast eat the slow'.
10. Adam Tooze, *Crashed. How a Decade of Financial Crisis Changed the World* (London, Allen Lane, 2018), p. 574.
11. King, *Grave New World*, p. 99.
12. https://www.weforum.org/agenda/2007/01/world_economic_-2/
13. King *Grave New World*, p. 27.
14. Ibid., p. 108,
15. See Tooze, *Crashed*.
16. See Philip G. Cerny, 'Plurality, Pluralism and Power: Elements of Pluralist Analysis in an Age of Globalization', in Rainer Eisfeld (ed.), *Pluralist Developments in the Theory and Practice of Democracy* (Opladen and Farmington Hills, Barbara Budrich Publishers on behalf of the International Political Science Association Research Committee, 2006), pp. 81-111.
17. Michael Oakeshott, *On Human Conduct* (Oxford, Oxford University Press, 1975), p. 136.
18. Ibid.
19. Danilo Zolo, 'The Singapore Model. Democracy, Communication and Globalization', *The Blackwell Companion to Political Sociology* (London, Wiley, 2004), ch. 38.
20. Walter Russell Mead, *Power, Terror, Peace and War. America's Grand Strategy in a World at Risk* (New York, Knopf, 2004), p. 74.
21. The Australian Secret Intelligence Organization, like MI5 and the Federal Bureau of Investigation, is responsible for internal security whereas Australian Secret Intelligence Service (ASIS), MI6, and the CIA are responsible for external intelligence.

22. Philip Bobbit, 'Everything We Think About the Wars on Terror is Wrong', *The Spectator*, 20 May 2006, p. 14.

23. King, *Grave New World*, p. 131.

24. As we saw in chapter 2.

25. Tooze, *Crashed*, p. 65.

26. Charles Mackay, *Memoirs of Extraordinary Popular Delusions and the Madness of Crowds* (London, National Illustrated Library, 1852), Vol. 1, Preface.

27. Mackay devotes an interesting chapter to John Law, the Scottish financial alchemist of his day, and his Mississippi scheme that bankrupted *ancien régime* France. See also C. Kindleberger and R. Aliber, *Manias, Panics and Crashes. A History of Financial Crises* (London, Wiley, 2005), pp. 33-104.

28. There was also a spectacular financial crisis in 1907, when the demand for cash led to a massive bank run in the US in the wake of the collapse of the Knickerbocker Trust in October. Significantly, J.P. Morgan played a vital role in coordinating the bank and trust bail-outs that followed. See Jon R. Moen and Ellis W. Tallman, 'The panic of 1907', *Federal Reserve History*, 4 Dec 2015 https://www.federalreservehistory.org/essays/panic_of_1907

29. Milton Friedman and Anne Jacobson Schwartz, *A Monetary History of the United States 1867–1960* (National Bureau of Economic Research, Princeton, Princeton University Press, 1971), p. 347.

30. See for example his theory of banking crises and financial instability available at http://www.levyinstitute.org/publications/hyman-minsky, especially 'The Financial Instability Hypothesis', Working Paper No. 74, pp. 6-8.

31. See George Soros, 'The Crisis and What To Do About It', *The New York Review of Books*, 6 Nov 2008, https://www.georgesoros.com/2008/11/06/the_crisis_what_to_do_about_it/; and George Soros, *The Alchemy of Finance* (London, Wiley, 1987), p.10.

32. King, *Grave New World*, p. 100.

33. Ibid., p. 105.

34. Thomas Piketty, *Capital in the Twenty First Century* (Boston, Harvard University Press, 2014); Paul Mason, *Post Capitalism: A Guide to Our Future* (London, Allen Lane, 2015).

35. Tooze, *Crashed*, p. 150.

36. Ibid., p. 159.

37. Ibid., p. 163.

38. *The Economist* as late as February 2008 proposed that the BRIC economies might have decoupled from the US induced financial crisis. See Satoshi Kambayashi, 'The Decoupling Debate', *The Economist*, 8 Mar 2008,

https://www.economist.com/finance-and-economics/2008/03/06/the-decoupling-debate

39. China and Japan in particular held large numbers of bonds in that curious hybrid public/private US mortgage initiative, Fannie Mae and Freddie Mac, the Government Sponsored Enterprises that received a $200 billion injection from the US government in August 2008: Tooze, *Crashed*, p. 57.

40. As Larry Summers described the relationship. See Tooze, *Crashed*, p. 41.

41. By a further irony, the low interest yen itself facilitated the leveraged merger and acquisition activities between 2002 and 2008 via the dollar-yen carry trade, the unwinding of which in October 2008 saw the yen the only currency, apart from the yuan, to rise against the US dollar.

42. The exception was Malaysia, which applied currency controls and froze foreign direct investment for two years. It earned international disapproval for its policy.

43. *New York Times*, 12 Nov 2008.

44. The credit agencies only downgraded Lehman Brothers in September 2008. A few days later it entered bankruptcy.

45. Tooze, *Crashed*, p. 203.

46. Ibid., p. 297.

47. Ibid., p. 316.

48. Ibid., p. 165.

49. King, *Grave New World*, p. 290.

50. Ibid., p. 306.

51. Ibid., p. 458.

52. Ibid., p. 290.

53. Ibid., p. 132.

54. This was best reflected in the S&P 500 index, which peaked before the global financial crisis at 1,557. It then plummeted to a low of 683. A handful of years later – partly a response to sustained pump-priming from the Federal Reserve – the index had jumped to a new high of 2,270. King, *Grave New World*, p. 133.

55. J.D. Vance, *Hillbilly Elegy. A Memoir of a Family and Culture in Crisis* (New York, Harper, 2016), p. 253.

56. Tooze, *Crashed*, p. 459.

57. John Rawls, *A Theory of Justice* (New York, Columbia University Press, 1971), p. 25. I have altered the penultimate word of Rawls' statement substituting 'most' for 'least' (in italics).

58. Democracies can be corrupted in two ways: by what Montesquieu calls 'the spirit of inequality' and 'the spirit of extreme equality'. See Louis de Secondat, Baron de Montesquieu, *The Spirit of the Laws*, 2 volumes (Glasgow, David Niven, 1794), vol. 1, book 8, p. 132.

59. The cast of the new utopians includes: Peter Thiel (Paypal and Palantir), Elon Musk (Tesla and Space X), Ray Kurzwiel and Larry Page (Google), Mark Zuckerberg (Facebook and Instagram), Jeff Bezos (Amazon), Travis Kalinick (Uber), and Robert Mercer (Cambridge Analytica).

60. See Jamie Bartlett's documentary, *The Secrets of Silicon Valley,* https://www.bbc.co.uk/programmes/b0916ghq

61. John Thornhill, 'Big Tech v Big Brother', *The Financial Times Weekend,* 19-20 Apr, 2017.

62. Robert Nozick, *Anarchy, State and Utopia* (New York, Basic Books, 1974), p. 334.

63. Martin Wolfe, 'Taming the masters of the tech universe', *Financial Times* 15 Nov 2017.

64. See James Titcomb, 'Google's growth heads for the cliff-edge as Amazon primes for advertising attack', *The Sunday Telegraph,* 21 Jul 2019.

65. Wolfe, 'Taming the masters.'

66. Jonathan Haskel and Stian Westlake, *Capitalism without Capital: The Rise of the Intangible Economy* (Oxford, Oxford University Press, 2017).

67. Carl Benedikt Frey and Michael A. Osborne, 'The Future of Employment: How Susceptible Are Jobs to Computerisation?', *Technological Forecasting and Social Change,* 114, 2017. Accessed online: Aug 2017. PDF: http://www.oxfordmartin.ox.ac.uk/downloads/academic/The_Future_of_Employment.pdf

68. Vilfredo Pareto, *Premier cours d'économie politique appliquée professé à l'Université de Lausanne* (1896), G. Busoni (ed.), (Geneva, Droz, 1982). See also Richard Koch, *The 80/20 Principle* (New York, Doubleday, 1998) and Robert Michels, *Political Parties; a Sociological Study of the Oligarchical Tendencies of Modern Democracy* (trans Eden and Cedar Paul) (Kitchener, Batoche Books, [1915] 2001). Michels formulated 'the iron law of oligarchy'.

69. Michels, *Political Parties.*

70. Morozov, Evgeny, 'Why the Internet of Things Could Destroy the Welfare State', *The Observer,* 19 July 2014, www.theguardian.com/technology/2014/jul/20/rise-of-data-death-of-politics-evgeny-morozov-algorithmic-regulation, accessed 1 Aug 2017.

71. Nick Bilton et al., 'The New Establishment', *Vanity Fair,* November 2017.

72. Josh Glancy, 'Interiew with J.D. Vance', *The Sunday Times,* 16 Jul 2017.

73. Tooze, *Crashed,* p.7 9.

74. Ibid., p. 117.

75. UK, Germany and France.

76. Irish banks' liabilities added up to 700 per cent of GDP. Tooze, *Crashed,* p. 110.

77. In 2009, the federal government introduced a constitutional amendment, the *Schuldenbremse,* restricting borrowing to no more than 0.35 per cent of GDP. See Tooze, *Crashed*, pp. 287-9.

78. It almost broke up in a disorderly and potentially globally damaging fashion in 2012, Ibid., p. 17.

79. King, *Grave New World,* p. 139.

80. Ibid., p. 240.

81. Yannis Varoufakis, *Adults in the Room. My Battle with Europe's Deep Establishment* (London, Bodley Head, 2017), p. 49.

82. Ibid., p. 447.

83. Somewhat predictably, Lagarde, the classic European insider, replaced Draghi at the ECB when his tenure ended in 2019.

84. Ibid., p. 246.

85. Ibid., p. 237.

86. Ibid., p. 481.

87. King, *Grave New World*, p. 309.

88. Tooze, *Crashed*, pp. 16-17.

89. George Soros, 'The Crisis.'

90. Joseph Schumpeter, *Capitalism, Socialism and Democracy* (London, Routledge, [1943] 2003). See also Paul Collier, *The Future of Capitalism* (London, Penguin, 2018), p. 21.

91. Karl Polanyi, *The Great Transformation* (Boston, Beacon Press, 2001), ch 1.

92. 'Mais ceci est-il une véritable bataille?': Stendhal (Henri-Marie Beyle), *The Charterhouse of Parma* (Penguin, London, 2006), p. 48.

93. The term Ortega y Gasset coined in 1930. See José Ortega y Gasset, *The Revolt of the Masses* (New York, Norton, 1957).

94. Richard Hofstadter, 'The Paranoid Style in American Politics', *Harpers Magazine*, November 1964, p. 77.

95. David Goodhart, *The Road to Somewhere. The Populist Revolt and the Future of Politics* (London, Hurst, 2017), p. 253; Vance, *Hillbilly Elegy*; Collier, *Future of Capitalism*; Christophe Guilluy, *Prosperity, the Periphery and the Future of France* (New Haven, Yale University Press, 2018).

96. Ibid., p. 253.

97. The hillbilly lifestyle was one of 'truly irrational behaviour'. As his mother, a qualified nurse, fed him Pepsi at nine months and asked him, as a young boy, to urinate into a bottle so she could pass a drug test, Vance clearly has a point, see p. 156.

98. Guilluy, *Prosperity*, p. 37.

99. Ibid.

100. Goodhart, p. 5.

101. Ibid., p. 63.

102. Ibid., p. 5.

103. Ibid., p. 61.

104. In the mid-1980s net migration to the UK had been almost zero. Ibid., p. 124.

105. Ibid., p. 123. The unofficial figures are of course much higher.

106. Ibid., p. 177.

107. Ibid., p. 135.

108. King, *Grave New World*, p. 145. See also Vance, *Hillbilly Elegy*.

109. Ibid., p. 15.

110. King, *Grave New World*, p. 227.

111. Ibid., p. 258. The Bourbon line is allegedly Talleyrand's on the restored French dynasty after 1815.

112. Ibid., p. 228.

113. See Anthony Giddens, *Turbulent and Mighty Continent: What Future for Europe?* (Cambridge, Polity, 2014); Mark Mazower, *Dark Continent. Europe's Twentieth Century* (London, Penguin, 1998); Douglas Murray, *The Strange Death of Europe* (London, Bloomsbury, 2017); Norman Davies, *Vanished Kingdoms* (London, Allen Lane, 2017).

7 ALL ROADS LEAD TO CHINA

1.   Stephen D. King, *Grave New World. The End of Globalization and the Return of History* (New Haven, CT, Yale University Press, 2017), p. 130.

2.   Japan was the only non-Western economy in the G7.

3.   G20 comprises Australia, Argentina, Brazil, Canada, China, Germany, France, India, Indonesia, Italy, Japan, the Republic of Korea, Mexico, Russia, Saudi Arabia, South Africa, Turkey, the UK, the US, and the EU.

4.   The Shanghai Cooperation Organisation (SCO) was established in 1996 as the Shanghai Five (China, Russia, Kazakhstan, Kyrgyzstan, Tajikistan). It evolved into the SCO in 2001 when Uzbekistan joined the group. It now has eight member states, including Pakistan and India.

5.   See Daniel A. Bell, *The China Model. Political Meritocracy and the Limits of Democracy* (Princeton, Princeton University Press, 2016).

6.   The CEE includes the eleven EU member countries of Bulgaria, Croatia, the Czech Republic, Estonia, Hungary, Latvia, Lithuania, Poland, Romania, Slovakia and Slovenia as well as five EU accession countries from the Western Balkans: Albania, Bosnia and Herzegovina, Macedonia (now North Macedonia), Montenegro and Serbia.

7.   'Brussels hits at China's loan pressure', *Financial Times*, 6 Mar 2019.

8.   'Italy ready to take China's road to the top', *The Times*, 7 Mar 2019.

9. Jason Horowitz, 'Italy's deal with China signals shift in geopolitics', *New York Times*, 1 Apr 2019.

10. See Thorston Benner et al., *Authoritarian Advantage: Responding to China's Growing Political Influence in Europe* (Joint Report by the Mercator Centre for China Studies and Global Public Policy Institute, February 2018), https://www.merics.org/en/publications/authoritarian-advance

11. 'Brussels hits at China's loan pressure', *Financial Times*.

12. Ibid.

13. Ibid.

14. O.N. Mehtra, 'NATO eastward expansion and Russian security', *Journal of Strategic Studies* 22, 8, 1998, p. 1225.

15. *National Security Strategy of the United States of America*, Washington DC, 2017, p. 47.

16. Australian Government, *Foreign Policy White Paper*, Canberra, 2017, p. 25.

17. 'James Mattis unveils new US military strategy focused on threat from Russia and China', 20 Jan 2018, http://www.abc.net.au/news/2018-01-20/china-and-russia-not-terrorism-main-threats-to-us-mattis-says/9345670

18. H.J. Mackinder, *Democratic Ideals and Reality* (Westport, CT, Greenwood Press, 1962), p. 70.

19. Ibid., p. 70.

20. Henry Kissinger, *Diplomacy* (New York, Simon and Schuster, 1994), p. 813.

21. Alain Minc coined the term 'durable disorder'. See his *Le nouvel moyen age* (Paris, Gallimard, 1993).

22. See Paul Valéry, *Orient et Occident*, vol 1. in *Les Lettres Modernes*, 3 vols. (Paris, Minard, 1998).

23. Hillary Clinton, 'America's Pacific Century', *Foreign Policy*, 11 Oct 2011, http://foreignpolicy.com/2011/10/11/americas-pacific-century/

24. Jeffrey Goldberg, 'The Obama Doctrine', *The Atlantic*, April 2016, http://www.theatlantic.com/magazine/archive/2016/04/the-obamadoctrine/471525/

25. See Walter Russell Mead, *Special Providence. American Foreign Policy and How it Changed the World* (New York, Routledge, 2002), pp. 223-227.

26. *Treaty of Amity and Cooperation*, Article 2: http://asean.org/treaty-amity-cooperation-southeast-asia-indonesia-24-february-1976/

27. Henry Kissinger, *World Order. Reflections on the Character of Nations and the Course of History* (London, Allen Lane, 2014), p. 178.

28. S. Rajaratnam, *The Prophetic and the Political*, in Chan Heng Chee and Obaid Ul Haq (eds.), (Singapore, ISEAS, 2007), p. 288.

29. Rosemary Foot, 'Identity politics and the US rebalance to Asia' (East Asia Institute, Seoul), March 2016. The other Asian signatories to the TPP are Brunei, Singapore, the Philippines, Vietnam, Australia, and New Zealand.

30. Yong Sun Ha & Yul Sohn, *The Co-evolution of Korea and Japan* (East Asia Institute, Seoul), August 2015.

31. 'Come together on the Abe Road', *The Economist*, 12 Dec 2015.

32. Majuri Mukherjee, 'India walking the line between China and the US', *The Diplomat*, 27 Apr 2016; *National Security Strategy*, p. 47.

33. *National Security Strategy*, p. 46.

34. Cited in Greg Sheridan, 'Sabre Rattling imbues Shangri-la with a growing sense of menace', *Straits Times*, 5 Jun 2014.

35. Author's translation. The Bahasa Indonesian reads: 'Kami sekarang mayat/Berikan kami arti/Berjagalah terus di garis batas pernyataan dan impian'. Karawang and Besaki are the regencies that bisect the Eastern suburbs of Jakarta and were sites of fierce resistance fighting in 1948. Anwar evidently drew heavily for his poem from the US poet Archibald Macleish's *The Young Dead Soldiers Do Not Speak* (1941).

36. J. Sun, 2018. 中国连续9年成东盟最大贸易伙伴去年交易5148 亿美元 [China is ASEAN's Largest Trading Partner for 9 Consecutive Years, Trading US$514.8 Billion Last Year]. 新浪网 [Sina]. Accessed at: http://finance.sina.com.cn/china/hgjj/2018-07-18/doc-ihfnsvyz 7227839.shtml.

37. Napoli, Ibid., p. 358.

38. Y. Cao, 2017. 财经观察：中国东盟携手共谱繁荣新篇章 [Financial Observation: China and ASEAN Join Hands to Share A New Chapter of Prosperity]. *Xinhua NewsAgency* [新华社]. Accessed at: http://www.gov.cn/xinwen/2017-11/12/content_5239121.htm.

39. S. Larkin, 'The Conflicted Role of the AIIB in South East Asia', *ISEAS Perspective*, 23, 2015, p. 6.

40. Larkin, Ibid. p. 4.

41. See *Master Plan on ASEAN Connectivity 2025* (Jakarta, the ASEAN Secretariat, 2016), https://asean.org/storage/2016/09/Master-Plan-on-ASEAN-Connectivity-20251.pdf

42. Ibid., p. 7.

43. B. Glaser and Deep Lal, cited in Benjamin Schreer, 'Should Asia be afraid?', *The National Interest* 20 Aug 2014, p. 2. https://nationalinterest. org/blog/the-buzz/should-asia-be-afraid-chinas-strategy-the-south-china-sea-11109

44. Achmad Fuad, 'Apa Untungnya Indonesia Masuk Belt and Road Initiative?' [What is Indonesia's Gain in Joining the Belt and Road Initiative?],

Watyuting, https://watyuting.com/topik/ekonomika/Apa-Untungnya-Indonesia-Masuk-Belt-and-Road-Initiative, accessed 23 Sep 2018.

45. J. Utama, and M. Kim, 'More than just economy: Maritime implications of China's investment', *The Jakarta Post*, 27 Jun 2016, http://www.thejakartapost.com/academia/2016/06/27/more-than-just-economy-maritime-implications-of-chinas-investment.html, accessed 23 Sep 2018.

46. Fuad, 'Apa Untungnya Indonesia'.

47. For instance, due to the hyperinflation of its currency and debt incurred to China, Harare struck a deal in 2015 which witnessed the cancellation of US$40 million worth of Chinese debt in exchange for solidifying the *renminbi* as legal tender. See A. Mustofa, Penjajahan Kuning Sedang Mengintai Indonesia [Yellow Colonization is Lurking in Indonesia], *Law Justice*, 2018, https://law-justice.co/penjajah-kuning-sedang-mengintai-indonesia-.html, accessed 28 Sep 2018].

48. D. Estrada, 'China's Belt and Road Initiative: Implications for the Philippines'. *Foreign Service Institute Insights,* 5, 3, 2018, http://www.fsi.gov.ph/wp-content/uploads/2018/03/Vol-5-No-3-China's-Belt-and-Road-Initiative-Implications-for-the-Philippines-Estrada1.pd, accessed 13 Oct 2018.

49. They include the North–South Railway in Southern Luzon (US$2.91 billion); the 70 km Subic-Clark Railway (US$947.64 million); the Davao City Expressway (US$424.81 million), and the Kaliwa Dam project (US$234.92 million). See A.J. Rabena, 'The Complex Interdependence of China's Belt and Road Initiative in the Philippines', *Asia and the Pacific Policy Studies,* 5, pp. 683-697.

50. R. Muggah, 'Duterte's Drug War in the Philippines is Out of Control, He Needs to be Stopped', *The Guardian*, 5 Jan 2017, https://www.theguardian.com/global-development-professionals-network/2017/jan/05/rodrigo-dutertes-drug-war-in-the-philippines-is-out-of-control-he-needs-to-be-stopped, accessed 13 Oct 2018].

51. Tom Wright and Simon Clark. 'Investigators Believe Money Flowed to Malaysian Leader Najib's Accounts Amid 1MDB Probe', *The Wall Street Journal*, https://www.wsj.com/articles/SB10130211234592774869404581083700187014570, accessed 5 Sep 2019.

52. J. Chin, 'MDB Sells Edra Power Assets to China Firm for Nearly RM10Billion Cash', *The Star*, 23 Nov 2015, https://www.thestar.com.my/business/business-news/2015/11/23/1mdb-sells-edra-power-assets-to-china-firm-for-nearly-rm10b-cash/ [6 Oct 2018].

53. N. Razak, 'Fruits Harvested from Seeds of Trust', *China Daily*, 2 Nov 2016, http://www.chinadaily.com.cn/opinion/2016-11/02/content_27245852.htm, accessed 6 Oct 2018.

54. M. Abi-Habib, 'How China Got Sri Lanka to Cough Up a Port', *New York Times*, 25 Jun 2018, https://www.nytimes.com/2018/06/25/world/asia/china-sri-lanka-port.html, accessed 5 Sep 2019.

55. S.K. Abu Bakar, 'Mukhriz: Najib Satu-Satunya PM Jual Tanah Hak Milik Kekal Kepada Warga Asing' ['Mukhriz: Najib the Only PM to Sell Permanent Land to Foreigners'], *Free Malaysia Today*, 19 Oct 2017, https://www.freemalaysiatoday.com/category/bahasa/2017/10/19/mukhriz-najib-satu-satunya-pm-jual-tanah-hak-milik-kekal-kepada-warga-asing/, accessed 13 October 2018.

56. — 不平等条 (bu ping deng tiao yue)

57. H. Lee and Y.Y. Huang, 对马来西亚投资：中国的机遇与风险 [Investment in Malaysia: China's Opportunities and Risks], 新华丝路 [Xinhua Silk Road], 2018. http://silkroad.news.cn/2018/0813/106248.shtml, accessed 13 Oct 2018.

58. The four ASEAN states are Singapore, Brunei, Malaysia, and Vietnam. The three South American states are Mexico, Peru, and Chile.

59. C. Emerson, *Australia Joins Launch of Massive Asian Regional Trade Agreement*, Department of Foreign Affairs and Trade. https://trademinister.gov.au/releases/2012/ce_mr_121120.html, accessed 14 Oct 2018.

60. D. Shira, 'RCEP Negotiations Reach Critical Stage – Likely to be Inked by Year-End'. *ASEAN Briefing*, 7 Sep 2018, https://www.aseanbriefing.com/news/2018/09/07/rcep-negotiations-reach-critical-stage-likely-inked-year-end.html, accessed 14 Oct 2018.

61. Y.H. Zhang, 没有TPP, 中国还有RCEP [No TPP, China Still Has the RCEP], 世界知识 [World Affairs], 8, 2018, pp. 64-66.

62. A free trade agreement with China would put pressure on the rupee and further exacerbate India's trade deficit with Beijing, which stood at US$59.4 billion in 2017. See Takashi Nakano, 'RCEP accord dims as India frets over trade liberalization', *Nikkei Asian Review*, 2018, https://asia.nikkei.com/Politics/International-Relations/RCEP-accord-dims-as-India-frets-over-trade-liberalization, accessed 5 Sep 2019.

63. X. Mao and X. Ding, 一带一路"倡议与区域经贸融合发展 [The 'Belt and Road' Initiative and the Development of Regional Economic and Trade Integration], 当代世界与社会主义 [Contemporary World and Socialism], 3, 2016.

64. Bonnie Glaser and Deep Lal, cited in Schreer, 'Should Asia be afraid?', p. 2.

65. *Foreign Policy White Paper* (Canberra), p. 46.

66. See inter alia, Michael Leifer, *The ASEAN Regional Forum: A Model for Cooperative Security in the Middle East* (Canberra, Dept. of International

Relations, Research School of Pacific and Asian Studies, Australian National University, 1998).

67. After issuing its nine red dash line outlining its territorial claim, China made the announcement at the Cambodian summit that the claim was uncontestable.

68. The tribunal sits in Hamburg and adjudicates according to the United Nations Convention on the Law of the Sea.

69. Tom Mitchell, 'UN tribunal rules against Beijing in South China Sea dispute', *Financial Times*, 12 Jul 2016.

70. 'China's overtures to cement ties with ASEAN', *Straits Times*, 12 Oct 2013.

71. As one Chinese diplomat described the ruling in July 2016. See Catherine Wong, 'Nothing more than a piece of paper', *South China Morning Post*, 6 Jul 2016. https://www.scmp.com/news/china/diplomacy-defence/article/1986029/nothing-more-piece-paper-former-chinese-envoy-dismisses

72. 'China's island building lacks strategic logic', *Financial Times*, 28 Oct 2015.

73. Henry Kissinger, *On China* (London, Allen Lane, 2011), p. 23.

74. *National Security Strategy* (Washington), p. 53.

75. James Bosco, 'The One China Policy, What would Nixon do?', *The Diplomat*, 5 Jan 2017.

76. Thucydides, *History of the Peloponnesian Wars* (trans. M.I. Finley) (London, Penguin, 1977), Book 1, p. 23.

77. Ibid., Book 6, p. 402.

78. Kishore Mahbubani, 'Qatar: Big Lessons from a Small Country', *The Straits Times*, 2 Jan 2017, https://www.straitstimes.com/opinion/qatar-big-lessons-from-a-small-country, accessed 12 Jun 2018. The piece caused controversy at the Singapore Ministry of Foreign Affairs, leading to Mahbubani 'stepping down' from his position as Dean of the Lee Kuan Yew School of Public Policy.

8 MAXIMS OR AXIOMS?

1. Francis Fukuyama, 'The End of History?', *The National Interest*, Summer 1989. Fukuyama replaced the question mark with a full stop in the book that evolved from the article, see Francis Fukuyama, *The End of History and the Last Man* (London, Penguin, 1992).

2. Charles Krauthammer, 'The unipolar moment', *Foreign Affairs* 70, 1, 1991.

3. John J. Mearsheimer, 'Imperial by design', *The National Interest*, 111, Jan/Feb 2011, p. 16.

4. Tony Blair, *A Journey* (London, Hutchinson, 2010), p. 689.

5. Mearsheimer, 'Imperial by design', p. 19.
6. James Kitfield, 'After bin Laden: is the war on terror winding down?' *National Journal*, 7 May 2011, http://www.nationaljournal. com/magazine/after-bin-laden-is-the-war-on-terror-winding-down--20110505, accessed 18 Oct 2014.
7. Mearsheimer, 'Imperial by design', p. 19.
8. Hans J. Morgenthau, *Politics among Nations: The Struggle for Power and Peace* (New York, Knopf, 1978), p. 1.
9. Morgenthau, *Politics Among Nations*, p. 4.
10. Francis Fukuyama, *The End of History and the Last Man* (London, Penguin, 1992), pp. 287-340.
11. Juan Linz and Alfred Stepan, *Problems of Democratic Transition and Consolidation: Southern Europe, South America, and Post-communist Europe* (Baltimore, MD, Johns Hopkins University Press, 1996), p. 5.
12. See Immanuel Kant, 'Perpetual Peace. A Philosophic Sketch', in H. Reiss (ed.), *Kant's Political Writings* (Cambridge, Cambridge University Press, 1970), pp.122-125. Influential examples of the post-Kantian IR genre are Alexander Wendt, 'Anarchy is What States Make of it: the Social Construction of Power Politics', *International Organization*, 46, 2, 1992, pp. 391-425; Alexander Wendt, *Social Theory of International Politics* (Cambridge, Cambridge University Press, 1999); Martha Finnemore and Kathryn Sikkink, 'Taking stock: the constructivist program in international relations and comparative politics', *Annual Review of Political Science*, 4, 2001, pp. 391-416. See also Anthony Giddens, *Modernity and Self-Identity: Self and Society in the Late Modern Age* (Cambridge, Polity Press, 1991).
13. See Kant, 'Perpetual Peace', p. 125; and inter alia, David Held and Anthony McGrew (eds.), *The Global Transformations Reader: An Introduction to the Globalization Debate* (Cambridge, Polity Press, 2000) and Peter Katzenstein, *A World of Regions: Asia and Europe in the American Imperium* (Ithaca, NY, Cornell University Press, 2005).
14. Walter Russell Mead, 'The Return of Geopolitics: the Revenge of the Revisionist Powers', *Foreign Affairs*, 93, 3, 2014, pp. 69-79.
15. Martin Wight, *Power Politics* (London, Penguin, 1979), p. 111.
16. 'A lurch onto the world stage', *The Economist*, 28 Feb 2015, p. 35.
17. Edward Lucas, 'Ukraine Protests: We're Letting Putin Win', *Daily Telegraph*, 20 Feb 2014.
18. Adam Tooze, *Crashed. How a Decade of Financial Crisis Changed the World* (London, Allen Lane, 2018), p. 491.
19. See Elise Giuliano, 'Is the risk of ethnic conflict growing in the Ukraine?', *Foreign Affairs*, 19 Mar 2019, https://www.foreignaffairs.com/articles/

ukraine/2019-03-18/risk-ethnic-conflict-growing-ukraine,　accessed 20 Mar 2019.

20. 'A lurch onto the world stage', *The Economist*, 28 Feb 2015, p. 36.

21. Charles Powell, 'The West will pay for losing its backbone in Iraq and Ukraine', *Daily Telegraph*, 19 Jun 2014.

22. Lucas, 'Ukraine protests'.

23. 'A lurch onto the world stage', *The Economist*.

24. R. Korteweg, 'Mogherini's mission: four steps to make EU foreign policy more strategic', Centre for European Reform, 19 Jan 2015.

25. Morgenthau, *Politics among nations*, p. 12.

26. See for example Gen. Donn A. Starry, 'Syria: one more reason for a return to grand strategy', *Information Dissemination*, 27 Aug 2013, http://www.informationdissemination.net/2013/08/syria-one-more-reason-for-return-of.html, accessed 19 Oct 2014; Patrick C. Docherty, 'A new US grand strategy', *New America Foundation*, 9 Jan 2013, http://newamerica.net/node/77134, accessed 19 Oct 2014.

27. Mearsheimer, 'Imperial by design', p. 12.

28. Mark Tran and Matthew Weaver, 'Isis announces Islamic caliphate in area straddling Iraq and Syria', *The Guardian*, 30 June 2014, http://www.theguardian.com/world/2014/jun/30/isis-announces-islamic-caliphate-iraq-syria, accessed 20 Oct 2014.

29. See Graeme Baker, 'The fierce ambition of ISIL's Baghdadi', AL Jazeera, 15 Jun 2014, http://www.aljazeera.com/news/middleeast/2014/06/fierce-ambition-isil-baghdadi-2014612142242188464.html,　accessed 20 Oct 2014.

30. *This is the promise of Allah*, Alhayat Media Center (IS/ISIS), no place, no date, circa 28 Jun 2014, p. 4, https://ia902505.us.archive.org/28/items/poa_25984/EN.pdf, accessed 20 Oct 2014.

31. *The promise of Allah*, p. 9.

32. Quoted in Tran and Weaver, 'Isis announces caliphate'.

33. See 'Al-Qaeda in Iraq confirms Syria's Nusra Front is part of its network', *Al-Arabiya*, 9 Apr 2013, http://english.alarabiya.net/en/News/middle-east/2013/04/09/Al-Qaeda-in-Iraq-confirms-Syria-s-Nusra-Front-is-part-of-its-network.html, accessed 20 Oct 2014.

34. Bassem Mroue, 'Here's a breakdown of the oil assets ISIS now controls', *Business Insider/Associated Press*, http://www.businessinsider.com/breakdown-of-the-oil-assets-isis-controls-2014-9,　accessed　20　Oct 2014.

35. See Max Weber, 'Politics as a vocation', in Max Weber, *The Vocation Lectures* (trans. Rodney Livingstone) (Indianapolis, Hackett, 2004).

36. 'The return of Khilafah', *Dabiq*, issue 1, Ramadan 1435, p. 13. See also James Barr, *A Line in the Sand. Britain, France and the Struggle that Shaped the Middle East* (Simon & Schuster, London, 2011), pp. 117-27.

37. 'The return of Khilafah', p. 7.

38. Ibid.

39. Quoted in Susan Crabtree, 'Flashback: Obama: al-Qaeda is on "a path to defeat"; calls for resetting terror policy', *Washington Times*, 23 May 2013, http://www.washingtontimes.com/news/2013/may/23/obama-al-qaeda-is-on-a-path-to-defeat/?page=all, accessed 22 Oct 2014.

40. See The White House, Office of the Press Secretary, 'Remarks by the President on the Middle East and North Africa', 19 May 2011, http://www.whitehouse.gov/the-press-office/2011/05/19/remarks-president-middle-east-and-north-africa, accessed 22 Oct 2014. See also David Ignatius, 'Hope for democracy in the Arab world', Washington Post, 9 Aug 2013, http://www.washingtonpost.com/opinions/david-ignatius-hope-for-democracy-in-the-arab-world/2013/08/09/df888f30-0043-11e3-96a8-d3b921c0924a_story.html, accessed 22 Oct 2014.

41. Michael Barone, 'Lessons from the Surge', *Townhall.com*, 29 Dec 2007, http://townhall.com/columnists/michaelbarone/2007/12/29/lessons_from_the_surge/page/full, accessed 14 May 2014; see also Peter D. Feaver, 'Anatomy of a surge', *Commentary*, 1 Apr 2008, http://www.commentarymagazine.com/article/anatomy-of-the-surge/, accessed 14 May 2014.

42. The White House, The Office of the Press Secretary, 'Remarks by the President and the First Lady on the End of the Iraq war', 14 Dec 2011, http://www.whitehouse.gov/the-press-office/2011/12/14/remarks-president-and-first-lady-end-war-iraq, accessed 22 Oct 2014.

43. See Chris Keeler, 'The end of responsibility to protect', *Foreign Policy Journal*, 12 Oct 2011, http://www.foreignpolicyjournal.com/2011/10/12/the-end-of-the-responsibility-to-protect/, accessed 22 Oct 2014.

44. See Thomas Raines, 'UK's Syria vote: a parliament of doves', *Chatham House*, 3 Sep 2013, https://www.chathamhouse.org/media/comment/view/194057, accessed 22 Oct 2014.

45. See Robert Kagan, 'US can't ignore the Middle East', *Washington Post*, 20 Nov 2012, http://www.washingtonpost.com/opinions/robert-kagan-us-cant-ignore-the-middle-east/2012/11/20/a2b4ede0-3331-11e2-bfd5-e202b6d7b501_story.html, accessed 25 Oct 2014.

46. See Daniel Trotta, 'Iraq war cost US more than $2 trillion: study', Reuters, 14 Mar 2013, http://www.reuters.com/article/2013/03/14/us-

iraq-war-anniversary-idUSBRE92D0PG20130314, accessed 25 Oct 2014; Ernesto Londoño, 'Iraq war costs to top $4 trillion', *Washington Post*, 28 Mar 2013, http://www.washingtonpost.com/world/national-security/study-iraq-afghan-war-costs-to-top-4-trillion/2013/03/28/ b82a5dce-97ed-11e2-814b-063623d80a60_story.html, accessed 25 Oct 2014.

47. Oliver Wright, 'Costly failures: wars in Iraq and Afghanistan cost UK taxpayers £30bn', *The Independent*, 27 May 2014, http://www.independent.co.uk/news/uk/politics/costly-failures-wars-in-iraq-and-afghanistan-cost-uk-taxpayers-30bn-9442640.html, accessed 25 Oct 2014.

48. See Kenneth M. Pollack and Ray M. Takeyh, 'Near Eastern promise: why Washington should focus on the Middle East', *Foreign Affairs*, May/June 2014, http://www.foreignaffairs.com/articles/141213/ kenneth-m-pollack-and-ray-takeyh/near-eastern-promises, accessed 25 Oct 2014.

49. See for example Ernest Gellner, *Muslim Society* (Cambridge, Cambridge University Press, 1981).

50. Cécile Fabre, *Cosmopolitan War* (Oxford, Oxford University Press, 2012), p. 3.

51. David Martin Jones, 'Peace through conversation', *The National Interest*, 79, 1, 2005, pp. 93-100.

52. James Alfred Aho, *German Realpolitik and American Sociology: An Inquiry into the Sources and Political Significance of the Sociology of Conflict* (Lewisburg, PA, Bucknell University Press, 1975), p. 20.

53. Aho, *German Realpolitik*, p. 21.

54. Thus in negotiations over the Ukraine in February 2015, German Chancellor Angela Merkel 'believes it is always better to keep talking than to stoke conflict', quoted in 'A lurch onto the world stage', *The Economist* 28 Feb 2015, p. 35.

55. David Richards, *Taking Command* (London, Headline 2014) cited in Tom Coughlan, 'A maverick goes into battle one last time', *The Times*, 6 Oct 2014.

56. Paddy Ashdown, 'We must embrace Putin to beat Islamic State', *The Times*, 30 Sep 2014.

57. United Nations General Assembly, 'Implementing the responsibility to protect: report of the Secretary-General, A3/63/677, 63rd session, agenda items 44-107', 12 Jan 2009, http://www.un.org/en/ga/ search/view_doc.asp?symbol=A/63/677, accessed 26 Oct 2014.

58. Stephen Toulmin, *Return to Reason* (Cambridge, MA, Harvard University Press, 2001), p. 117.

59. Morgenthau, *Politics Among Nations*, p. 15.

60. S. Toulmin, *Return to Reason*, p. 117.

61. Alexis de Tocqueville, *Democracy in America* (Pittsburgh, Pennsylvania State Classics, 2002), vol. 1, pp. 261-62.

62. Reinhold Niebuhr, *Moral Man and Immoral Society* (New York, Charles Scribner, 1960), pp. 83–112. See also A. R. Colli, 'Normative Prudence as a Tradition of Statecraft', *Ethics and International Affairs* 5 (2), 1991.

63. Aristotle, *Nichomachean Ethics* (Oxford, Oxford University Press, 2009), Book 6, 8, p.112.

64. Aristotle, *Rhetorica* (trans W. Rhys Roberts) (Oxford, OUP, 1924), 1.5, 1362, p. 24.

65. Thomas Aquinas, 'Question 47. Of Prudence considered in itself', *Secunda Secundae, Summa Theologica* (1225–1274), translated by the Fathers of the English Dominican Province, http//www.microbooks. studio.com.

66. Ibid.

67. In the collection of the British National Gallery.

68. Peter H. Wilson, *Europe's Tragedy. A New History of The Thirty Years War* (London, Allen Lane, 2010), p. 9.

69. Wilson, *Europe's Tragedy*, p. 800.

70. Ibid., pp. 784-95.

71. C.P. Kindelberger, 'The economic crisis of 1619–1623', *Journal of Economic History* 51, 1999, pp. 149-175.

72. See C. Needham, 'Freedom, Community, and Function: Communitarian Features of Medieval Political Theory', *American Political Science Review*, 6, 4, 1992, pp. 977-986.

73. See J.H. Plumb, 'The City and the State', in J.H. Plumb (ed.), *The Penguin Book of the Renaissance* (London, Penguin, 1964), pp. 34-40.

74. Francesco Guicciardini, *Selected Writings,* Cecil Grayson (ed.), (Oxford, Oxford University Press, 1965), p. 20.

75. Plumb, 'City and State', p. 35. See also Garrett Mattingly, *Renaissance Diplomacy* (London, Cape, 1955).

76. Niccolò Machiavelli, *The Prince* (London, Penguin, 1982), p. 91.

77. Ibid., p. 87.

78. J.R. Hale, 'War and public opinion in Renaissance Italy', in E.F. Jacob (ed.) *Italian Renaissance Studies* (London, Faber and Faber, 1960), p. 116.

79. Niccolò Machiavelli, *The Art of War*, cited in Hale, 'War and public opinion', p. 120.

80. Niccolò Machiavelli, *The Art of War*.

81. Richard Tuck, *Philosophy and Government, 1572–1651* (Cambridge, Cambridge University Press, 1993), pp. 55-56.

82. Giovanni Botero's *Della ragion di stato* (1589) shares this concern with prudence and the desire to secure and expand the state. See Giovanni Botero, *The Reason of State and the Greatness of Cities* (trans. P.J. and D.P. Waley) (London, Routledge and Kegan Paul, 1956), pp. 34-72.

83. The most significant twentieth century treatment of reason of state thinking, Friedrich Meinecke's *Machiavellism. The Doctrine of raison d'état and its Place in Modern History* (New Haven, Yale University Press, 1957), mentions Lipsius but accords more space to less influential thinkers in the genre like his Venetian admirer Traiano Boccalini (see chapter 3).

84. Justus Lipsius, *Politicorum sive civilis doctrinae libri sex* (1589). All references are from Justus Lipsius, *Politica: six books of politics or political instruction*, Jan Waszink (ed.) (Assen, Royal Van Gorcum, 2004). On the centrality of Tacitus to this understanding of politics see Jan Waszink, Introduction, *Politica*, pp. 93-8.

85. Marshall McLuhan, *Gutenberg Galaxy: The Making of Typographic Man* (London, Routledge and Kegan Paul, 1962). See also Stephen Greenblatt, *The Swerve. How the Renaissance Began* (London, Vintage, 2012), pp. 226-41.

86. This could translate into a vernacular idiom as: right or justice, law, authority, peace, conscience, the safety of the people as the supreme good, and the public good.

87. La Rochefoucauld compiled his maxims between 1665–78. See Francois, Duc de la Rochefoucauld, *Maxims* (trans L.W. Tanock) (London, Penguin, 1959), maxim 218, p. 62.

88. Lipsius, *Politica*, 3.3, p. 391.

89. Hannah Arendt, *On Revolution* (Penguin, London, 1990), p. 36.

90. Edward Hyde, 'Of Conscience', in *A Collection of Several Tracts of Edward Earl of Clarendon* (London, 1727), pp. 162-3.

91. Lipsius, 'Preliminary matter', *Politica*, p. 231.

92. Lipsius, *Politica*, 4.3., p. 395.

93. See J.H. Hexter, *The Vision of Politics on the Eve of the Reformation* (London, Routledge and Kegan Paul, 1973), p. 168. Robert Bireley writes that for Botero, 'the term *reason* carried a particular implication... He argued that the ruler who sought a powerful state did best to seek the well-being of his subjects in a fashion that was moral and so reasonable'. See Robert L. Bireley, *The Refashioning of Catholicism 1450–1700: A Reassessment of the Counter-Reformation* (New York, St. Martin's, 1999), p. 183.

94. Justus Lipsius, *On Constancy* (1595), (Phoenix Press, Bristol, 2006), p. 58.

95. Aristotle, *Nichomachean Ethics*.

96. Lipsius, *Politica*, 1.7, p. 283.

97. Lipsius, *Politica* (capitals in original), p. 283 and pp. 233-262.

98. Lipsius, *Politica* 3.1, p. 347.

99. R.M. Wenley, 'Casuistry', in *The Encyclopaedia of Religion and Ethics* (Edinburgh,1910), p. 239.

100. Cited in A.R. Jonsen and S. Toulmin, *The Abuse of Casuistry. A History of Moral Reasoning* (Berkeley, University of California, 1988), p. 130. See also T.C. Potts, *Conscience in Medieval Philosophy* (Cambridge, 1980).

101. Jonsen and Toulmin, *The Abuse of Casuistry*, p. 2. The case of murder and the circumstances governing it regularly featured in books of case divinity. See D. Cathcart, *Doubting Conscience Donne and the Poetry of Moral Argument* (Ann Arbor, University of Michigan, 1974), p. 35.

102. H. Hopfl, *Jesuit Political Thought. The Society of Jesus and the State, c. 1560– 1630* (Cambridge, Cambridge University Press, 2004), p. 5.

103. Conal Condren, *Argument and Authority in Early Modern England: The Presupposition of Oaths and Offices* (Cambridge, Cambridge University Press, 2006), p. 174.

104. Jonsen and Toulmin, *The Abuse of Casuistry*, p. 2.

105. Lipsius, *Politica*, 3.2, p. 349.

106. Lipsius, *Politica*, 4.1, pp. 383-85.

107. Lipsius, *Politica* 4,2.p. 387. Capitals in original.

108. Lipsius, *Politica*, 4.5, pp. 403-409.

109. Lipsius, *Politica*, 4.13, p. 509.

110. Lipsius, *Politica* 4.13, p. 511.

111. Lipsius, *Politica* 5.1, p. 513.

112. Lipsius, *Politica*, 5.2, p. 539.

113. Lipsius, *Politica* 5.3, p. 541.

114. Lipsius, *Politica* 5.19, pp. 657-59.

115. Lipsius, *Politica*, 5.17, p. 645.

116. Lipsius, *Politica*, 3.4, p. 355.

117. Jonsen and Toulmin, *The Abuse of Casuistry*, p. 27.

118. See Cécile Fabre, Ibid and Alex Bellamy, *Just War from Cicero to Iraq* (Cambridge, Polity Press, 1996). In fact Michael Walzer had already elaborated an updated modern, liberal version of Just War in the context of Vietnam. See M. Walzer, *Just and Unjust War. A Moral Argument with Historical Illustrations* (New York, Basic Books, 1977).

119. David Fisher, *Morality and War: Can War Be Justified in the Twenty-first Century?* (Oxford, Oxford University Press, 2011), p. 258.

120. Fisher, *Morality and War*, p. 247.

121. Fisher, *Morality and War*, p. 253.

122. Thomas Aquinas, 'On War. Q.40, articulus 1, Secunda Secundae', *Summa Theologiae* (1274). See also Thomas Aquinas, *Aquinas' Political*

Writings, R.W. Dyson (ed.), (Cambridge, Cambridge University Press, 2002), p. 239.

123. Fisher, *Morality and War,* p. 247.

124. Fisher, *Morality and War,* p. 62.

125. Jack Spence, 'Does Morality Matter in Security Policy? A Reply to David Fisher', *Survival*, 55, 5, 2013, p. 151.

126. Spence, 'Does Morality Matter ?', p. 151.

127. Edmund Burke, *Reflections on the Revolution in France and on the Proceedings of certain Societies in London Relative to that Event* (1790) (London, Penguin, 2003), p. 97.

128. Edmund Burke, 'Letters on a Regicide Peace', *The Works of Edmund Burke*, 3 vols. (New York, Harper Brothers, 1837), vol. 2, p. 215.

129. Burke 'Letters', p. 216.

130. Burke, 'Letters', p. 217.

131. Dennis Judd, *Palmerston* (London, I.B. Tauris, 2015), pp. 109-110.

132. M. Oakeshott, *The Politics of Faith and the Politics of Scepticism* (New Haven, Yale University Press, 1996), p. 9.

133. Ibid., p. 13. See also M. Oakeshott, 'On the Civic Condition', in *On Human Conduct* (Oxford, Oxford University Press, 1975), part 2.

134. See Garrett Mattingly, *The Armada* (New York, Houghton Mifflin, 1987), p. 11; and *Renaissance Diplomacy*, p. 207.

135. Niccolò Machiavelli, *The Prince* (London, Penguin, 1966), p. 40.

136. Lipsius, *Politica* 2.6., p. 309.

137. Lipsius, *Politica* 4.1, p. 383.

138. Lipsius, *Politica*, 4.14, p. 513.

139. Lipsius, *Politica*, 4.14, p. 517.

140. Lipsius, *Politica*, 1.1, p. 261.

141. Lipsius *Politica*, 1.7, p. 285.

142. Lipsius, *Politica*, 4.1, p. 385.

143. Such nescience peaked when the then Foreign Secretary in the Blair government, David Milliband, decided to close the Foreign Office diplomatic archive.

144. Lipsius, *Politica*, 3.2, p. 391.

145. Lipsius, *Politica*, 4.14, p. 531.

146. As Lipsius described Europe in the 1580s.

147. 'How often have statesmen been motivated by the desire to improve the world, and ended by making it worse?' Morgenthau, *Politics among Nations*, p. 4. See also Friedrich Meinecke's *Machiavellism*. The German title more accurately conveys Meinecke's concern: *Die Idee der Staatsrason in neuren Gesichte* (1924).

148. Abu Bakr al Naji, *The Management of Savagery: The Most Critical Stage Through Which the Umma Will Pass* (trans. William McCants), Cambridge MA, Harvard University Press, 2006). See Hassan Hassan and Michael Weis, *ISIS: Inside an Army of Terror* (New York, Regan, 2015).

149. Matthew d'Ancona, '"None of our business" is no answer to Islamist terror', *Daily Telegraph*, 5 July 2014.

150. See David Martin Jones, *Conscience and Allegiance in Seventeenth Century England* (New York, University of Rochester Press, 1999), chapter 1.

151. 'Mosques harbouring Islamic extremists to be closed down', *The Times*, 24 Mar 2015.

152. Lawrence Freedman, 'The master strategist is still a myth', *War on the Rocks*, 14 Oct 2014, http://warontherocks.com/2014/10/the-master-strategist-is-still-a-myth/, accessed 29 Oct 2014.

153. K.R. Minogue, 'Prudence', in Digby Anderson (ed.) *Decadence* (The Social Affairs Unit, London, 2005), p. 36.

154. David Brooks, 'A Gift for Donald Trump', *The New York Times*, 10 Feb 2017. Accessed 2 Aug 2019 https://www.nytimes.com/2017/02/10/opinion/a-gift-for-donald-trump.html

155. Brooks, 'A Gift'. See also John Bew and David Martin Jones, 'A Trump Doctrine?' *The National Interest* 153, Jan/Feb 2018.

156. Glenn Paskin, 'Interview with Donald Trump', *Playboy*, 1 Mar 1990, https://www.playboy.com/read/playboy-interview-donald-trump-1990.

157. Susan B. Glaser, 'Michael Anton: The Full Transcript', *Global Politico* 17 Apr 2017, https://www.politico.com/magazine/story/2017/04/michael-anton-the-full-transcript-215029

158. Morgenthau, *Politics Among Nations*, p. 4.

9 THE REVENGE OF POLITICS AND THE SEARCH FOR ORDER

1. John Gray, *Enlightenment's Wake. Politics and Culture at the End of the Modern Age* (London, Routledge, 1995), p. 21.

2. José Ortega y Gasset, *The Revolt of the Masses* (1930) (New York, Norton, 1957), p. 56.

3. Bernard-Henri Levy, *Left in Dark Times: A Stand Against the New Barbarism* (New York, Random House, 2008). Alt right activist Richard B. Spencer launched *The Alternative Right* webzine in 2010.

4. Ortega y Gasset, *The Revolt of the Masses*. As Ortega y Gasset noted, 'when the mass acts on its own, it lynches': p. 116.

5. Eric Voegelin, *In Search of Order*, in *Order and History* (Baton Rouge, Louisiana University Press, 1987), vol. 5, p. 6.

6. Augustine of Hippo, *The City of God Against the Pagans* (Cambridge, Cambridge University Press, 1998), Book 2.21, p. xxii.

7. See Norman Cohn, *The Pursuit Of The Millennium. Revolutionary Millenarians And Mystical Anarchists of the Middle Ages* (London, Paladin, 1970).

8. See Voegelin, *Political Religions* and *The Ecumenic Age*, in *Order and History*, vol. 4, p. 268. See also Cohn, *Pursuit of the Millennium*, and R.I. Moore, *The War on Heresy* (Cambridge, MA, Harvard University Press, 2012).

9. Eric Voegelin, *The New Science of Politics* (Chicago, University of Chicago Press, 1952), p. 167.

10. Ernest Sternberg, 'Purifying the World: What The New Radical Ideology Stands For', *Orbis*, Winter, 2010, p. 64.

11. Emilio Gentile, 'The Sacralization of Politics: Definitions, Interpretations and Reflections on the Question of Secular Religion and Totalitarianism', *Totalitarian Movements and Political Religions*, 1, 1, 2000, pp. 18-19. See also the recent claims of Extinction Rebellion and the curious cult of Greta Thunberg, *No One is Too Small to Make a Difference* (London, Penguin, 2019); and Julie Burchill, 'Extinction Rebellion's splitters point to a deeper divide,' *The Sunday Telegraph*, 20 Jul 2019.

12. Hannah Arendt, *The Origins of Totalitarianism* (New York, Houghton, Mifflin Harcourt, 1951), pp. 472-9.

13. Roger Griffin, *The Nature of Fascism* (London, Pinter, 1991), p. 32.

14. See Paul Collier, *The Future of Capitalism. Facing the New Anxieties* (London, Penguin, 2018), pp. 17-20.

15. Guy Standing, *The Precariat: The New Dangerous Class* (London, Bloomsbury, 2011), pp. 1-5.

16. Richard Hofstadter, 'The Paranoid Style in American Politics', *Harpers Magazine*, November 1964.

17. Church of Jesus Christ Christian Aryan Nations, Converse, Louisiana https//:www.aryan-nations.org.

18. Bruce Hoffman, *Terrorism in the United States and the Potential Threat to Nuclear Facilities* R-3351-DOE (Santa Monica, RAND Corp, 1986), p. v.

19. American neo-Nazi Eric Thomson coined the term in 1976.

20. For an excellent account of the paranoid style see Jon Ronson, *Them: Adventures with Extremists* (London, Picador, 2001).

21. Andrew Macdonald (a.k.a. William Luther Pierce), *The Turner Diaries* (Hillsboro, WV, National Vanguard Books, 1978).

22. It was white extremists Alex Curtis and Tom Metzger who originated the term 'lone wolf' in the mid–1990s.

23. Louis Beam, 'Leaderless Resistance', *The Seditionist* 12, January 1992, p. 1. Beam first promulgated the notion in 1983 to the Ku Klux Klan. See

also Southern Poverty Law Center, 'Louis Beam', at spl.org, and George Michael, *Lone Wolf Terror and the Rise of Leaderless Resistance* (Nashville, Vanderbilt University Press, 1995), pp. 5-15.

24. There is currently a move by the ruling coalition government to ban the party. A previous attempt to ban the party as unconstitutional failed in 2003. See: http://www.spiegel.de/international/topic/right_wing_extremism/.

25. http://www.spiegel.de/international/topic/right_wing_extremism/.

26. Franz Stefan Gady, 'Corruption and Scandal can't stop Austria's Far Right', *Foreign Policy*, 23 May 2019, https://foreignpolicy.com/2019/05/23/corruption-and-collusion-cant-stop-austrias-far-right/ accessed 5 Aug 2019.

27. http://blogs.telegraph.co.uk/news/douglascarswellmp/100242451/the-front-national-is-the-most-popular-party-in-france-are-you-happy-now-eurocrats/.

28. For the gravity of the recession and the weakness of the Greek recovery to insipid growth, see Martin Wolf, 'Greek economy shows promising signs of growth', *Financial Times* 20 May 2019, https://www.ft.com/content/b42ee1ac-4a27-11e9-bde6-79eaea5acb64

29. https://www.politico.eu/article/thierry-baudet-forum-for-democracy-netherlands-5-things-to-know-about-dutch-far-rights-new-figurehead/, accessed 27 Mar 2019.

30. As opposed to parties like the Dutch Forum for Democracy or Italy's Five Star movement, which want to restrict immigration and reassert a cultural, as opposed to a racial, identity.

31. See Alexander Meleagrou-Hitchens and Hans Brun, *A Neo-Nationalist Network: The English Defence League and the European Counter Jihad Movement* (International Centre for the Study of Radicalization and Political Violence, London, 2013), p. 3.

32. Robinson was 'the rock star' of the UK extreme right.

33. Hitchens and Brun, Ibid., p. 5.

34. Camus was a close friend of Roland Barthes and spent time at Andy Warhol's Factory in Greenwich Village, New York in the 1970s. The influence of Jean Raspail's *Le Camp des Saints* (1973) is evident upon Camus *Le Grand Replacement* (2012).

35. Ye'or Bat (a.k.a. Giselle Litman), *Eurabia.The Euro-ArabAxis* (New Jersey, Fairleigh Dickinson University Press, 2005).

36. 'Murder of Lee Rigby provokes anti-Muslim attacks', *The Daily Telegraph*, 23 May 2013; 'Islamophobia attacks rise dramatically after the murder of Lee Rigby', *The Independent*, 28 May 2013.

37. Andrew Berwick, *2083: A European Declaration of Independence* (London, 2013), pp. 595-645.

38. According to the Southern Poverty Law Center's Hatewatch site: https://www.splcenter.org/hatewatch/2016/06/16/alleged-killer-british-mp-was-longtime-supporter-neo-nazi-national-alliance

39. Raffaello Pantucci and Clare Ellis, *Lone Actor Terrorism* (RUSI, London 2016).

40. Ernest Gellner, *Nations and Nationalism* (London, Phoenix, 1997).

41. Ibid., p. 104.

42. Ibid. p. 106.

43. Levy, *Left in Dark Times*.

44. K.R. Minogue, 'Christophobia and the West', *The New Criterion*, June, 2003.

45. John Fonte, 'Liberal Democracy versus Transnational Progressivism: The Future of the Ideological Civil War Within the West', *Orbis*, Summer 2002, pp. 1-14.

46. See David Martin Jones, 'Peace Through Conversation', *The National Interest*, 79, 1, Spring, 2005.

47. Redemptive social movements like Greenpeace, the World Social Forum, Extinction Rebellion or other vehicles of emancipatory global ethics are to be distinguished from white supremacist or Islamist social movements that might also consider their activities in some sense redemptive.

48. Sternberg, 'Purifying the World', p. 61.

49. Michael Hardt and Antonio Negri, *Empire* (Cambridge, MA, Harvard University Press, 2001). See also Noam Chomsky, *Hegemony and Survival: America's Quest for Global Dominance* (London, Penguin, 2004), and Alexander Del Valle, *I Rossi Neri, Verdi: la convergenza degli Estremi opposti. Islamismo, comunismo, neonazismo* (Torino, Lindau, 2010).

50. See Levy, *Left in Dark Times*, p. 24 and Sternberg, 'Purifying the World', p. 63.

51. Levy, ibid., pp. 23-30.

52. Nick Cohen, *What's Left? How the Left Lost Its Way* (London, Harper, 2007), pp. 4-14.

53. John Ware, 'Is Labour Anti-Semitic?', *Panorama*, July 2019, https://www.bbc.co.uk/programmes/m0006p8c

54. Cohen, *What's Left*, p. 61.

55. Sternberg, 'Purifying the World', p. 74.

56. The slogan appeared on the Tumblr blog page in August 2011.

57. Anonymous conducted cyber-attacks in support of whistle blowers like Edward Snowden, Bradley Manning and Julian Assange. http://www.youtube.com/watch?v=AcDnjFemPuc.

58. http://www.youtube.com/watch?v=o74sMCU_kPQ.

59. Fonte, 'Liberal Democracy vs Transnational Progressivists', p. 1. Levy, *Left in Dark Times,* pp. 137-145.

60. Sternberg, 'Purifying the World', p. 66.

61. http://www.forumsocialmundial.org.br/noticias_1.php?cd_news=2556&cd_language=2.

62. Sternberg, 'Purifying the World', p. 76.

63. Ibid.

64. Cohen, *What's Left?,* p. 301.

65. An important and necessary term in the Olympian vocabulary. Originally coined by Antonio Gramsci, the subaltern or minority voice came to be used by postcolonial discourse theorists to show how that voice has been silenced, both by colonialism and in the postcolonial treatment of the non-Western other. Empathetic and emancipatory communicatory reason, however, enables it to articulate its grievances and pain. See Gayatri Chakravorty Spivak, 'Can the Subaltern Speak?', in *Colonial Discourse and Post-Colonial Theory: A Reader*, in Patrick Williams and Laura Chrisman (eds.), (Hertfordshire, Harvester Wheatsheaf, 1994), p. 93.

66. Levy, *Left in Dark Times,* pp. 137-145.

67. Sternberg, 'Purifying the World', p. 83.

68. Yoram Hazony, *The Virtue of Nationalism* (New York, Basic Books, 2018) (all citations taken from the Amazon Kindle edition).

69. Ibid loc 2782.

70. Immanuel Kant, 'Idea for a universal history with a cosmopolitan purpose', in *Kant's Political Writings*, p. 37.

71. See Hazony, *The Virtue of Nationalism*, loc 2784.

72. Ibid., loc 2490.

73. Alexandre del Valle, *Le Totalitarisme Islamiste à l'assaut des Démocraties* (Paris, Syrtes, 2002).

74. Albert Camus, *The Rebel* (London, Penguin, 1967), p. 191.

75. James Burnham, *Suicide of the West: An Essay on the Meaning and Destiny of Liberalism* (1964) (New York, Encounter Books, 2014). More recently, see Jonah Goldberg, *Suicide of the West. How the Rebirth of Tribalism, Populism, Nationalism, and Identity Politics is Destroying American Democracy* (New York, Crown Publishers, 2018); and David Marquand, *The End of the West: the Once and Future Europe* (Princeton, Princeton University Press, 2011).

76. Leo Strauss, *The City and Man* (Chicago, Chicago University Press, 1964), p. 6.

77. See in this context, Albert Camus, *The Rebel*.

78. Minogue, *The Liberal Mind*, p. 200.

79. Pascal Bruckner, *The Tyranny of Guilt. An Essay on Western Masochism* (Princeton, Princeton University Press, 2010).

80. Yascha Mounck, *The People versus Democracy. Why our Freedom is in Danger and How to Save It* (Cambridge MA, Harvard University Press, 2018), p. 161.

81. Ernest Gellner, *Conditions of Liberty. Civil Society and its Rivals* (London, Hamish Hamilton, 1994), p. 185.

82. See in this context, Hannah Arendt, 'Truth and Politics', in Peter Baehr (ed.) *The Portable Hannah Arendt* (London, Penguin, 2000); George Orwell, *Politics and the English Language* (London, Penguin Classics, 2013); Albert Camus, *The Myth of Sisyphus* (London, Penguin, 2005), and *The Rebel. An essay on man in revolt* (New York, Alfred A. Knopf, 1956).

83. Max Weber, *Economy and Society* (Berkeley, University of California Press, 1978), 54.

84. Alexander Hamilton, John Jay and James Madison, *The Federalist,* 85 (Indianapolis, Liberty Fund, 2001), p. 458.

85. David Runciman, *The Confidence Trap: A History of Democracy in Crisis from World War I to the Present* (Princeton, Princeton University Press, 2013). Runciman became more pessimistic five years later contemplating *How Democracy Ends* (London, Profile, 2018).

86. John Milton, *The Ready and Easy Way to establish a Free Commonwealth and the excellences thereof compared with the inconveniencies and dangers of readmitting kingship in this nation* (London, 1660).

87. Tom Paine, *Common Sense* (Philadelphia, 1776), p. 122.

88. Madison, *The Federalist*, No. 14, p. 170.

89. Arendt, *On Revolution* (Penguin, London, 1990), p. 93.

90. Jean Jacques Rousseau, *The Social Contract and Discourses* (London, Everyman, 1973), p. 193.

91. Arendt, *On Revolution*, p. 275.

92. Bernard Crick's *In Defence of Politics* (London, Weidenfeld & Nicholson, 1992) was the standard introduction to the field in Commonwealth universities during the Cold War. It went through six editions between 1962 and 2005.

93. See Hannah Arendt, *The Promise of Politics* (New York, Random House, 2005).

94. See Richard S. Katz & Peter Mair, 'Changing Models of Party Organization and Party Democracy: The Emergence of the Cartel Party', *Party Politics*, 1, 1, 1995.

95. Kenneth R. Minogue, *Politics: A Very Short Introduction* (Oxford, Oxford University Press, 1995), p. vii. See also Crick, *In Defence of Politics* (1962); Michael Oakeshott, *Rationalism in Politics and Other Essays*

(London, Methuen, 1981); Hannah Arendt, *Between Past and Future* (1954) (London, Penguin, 1993); Arendt, *The Promise of Politics*; Leo Strauss and Joseph Cropsey, *History of Political Philosophy* (Chicago, Chicago University Press, 1986).

96. George Gale, cited in Paul Johnson, 'A Gale for All Seasons', *The Spectator*, 10 Nov 1990, p. 22.

97. Strauss and Cropsey, *History of Political Philosophy*, p. 3.

98. Ibid., p. 3.

99. Ibid., p. 5.

100. Aristotle, *The Politics* (Penguin, London, 1979), Book V, p. 206.

101. Ibid., p. 209.

102. Ibid., Book IV, p. 171.

103. Crick, *In Defence of Politics*, p. 23.

104. Albert Camus, *The Rebel* (London, Peregrine, 1967), p. 266.

105. Aristotle, *The Politics*.

106. John Fortescue, *De Laudibus Legum Angliae* (London, 1543).

107. G. R. Elton, 'The Political Creed of Thomas Cromwell', *Transactions of the Royal Historical Society*, 6, 1956, pp. 69-92.

108. The title of Anthony Ascham's influential Commonwealth pamphlet, *Of the Confusions and Revolutions of Government* (London, 1649).

109. Charles Louis de Secondat, Baron de Montesquieu 'Of the Corruption of the Principles of Democracy', *The Spirit of the Laws* in *The Complete Works of M. de Montesquieu*, 7 vols., vol.1, Book VIII, ch. 2, p. 143. https://oll.libertyfund.org/titles/montesquieu-complete-works-vol-1-the-spirit-of-laws

110. Montesquieu, 'That the laws given by the legislator ought to be relative to the principles of government', *The Spirit of the Laws*, vol. 1, Book V, ch.5, p. 54.

111. Arendt, *On Revolution*, p. 218.

112. Ibid., p. 153.

113. Oakeshott, *The Politics of Faith and the Politics of Scepticism*, p. 30.

114. Ibid., p. 128. Oakeshott evidently derived this understanding from the writings of the Restoration politician George Savile, Marquess of Halifax. See particularly George Savile, 'The Character of a Trimmer' in *The Complete Works of George Savile, First Marquess of Halifax*, Walter Raleigh (ed.), (Oxford, Clarendon Press, 1912), pp. 47-124.

115. Oakeshott, *Politics of Faith*, p. 128.

116. Ibid., p. 125.

117. Arendt, *On Revolution*, p. 231.

118. Steven Pinker, *The Better Angels of our Nature: Why Violence has Declined* (London, Penguin, 2011), p. xxvi and pp. 682-683.

119. Arendt, *On Revolution*, p. 231.
120. Eric Voegelin cited in Barry Cooper, *Eric Voegelin and the Foundations of Modern Political Science* (Columbia, MO, University of Missouri, 1999), p. 39.
121. Ibid.
122. Arendt, *On Revolution*, p. 20
123. Minogue, *Politics*, p. 4.
124. Arendt, *On Revolution*, p. 269.
125. Maurice Duverger, *Political Parties* (Oxford, Oxford University Paperbacks, 1954); for Otto Kircheimer, see André Krouwel, 'Otto Kircheimer and the Catch All Party', *West European Politics*, 26, 2, 2003, p. 23.
126. Arendt, *On Revolution*, p. 268.
127. Richard S. Katz and Peter Mair, 'Changing Models of Party Organization and Party Democracy: The Emergence of the Cartel Party', *Party Politics*, 1, 1, 1995, pp. 5-31.
128. Anthony Barnett, 'Corporate Populism and Partyless Democracy', *New Left Review*, May–June, 2000.
129. Peter Oborne, *The Triumph of the Political Class* (London, Pocket Books, 2007), p. xviii.
130. Anthony Barnett coined the phrase 'manipulative corporate pluralism.'
131. Peter Mair, *Ruling the Void: The Hollowing out of Western Democracy* (London, Verso, 2013), p. 1.
132. Ibid., pp. 125-130.
133. Ibid., p. 16.
134. Ibid., p. 3.
135. Ibid., p. 98.
136. Peter Oborne, 'Europe is slowly strangling the life out of national democracy', *Daily Telegraph*, 1 Jan 2014, p. 1.
137. Runciman, *The Confidence Trap*, p. 265.
138. Hew Strachan, *The Direction of War Contemporary Strategy in Historical Perspective* (Cambridge, Cambridge University Press, 2014), p. 3.
139. Lord Ashdown cited in Sam Coates, 'Voters' trust in society is collapsing, says Ashdown', *The Times*, 4 Jan 2014, p. 1.
140. 'Communities "taking law into their own hands", says police chief inspector', *The Guardian*, 19 Jan 2014.
141. Ibid.
142. Runciman, *The Confidence Trap*, p. 296.
143. Ibid.

10 CONCLUSION

1. René Char, 'Notre heritage n'est précédé d'aucun testament', cited in Hannah Arendt, *On Revolution* (Penguin, London, 1990), p. 275.

2. Douglas Murray, *The Strange Death of Europe* (London, Bloomsbury, 2017); David Goodhart, *The Road to Somewhere. The Populist Revolt and the Future of Politics* (London, Hurst, 2017); Kevin Rudd, 'The Rise of Authoritarian Capitalism', *The New York Times*, 16 Sep 2018.

3. The decline of the West is an enduring theme and may be traced back to St Augustine. James Burnham already coined the title *Suicide of the West. An Essay on the Meaning and Destiny of Liberalism*, a title and theme which Goldberg repeats. Leo Strauss presciently forecast the current mood in *The City and Man* (Chicago, University of Chicago Press, 1964).

4. Jonah Goldberg, *The Suicide of the West. The rebirth of tribalism, populism, nationalism, and identity politics* (New York, Random House 2018) (all citations from the i-book edition).

5. Yoram Hazony, *The Virtue of Nationalism* (New York, Basic Books, 2018).

6. Norman Davies, *Vanished Kingdoms. The History of Half-forgotten Europe* (London, Allen and Lane, 2012), p. 687.

7. Ibid., pp. 731-2. See also recent literature in comparative political science, like Steven Levitsky and Daniel Ziblatt, *How Democracies Die. What History Reveals about our Future* (London, Penguin, 2018); and David Runciman, *How Democracy Ends* (London, Profile, 2018).

8. In this context, see Runciman, *How Democracy Ends*, and Levitsky and Ziblatt, *How Democracies Die*.

9. Aristotle, *The Politics*. See particularly Book 5, p. 189; Plato, *The Republic* in *The Portable Plato* (London, Penguin, 1979) especially Book 8.

10. Thomas Hobbes, *Behemoth: the history of the causes of the civil wars of England, and of the counsels and artifices by which they were carried on from the year 1640 to the year 1660*, Paul Seaward (ed.), (Oxford, Oxford University Press, 2009); John Locke, *Two Treatises of Civil Government*, Peter Laslett (ed.) (Cambridge, Cambridge University Press, 1988).

11. See particularly the extended analogy of the state 'as an artificial man' in the 'Introduction' to *The Leviathan* (1651) C.B. Macpherson (ed.), (London, Penguin, 1977).

12. Ibn Khaldun, *The Muqaddimah. An Introduction to History*, N.J. Dawood (ed.), (Princeton, Princeton University Press, 2015), pp. 244-61.

13. Davies, *Vanished Kingdoms*, p. 258.

14. *Consolidated Texts of the EU Treaties as Amended by The Treaty of Lisbon* (Cm7310, Norwich, HMSO, 2008), p. 3.

15. J. Ortega y Gasset, *The Revolt of the Masses*.

16. Michael Oakeshott, 'The Tower of Babel', in *On History and Other Essays* (Oxford, Blackwell, 1985), p. 165.

17. Stefan Zweig, *Messages from a Lost World. Europe on the Brink* (London, Pushkin Press, 2016), p. 53.

18. Ibid.

19. Ibid., p. 54.

20. Ibid., p. 54.

21. Ibid., p. 56.

22. Ibid., p. 58. See John Gray's 'Foreword', pp. 27-28.

23. Ibid., p. 58.

24. Ibid., p. 58.

25. Oakeshott, 'Tower of Babel', pp. 179-180.

26. Ibid., p. 181.

27. Ibid., p. 182.

28. Ibid., p. 194.

29. See Samuel R. Delany, *Babel 17* (New York, Ace Books, 1966).

30. Aldous Huxley's epsilon minus semi-morons come to mind. See A. Huxley, *Brave New World* (New York, Vintage, 2007).

31. Pico della Mirandola, *An Oration on the Dignity of Man* (1487) (Gateway, Chicago, 1956), p. 3.

32. Thomas More, *Utopia* (1516) (Penguin, London, 1956), p. 84.

33. Francis Bacon, *New Atlantis begun by Lord Verulam* (London, 1660), p. 4.

34. Søren Kierkegaard, *The Journals of Søren Kierkegaard, 1834–1854*, Alexander Dru (ed.), (Fontana, London, 1956), p. 156.

35. Thomas Hardy, 'God's Funeral', in *Poems of Thomas Hardy. A New Selection*, Ned Halley (ed.), (London, Pan Macmillan, 2017), pp. 262-5.

36. Eric Voegelin, *In Search of Order* in *Order and History*, 5 vols. (Baton Rouge, Louisiana State University Press, 1987), vol. 5, p. 6.

37. Albert Camus, *The Myth of Sisyphus* (Penguin, London, 1955), p. 11.

38. Interestingly Camus takes his dedication to the *Myth* from Pindar: 'O my soul, do not aspire to immortal life, but exhaust the limits of the possible'.

39. For Babel, see Genesis 11:1-9. For Faust, see Christopher Marlowe's *The Tragical History of Dr Faustus* (1592) and Johann Wolfgang von Goethe's *Faust*. Karel Kapek revived the idea in his play *The Makropulos Affair* (1922), which Janáček turned into an opera (1925).

40. Yuval Harari, *Homo Deus* (London, Harper Collins, 2017).

41. Marshall McLuhan, *The Gutenberg Galaxy* (Routledge, London, 1962).

42. Marshall McLuhan and Quentin Fiore, *War and Peace in the Global Village* (Bantam, London, 1968), p. 61.

43. Ibid., p. 190.

44. G.E. Stearn (ed.), *McLuhan Hot and Cool* (Penguin, London, 1968), p. 336.

45. Daniel C. Dennett, *From Bacteria to Bach and Back* (London, Allen Lane, 2017).

46. Harari, *Homo Deus*.

47. Robert Nozick, *Anarchy, State and Utopia* (Basic Books, New York, 1974), p. 42.

48. George Zarkadakis, *In Our Own Image: Will Artificial Intelligence Save or Destroy Us?* (London, Rider, 2015).

49. Nick Bostrom, *Superintelligence, Path, Danger, Strategies* (Oxford, Oxford University Press, 2014).

50. See Franklin Foer, *World Without Mind* (Cape, London, 2017), p. 230.

51. Meghan O'Gieblyn, 'God in the Machine', *The Guardian*, 18 Apr 2017. See also Mark O'Connell, *To Be a Machine* (Granta, Cambridge, 2017).

52. Nick Bostrom, 'Are you living in a computer simulation?' *Philosophical Quarterly* 53, 211, 2003, pp. 243-55.

53. George Packer, 'No Death, No Taxes', *The New Yorker*, 28 Nov 2011.

54. Charlotte Allen, 'So You Want To Live Forever', *The Weekly Standard*, 12 May 2014.

55. Neil Strauss, 'Elon Musk, the architect of tomorrow', *Rolling Stone*, Dec 2017. The method, Musk explains, requires 1. Ask a question. 2. Gather as much evidence as possible about it. 3. Develop axioms based on the evidence, and try to assign a probability of truth to each one. 4. Draw a conclusion based on cogency in order to determine: Are these axioms correct, are they relevant, do they necessarily lead to this conclusion, and with what probability? 5. Attempt to disprove the conclusion. Seek refutation from others to further help break your conclusion. 6. If nobody can invalidate your conclusion, then you're probably right.

56. Michael Oakeshott, 'Rationalism in Politics', in *Rationalism in Politics and Other Essays* (London, Methuen, 1981), pp. 5-6.

57. Ibid., p. 12.

58. Ibid., p. 21.

59. Joao Carlos Espada, *The Anglo-American Tradition of Liberty. A View from Europe* (London, Routledge, 2016), p. 67.

60. Oakeshott, *Rationalism in Politics and Other Essays*, p. 6.

61. Ibid., p. 8.

62. Foer, *World Without Mind*, p. 3.

63. See Stein Ringen, *The Perfect Dictatorship. China in the Twenty-first Century* (Hong Kong, Hong Kong University Press, 2018). See also David Alayon, 'Exposing China's Digital Dictatorship', *The Medium*, Oct 2018 https://medium.com/future-today/exposing-chinas-digital-dystopian-dictatorship-88df1c443cc6

64. Vilfredo Pareto, *Les Systèmes Socialistes. Cours professé à l'Université de Lausanne.* (Paris, Giard et Brière, 1902). See Hugo Drachan, 'Why the Elites always rule', *The New Statesman*, 18 Jan 2017 https://www.newstatesman.com/politics/uk/2017/01/why-elites-always-rule

65. Pareto distinguished two elite types: 'foxes' that manipulated the masses and 'lions' that exerted power over them. Silicon Valley manipulation is of the fox variety.

66. Paul Lewis, 'Our minds can be hacked', *The Guardian,* 6 Oct 2017.

67. Decca Aikenhead, 'A Digital Frankenstein is sending us crazy. Only the law can tame it', *The Sunday Times*, 7 Jul 2019.

68. Ibid.

69. Lewis, 'Our minds can be hacked'.

70. William A. Gorton, 'Manipulating Citizens: How Political Campaigns' Use of Behavioral Social Science Harms Democracy', *New Political Science* 38, 1, 2016, pp. 61-80.

71. Aikenhead, 'A Digital Frankenstein'.

72. Quoted in ibid.

73. See http://europa.eu/rapid/press-release_IP-19-1770_en.htm and James Titcomb, 'Google's Growth heads for the cliff-edge as Amazon primes for advertising attack', *The Sunday Telegraph*, 21 Jul 2019. Also see Tom Keatinge and Florence Keane, *Social Media and Terrorist Fund Raising* (Global Research Network on Terrorism and Technology Paper 10, London, RUSI, July 2019).

74. https://www.judiciary.senate.gov/meetings/facebook-social-media-privacy-and-the-use-and-abuse-of-data

75. Gorton, 'Manipulating Citizens', p.3.

76. Roger Scruton, *Where We Are? The State of Britain Now* (Bloomsbury, London, 2017).

77. Oakeshott, 'The Tower of Babel', p. 61.

78. Ibid.

79. Ibid., p. 60.

80. Ibid., p. 74.

AFTERWORD

1. This afterword is a response to an anonymous reader's comment asking: Has there really been a collapse of academic integrity? When attacking the grant success rate of IR projects aligning with normative transnational ideas, evidence would be required.

2. See Stefan Collini, 'In UK universities there is a daily erosion of integrity', *The Guardian* 18 Apr 2018, accessed 30 Jul 2019. https://

www.theguardian.com/education/2018/apr/24/uk-universities-erosion-integrity-bologna-statement

3. See Organization of Economic Cooperation and Development (OECD), *Education at a Glance* (Paris, 2008), p. 273 and p. 279; and Australian Government Department of Education, Employment and Workplace Relations, *Finance 2007: Financial Reports of Higher Education Providers* (Canberra, September 2008), p. 3. The total Australian figure, AUS$15,912,116,000 in 2007, comprised state and local contributions, fees and consultancies, investments and the government-subsidized Higher Education Contribution Scheme (HECS). The latter after its reform in 1997 currently contributes a further thirty-two per cent of 'private' funding, as the Organization of Economic Cooperation and Development unhelpfully terms it. As the OECD report *Education at a Glance* (2007) explains, the developed economies saw 'expenditure on educational institutions per tertiary student remain stable over the period 1995–2000, but then increase by 11% on average in OECD countries from 2000–2005 as governments invested massively in response to the expansion of tertiary education. Australia together with the Nordic countries and the UK 'followed this pattern': p. 273.

4. In Australia student numbers grew from 390,000 in 1987 to 950,000 in 2005. See Australian Government, *Our Universities. Backing Australia's Future* (Canberra, 2003), pp. 3-5. By 2009, the overseas student market was worth $15.5 billion, *The Australian Higher Education*, 9 Jun 2009. See in this context James Allan, 'Misgoverning the Universities' in Keith Windschuttle, David Martin Jones and Ray Evans (eds.), *The Howard Years* (Sydney, Quadrant, 2009). See also John Lodewijks, 'What managerialism has wrought', in William Coleman (ed.), *Campus Meltdown: the deepening crisis in Australian universities* (Brisbane, Connor Court, 2019).

5. Stefan Collini, *Speaking of Universities* (London, Verso, 2017), p. 4. See also his *What are Universities for?* (London, Verso, 2012).

6. Frank Furedi, *What Happened to the University? A Sociological Explanation of its Infantilization* (London, Routledge, 2017).

7. A.W. Gouldner, *The Future of Intellectuals and the Rise of the New Class* (London, Macmillan, 1979).

8. See Matthew Taylor, 'Ministers failing to halt tide of university science closures', *The Guardian*, 4 May 2006; BBC News, 'Reading confirms physics closure', 21 Nov 2006, available at http://news.bbc.co.uk/1/hi/education/6159106.stm (accessed 18 Nov 2011).

9. See Nina Power, 'A blow to philosophy', *The Guardian*, 29 Apr 2010; Jessica Shepherd, 'London Met may cut more than half degree courses',

The Guardian, 15 Apr 2011; John Gill, 'Public debate on future of classics "will only worsen situation," principal claims', *Times Higher Education*, 1 Jul 2011.

10. Furedi, *What Happened*, p. 2. See also his *The Culture of Fear* (London, Cassell, 1997).

11. Furedi, *What Happened*, p. 6.

12. See Allan Bloom, Foreword by Saul Bellow, *The Closing of the American Mind. How Higher Education has Failed Democracy and Impoverished the Souls of Today's Students* (Chicago, Chicago University Press, 1987).

13. Ibid, p. vii.

14. See Collini, *Speaking of Universities*, p. 7. In particular see Terence Karran and Lucy Mallinson, *Academic Freedom in the UK: Legal and normative protection in a comparative context: Report for the University and College Union*, 2017. Accessed 28 Jul 2019 https://www.ucu.org.uk/academic-freedom-in-2017

15. Ibid., p. 3. See also Richard Bean's prescient satire *The Heretic*, Royal Court Theatre, London, 2011.

16. Collini, 'In UK universities'.

17. In Australia by 2007, the Department of Education and Workplace Relations (DEEWR) noted that the higher education sector employed close to 100,000 academics at various levels. DEEWR now categorized academics not only according to their status, ranging from Professor down to the humble junior and part-time sessional lectureate, but also according to their function: research only; research and teaching; and teaching only. Consequently academia became increasingly hierarchical. The privileged twenty-seven per cent of academics destined only for research reached this status through their success, individually or in 'research teams', in achieving large grants dispensed via the Commonwealth's increasingly bureaucratized Australian Research Council mechanism. At the same time, more than half of all staff employed by the sector engaged in non–academic activity. By 2009, as former University of Canberra Vice Chancellor Don Aitkin observed, the higher education sector had achieved 'world leadership' in this area, an expression of 'a native genius in regulative mechanisms'. Don Aitkin, 'Research Wins Budget Favour', *Australian Financial Review*, 25 May 2009, p. 28.

18. See Allan, 'Misgoverning the Universities', for the illogical absurdity of this process. As Allan explains, it is not so much double counting. It is worse than that, because it involves counting something that should not be counted at all. Grant monies are aimed at facilitating research that might lead to publications. But it is those publications that ought to be judged or assessed, p. 457.

19. Collini, 'In UK Universities'. This fetishization reflects the fact not only that there are large sums involved, it also requires a small team of university administrators to help with the data required for filling in the application form that extends, in the ARC and ERC cases, to over twenty pages in several sections. It also means that for providing these resources, the university takes a cut of between 45-50% of the total grant. The Australian experience is comparative and salutary. In the Liberal coalition government's second term, performance based research received larger public doles. In January 2001, the government announced a $2.9 billion package, *Backing Australia's Ability*. Funds for ARC administered research doubled over a five-year period. By the time Brendan Nelson presented *Higher Education at the Crossroads* (2002) and *Our Universities: Backing Australia's Future* (2003), culminating in *The Higher Education Support Act* (2003), the coalition presided over a much expanded, centrally funded tertiary sector. Despite six years of reform, Nelson's reports nevertheless found the framework for funding and policy 'unwieldy, complex and inflexible'. Yet as Nelson's report also observed, it entailed 'perverse incentives'. The 'heavily centralized Commonwealth bureaucratic arrangements' had produced a sector that was still 'not maximising its potential and is limited in its ability to be internationally competitive'.

20. Collini makes this point in both his books. See *Speaking of Universities,* p. 4.

21. See for example, Martin Kramer, *Ivory Towers on Sand: The Failure of Middle Eastern Studies in America* (Washington DC, Washington Institute for Near East Policy, 2001).

22. Rob Jones, 'UK universities: concern over foreign donations', BBC News Education and Family, 4 March 2011, available at http://www.bbc.co.uk/news/education-12644749 (accessed 17 Nov 2011).

23. Christopher Davidson, 'It's hard to bite the hand that feeds', *Times Higher Education*, 16 Nov 2011.

24. Davidson, 'It's hard to bite the hand that feeds'.

25. On 24 July 2019, after demonstrations at the University of Queensland about the funding and teaching of its Confucius Institute, Foreign Minister Marise Payne 'warned that the Morrison government won't tolerate foreign interference in the exercise of free speech in Australia, after a senior Chinese diplomat backed "patriotic behaviour" by Chinese students who clashed violently with pro-Hong Kong protesters at the University of Queensland'. Ben Packham, 'The Government won't tolerate interference in the exercise of free speech', *The Australian*, 24 Jul 2019. See also Mark Harrison, 'Xi Jingping and the Australian Left's Dilemma', *Sydney Moring Herald*, 29 Jan 2019, accessed 31 Jul 2019,

https://www.smh.com.au/world/asia/xi-jinping-s-china-and-the-australian-left-s-dilemma-20190128-p50u3r.html

26. Examples of EU sponsored research projects are GR:EEN (Global Re-ordering: Evolution Through European Networks), http://www2.warwick.ac.uk/fac/soc/csgr/green/ and the GARNET network (Global Governance, Regionalisation and Regulation: The Role of the EU), which comprises forty-two educational institutions and is funded by the EU Commission's 6th Framework programme co-ordinated by the Centre for the Study of Globalisation and Regionalisation, University of Warwick: http://www2.warwick.ac.uk/fac/soc/garnet/.

27. The ERC funding website shows that early career researchers can receive starting grants of €1.5 million for five years. ERC consolidator grants are for €2 million for five years. Advanced grants for established research leaders also go for €2.5 million for five years. See https://erc.europa.eu/

28. Project name: Gendered Peace Project. A Gendered International Law of Peace. Researcher (PI) Christine Chinkin, Host Institution (HI), London School of Economics and Political Science. Advanced Grant (AdG), SH2, ERC-2017-ADG. The project runs from 2018-2022.

29. Thus Dominic Rohner's project on 'The economics of lasting peace: The role of policies and institutions', SH1, ERC-2015-ST will receive €1,013,720 between 2016–21. Tineke DeStrooper at the University of Ghent was awarded €1,497,407 between 2019-2024 for 'Righting Victim Participation in Transitional Justice', Starting Grant (StG), SH2, ERC-2018-STG. Equally interestingly, Monica Salzbrunn's project on 'Art and Activism: Creativity and Performance as Subversive Forms of Political Expression in Super-Diverse Cities', Consolidator Grant (CoG), SH5, ERC-2015-CoG receives €1,999,287 from 2016 to 2021. Shanshan Lan's project, 'The Reconfiguration of Whiteness in China: Privileges, Precariousness, and Racialized Performances', Consolidator Grant (CoG), SH3, ERC-2018-COG received €2 million a year from 2019 to 2024. Susanna Clay, at Durham University, receives an early career starting grant of €1.499 million per annum from 2019–24 to find 'What are the origins of empathy? A comparative developmental investigation'. Rodrigo Maeso's project 'The politics of anti-racism in Europe and Latin America: knowledge production, decision-making and collective struggles', received a grant of €1,915, 317 euros a year from 2017–22, and Veronika Fikfak for her project 'A nudge in the rights direction? Redesigning the architecture of human rights remedies', Starting Grant (StG), SH2, ERC-2018-STG will get €1,493,796 euros between 2019–24. These are a representative sample of the ESRC awards between 2015-18.

30. The portal is available at: https://dataportal.arc.gov.au/NCGP/Web/ Grant/Grants#/20/1/International%20relations/

31. F140100154—University of Canberra, awarded to Professor John Drysek, an 'Australian Laureate Fellow'.

32. Grant LP160100085—Monash University https://dataportal.arc.gov. au/NCGP/Web/Grant/Grant/LP160100085

33. DP160101277—The University of Sydney https://dataportal.arc.gov. au/NCGP/Web/Grant/Grant/DP160101277

34. DP0346176—The University of New South Wales, https://dataportal. arc.gov.au/NCGP/Web/Grant/Grant/DP0346176

35. DP140103945—Swinburne University of Technology https:// dataportal.arc.gov.au/NCGP/Web/Grant/Grant/DP140103945

36. The Centre's scholars have received several large ARC grants together with two rounds of funding from the Department of Foreign Affairs and Trade between 2012–18. See particularly regarding DFAT awards: https://dfat.gov.au/about-us/publications/Pages/results. aspx?ak=Responsibility+to+protect&acat=&at=&ac=&ar=&adf= &adt=&ai=

    See also: https://dfat.gov.au/about-us/publications/Documents/ r2p-global-centre-proposal-core-funding.pdf and https://dataportal. arc.gov.au/NCGP/Web/Grant/Grant/DP0986159

    http://researchers.uq.edu.au/research-project/15000

    For the global reach of the endeavour, see *The International Coalition for the Responsibility to Protect* (New York, DFAT, 2012): https://dfat.gov. au/about-us/publications/Documents/r2p-international-coalition- proposal-core-funding.pdf

37. Peter Mair, *Ruling the Void. The Hollowing out of Western Democracy* (London, Verso, 2001), pp. 115-37; and Richard Katz and Peter Mair, 'Changing Models of Party Organization and Party Democracy: The Emergence of the Cartel Party', *Party Politics*, 1, 1, 1995, pp. 5-31.

38. John Gray, *Enlightenment's Wake* (London, Routledge, 1995); Brian Barry, *Culture and Diversity* (Cambridge, Polity Press, 1991).

39. Furedi, *What's happening to our universities?*, p. 4.

40. Allan, 'John Howard and the Universities'.

41. Examining the ERC and ARC websites my research assistant and I could not find any.

42. Allan, 'John Howard'.

43. See Jon Shield, 'The Disappearing Conservative Professor', *National Affairs*, Fall 2019. Accessed 31 Jul 2019: https://www.nationalaffairs. com/publications/detail/the-disappearing-conservative-professor

44. Veblen cited in Collini, *Speaking of Universities*, p. 3.

45. 'Why Exeter University defends the closure of its chemistry department', *The Independent,* 8 Jun 2006.

46. F.A. Hayek, 'The New Confusion about "Planning"', in *New Studies in Philosophy, Politics, Economics, and the History of Ideas* (London, Routledge, 1978), p. 240.

47. F.A. Hayek, 'Education and Research', in *The Constitution of Liberty* (London, Routledge, 1965), ch. 24.

48. Ibid., pp. 391-95.

49. Ibid., p. 391.

BIBLIOGRAPHY

BOOKS, CHAPTERS IN BOOKS, AND ACADEMIC ARTICLES

Addison, Joseph. *The Spectator* 185, 2 Oct 1711. In *The Works of Joseph Addison*, 3 vols., vol. 1. New York, Harper, 1842.

Aho, James Alfred. *German Realpolitik and American Sociology: an Inquiry into the Sources and Political Significance of the Sociology of Conflict.* Lewisburg, PA, Bucknell University Press, 1975.

Akamatsu, K. 'A historical pattern of economic growth in developing countries'. *Journal of Developing Economies* 1:1, 1962.

Alexander, Yonah, and Michael S. Swetnam. *Usama bin Laden's al-Qaeda: Profile of a Terrorist Network.* Ardsley, NY, Transnational Publishers, 2001.

Ali, Tariq. *Rough Music: Blair, Bombs, Baghdad, London, Terror.* London, Verso, 2005.

Allan, James. 'Misgoverning the Universities' in Keith Windschuttle, David Martin Jones and Ray Evans eds., *The Howard Years.* Sydney, Quadrant, 2009.

Allison, Graham. *Destined for War. Can America Escape the Thucydides Trap?* New York, Houghton Mifflin Harcourt, 2017.

Almond, G.A. & Coleman, J. *The Politics of Developing Areas.* Princeton, Princeton University Press, 1960.

Anon. *The Koran,* trans. N.J. Dawood. London, Penguin. 1990.

Aquinas, Thomas. *Aquinas Political Writings.* R.W. Dyson, ed. Cambridge, Cambridge University Press, 2002.

Arendt, Hannah. *Between Past and Future.* London, Penguin, 1993.

—— *On Revolution.* London, Penguin, 1990.

—— *The Origins of Totalitarianism.* New York, Houghton Mifflin Harcourt, 1951.

—— *The Promise of Politics.* New York, Random House, 2005.

—— 'Truth and Politics'. In Peter Baehr, ed., *The Portable Hannah Arendt.* London, Penguin, 2000.

Aristotle. *Rhetorica,* trans W. Rhys Roberts. Oxford, Oxford University Press, 1924.

357

BIBLIOGRAPHY

—— *The Nichomachean Ethics.* Oxford, Oxford University Press, 2009.

—— *The Politics.* London, Penguin, 1979

Aron, Raymond. *On War.* London, Secker and Warburg, 1958.

Ashan M.M. and Kidwai, A.R. *Sacrilege Versus Civility: Muslim Perspectives on the Satanic Verses Affair.* Markfield, UK, Islamic Foundation, 1993.

Augustine. *The City of God Against the Pagans*, R.W. Dyson ed., Cambridge, Cambridge University Press, 1998.

Ayubi, Nazih N. *Political Islam. Religion and Politics in the Arab World.* London, Routledge, 1991.

Bacon, Francis. *New Atlantis begun by Lord Verulam.* London, 1660.

al-Banna, Hasan. *Five Tracts of Hasan al-Banna,* trans Charles Wendell. Berkeley, CA, University of California Press, 1988.

Bankoff, Greg. 'Regions of Risk: Western discourse on terrorism and the significance of political Islam'. *Studies in Conflict and Terrorism*, 26:1, 2003.

Barber, Benjamin. *Jihad vs McWorld: How Globalism and Tribalism Are Reshaping the World.* New York, New York Times Books, 1995.

Barkawi, Tarak. 'On the pedagogy of 'small wars'. *International Affairs.* 80:1, 2004.

Barnett, Anthony. 'Corporate Populism and Partyless Democracy', *New Left Review*, May–June 2003.

Barr, James. *A Line in the Sand. Britain, France and the Struggle that Shaped the Middle East.* London, Simon & Schuster, 2011.

Barry, Brian. *Culture and Equality. An Egalitarian Critique of Multiculturalism.* Cambridge, Polity Press, 1991.

Bayliss, John, and Steve Smith. 'Introduction', in Bayliss, John, and Steve Smith, eds. *The Globalization of World Politics. An Introduction to International Relations.* Oxford, Oxford University Press, 2001.

Beam, Louis. 'Leaderless Resistance'. *The Seditionist* 12, 1992. http: www.crusader.net/texts/ bt/bt04.html.

Beitz, Charles. *Political Theory and International Relations*, Princeton, Princeton University Press, 1973.

Beitz Charles ed. *International Ethics*, Princeton, Princeton University Press, 1983.

Bell, Daniel, A. *The China Model. Political Meritocracy and the Limits of Democracy.* Princeton, Princeton University Press, 2016.

—— *Communitarianism and its Critics.* Oxford, Oxford University Press, 1993.

Bell, Duncan. 'What is Liberalism?' *Political Theory*, 2:6, 2014.

Bellamy, A. *Just Wars From Cicero to Iraq.* Cambridge, Polity Press, 1996.

Benner, Thorston, et al. 'Authoritarian Advantage: Responding to China's Growing Political Influence in Europe.' *Joint Report by the Mercator Centre for China Studies and Global Public Policy Institute.* New York, Global Policy Institute, February, 2018.

Berman, Paul. *Terror and Liberalism.* New York, Norton, 2003.

Berlin, Isaiah. 'Empirical Propositions and Hypothetical Statements' in Henry Hardy ed., *Concepts and Categories. Philosophical Essays.* London, Pimlico, 1999.

Berwick, Andrew. *2083: A European Declaration of Independence.* London, 2013.

Bew, John, and David Martin Jones, 'A Trump Doctrine?' *The National Interest* 153, Jan/Feb 2018.

Beyle, Henri-Marie (Stendhal). *The Charterhouse of Parma.* London, Penguin, 2006.

Bireley, R. *The Refashioning of Catholicism, 1450–1700.* London, Macmillan, 1999.

Blair, Tony. *A Journey.* London, Hutchinson, 2010.

Bloom, Allan. *The Closing of the American Mind. How Higher Education has Failed Democracy and Impoverished the Souls of Today's Students.* Chicago, Chicago University Press, 1987.

BIBLIOGRAPHY

Booth, Ken. 'International Relations versus the Future', in Booth, K. and Smith, S. eds., *International Relations Theory Today*. Cambridge, Polity Press, 1998.

—— 'The Human Faces of Terror: Reflections in a Cracked Looking Glass'. *Critical Studies on Terrorism*. 1:1, 2008.

Booth, Ken and Tim Dunne. 'Worlds in Collision. Terror and the Future of Global Order', in Booth, Ken and Tim Dunne eds., *Worlds in Collision. Terror and the Future of Global Order*. London, Palgrave, 2002.

Booth, Ken, Tim Dunne and Michael Cox eds. *How Might We Live? Global Ethics in a New Century*. Cambridge, Cambridge University Press, 2001.

Borradori, Giovanna. *Philosophy in a Time of Terror. Dialogues with Jürgen Habermas and Jacques Derrida*. Chicago, University of Chicago Press, 2003.

Bostrom, Nick. 'Are you living in a computer simulation?' *Philosophical Quarterly* 53:211, 2003.

—— *Superintelligence, Path, Danger, Strategies*. Oxford, Oxford University Press, 2014.

Botero, Giovanni. *The Reason of State and the Greatness of Cities*, trans. P.J. and D.P. Waley. London, Routledge and Kegan Paul, 1956.

Brinkley, D. 'Dean Ascheson and the Special Relationship. The West Point Speech of December 1962'. *Historical Journal* 33:3, 1990.

Brown, Chris. *International Relations Theory. New Normative Approaches*. Hemel Hempstead, Harvester Wheatsheaf, 1992.

Brown, Chris. Terry Nardin and Nicholas Rengger. *International Relations in Political Thought*. Cambridge, Cambridge University Press, 2002.

Bruckner, Pascal. *The Tyranny of Guilt. An Essay on Western Masochism*. Princeton, Princeton University Press, 2011.

Bull, H. *The Anarchical Society. A Study of Society in World Politics*. New York, Columbia University Press, 1977.

Burke, Anthony. *Beyond Security, Ethics and Violence: War against the Other*. London, Routledge, 2007.

—— 'Against The New Internationalism. *Ethics & International Affairs*, 19:2, 2005.

—— 'The End of Terrorism Studies'. *Critical Studies on Terrorism*. 1:1, 2008.

Burke, Edmund (1790), Conor Cruise O'Brien ed. *Reflections on the Revolution in France and on the Proceedings of Certain Societies in London Relative to that Event*. London, Penguin, 2003.

—— 'Letters on a Regicide Peace' (1795), in *The Works of Edmund Burke*, vol. 3. Indianapolis, Liberty Fund, 2009.

Burnham, James. *Suicide of the West: An Essay on the Meaning and Destiny of Liberalism*. New York, Encounter Books, (1964) 2014.

Campbell, David. *Writing Security: United States Foreign Policy and the Politics of Identity*. Manchester, Manchester University Press, 1998.

Camus, Albert. *The Myth of Sisyphus*. New York, Alfred Knopf, 1955.

Camus, Albert. *The Rebel*. London, Peregrine, 1967.

Campbell, David. *Writing Security. United States Foreign Policy and the Politics of Identity*. Minneapolis, University of Minnesota Press, 1992.

—— *National Deconstruction: Violence, Identity, and Justice in Bosnia*. Minneapolis, University of Minnesota Press, 1998.

Cerny, Philip G. 'Paradoxes of the Competition State: The Dynamics of Political Globalization'. *Government and Opposition*. 32:2, 1997.

—— 'Plurality, Pluralism and Power: Elements of Pluralist Analysis in an Age of Globalization', in Rainer Eisfeld, ed. *Pluralist Developments in the Theory and Practice of Democracy*, Farmington Hills, Barbara Budrich Publishers, 2006.

BIBLIOGRAPHY

Chan Heng Chee, 'Democracy: Evolution and Implementation', in R. Bartley, H.C. Chan, S. Huntington, & S. Ogata, eds. *Democracy and Capitalism: Asian and American Perspectives.* Singapore, ISEAS,1993.

Chomsky, Noam. 'Who are the global terrorists?', in K. Booth and Tim Dunne eds. *Worlds in Collision. Terror and the Future of Global Order.* London, Palgrave, 2002.

—— *Hegemony and Survival: America's Quest for Global Dominance.* London, Penguin, 2004.

Cioran, E.M. *The Temptation to Exist.* Chicago, Quadrangle Books, 1968.

Clark, J.C.D. *Our Shadowed Present: Modernism, Postmodernism and History.* Stanford, Stanford University Press, 2003.

Clinton, Hillary. 'America's Pacific Century'. *Foreign Policy* 11 Oct 2011. http://foreignpolicy. com/2011/10/11/americas-pacific-century/.

Cohen, Nick. *What's Left? How the Left Lost Its Way.* London, Harper, 2007.

Cohn, Norman. *The Pursuit Of The Millennium Revolutionary Millenarians and Mystical Anarchists of the Middle Ages,* London, Palladin,1970.

Coleman, J. & Almond G.A. *The Politics of Developing Areas.* Princeton, Princeton University Press, 1960.

Colli, A. R. 'Normative Prudence as a Tradition of Statecraft', *Ethics and International Affairs,* 5:2, 1991.

Collier, Paul. *The Future of Capitalism. Facing the New Anxieties.* London, Penguin, 2018.

Collini, Stefan. *Speaking of Universities.* London, Verso, 2017.

—— *What are Universities for?* London, Verso, 2012.

Collins, Michael. *The Likes of Us: A Biography of the White Working Class.* London, Granta, 2004.

Condren, Conal. *Argument and Authority in Early Modern England: The Presupposition of Oaths and Offices.* Cambridge, Cambridge University Press, 2006.

Cooper, Barry. *New political religions, or, An analysis of Modern Terrorism.* Columbia, University of Missouri Press, 2004.

—— *Eric Voegelin and the Foundations of Modern Political Science.* Columbia, University of Missouri Press, 2004.

Cox, Robert. 'Social Forces, States and World Orders: Beyond International Relations Theory' *Millennium Journal of International Studies* 10:2, 1981.

Crick, Bernard. *In Defence of Politics.* London, Weidenfeld & Nicholson, 1992.

Dahl, Robert. *Polyarchy: Participation and Opposition.* New Haven, Yale University Press, 1971.

Dahrendorf, Ralf. 'The Third Way and Liberty. An Authoritarian streak in Europe's new Center'. *Foreign Affairs,* 79:5, October 1999.

Davies, James C. 'Toward a Theory of Revolution.' *American Sociological Review* 27:1, 1962.

—— 'The J-curve of Rising and Declining Satisfaction as a Source of Some Great Revolutions and a Contained Rebellion'. In Hugh Davis Graham and Ted Robert Gurr, eds., *The History of Violence in America.* New York, Bantam, 1969.

Davies, Norman. *Vanished Kingdoms. The History of Half-Forgotten Europe.* London, Allen and Lane, 2012.

Delong-Bas, Natana J. *Wahhabi Islam: From Revival to Reform to Global Jihad.* London, IB Tauris, 2004.

Dennett, Daniel C. *From Bacteria to Bach and Back.* London, Allen Lane, 2017.

Der Derian, James. *Anti-Diplomacy: Spies, Terror, Speed and War.* Oxford, Blackwell, 1992.

Derrida, Jacques. *Of Grammatology.* Baltimore, Johns Hopkins University Press, 1997.

Derrida, Jacques, and Jürgen Habermas. 'What Binds Europeans together: a plea for a common Foreign Policy, beginning in the core Europe.' *Constellations,* 50:3, February 2003.

Docherty, Patrick C. 'A new US grand strategy', *New America Foundation,* 9 Jan 2013 Accessed 2014. http://newamerica.net/node/77134.

BIBLIOGRAPHY

Doyle, Michael. 'Kant, Liberal legacies and foreign affairs.' *Philosophy and Public Affairs* 12:3, Summer 1983.

Dunne, Tim. 'Liberalism', in John Bayliss and Steve Smith eds., *The Globalization of World Politics. An Introduction to International Relations*. Oxford, Oxford University Press 2001.

Durodié, Bill. 'Terrorism and community resilience – a UK perspective.' in *Terrorism in the UK*. Briefing paper 05/01, London, Chatham House, July 2005.

Duverger, Maurice. *Political Parties*. Oxford, Oxford University Paperbacks, 1954.

Dworkin, Ronald. *Taking Rights Seriously*. London, Duckworth, 1977.

Espada, Joao Carlos. *The Anglo-American Tradition of Liberty. A View from Europe*. London, Routledge, 2016.

Fabre, Cécile. *Cosmopolitan War*. Oxford, Oxford University Press, 2012.

Fakner, Yolam. 'Radical Islamist Profiles: Omar Bakri Mohammed.' *Middle East Media Research Institute,* 24 Oct 2001.

Falk, Richard. *On Humane Governance: Toward a New Global Politics*. Cambridge, Polity Press, 1995.

Finnemore, Martha and Kathryn Sikkink. 'Taking stock: the constructivist program in international relations and comparative politics', *Annual Review of Political Science*, 4, 2001.

Fisher, David. *Morality and War: Can War Be Justified in the Twenty-first Century?* Oxford, Oxford University Press, 2011.

Foer, Franklin. *World Without Mind*. London, Cape, 2017.

Fonte, John. 'Liberal Democracy versus Transnational Progressivism: The Future of the Ideological Civil War Within the West,' *Orbis*, Summer 2002.

Foot, Rosemary. *Identity Politics and the US Rebalance to Asia*. Seoul, East Asia Institute, 2016.

Fortescue, John. *De Laudibus Legum Angliae*. London, 1543.

Foucault, Michel. *Discipline and Punish*. London, Penguin, 1977.

—— *Power Knowledge. Selected Interviews and Other Writings 1972–1977*, Colin Gordon ed. Brighton, Harvester Wheatsheaf, 1977.

Fourest, Caroline. *In Praise of Blasphemy*. Kindle edition, Paris, Grasset, 2015.

Frank, Robert H. and Phillip J. Cook. *The Winner Take All Society. Why the Few at the Top Get So Much More than the Rest of Us*. London, Penguin, 1995.

Frey, Carl Benedikt, and Michael A. Osborne. 'The Future of Employment: How Susceptible Are Jobs to Computerisation?' *Technological Forecasting and Social Change,* 114, 2017.

Friedman, Milton, and Anne Jacobson Schwartz. *A Monetary History of the United States, 1867–1960*. National Bureau of Economic Research, Princeton, Princeton University Press. 1993.

Friedman, T. L. *The Lexus and the Olive Tree*. London, Harper Collins, 2000.

Fukuyama, Francis. 'The end of history?' *The National Interest*, 16, Summer 1989.

—— 'History and September 11'. In K. Booth and T. Dunne, eds., *Worlds in Collision Terror and the Future of Global Order*. London, Palgrave, 2002.

—— *The End of History and The Last Man*. London, Penguin, 1992.

Furedi, Frank. *What Happened to the University? A Sociological Explanation of its Infantilization*. London, Routledge, 2017.

Galston, William. *Liberal Purposes,* Cambridge, Cambridge University Press, 1991.

Gellner, Ernest. *Conditions of Liberty. Civil Society and its Rivals*. London, Hamish Hamilton, 1994.

—— *Muslim Society*. Cambridge, Cambridge University Press, 1981.

—— *Nations and Nationalism*. Ithaca, NY, Cornell University Press, 1983.

—— *Postmodernism, Reason and Religion*. New York, Routledge, 1992.

—— *Relativism in the Social Sciences*. Cambridge, Cambridge University Press, 1985.

—— *Spectacles and Predicaments. Essays in Social Theory.* Cambridge, Cambridge University Press, 1979.

Gentile, Emilio. 'The Sacralization of Politics: Definitions, Interpretations and Reflections on the Question of Secular Religion and Totalitarianism', *Totalitarian Movements and Political Religions*, 1:1, 2000.

Geyl, Pieter. 'From Ranke to Toynbee: Five Lectures on Historians and Historiographical Problems'. *Studies in History*, Northampton, MA, Smith College History Department, 1952.

Gibbon, Edward. 'General Observations on the Fall of the Roman Empire in the West', in *The History of the Decline and Fall of the Roman Empire*, 12 vols., New York, Fred de Fau & Co., 1906.

Gidden, Anthony. *The Third Way: The Renewal of Social Democracy.* Cambridge, Polity Press, 1998.

—— *Modernity and Self-Identity: Self and Society in the Late Modern Age.* Cambridge, Polity Press, 1991.

—— *Turbulent and Mighty Continent. What Future for Europe?* Cambridge, Polity Press, 2014.

Giuliano, Elise. 'Is the risk of Ethnic conflict growing in the Ukraine?' *Foreign Affairs*, 2019, March. https://www.foreignaffairs.com/articles/ukraine/2019-03-18/risk-ethnic-conflict-growing-ukraine. Accessed 20 Mar 2019.

Goldberg, Jonah. *The Suicide of the West. The Rebirth of Tribalism, Populism, Nationalism, and Identity Politics.* New York, Random House, 2018.

Gomez, E.T. *Political Business. Corporate Involvement of Malaysian Political Parties.* Townsville, James Cook University Press, 1994.

Goodhart, David. *The Road to Somewhere. The Populist Revolt and the Future of Politics.* London, Hurst, 2017.

Gorton, William A. 'Manipulating Citizens: How Political Campaigns Use of Behavioral Social Science Harms Democracy', *New Political Science* 38:1, 2016, pp. 61-80.

Gouldner, A.W. *The Future of Intellectuals and the Rise of the New Class.* London, Macmillan, 1979.

Gray, John. *Enlightenment's Wake. Politics and Culture at the Close of the Modern Age.* London, Routledge, 1995.

—— *False Dawn: The Delusions of Global Capitalism.* London, Granta, 2002.

—— *The New Market Ideology.* Lanham MD, Rowman, 2002.

Gregory, Frank, and Paul Wilkinson. 'Riding pillion for tackling terrorism is a high risk policy.' *Terrorism in the UK, Briefing Paper 05/01.* London, Chatham House, July 2005.

Griffin, Roger. *The Nature of Fascism.* London, Pinter, 1991.

Guicciardini, Francesco. *Selected Writings*, Cecil Grayson ed. Oxford, Oxford University Press, 1965.

Guilluy, Christophe. *Prosperity, the Periphery and the Future of France.* New Haven, Yale University Press, 2018.

Gurr, Ted Robert. *Why Men Rebel.* Princeton, NJ, Princeton University Press, 1970.

Ha, Yong Sun, and Yul Sohn. *The Co-evolution of Korea and Japan.* Seoul, East Asia Institute, 2015.

Habermas, Jürgen. 'Reconciliation through the Public Use of Reason: Remarks on John Rawls's Political Liberalism'. *Journal of Philosophy*, XCII:3, March 1995.

—— 'Why Europe needs a Constitution'. *New Left Review* 11, September/October 2001.

—— *Legitimation Crisis.* London, Heinemann, 1976.

—— *Moral Consciousness and Communicative Action.* Cambridge, Polity Press, 1990.

—— *The Philosophic Discourse of Modernity.* Cambridge, Polity Press, 1987.

—— *Between Facts and Norms: Contributions to a Discourse Theory of Law and Democracy.* Cambridge, Polity Press, 2005.

BIBLIOGRAPHY

——— *A Berlin Republic: Writings on Germany*. Cambridge, Polity Press, 1998.

——— *The Theory of Communicative Action*. 2 Vols. Boston, Beacon Press, 1984.

Hale, J.R. 'War and Public Opinion in Renaissance Italy', in E.F. Jacob ed. *Italian Renaissance Studies*. London, Faber and Faber, 1960.

Halliday, Fred. 'The Politics of Islamic Fundamentalism'. In Akbar S. Ahmed and Hastings Donnan, eds. *Islam, Globalization and Postmodernity*. London, Routledge, 1996.

Hamilton, Alexander, John Jay and James Madison, *The Federalist Papers*. Indianapolis, Liberty Fund, 2001.

Hallaq, Wael. 'Was the Gate of Ijtihad Closed?' *International Journal of Middle East Studies* 16:1, 1984.

Harari, Yuval. *Homo Deus*. London, Harper Collins, 2017.

Hardt, Michael and Antonio Negri. *Empire*. Cambridge, MA, Harvard University Press, 2001.

Harries, Owen. 'An End to Nonsense'. *The National Interest*. 65:5, 2001.

Haskel, Jonathan and Stian Westlake. *Capitalism without Capital: The Rise of the Intangible Economy*. Oxford, Oxford University Press, 2017.

Hassan, Hassan and Michael Weis. *ISIS: Inside an Army of Terror*. New York, Regan, 2015.

Hastings, Tom H. *Nonviolent Response to Terrorism*. Jefferson, NC, McFarland, 2004.

Hayek, F.A. *The Constitution of Liberty*. London, Routledge, 1965.

Hazony, Yoram. *The Virtue of Nationalism*. New York, Basic Books, 2018.

He, Baogang. *The Democratization of China*. Routledge, 1996.

——— *The Democratic Implications of Civil Society in China*. London, Routledge, 1997.

Heath, Anthony and David Sanders. *Ethnic Minority British Electoral Survey*. Oxford, Oxford University Press, 2012.

Hefner, Robert. *Civil Islam*. Princeton, Princeton University Press, 2000.

Held, David and Anthony McGrew, eds. *The Global Transformations Reader: An Introduction to the Globalization Debate*. Cambridge, Polity Press, 2000.

——— *Democracy and the Global Order: from the Modern State to Cosmopolitan Governance*. Cambridge, Polity Press, 1995.

——— *Political Theory Today*. Stanford, Stanford University Press, 1991.

Hexter, J.H. *The Vision of Politics on the Eve of the Reformation*. London, Routledge and Kegan Paul, 1973.

Hippel, Karin Von. 'The Roots of Terrorism: Probing the Myths'. In Lawrence Freedman, ed. *Superterrorism: Policy Responses*. Oxford, Blackwell, 2002.

Hiro, Dilip. *War Without End: The Rise of Islamist Terrorism and the Global Response*. London, Routledge, 2002.

Hobbes, Thomas. *Leviathan*, C.B. Macpherson ed. London, Penguin, 1981.

——— *Behemoth: the history of the causes of the civil wars of England, and of the counsels and artifices by which they were carried on from the year 1640 to the year 1660*, Paul Seaward ed. Oxford, Oxford University Press, 2009.

Hoffman, Bruce. *Terrorism in the United States and the Potential Threat to Nuclear Facilities*. R-3351-DOE, Santa Monica, RAND Corp, 1986.

Hollis, Rosemary. 'Isolating extremists'. *World Today* 21, August/September 2004.

Hopfl, H. *Jesuit Political Thought. The Society of Jesus and the State, c. 1560–1630*. Cambridge, Cambridge University Press, 2004.

Horkheimer, Max and Theodor Adorno. *Dialektik der Aufklärung*. Amsterdam, Querido Verlag 1947.

Horne, Cale and Bestvater, Samuel. 'Assessing the effects of changes in British counterterrorism policy on radical Islamist networks in the UK 1999–2008', *Behavioural Science of Terrorism and Political Aggression*, 8:2, 2015.

BIBLIOGRAPHY

Hoy, D. 'Jacques Derrida'. In Q. Skinner ed. *The Return of Grand Theory in the Social Sciences.* Cambridge, Cambridge University Press, 1985.

Hume, David. 'On Superstition and Enthusiasm'. In *Essays Moral, Political and Literary, 1742– 54.* Indianapolis, Liberty Fund, 1987.

Huntington, Samuel P. *Political Order in Changing Societies.* New Haven, Yale University Press, 1968.

—— *The Third Wave. Democratization in the Late Twentieth Century.* Norman, OK, University of Oklahoma Press, 1991.

—— *The Clash of Civilizations and the Remaking of World Order.* New York, Simon & Schuster, 1996.

—— 'Democracy's third wave'. *Journal of Democracy*, 2:2, 1991.

Husain, Ed. *The Islamist. Why I Joined Radical Islam In Britain, What I Saw And Why I Left.* London, Penguin, 2007.

Hutchings, K. 'Towards a Feminist International Ethics', in K. Booth, T. Dunne and M. Cox eds. *How Might We Live? Global Ethics in a New Century.* Cambridge, Cambridge University Press, 2001.

Hyde, Edward. 'Of Conscience', in *A Collection of Several Tracts of Edward Earl of Clarendon.* London, 1727.

Ibn Khaldun. *The Muqaddimah. An Introduction to History,* tr. Franz Rosenthal, N.J. Dawood ed., Princeton, Princeton University Press, 2015.

Ibn Taymiyah, Shaykh. *Al-'Ubudiyyah: Being a True Slave of Allah.* London, Ta-Ha, 1999.

Ibrahim, Anwar. *The Asian Renaissance.* Kuala Lumpur, Pelanduk, 1996.

Ikenberry, G. John. *After Victory: Institutions, Strategic Restraint and the Rebuilding of Order after Major Wars.* Princeton, Princeton University Press, 2000.

Islamic State. 'The Return of Khilafah', *Dabiq.* 1:1. Ramadan 1435AH/June-July 2010.

Jackson, Richard. *Writing the War on Terror: Language, Politics and Counter-terrorism.* Manchester, Manchester University Press, 2005.

Jansen, Johannes J.G. *The Neglected Duty: The Creed of Sadat's Assassins and Islamic Resurgence in the Middle East, with a translation of Muhammad Abd al-Salam Faraj, al-Faridah al-Gha'ibah.* London, Macmillan, 1986.

Jenkins, Sir John. *Defining Islamophobia. Research Note.* Westminster, Policy Exchange, 2018.

Jones, David Martin. *The Image of China in Western Social and Political Thought.* London, Palgrave, 2001.

—— 'Democratization, Civil Society and Middle Class Culture in Contemporary Pacific Asia', *Comparative Politics* 30:1, 2011.

—— 'Peace through conversation.' *The National Interest,* 79:1, 2005, pp. 93-100.

Jones, David Martin, and Mike Lawrence Smith. 'From Konfrontasi to Disintegrasi: ASEAN and the Rise of Islamism in Southeast Asia.' *Studies in Conflict and Terrorism,* 25:6,2002.

—— 'Franchising Terror.' *World Today.* 57:1, October 2001.

Judd, Dennis. *Palmerston.* London, I.B. Tauris, 2015.

Judt, Tony. *Past Imperfect.* Stanford, University of California Press, 1992.

Jurgensmeyer, Mark. *Terror in the Mind of God. The Global Rise of Religious Violence.* Oakland, University of California Press, 2017.

Kant, Immanuel. 'Perpetual Peace. A Philosophical Sketch' (1795). In Hans Reiss, ed., *Kant's Political Writings.* Cambridge, Cambridge University Press, 1970.

—— 'Idea for a universal history with a cosmopolitan purpose' (1784), in Hans Reiss, ed., *Kant's Political Writings.* Cambridge, Cambridge, University Press,1970.

Karpat, Kemal H. *The Politicization of Islam: Reconstructing Faith, State and Community in the Late Ottoman Empire.* Oxford, Oxford University Press. 2001.

Karram, Azza, 'Islamisms, Globalisation, Religion and Power.' In Ronaldo Munck and Purnaka de Silva ed., *Postmodern Insurgencies: Political Violence, Identity Formation and Peacemaking in Comparative Perspective*. London, Macmillan, 2000.

Karstadt, Susanne. 'Terrorism and "new wars".' In Bülent Gökay and R.B.J. Walker, eds., *11 September: War, Terror and Judgement*. London, Frank Cass, 2003.

Katz, Richard S. and Peter Mair. 'Changing Models of Party Organization and Party Democracy: The Emergence of the Cartel Party', *Party Politics*, 1:1, 1995.

Katzenstein, Peter. *A World of Regions: Asia and Europe in the American Imperium*. Ithaca, NY, Cornell University Press, 2005.

Keating, Tom and Florence Keane. 'Social Media and Terrorist Fund Raising', *Global Research Network on Terrorism and Technology*, Paper 10. RUSI, London, July 2019.

Keddie, Nikki R. *An Islamic Response to Imperialism: Political and Religious Writings of Sayyid Jamal al-Din "al-Afghani"*. Berkeley, CA, University of California Press, 1968.

Kedourie, Elie. *Afghani and Abduh: An Essay on Religious Unbelief and Political Activism in Modern Islam*. London: Frank Cass, 1966.

Kierkegaard, Søren. *The Journals of Søren Kierkegaard 1834–1854*, Alexander Dru ed. Fontana, London, 1956.

Kindelberger, C.P. 'The economic crisis of 1619–1623', *Journal of Economic History* 51, 1999.

Kindleberger, C.P. and R. Aliber, R. *Manias, Panics and Crashes. A History of Financial Crises*. London, Wiley, 2005.

King, Stephen D. *Grave New World. The End of Globalization and the Return of History*. New Haven, CT, Yale University Press, 2017.

Kissinger, Henry. *Diplomacy*. New York, Simon and Schuster, 1994.

——— *On China*. London, Allen Lane, 2011.

——— *World Order. Reflections on the Character of Nations and the Course of History*. London, Allen Lane, 2014.

Kitfiel, James. 'After bin Laden: is the war on terror winding down?' *National Journal,* 7 May 2011.

Koch, Richard. *The 80/20 Principle*. New York, Doubleday, 1998.

Korteweg, R. 'Mogherini's mission: four steps to make EU foreign policy more strategic'. *Centre for European Reform*, 19 Jan 2011. http://www.nationaljournal.com/magazine/after-bin-laden-is-the-war-on-terror-winding-down--20110505.

Krauthammer, Charles. 'The unipolar moment', *Foreign Affairs*, 70:1, 1991.

Kropotkin, Peter. *Paroles d'un Révolte*. Paris, Marpon and Flammarion, 1885.

Krouwel, André. 'Otto Kircheimer and the Catch All Party'. *West European Politics*. 26:2, 2003.

Kuhn, Thomas. *The Structure of Scientific Revolutions*. Chicago, Chicago University Press, 1962.

Kymlicka, Will. *Contemporary Political Philosophy*. Oxford, Oxford University Press, 2002.

——— *Contemporary Political Philosophy: an Introduction*. Oxford, Clarendon Press, 1990.

——— *Multicultural Citizenship. A Liberal Theory of Multicultural Rights*. Oxford, Oxford University Press, 1995.

Larkin, S. 'The Conflicted Role of the AIIB in South East Asia.' *ISEAS Perspective,* Singapore, 23:6, 2015.

Lasch, Christopher. *The Culture of Narcissism. American Life in an Age of Diminishing Returns*. New York, Norton, 1979.

Lawrence, Bruce, ed. *Messages to the World: The Statement of Osama bin Laden*. London, Verso, 2005.

Lebow, Richard Ned, and Thomas Risse-Kappen. *International Relations Theory and the End of the Cold War*. New York, Columbia University Press, 1995.

Lerner, Daniel. *The Passing of Traditional Society. Modernizing the Middle East*. New York, Free Press, 1958.

Levitsky Steven and Daniel Ziblatt. *How Democracies Die: What History Reveals about our Future.* London, Penguin, 2018.

Levy, Bernard-Henri. *Left in Dark Times: A Stand Against the New Barbarism.* New York, Random House, 2008.

Lilla, Mark. *The Reckless Mind.* New York, New York Review of Books, 2001.

Linklater, Andrew. *Critical Theory and World Politics. Citizenship, Sovereignty and Humanity.* London, Routledge, 2007.

Linz, Juan, and Alfred Stepan. *Problems of Democratic Transition and Consolidation: Southern Europe, South America, and Post-communist Europe.* Baltimore, MD, Johns Hopkins University Press, 1996.

Lipsius, Justus. *Politicorum sive civilis doctrinae libri sex* (1589) in Jan Waszink, ed. *Politica: Six Books of Politics or Political Instruction.* Assen, Royal Van Gorcum, 2004.

—— (1595) *On Constancy*, Bristol, Phoenix Press, 2006.

Locke, John. *Two Treatises of Civil Government*, Peter Laslett ed. Cambridge, Cambridge University Press 1988.

—— *A Letter Concerning Toleration and Other Writings*, Mark Goldie ed. Indianapolis, Liberty Fund, 2010 https://oll.libertyfund.org/titles/locke-a-letter-concerning-toleration-and-other-writings

Lodewijks, John. 'What managerialism has wrought', in William O. Coleman, ed., *The Deepening Crisis in Australian Universities.* Connor Court, Brisbane, 2019.

Ludendorf, Erich. *The Nation at War [Der Totale Krieg]*, A.S. Rappoport ed. London, Hutchinson, 1936.

Lutz, James M., and Brenda J. Lutz. *Global Terrorism.* London, Routledge, 2013.

Macdonald, Andrew (a.k.a. William Luther Pierce). *The Turner Diaries.* Hillsboro, WV, National Vanguard Books, 1978.

Machiavelli, Niccolò. *The Art of War* (1521). Chicago, Chicago University Press, 2013.

—— *The Prince.* London, Penguin, 1966.

—— *The Discourses.* London, Penguin, 1998.

Mackay, Charles. *Memoirs of Extraordinary Popular Delusions and the Madness of Crowds.* London, National Illustrated Library, 1852.

Mackinder, H.J. *Democratic Ideals and Reality.* Westport, Greenwood Press, 1962.

Mahathir, Mohamad. *The Challenge.* Petaling Jaya, Pelanduk Publishing, 1993.

Mahathir Mohamad and S. Ishihara. *The Voice of Asia: Two Leaders Discuss the Coming Century.* Tokyo, Kodansha International, 1995.

Mahbubani, K. 'The Pacific Way'. *Foreign Affairs*, 74:1, 1995.

—— 'The United States: Go East Young Man', *The Washington Quarterly*, 17:2, 1994.

Maher, Shiraz. *Salafi-Jihadism. The History of an Idea.* London, Hurst, 2016.

Mair, Peter. *Ruling the Void. The Hollowing of Western Democracy.* London, Verso, 2013.

Mani, Rama. 'The root causes of terrorism and conflict prevention.' In Jane Boulden and Thomas G. Weiss eds. *Terrorism and the UN: Before and After September 11.* Bloomington, Indiana University Press, 2004.

Mao, X. "一带一路"倡议与区域经贸融合发展 [The "Belt and Road" Initiative and the Development of Regional Economic and Trade Integration]. 当代世界与社会主义 *Contemporary World and Socialism*, 3:1, 2016.

Marcuse, Herbert. *One Dimensional Man. Studies in the Ideology of Advanced Industrial Society.* New York, Beacon Press, 1964.

Mattingly, Garrett. *The Armada.* New York, Houghton Mifflin, 1987.

—— *Renaissance Diplomacy.* New York, Dover, 1988.

Mazower, Mark. *Dark Continent. Europe's Twentieth Century.* London, Penguin, 1998.

BIBLIOGRAPHY

McLuhan, Marshall. *The Gutenberg Galaxy*. London, Routledge, 1962.

McLuhan, Marshall, and Quentin Fiore. *War and Peace in the Global Village*. London, Bantam, 1968.

McNeill, W.H. *Arnold Toynbee: A Life*. Oxford, Oxford University Press, 1989.

Mead, Walter Russell. 'The return of geopolitics: the revenge of the revisionist powers', *Foreign Affairs*, 93:3, 2014.

Mearsheimer, John J. 'Imperial by design.' *The National Interest* 11:16, Jan-Feb 2012.

—— 'E.H. Carr vs Idealism: The Battle Rages On'. *International Relations* 19:2, 2005.

—— *The Tragedy of Great Power Politics*, London, Norton, 2001.

Mehtra, O.N. 'NATO eastward expansion and Russian security'. *Journal of Strategic Studies* 22:8, 1992.

Meinecke, Friedrich. *Machiavellism. The Doctrine of raison d'état and its Place in Modern History*. New Haven, Yale University Press, 1957.

Mead, Walter Russell. *Power, Terror, Peace and War. America's Grand Strategy in a World at Risk*. New York, Knopf, 2004.

—— *Special Providence. American Foreign Policy and How it Changed the World*. New York, Routledge, 2002.

Meleagrou-Hitchens, Alexander. *The Global Jihadist Movement in the West. A Study of Anwar al-Awlaki and His Followers in the Context of Homegrown Radicalisation and the Global Jihadist Western Recruitment Strategy*. University of London, unpublished PhD thesis, 2015.

Meleagrou-Hitchens Alexander and Hans Brun, *A Neo-Nationalist Network: The English Defence League and the European Counter Jihad Movement*. International Centre for the Study of Radicalization and Political Violence, London, 2013.

Michael, George. *Lone Wolf Terror and the Rise of Leaderless Resistance*. Vanderbilt University Press, Nashville 1995.

Michels, Robert (1911). *Political Parties. A Sociological Study of the Oligarchical Tendencies of Modern Democracy*. Kitchener, ON, Batoche Books, 2001.

Minc, Alain. *Le nouvel moyen age*. Paris, Gallimard, 1993.

Minogue, K.R. *Alien Powers. The Pure Theory of Ideology*. Wilmington, ISI Books, 2008.

—— *The Liberal Mind*. London, Methuen, 1963.

—— *Politics: A Very Short Introduction*. Oxford, Oxford University Press, 1995.

—— 'Prudence', in Digby Anderson, ed. *Decadence*. The Social Affairs Unit, London, 2005.

—— 'Ideology after the collapse of communism'. *Political Studies* xli:7, 1993.

—— 'Christophobia and the West'. *New Criterion*, June 2003.

Minsky, Hyman P. 'The Financial Instability Hypothesis' Working Paper No 74. Bard College, Levy Economics Institute, 1992.

Mirandola, Pico della. *An Oration on the Dignity of Man* (1487). Gateway, Chicago, 1956.

Montesquieu, Louis de Secondat, Baron de. *The Spirit of the Laws*. Glasgow, David Niven, 2 vols. 1794.

Moore, Michael. *Dude, Where's My Country?* New York, Warner Books, 2003.

Moore, R.I. *The War on Heresy*. Cambridge, MA, Harvard University Press, 2012.

More, Thomas. *Utopia* (1516). Penguin, London, 1956.

Morgenthau, Hans J. and Kenneth W. Thompson. *Politics among Nations: the Struggle for Power and Peace*. New York, McGraw-Hill, 1993.

Morris, Meaghan. 'White panic or Mad Max and the sublime.' In Chen Kuan-Hsing ed., *Trajectories: Inter-Asian Cultural Studies*. London, Routledge, 1998.

Mounck, Yascha. *The People versus Democracy. Why Our Freedom is in Danger and How to Save It*. Cambridge MA, Harvard University Press, 2018.

367

Murray, Douglas. *The Strange Death of Europe*. London, Bloomsbury, 2018.

Mustofa, S. 'Penjajahan Kuning Sedang Mengintai Indonesia' [Yellow Colonisation is Lurking in Indonesia], *Law Justice*, Jakarta, 2018. https://law-justice.co/penjajah-kuning-sedang-mengintai-indonesia-.html.

Naji, Abu Bakr. *The Management of Savagery: The Most Critical Stage Through Which the Umma Will Pass* (tr. William McCants). Cambridge, MA, Harvard Institute of Strategic Studies, Harvard University Press, 2006.

Nakano, T. 'RCEP accord dims as India frets over trade liberalization'. *Nikkei Asian Review*, 2018.https://asia.nikkei.com/Politics/International-Relations/RCEP-accord-dims-as-India-frets-over-trade-liberalization.

Needham, C. 'Freedom, Community, and Function: Communitarian Features of Medieval Political Theory'. *American Political Science Review*, 86:4, 1992.

Niebuhr, Reinhold. *Moral Man and Immoral Society*. New York, Charles Scribner, 1960.

Norris, Pippa, and Ronald Inglehart. 'Public opinion among Muslims in the West', in Pippa Norris, Marion Just and Montague Kern eds. *Framing Terrorism: The News Media, the Government and Terrorism*. London, Routledge, 2003.

Nozick, Robert. *Anarchy, State and Utopia*. New York, Basic Books, 1974.

Nye, Joseph S. *Soft Power. The Means to Success in World Politics*. New York, Public Affairs, 2004.

—— 'Soft Power' *Foreign Policy*, Autumn 1990.

Oakeshott, Michael. *On Human Conduct*. Oxford, Oxford University Press, 1975.

—— *Rationalism in Politics and Other Essays*. London, Methuen, 1981.

—— *The Politics of Faith and the Politics of Scepticism*. New Haven, Yale University Press, 1996.

—— *Experience and its Modes* (1933). Cambridge, Cambridge University Press, 2015.

Oates, Sarah. *Selling fear? The Framing of the Terrorist Threat in Elections*. London, Chatham House, 2005.

O'Connell, Mark. *To Be a Machine*. Cambridge, Granta, 2017.

Ohmae, Kenichi. *The Borderless World Power and Strategy in the Interlinked Economy*. London, HarperCollins, 1991.

Ortega y Gasset, José (1930). *The Revolt of the Masses*. New York, Norton, 1957.

Orwell, George. *Ninety Eighty Four*. London, Penguin, 2019.

—— 'Politics and the English Language', in *Essays*. Bernard Crick ed. London, Penguin, 2000.

Overholt, William H. *The Rise of China: How Economic Reform is Creating a New China*. New York, Norton, 1994.

Paine, Thomas. *Common Sense* (1776). London, Penguin, 1978.

Pantucci, Raffaello and Ellis Clare. *Lone Actor Terrorism*. RUSI, London, 2016.

Pape, Robert. *Dying to Win. The Strategic Logic of Suicide Terrorism*. London, Penguin, 2005.

Parekh, Bhiku. *The Future of Multi-Ethnic Britain — The Parekh Report*. London, Profile Books/The Runnymede Trust, 2000.

—— 'The Cultural Particularity of Liberal Democracy'. In David Held ed., *Prospects for Democracy*. Cambridge, Polity Press, 1993.

Pareto, Vilfredo. *Cours d'économie politique*. Lausanne, 1896.

—— *Les Systèmes Socialistes. Cours professé à l'Université de Lausanne*. Paris, Giard et Brière, 1902.

Parker, Andrew. *Address on the evolving security threat*. London, RUSI, 2013. http://www.rusi.org/events/past/ref:E5254359BB8F44.

Parsons, Talcott. *On Institutions and Social Evolution*. Chicago, Chicago University Press, 1982.

—— *The Social System*. New York, Free Press, 1951.

Peters, Rudolph. *Jihad in Classical and Modern Islam: A Reader*. Princeton, NJ, Marcus Wiener, 1996.

Petit, Robert Goodin and Philip Petit. 'Introduction', in R. Goodin and P. Petit ed., *A Cambridge Companion to Political Philosophy*. Cambridge, Cambridge University Press, 1993.

Phillips, Trevor. 'Foreword' in Jenkins, Sir John, *Islamophobia. A Research Note*. London, Policy Exchange, 2019.

Pinker, Steven. *The Better Angels of our Nature: Why Violence has Declined*. London: Penguin, 2011.

Plato. 'The Republic', in *The Portable Plato*. London, Penguin, 1979.

Plenel, Edwy. *Pour Les Mussulmans*. Paris, Babelio, 2014.

Plumb, J.H. 'The city and the state', in J.H. Plumb ed., *The Penguin Book of the Renaissance*, London, Penguin, 1964.

Pogge, Thomas. *Realizing Rawls*. Ithaca, Cornell University Press, 1989.

Polanyi, Karl. *The Great Transformation: the Political and Economic Origins of our Time*. Boston, MA, Beacon Press, 2001.

Pollack, Kenneth M., and Ray M. Takeyh. 'Near Eastern promise: why Washington should focus on the Middle East', *Foreign Affairs,* May/June 2014. http://www.foreignaffairs.com/articles/141213/kenneth-m-pollack-and-ray-takeyh/near-eastern-promises.

Pope, Alexander. *Essay on Man*. London, 1734.

Popper, Karl. *The Logic of Scientific Discovery* (1935). London, Routledge, 2002.

—— *The Open Society and Its Enemies*. London, Routledge & Kegan Paul, 2 vols., 1962.

Potts, T.C. *Conscience in Medieval Philosophy*. Cambridge, Cambridge University Press, 1980.

Powell, Jonathan. *Talking to Terrorists. How to End Armed Conflicts*. London, Bodley Head, 2014.

Qutb, Sayyid. *Islam: The Misunderstood Religion*. Kuwait, Ministry of Awqaf and Islamic Affairs, 1967.

—— *Islam The Religion of the Future*. Kuwait, International Islamic Federation of Student Organizations, 1971.

—— *Milestones (Ma'alim fi al-tariq)*. Damascus, 1985.

Rabena, A.J. 'The Complex Interdependence of China's Belt and Road Initiative in the Philippines'. *Asia and the Pacific Policy Studies*, 5:2, 2018.

Rajaratnam, S. *The Prophetic and the Political*. Chan Heng Chee and Obaid Ul Haq, eds. Singapore, ISEAS, 2007.

Raphaeli, Nimrod. 'Radical Islamist Profiles (3). Ayman Muhammad Rabi al Zawahiri: The Making of an Arch Terrorist.' *Middle East Research Institute Inquiry and Analysis Series.* 127:11, March 2003.

Rawls, John. *A Theory of Justice*. Oxford, Oxford University Press, 1971.

—— *Political Liberalism*. New York, Columbia University Press, 1993.

—— *The Law of Peoples, with The Idea of Public Reason Revisited*. Cambridge, MA, Harvard University Press, 1999.

Richards, David. *Taking Command*. London, Headline, 2014.

Richardson, Louise. *What Terrorists Want*. London, Random House, 2006.

Richardson, Louise, ed. *The Root Causes of Terrorism*. London, Routledge, 2006.

Ringen, Stein. *The Perfect Dictatorship, China in the Twenty-first Century*. Hong Kong, Hong Kong University Press, 2018.

Rochefoucauld, Francois, Duc de la. *Maxims*, tr. L.W. Tanock. London, Everyman, 1959.

Rorty, Richard. *Contingency, Irony and Solidarity.* Cambridge, Cambridge University Press, 1989.

Rostow, W.W. *The Stages of Economic Growth*. Cambridge, Cambridge University Press, 1978.

Roy, Olivier. *Jihad and Death. The Global Appeal of Islamic State*. London, Hurst, 2017.

—— 'EuroIslam: The Jihad Within?' *The National Interest* 71, Spring, 2003.

Runciman David. *The Confidence Trap. A History of Democracy in Crisis*. Princeton, Princeton University Press, 2013.

—— *How Democracy Ends*. London, Profile, 2018.

Said, Edward. *Out of Place: A Memoir*. New York, Vintage, 2000.

——*Orientalism*. New York, Pantheon Books, 1978.

Sandall, Roger. *The Culture Cult: Designer Tribalism and Other Essays*. Boulder CO, Westview, 2001.

Sandel, M. *Liberalism and the Limits of Justice*. Cambridge, Cambridge University Press, 1992.

Sardar, Ziauddin and Merryl Wynn Davies. *Why Do People Hate America?* London, Icon Books, 2003.

Savile, George. 'The Character of a Trimmer', in *The Complete Works of George Savile First Marquess of Halifax*, Walter Raleigh ed., Oxford, Clarendon Press, 1912.

Schreer, B. 'Should Asia be afraid?' *The National Interest*, 20 Aug 2014. https://nationalinterest. org/blog/the-buzz/should-asia-be-afraid-chinas-strategy-the-south-china-sea-11109

Schumpeter, Joseph. *Capitalism, Socialism and Democracy*. London, Routledge, 2003.

Scruton, Roger. *Fools, Fraudsters and Firebrands: Thinkers of the New Left*. London, Bloomsbury, 2016.

—— *Where We Are? The State of Britain Now*. London, Bloomsbury, 2017.

Shaw, Martin. *Global Society and International Relations*. Cambridge, Polity Press, 1994.

Shepard, William E. *Sayyid Qutb and Islamic Activism*. Leyden, E.J. Brill, 1996.

Shira, D. 'RCEP Negotiations Reach Critical Stage – Likely to be Inked by Year-End.' 14 Oct 2018. *ASEAN Briefing*. Accessed 2018: https://www.aseanbriefing.com/ news/2018/09/07/rcep-negotiations-reach-critical-stage-likely-inked-year-end.html.

Sifaoui, Mohamed. *Inside al-Qaeda: How I Infiltrated the World's Deadliest Terror Organization*. London, Granta, 2003.

Skinner, Quentin. 'Introduction', in Q. Skinner, ed., *The Return of Grand Theory in the Social Sciences*. Cambridge, Cambridge University Press, 1985.

Smelser, Neil J., and Mitchell Faith. *Terrorism: Perspectives from the Behavioral and Social Sciences*. Washington DC, National Academies Press, 2002.

Smith, Steve. 'The Self-Images of a Discipline: A Genealogy of International Relations Theory', in Booth, K. and S. Smith eds., *International Relations Theory Today*. Cambridge, Polity Press, 1998.

Smith, Steve. 'Unanswered Questions.' In Ken Booth and Tim Dunne, eds., *Worlds in Collision: Terror and the Future of Global Order*. Basingstoke, Palgrave, 2002.

Sopiee, N. 'The New World Order: What Southeast Asia should strive for'. In R. Mahmood and T. Ramnath eds., *Southeast Asia. The Way Forward*. Kuala Lumpur, Friedrich Ebert Stiftung, 1992.

Soros, George. *On Globalization*. Oxford, Public Affairs, 2002.

—— *The Alchemy of Finance*. London, Wiley, 2007.

Spengler, Oswald. *The Decline of the West*. 2 vols. New York, Alfred A. Knopf, 1939.

Spivak, Gayatri Chakravorty. 'Can the Subaltern speak?', in Patrick Williams and Laura Chrisman, eds. *Colonial Discourse and Post-Colonial Theory: A Reader*. Hertfordshire, Harvester Wheatsheaf, 1994.

Standing, Guy. *The Precariat: The New Dangerous Class*. London, Bloomsbury, 2011.

Stearn, G.E. (ed.). *McLuhan Hot and Cool*. London, Penguin, 1968.

Sternberg, Ernest. 'Purifying the World: What The New Radical Ideology Stands For'. *Orbis*, Winter 2014.

Strachan, Hew. *The Direction of War. Contemporary Strategy in Historical Perspective*. Cambridge, Cambridge University Press, 2014.

Strauss, Leo. *The City and Man*. Chicago, Chicago University Press, 1964.

—— *The Rebirth of Classical Political Rationalism. An Introduction to the Thought of Leo Strauss*. Chicago, Chicago University Press, 1989.

BIBLIOGRAPHY

Strauss, Leo, and Joseph Cropsey. *History of Political Philosophy*. Chicago, Chicago University Press, 1986.

Studwell, Joe. *Asian Godfathers: Money and Power in Hong Kong and South East Asia*. London, Profile Books, 2007.

Swift, Adam. *Political Philosophy: A Beginner's Guide for Students and Politicians*. Cambridge, Polity Press, 2001.

Tan, Seng. 'An enemy of their making: US security discourse on the September 11 terror problematique.' In Kumar Ramakrishnan and See Seng Tan, eds. *After Bali: The Threat of Terrorism*. Singapore, World Scientific Publishing, 2003.

Taylor, Charles. 'The Politics of Recognition'. In Amy Gutman ed., *Multiculturalism. Examining the Politics of Recognition*. Princeton, Princeton University Press, 1994.

—— *Sources of the Self. The Making of the Modern Identity*. Cambridge, Cambridge, University Press, 1989.

—— *The Ethics of Authenticity*. Harvard, Harvard University Press, 1992.

Thompson, Grahame and Paul Hirst. *Globalization in Question*. Cambridge, Polity Press, 1997.

Thucydides. *History of the Peloponnesian Wars*. tr. J. Finley. London, Penguin, 1977.

Thunberg, Greta. *No One is Too Small to Make a Difference*. London, Penguin, 2019.

Tickner, J. Ann. 'Revisioning Society', in Booth, K. and Smith, S. eds., *International Relations Theory Today*. Cambridge, Polity, 1998.

Tocqueville, Alexis de. *Democracy in America*. 2 vols. Pittsburgh, Pennsylvania State Classics, 2002.

Tooze, Adam. *Crashed: How a Decade of Financial Crisis Changed the World*. London, Allen Lane, 2018.

Toulmin, Stephen. *Cosmopolis. The Hidden Agenda of Modernity*. Chicago, Chicago University Press, 1990.

—— *Return to Reason*. Cambridge, MA, Harvard University Press, 2001.

Toynbee, Arnold. *A Study of History*. 12 vols. Oxford, Oxford University Press, 1948–61.

Tu Wei Ming ed. *The Triadic Chord: Confucian Ethics, Industrial East Asia and Max Weber*. Singapore, Institute of East Asian Philosophies, 1991.

Tuck, Richard. *Philosophy and Government, 1572–1651*. Cambridge, Cambridge University Press, 1993.

Tully, James. *Strange Multiplicity. Constitutionalism in an Age of Diversity*. Cambridge, Cambridge University Press, 1995.

Valéry, Paul. 'Orient et Occident', in *Les Lettres Modernes*. 3 vols. Paris, Minard, 1998.

Valle, Alexander Del. *I Rossi Neri, Verdi: la convergenza degli Estremi opposti. Islamismo, comunismo, neonazismo*. Torino, Lindau, 2010.

Vance, J.D. *Hillbilly Elegy. A Memoir of a Family and Culture in Crisis*. New York, Harper, 2016.

Varoufakis, Yannis. *Adults in the Room. My Battle with Europe's Deep Establishment*, London, Bodley Head, 2017.

Voegelin, Eric. *The New Science of Politics; and Science, Politics and Gnosticism,* vol. 5, in Manfred Henningsen, ed. *The Collected Works of Eric Voegelin*. 28 vols. Columbia, MO, University of Missouri Press, 2000.

—— 'The Eclipse of Reality', in *What is History and Other Late Unpublished Writings*, vol. 28. Thomas A. Holweck and Paul Caringella, eds., *The Collected Works of Eric Voegelin*, 28 vols. Baton Rouge, Louisiana State University Press, 1975.

—— *Political Religions* and *The Ecumenic Age*, vol. 4 in *Order and History*, 5 vols. Baton Rouge, Louisiana University Press, 1974.

—— *In Search of Order*, vol. 5 in *Order and History*, 5 vols. Baton Rouge, Louisiana University Press, 1987.

—— *Modernity Without Restraint, What is History and Other Late Unpublished Writings*. Vol. 28 in *The Collected Works of Eric Voegelin*, 28 vols Columbia, MO, University of Missouri Press, 1990.

—— *The New Science of Politics*. Chicago, University of Chicago Press, 1952.

Vogel E. & Lodge G. *Ideology and National Competitiveness: A Comparison of Nine Different Countries*. Boston, Harvard Business School Press, 1987.

Walker, R.J. B. *Inside Outside. International Relations as Political Theory*. Cambridge, Cambridge University Press, 1993.

Wallerstein, Immanuel. *The Capitalist World Economy*. Cambridge, Cambridge University Press. 1980.

—— *The Modern World System. Mercantilism and the Consolidation of the European World Economy*. 2 vols. New York, Academic Press, Vol. 2, 1980.

—— *The Modern World System. Capitalist Agriculture and the Origin of the European World Economy*. 2 vols. New York, Academic Press, Vol. 1, 1974.

Waltz, Kenneth. 'International Politics is not foreign policy'. *Security Studies* 6:1, 1996.

Walzer, Michael. *Just and Unjust War. A Moral Argument with Historical Illustrations*. New York, Basic Books, 1977.

—— *Spheres of Justice*. New York, Basic Books, 1983.

Weber, Max. 'Politics as a vocation'. In *The Vocation Lectures,* trans Rodney Livingstone. Indianapolis, Hackett, 2004.

Weber, Max. *Economy and Society*. Berkeley, University of California Press, 1978.

Weiss, Thomas G., Margaret E. Crahern, and John Goering. *Wars on Terrorism and Iraq: Human Rights, Unilateralism and U.S. Foreign Policy*. London, Routledge, 2004.

Wendt, Alexander. *Social Theory of International Politics*. Cambridge, Cambridge University Press, 1999.

——'Anarchy is what states make of it: the social construction of power politics', *International Organization*, 46:2, 1992.

Wenley, R.M. 'Casuistry', in *The Encyclopaedia of Religion and Ethics*. Edinburgh, 1910.

Wight, Martin. *Power Politics*. London, Penguin, 1979.

Williams, Jody. 'The War in Iraq and Its Consequences: Thoughts of Nobel Laureates and Eminent Scholars'. In Abrams, Irwin and Wang Gungwu, eds. *The Iraq War and Its Consequences*, Singapore, World Scientific, 2004.

Wilson, Peter H. *Europe's Tragedy. A New History of The Thirty Years War*. London, Allen Lane, 2010.

Wolin, Sheldon. *The Seduction of Unreason*. Princeton, Princeton University Press, 2004.

Ye'or Bat (a.k.a. Litman, Giselle). *Eurabia: the Euro-Arab Axis*. New Jersey, Fairleigh Dickinson University Press, 2005.

Young, Alwyn. 'A Tale of Two Cities: Factor Accumulation and Technical Change in Hong Kong and Singapore', in O. Blanchard and S. Fisher eds., *N.B.E.R. Macroeconomics Annual 1992*. Cambridge (MA), MIT Press, 1992.

Yunus, Mohammad. *Commonwealth Lecture 2003: Halving Poverty by 2015*. London, The Commonwealth Yearbook, 2004.

Zalewski Marysia and Cynthia Enloe. 'Questions about identity in international relations', in Booth K. and Smith S. eds. *International Relations Theory Today*. Cambridge, Polity Press, 1998.

Zarkadakis, George. *In Our Own Image: Will Artificial Intelligence Save or Destroy Us?* London, Rider, 2015.

al-Zayyyat, Montasser. *The Road to al-Qaeda: The Story of Bin Laden's Right-Hand Man*, London, Pluto Press, 2004.

BIBLIOGRAPHY

Zhang, Y.H. "没有TPP,中国还有RCEP [No TPP, China Still Has the RCEP]." 世界知识 *World Affairs*, 64–66, 2016.

Zolo, Danilo. 'The Singapore Model Democracy, Communication and Globalization.' In *The Blackwell Companion to Political Sociology*. London, Wiley, 2004.

Zweig, Stefan. *Messages From a Lost World. Europe on the Brink*. London, Pushkin Press, 2016.

SELECTED NEWSPAPER AND JOURNAL ARTICLES

Aaronovitch, David. 'If we don't provoke them, maybe they will leave us alone. You reckon so?' 12 Jul 2005. *The Times*.

Adebolajo, Michael. 'Why carnage is hitting our towns'. Letter, 14 Dec 2013, *The Times*.

Abi-Habib, M. 'How China Got Sri Lanka to Cough Up a Port'. 25 Jun 2018. *New York Times*. https://www.nytimes.com/2018/06/25/world/asia/china-sri-lanka-port.html.

Abu Bakar, S.K. 'Najib Satu-Satunya PM Jual Tanah Hak Milik Kekal Kepada Warga Asing' [Mukhriz: Najib the Only PM to Sell Permanent Land to Foreigners]. 19 Oct 2017. *Free Malaysia Today*. Accessed October 2018. https://www.freemalaysiatoday.com/category/bahasa/2017/10/19/mukhriz-najib-satu-satunya-pm-jual-tanah-hak-milik-kekal-kepada-warga-asing/.

Adams, Christopher. 'Growing fears of backlash as BNP seeks to make capital'. 14 Jul 2005. *Financial Times*.

Aikenhead, Decca. 'A Digital Frankenstein is sending us crazy. Only the law can tame it', 7 Jul 2019. *The Sunday Times*.

Allen, Charlotte. 'So You Want To Live Forever'. 12 May 2014. *The Weekly Standard*.

Ali, Ayaan Hirsi. 27 May 2013. 'The Problem of Muslim Leadership.' *The Wall Street Journal*.

Armstrong, Karen. 'The label Catholic terror was never used about the IRA.' 11 Jul 2005. *The Guardian*.

Ashdown, Paddy. 'We must embrace Putin to beat Islamic State.' 30 Sep, 2014. *The Times*.

Alayon, David. 'Exposing China's Digital Dictatorship', Oct 2018. *The Medium*. https://medium.com/future-today/exposing-chinas-digital-dystopian-dictatorship-88df1c443cc6

Baker, Graeme. 'The fierce ambition of ISIL's Baghdadi'. *Aljazeera*. 15 Jun 2014. Accessed October 2014. http://www.aljazeera.com/news/middleeast/2014/06/fierce-ambition-isil-baghdadi-2014612142242188464.html.

Baldwin, Tom. 'BNP fans flames with "sick" by-election leaflet.' 14 Jul 2005. *The Times*.

Bartlett, Jamie. *The Persuasion Machine*. BBC2, 19 Mar 2019. Accessed 20 Jul 2019 https://www.bbc.co.uk/programmes/b091zhtk

Beeston, Richard, and Michael Binyon. 'Blair Repeatedly Failed to Tackle Radical Muslims in his Backyard'. 10 Aug 2005. *The Times*.

Bilton, Nick. 'Is Mark Zuckerberg Facebook's Last True Believer?' 7 Nov 2017. *Vanity Fair*. https://www.vanityfair.com/news/.../is-mark-zuckerberg-facebooks-last-true-believer

Blair, Tony. 'Work Together to a Brave New World'. *Speech to Labour Party Conference*, 3 Oct 2001. *The Times*.

Brady, Brian. 'Hooked at Last'. 30 May 2004. *Scotland on Sunday*.

Brooks, David. 'A Gift for Donald Trump'. 10 Feb 2017. *The New York Times*. https://www.nytimes.com/2017/02/10/opinion/a-gift-for-donald-trump.html

Bobbit, Phillip. 'Everything We Think About the War on Terror is Wrong.' 20 May 2006. *The Spectator*.

Bosco, James. 'The One China Policy, What would Nixon do?' 5 Jan 2017. *The Diplomat*.

BIBLIOGRAPHY

Britten, Nick. 'Leading cleric rails at injustice of "Muslim" bashing.' 28 Jul 2005. *Daily Telegraph*.

Bucci, Nino. 'Fine Tuning Push on Terror Laws'. 14 May 2013. *Sydney Morning Herald*.

Campbell, Jamie. 'Why Terrorists Love Britain.' 9 Aug 2004. *New Statesman*.

Cao, Y. 财经观察：中国东盟携手共谱繁荣新篇章 [Financial Observation: China and ASEAN Join Hands to Share A New Chapter of Prosperity. 12 Nov 2017. *Xinhua News Agency [新华社]*.http://www.gov.cn/xinwen/2017-11/12/content_5239121.htm.

Chin, J. '1MDB Sells Edra Power Assets to China Firm for Nearly RM10Billion Cash'. *The Star*, 23 Nov 2013. Accessed 6 Oct 2018. https://www.thestar.com.my/business/business-news/2015/11/23/1mdb-sells-edra-power-assets-to-china-firm-for-nearly-rm10b-cash.

Clark, David. 'This Terror Will Continue Until We Take Arab Grievances Seriously.' 9 Jul 2005. *The Guardian*.

Coates, Sam. 'Voters' trust in society is collapsing, says Ashdown'. 4 Jan 2014. *The Times*.

Cohen, David. 'Terror on the Dole'. 20 Apr 2004. *The Evening Standard*.

Coll, Steve, and Susan B. Glasser. 'Islamic radicals found a haven'. 10 Jul 2005. *The Washington Post*.

Colombani, Jean Marie. 'Nous sommes tous Américains'. 2 Sep 2001. *Le Monde*.

Corbett, James. 'London's New Villains'. 31 Oct, 2005, *Al-Ahram Weekly*.

Cowan, Rosie. 'Attack on London is Inevitable', 17 Mar 2004. *The Guardian*.

Crabtree, Susan. 'Flashback: Obama: al-Qaeda is on "a path to defeat"; calls for resetting terror policy'. 23 May 2013, *Washington Times* http://www.washingtontimes.com/news/2013/may/23/obama-al-qaeda-is-on-a-path-to-defeat/?page=all.

Durodié, Bill. 'Al-Qaeda: a conspiracy of dunces?' Apr 14, 2005. *Spiked*. http:www.spiked-online.com/Articles/0000000CA90.htm.

Drachan, Hugo. 'Why the Elites always rule', 18 Jan 2017. *The New Statesman*. https://www.newstatesman.com/politics/uk/2017/01/why-el/

Eco, Umberto. 'Ur Fascism', 22 Jun 1995. *The New York Review of Books*, https://www.nybooks.com/articles/1995/06/22/ur-fasci

Estrada, D. ' China's Belt and Road Initiative: Implications for the Philippines, Manila'. *Foreign Service Institute Insights*, Oct 2018. Accessed 1 Nov 2018. http://www.fsi.gov.ph/wp-content/uploads/2018/03/Vol-5-No-3-China's-Belt-and-Road-Initiative-Implications-for-the-Philippines-Estrada1.pdf.

Ford, Richard. 'Two communities that hardly ever mix'. 13 Jul 2005. *The Times*.

Freedman, Lawrence. 'The master strategist is still a myth', *War on the Rocks*, 14 Oct 2014. http://warontherocks.com/2014/10/the-master-strategist-is-still-a-myth/, accessed 29 October 2014.

Fuad, A. 'Apa Untungnya Indonesia Masuk Belt and Road Initiative?' [What is Indonesia's Gain in Joining the Belt and Road Initiative?] 5 Oct 2018. *Watyuting*, Jakarta. Accessed 5 Oct Watyutink. https://watyuting.com/topik/ekonomika/Apa-Untungnya-Indonesia-Masuk-Belt-and-Road-Initiative.

Gady, Franz Stefan. 'Corruption and Scandal can't stop Austria's Far Right'. 23 May 2019, *Foreign Policy*. https://foreignpolicy.com/2019/05/23/corruption-and-collusion-cant-stop-austrias-far-right/

Gardham, Duncan. 'Preachers of Hate Could be Charged with Treason'. 8 Aug 2005. *The Daily Telegraph*.

Giddens, Anthony. 'Scaring people may be the only way to avoid the risks of new-style terrorism'. 10 Jan 2005. *The New Statesman*.

Gillan, Audrey. 'Detained Muslim Cleric is Spiritual Leader to Militants, Hearing Told'. 20 Nov 2003. *The Guardian*.

BIBLIOGRAPHY

Glancy, Josh. 'J.D. Vance Interview', 16 Jul 2016. *The Sunday Times Magazine.*

Goldberg, Jeffrey. 'The Obama Doctrine.' April 2016. *The Atlantic.* http://www.theatlantic. com/magazine/archive/2016/04/the-obamadoctrine/471525/.

Goodhart, David. 'It's paranoia, not Islamophobia.' 15 Jul 2005. *The Guardian.*

Grant, S. and Davies, J. 'Capital Market pariahs'. 12 Aug 1998. *Financial Times.*

Guthrie, Jonathan, and Chris Tighe. 'The eerily ordinary extremists.' 15 Jul 2005. *Financial Times.*

Heath, Anthony. 'Has Multiculturalism failed in the UK? Not Really'. 10 Aug 2012. *The Guardian.* http://www.theguardian.com/commentisfree/2012/aug/10/multiculturalism-uk-research.

Hitchens, Christopher. 'Assassins of the Mind'. February 2009. *Vanity Fair.*

Hofstadter, Richard. 'The Paranoid Style in American Politics.' November 1964. *Harper's Magazine.*

Horowitz, Jason. 'Italy's deal with China signals shift in geopolitics', *New York Times,* 1 Apr 2019.

Howden, Saffron. 'Muslim children should not be forced to sing the national anthem says Hizbut-Tahrir'. *The Sydney Morning Herald,* 1 Nov 2015.

https://www.smh.com.au/national/muslim-children-should-not-be-forced-to-sing-national-anthem-says-hizb-uttahrir-20151101-gknwy9.html

Hume, Mick. 'The age of intolerant tolerance'. 19 Aug 2005. http://www.spiked-online. com/Articles/0000000CAD0A.htm.

Ignatius, David. 'Hope for Democracy in the Arab World'. 9 Aug 2013. *Washington Post.* http://www.washingtonpost.com/opinionshttp://www.washingtonpost.com/ opinions/david-ignatius-hope-for-democracy-in-the-arab-world/2013/08/09/df88/ david-ignatius-hope-for-democracy-in-the-arab-world/2013/08/09/df888f30-0043-11e3-96a8-d3b921c0924a_story.html.

Jenkins, Simon. 'Panic in the face of fanatics is making Britain dangerous'. 31 Jul 2005. *The Sunday Times.*

Johnston, Philip. 'Hardline Cleric Faces Explusion from Finsbury Park Mosque'. 17 January 2003. *The Daily Telegraph.*

Jenkins, Jolyon. 'The green sheep in Colonel Gadaffi Drive'. 8 Sep 1987. *New Statesman.*

Kaletsky, Anatole. 'The act of small-time losers'. 14 Jul 2005. *The Times.*

Kagan, Robert. 'US can't ignore the Middle East', 20 Nov 2012. *Washington Post* http:// www.washingtonpost.com/opinions/robert-kagan-us-cant-ignore-the-middle-east/2012/11/20/a2b4ede0-3331-11e2-bfd5-e202b6d7b501_story.html, accessed 25 Oct 2014.

Kennedy, Dominic. 'British Activist was behind Iran's Fatwa on Salman Rushdie', 25 Feb 2019. *The Times.* https://www.thetimes.co.uk/article/british-activist-was-behind-iran-s-call-to-kill-salman-rushdie-7cd22753s Accessed 27 Jul 2019.

Lee, H. & Huang, Y.Y. 对马来西亚投资：中国的机遇与风险 [Investment in Malaysia: China's Opportunities and Risks]. 新华丝路 1 Oct 2018. *Xinhua.* Accessed 13 Oct 2018. http://silkroad.news.cn/2018/0813/106248.shtm.

Leppard, David, and Robert Winnet. 'Blair's Extremism Proposals Attacked as the Hunt Continues for Terror's New Breed.' 7 Aug 2005. *The Sunday Times.*

Lewis, Paul. 'Our minds can be hacked'. *The Guardian.* 6 Oct 2017.

Londoño, Ernesto. 'Iraq war costs to top $4 trillion.' 28 Mar 2013. *Washington Post.*

Lone, Salim. 'Withdrawal would curb terrorism.' 12 Jul 2005. *The Guardian.*

Lucas, Edward. 'Ukraine: protests: we're letting Putin win'. 20 Feb 2014. *Daily Telegraph.*

Mahbubani, K. 'Qatar: Big Lessons from a Small Country'. 2 Jan 2017. *The Straits Times* Accessed June 2018. https://www.straitstimes.com/opinion/qatar-big-lessons-from-a-small-country.

BIBLIOGRAPHY

Malik, Shiv. 'The Muslim community'. 24 Jul 2005. *The Independent.*

Marin, Minnette. 'Confronted with our own decadence'. 31 Jul 2005. *The Sunday Times.*

Mendick, Robert. 'Now Bakri Attacks Hypocrite Muslims'. 21 Jul 2005. *The Evening Standard.*

Mitchell, Tom. 'UN tribunal rules against Beijing in South China Sea dispute'. 12 Jul 2016. *Financial Times.*

Moore, Charles. 'Where is the Gandhi of Islam?' 9 Jul 2005. *The Daily Telegraph.*

Morozov, Evgeny. 'Why the Internet of Things Could Destroy the Welfare State'. 19 Jul 2014. *The Observer, Guardian News and Media.* Accessed August 2017. www.theguardian.com/ technology/2014/jul/20/ rise-of-data-death-of-politics-evgeny-morozov-

Mroue, Bassem. 'Here's a breakdown of the oil assets ISIS now controls'. 20 Oct 2014. *Business Insider/Associated Press.* http://www.businessinsider.com/breakdown-of-the-oil-assets-isis-controls-2014-9.

Muggah, R. 'Duterte's Drug War in the Philippines is Out of Control, He Needs to be Stopped', 5 Jan 2017. *The Guardian.* Accessed 13 Oct 2018. https://www.theguardian. com/global-development-professionals-network/2017/jan/05/rodrigo-dutertes-drug-war-in-the-philippines-is-out-of-control-he-needs-to-be-stopped.

Mukherjee, Majuri. 'India walking the line between China and the US'. 27 Apr 2016. *The Diplomat.*

Newman, Cathy, and James Blitz. 'MPs urge fellow Muslims to drive out evil.' 14 Jul 2005. *Financial Times.*

Norfolk, Andrew, and Russell Jenkins. 'A legacy of deprivation.' 15 Jul 2005. *The Guardian.*

Oborne, Peter. 'Don't be misled – the London bombs were a direct response to the Iraq war.' 30 Jul 2005. *The Spectator.*

O'Gieblyn, Meghan. 'God in the Machine'. 18 Apr 2017. *The Guardian.*

Packer, George. 'No Death, No Taxes'. 28 Nov 2011. *The New Yorker.*

Parris, Matthew. 'Suicide bombings will pass – they are just a grisly terrorist fashion'. 6 Aug 2005. *The Times.*

Powell, Charles. 'The west will pay for losing its backbone in Iraq and Ukraine'. 19 Jun 2014. *Daily Telegraph.*

Purves, Libby. 'The land that lost its pride'. 26 Jul 2005. *The Times.*

Ramadan, Tariq. 'Islam et Occident: Interview with Tariq Ramadan'. 22 Apr 2004. *Le Point.*

Razak, N. 'Fruits Harvested from Seeds of Trust'. 2 Oct 2016. *China Daily.* Accessed 6 Oct 2018. http://www.chinadaily.com.cn/opinion/2016-11/02/content_27245852.htm.

'Rise in Hate Crimes Against Muslims After Attacks.' 11 Jul 2005. *Reuters News Report.*

Rose, David. 'Flashy tactics won't defeat the terrorists.' 4 Jul 2005. *Observer.*

Said, Edward. 'A Window on the World'. 2 Aug 2003. *The Guardian.*

Sheridan, Greg. 'Sabre Rattling imbues Shangri-la with a growing sense of menace'. 5 Jun 2014. *Straits Times.*

Soros, George. 'The Crisis and What to do about it', *The New York Review of Books*, 6 Nov 2008. https://www.georgesoros.com/2008/11/06/the_crisis_what_to_do_about_it/

Starry, General Donn A. 'Syria: one more reason for a return to grand strategy', 27 Aug 2013. *Information Dissemination.* Accessed 19 Oct 2014. http://www.informationdissemination. net/2013/08/syria-one-more-reason-for-return-of.html.

Strauss, Neil. 'Elon Musk the architect of tomorrow.' December 2017. *Rolling Stone.*

Steltzer, Irwin. 'Letter from Londonistan'. 1 Aug 2005. *Weekly Standard.*

Sun, J. 中国连续9年成东盟最大贸易伙伴去年交易5148亿美元 [China is ASEAN's Largest Trading Partner for 9 Consecutive Years, Trading US$514.8 Billion Last Year]. 18 Jul 2018. 新浪网 *Finance Sina.* http://finance.sina.com.cn/china/hgjj/2018-07-18/ doc-ihfnsvyz7227839.shtml.

BIBLIOGRAPHY

Tahiri, Amir. 'Beards and Scarves aren't Muslim, They're Simply Adverts for al-Qaeda'. 27 Jul 2005. *The Times.*

Thornhill, John. 'Big Tech v Big Brother'. 19-20 Apr 2017. *The Weekend Financial Times.*

Titcomb, James. 'Google's Growth heads for the cliff-edge as Amazon primes for advertising attack', 21 Jul 2019. *The Sunday Telegraph.*

Tran, Mark, and Matthew Weaver., 'Isis announces Islamic caliphate in area straddling Iraq and Syria'. 30 Jun 2014. *The Guardian.* http://www.theguardian.com/world/2014/jun/30/isis-announces-islamic-caliphate-iraq-syria.

Travis, Alan. 'Judges Quash Extradition of Suspect'. 28 Jun 2002. *The Guardian.*

Trotta, Daniel. 'Iraq war cost US more than $2 trillion: study'. 14 Mar 2013. *Reuters.*

Tsang, D. 'Asia Needs a Bond market'. 17-18 Jul 1998. *Asia Wall Street Journal.*

Utama, J. & Kim, M. 'More than just economy: Maritime implications of China's investment'. 27 Jun 2016. *The Jakarta Post.* Accessed January 2019: http://www.thejakartapost.com/academia/2016/06/27/more-than-just-economy-maritime-implications-of-chinas-investment.html.

Wazier, Burhan. 'People look at me on the tube'. 14 Jul 2005. *London Metro.*

Weaver, Tran. 'Isis announces caliphate in area straddling Iraq and Syria'. 30 June 2014. *The Guardian.* https://www.theguardian.com/world/2014/jun/30/isis-announces-islamic-caliphate-iraq-syria.

Ware, John. 'Is Labour Anti-Semitic?' *Panorama,* Jul 2019. https://www.bbc.co.uk/programmes/m0006p8c

Weissman, Ed. 'The vote Ed Snowden needs to turn back the surveillance state'. 27 Nov 2013. *Oped News.*

Whitlock, Craig. 'Briton Used Internet as His Bully Pulpit'. 8 Aug 2005. *The Washington Post.*

Willing, Richard. 'Radical Cleric Fighting Extradition to USA on Terror Charges'. 27 May 2004. *USA Today.*

Winter, Charlie. 'Inside the Collapse of Islamic State's propaganda machine'. 20 Dec 2017. *Wired.*

Wolf, Martin. 'Taming the masters of the tech universe'. 15 Nov 2017. *Financial Times.*

Wolfe, Tom. 'The Me Decade'. 26 Aug 1973. *New York Magazine.*

Woods, Richard, and David Leppard. 'Focus: How liberal Britain let hate flourish'. 12 Feb 2006. *Sunday Times.*

Wright, Oliver. 'Costly failures: wars in Iraq and Afghanistan cost UK taxpayers £30bn', 27 May 2014, *The Independent* http://www.independent.co.uk/news/uk/politics/costly-failures-wars-in-iraq-and-afghanistan-cost-uk-taxpayers-30bn-9442640.html.

Wright, T. & Clark, S. 'Investigators Believe Money Flowed to Malaysian Leader Najib's Accounts Amid 1MDB Probe'. 6 Jun 2015, *The Wall Street Journal.* https://www.wsj.com/articles/SB10130211234592774869404581083700187014572

NEWSPAPER JOURNALS AND OTHER MEDIA (NO AUTHOR)

'Abu Qatada Deported'. 7 Jul 2013, *The Guardian.* http://www.theguardian.com/world/2013/jul/07/abu-qatada-deported-from-uk.

'Al-Qaeda in Iraq confirms Syria's Nusra Front is part of its network'. 9 Apr 2013, *Al Arabiya,* Accessed October 20, 2013. http://english.alarabiya.net/en/News/middle-east/2013/04/09/Al-Qaeda-in-Iraq-confirms-Syria-s-Nusra-Front-is-part-of-its-network.html.

'A lurch onto the world stage.' 8 Feb 2015, *The Economist.*

'Anti-Terror Police Raid London Mosque'.20 Jan 2003, BBC News. Accessed August 19, 2005. http://news.bbc.co.uk/2/hi/uk_news/england/2675223.stm.

BIBLIOGRAPHY

'Blair Pays Tribute to Resilience'. 9 Jul 2004, BBC News. Accessed 24 Aug 2005. http://news.bbc.co.uk/1/hi/uk_politics/4666311.stm.

'Brussels hits at China's loan pressure'. 6 Mar 2019, *Financial Times.*

'Calling Terrorist Traitors is no answer', 9 Aug 2005, *The Daily Telegraph.*

'China's island building lacks strategic logic.' 28 Oct 2015. *Financial Times.*

'China's overtures to cement ties with ASEAN.' 12 Oct 2013. *Straits Times.*

'Cooling Towards Britannia, Not Blair'. 12 Oct 2003, *The Observer.*

'Come together on the Abe Road'. 12 Dec 2015, *The Economist.*

'David Cameron: State Multiculturalism has failed'. 5 Feb 2011. Accessed 27 Jul 2019, https://www.bbc.co.uk/news/uk-politics-12371994.

'Deporting Hatred'. 6 Aug 2005. *The Times.*

'Edward Snowden Revelations prompt UN investigation of Surveillance'. 2 Dec 2013, *The Guardian.*

'Hundreds of UK jihadists in Syria.' 4 Dec 2013, *The Daily Telegraph.*

'The Iraq connection'. 20 Jul 2005, *The Guardian.*

'In Full: Blair on Bomb Blasts'. 7 Jul 2005. Accessed 24 Aug 2005. http://news.bbc.co.uk/1/hi/uk/4659953.stm

'Inside the sect that loves terror', 7 Aug 2005, *Sunday Times.*

'Italy ready to take China's road to the top'. 7 Mar 2019, *The Times.*

'MI5 chief Andrew Parker says Edward Snowden's leaks are a gift to terrorists'. 14 Oct 2013, *The Huffington Post.*

'Muslim Cleric Says Groups Plan to Strike London', 19 Apr 2004, *The Boston Globe.*

'Profile: Omar Saeed Sheikh'. 16 Jul 2002. Accessed 3 Sep 2005. http://news.bbc.co.uk/1/hi/uk/1804710.stm.

'Statement Claiming London Attacks'. 7 July 2005, BBC News. http://news.bbc.co.uk/2/hi/uk_news/4660391.stm. Accessed 12 Sep 2019.

'Terror Attack "A Matter of Time"'. 17 Jun 2003, BBC News. Accessed 21 Nov 2005. http://news.bbc.co.uk/1/hi/uk/2997146.stm.

'The judiciary should not patrol our borders'. 30 Jul 2005, *Daily Telegraph.*

'The power of nightmares: Baby it's cold outside'. 14 Jan 2005. BBC News: http://news.bbc.co.uk/go/pr/fr/-/1/hi/programmes/3755686/stm.

'We Have The Laws: Use Them'. 17 Jul 2005, *The Sunday Telegraph.*

'Who Will be Deported and Who Decides?' 6 Aug 2005, *The Guardian.*

PRIMARY SOURCES

All Party Parliamentary Group on British Muslims (APPG). *Report on the Inquiry into a working definition of Islamophobia: Anti-Muslim Hatred.* Norwich, Westminster, 2018. https://static1.squarespace.com/static/599c3d2febbd1a90cffdd8a9/t/5bfd1ea3352f531a6170ceee/1543315109493/Islamophobia+Defined.pdf

Australian Government. *Living Safe Together. Building Community Resilience to Violent Extremism.* Canberra, 2015. https://www.livingsafetogether.gov.au/pages/home.aspx

Department of Defence, Government of Australia. *2016 Defence White Paper,* Canberra, Commonwealth of Australia, 2016.

ASEAN Treaty of Amity and Cooperation, 1976. http://asean.org/treaty-amity-cooperation-southeast-asia-indonesia-24-february-1976/.

Master Plan on ASEAN Connectivity 2025 Jakarta, The ASEAN Secretariat, 2016. https://asean.org/storage/2016/09/Master-Plan-on-ASEAN-Connectivity-20251.pdf

BIBLIOGRAPHY

Bush, President George W. *Address to a Joint Session of Congress and the American People.* Washington DC, White House Office of the Press Secretary, 20 Sep 2001.

United Nations General Assembly. *Implementing the responsibility to protect: report of the Secretary-General,* A3/63/677, 63rd session, agenda items 44-107, 12 Jan 2009. *http://www.un.org/en/ga/search/view_doc.asp?symbol=A/63/677*

Consolidated Texts of the EU Treaties as Amended by the Treaty of Lisbon. CM 7310, Norwich, HMSO, 2008.

CONTEST 3.0. The United Kingdom's strategy for countering terrorism. CM 9608, Norwich, HMSO, 2018.

House of Commons. *Racial and Religious Hatred Act, 2006.* London, Office of Public Sector Information, http://www.opsi.gov.uk/acts/acts2006/ukpga_20060001_en_1.

Emerson, C. *Australia Joins Launch of Massive Asian Regional Trade Agreement.* Department of Foreign Affairs and Trade Canberra, 2012. Trademinister.gov.au/releases/2012/ce_mr_121120.html.

Obama, Barack. *Remarks by the President on the Middle East and North Africa.* Washington, DC, The White House Office of the Press Secretary, 19 May 2011. http://www.whitehouse.gov/the-press-office/2011/05/19/remarks-president-middle-east-and-north-africa.

2017 National Security Strategy of the United States of America. Washington, DC, White House, 2017.

Kean, Thomas H. et al., *The 9/11 Commission Report. Final Report of the National Commission on Terrorist Attacks on the United States.* Washington, DC, 2004.

Silber Mitchell D. and Bhatt Arvin. *Radicalization in the West. The Homegrown Threat.* New York, NYPD, 2007. https://seths.blog/wp-content/uploads/2007/09/NYPD_Report-Radicalization_in_the_West.pdf

Mayor of London. *Why the Mayor Will Maintain Dialogues With All of London's Faiths and Communities.* London, Greater London Authority, 2005.

Home Office. *Building Cohesive Communities.* Report of the Ministerial Group on Public Order and Community Cohesion, (The Denham Report), Norwich, HMSO 2001.

Working Together to Prevent Extremism. A Report of the Independent Review Team, Norwich HMSO April 2005. https://webarchive.nationalarchives.gov.uk/20120920045201/http://www.communities.gov.uk/documents/communities/pdf/152164.pdf

INDEX

civil war, Syria, 91, 92, 154, 182, 185, 186, 206, 223, 230
civil war, Ukraine, 181
civilization and its discontents, 43–6
Clash of Civilizations and the Remaking of World Order, The (1996), 3
Clegg, Nick, 277
Clinton, Bill, 23, 29, 126, 136, 180, 257, 280
　His administration, 74
　Somalia adventure (1993), 25
Clinton, Hillary, 163
CNN (TV channel), 107
CNN effect, 15
Cohen, Nick, 104, 236
Cohen, Stephen P., 22
COIN. *See* counter-insurgency (COIN)
Cold War, 1, 22, 34, 37, 67, 69, 163, 190, 236
　era, 32
　methodological edifice, 6–7
　post-Cold War, 36–7
　terrorism, 37
Collateralized Debt Obligations (CDOs), 19, 122, 134
Collectif Contre l'Islamophobie en France (CCIF), 106
Collier, Paul, 150
Collins, Justice, 306n30
Commission on the Future of Multi-ethnic, 307n43
Communist Party of China (CPC), 20, 125
Comte-Sponville, André, 211
Conseil Francais du Culte Musulman (CFCM), 106
Conservative People's Party, 224
Constants (journal), 57
Convention on Human Rights (Europe), 78, 91

Cook, Philip J., 21
　Winner Takes All Society, The, 21
Cooks, Tim, 274
Cool Britannia, 81, 299n55
Cope, Abiezer, 115
Copeland, David, 229
Corbyn, Jeremy, 90, 105, 150, 152, 237
cosmopolitan
　democracy, 31
　ethics, casuistry, and just war, 202–8
　norms and grand historical narratives, 187–8
cosmopolitanism, 241
Coulibaly, Ahmedy, 104
counter-insurgency (COIN), 67
Court of Human Rights (Europe), 31, 88
Court of Justice (Europe), 78, 88
Cox, Jo, 229, 233
CPC. *See* Communist Party of China (CPC)
CRC. *See* China Railway Corp (CRC)
Credit Default Swaps (CDSs), 134
Crick, Bernard, 249
　In Defence of Politics, 343n92
Crimean peninsula, 182
Critical Studies on Security (journal), 73, 84
Critical Studies on Terrorism (journal), 84, 105
Cromwell, Thomas, 251
Curtis, Alex, 339n22
cyber-caliphate, 52–7

Dabiq (journal), 60, 184, 303n115
Dahl, Robert, 249
　polyarchy, 11
Dahrendorf, Ralf, 30, 32